Intelligence and national security policymaking on Iraq

Intelligence and national security policymaking on Iraq

British and American perspectives

Edited by
JAMES P. PFIFFNER AND MARK PHYTHIAN

For my friends Nat & Sue Tinkler

Jim Pfiffner

1/18/2020

Texas A&M University Press
College Station

This paper meets the requirements of ANSI/NISO Z39.48-1992
(Permanence of Paper).
Binding materials have been chosen for durability.

Library of Congress Cataloging-in-Publication Data

Intelligence and national security policymaking on Iraq : British and
American perspectives / edited by James P. Pfiffner and Mark Phythian. —
1st North American ed.
    p. cm. — (Joseph V. Hughes Jr. and Holly O. Hughes series on the
presidency and leadership)
    Includes bibliographical references and index.
    ISBN-13: 978-1-60344-067-7 (cloth : alk. paper)
    ISBN-10: 1-60344-067-4 (cloth : alk. paper)
    ISBN-13: 978-1-60344-093-6 (pbk. : alk. paper)
    ISBN-10: 1-60344-093-3 (pbk. : alk. paper)
    1. Iraq War, 2003—Military intelligence—United States.   2. Iraq War,
    2003—Military intelligence—Great Britain.   3. National
security—United States—Decision making.   4. National security—Great
Britain—Decision making.   5. United States—Military relations—Iraq.
6. Great Britain—Military relations—Iraq.   7. United States—Military
policy.   8. Great Britain—Military policy.   9. Iraq War, 2003—Causes.
    I. Pfiffner, James P.   II. Phythian, Mark.   III. Series: Presidency and
leadership (Unnumbered)
    DS79.764.U6I57   2008
    956.7044'31—dc22
    2008025298

Contents

Figures

Acknowledgements

The editors would like to thank all of the contributors for agreeing to write for this book, Tony Mason at Manchester University Press for his interest in the project, and Jenny Howard and Stephanie Matthews of Manchester University Press for their professionalism in shepherding the book into print.

For the time and support necessary to work on this volume, James Pfiffner would like to thank the School of Advanced Study at the University of London where he was a Professorial Fellow in the Institute for the Study of the Americas from January through June 2007. Nicholas Mann, Dean of SAS and James Dunkerley, Dean of ISA were generous in making the Fellowship possible. He would also like to thank the School of Public Policy at George Mason University, particularly Dean Kingsley Haynes, for the study leave that made the visit possible. Several colleagues provided help and advice for this project for which he is grateful: Lara Brown, Tom Coghlan, Phil Davies, John Dumbrell, George C. Edwards, James Finkelstein, John Gordon, Don Kash, Timothy Lynch, Jeremy Mayer, Iwan Morgan, John Owens, and Jon Roper.

Mark Phythian would like to thank Peter Gill, his former colleagues in the History and Governance Research Institute at the University of Wolverhampton, Diane Evans—particularly for invaluable help with the appendices—and James and Hayley.

The editors would also like to thank the publishers and authors for permission to reprint the following:

James P. Pfiffner, "Did George Bush Mislead the United States in his Arguments for War in Iraq?," *Presidential Studies Quarterly* Vol. 34, No. 1 (March 2004), pp. 25–46. [Chapter 4]

Richard J. Kerr et al., "Intelligence and Analysis on Iraq: Issues for the Intelligence Community," *Studies in Intelligence* Vol. 49, No. 3 (2005), pp. 1–9. [Chapter 8]

Robert Jervis, "The Politics and Psychology of Intelligence and Intelligence Reform," *The Forum* Vol. 4, Issue 1 (2006), pp. 1–9. [Chapter 9]

Paul R. Pillar, "Intelligence, Policy, and the War in Iraq," *Foreign Affairs* (March/April 2006), pp. 15–27. [Chapter 13]

Contributors

Rebecca Donnegan was Deputy Inspector General of the Central Intelligence Agency in 1989, and also in 2001.

John Dumbrell is Professor of Government in the School of Government and International Affairs at Durham University (UK). His most recent books are *A Special Relationship: Anglo-American Relations from the Cold War to Iraq* (Palgrave, 2006) and *President Lyndon Johnson and Soviet Communism* (Manchester University Press, 2004: winner of the Richard E. Neustadt book prize for 2005). He is currently researching the foreign policy of the administration of Bill Clinton.

Robert Jervis is the Adlai E. Stevenson Professor of International Politics at Columbia University. He has also held professorial appointments at the University of California at Los Angeles and Harvard University. In 2000–1, he served as the President of the American Political Science Association. His books include *Perception and Misperception in International Politics, The Meaning of the Nuclear Revolution, System Effects: Complexity in Political and Social Life,* and *American Foreign Policy in a New Era.*

Loch K. Johnson is Regents Professor of Public and International Affairs at the University of Georgia. He is author of several books and over 100 articles on US intelligence and national security. His books include *The Making of International Agreements* (1984); *A Season of Inquiry* (1985); *America's Secret Power* (1989); *America as a World Power* (1995); *Secret Agencies* (1996); *Bombs, Bugs, Drugs, and Thugs* (2000); *Seven Sins of American Foreign Policy* (2007); *Handbook of Intelligence Studies* (2007, editor); and *Strategic Intelligence* (2007, 5 volumes, editor). He has served as a special assistant to the chair of the Senate Select Committee on Intelligence (1975–76), staff director of the House Subcommittee on Intelligence Oversight (1977–79), and special assistant to the chair of the Aspin-Brown Commission on Intelligence (1995–96). He is the senior editor of the international journal *Intelligence and National Security.*

Richard J. Kerr is an international consultant. He joined the Central Intelligence Agency in 1960; was appointed deputy director for intelligence of the CIA in 1986; acting director of Central Intelligence in 1991; and deputy director of Central Intelligence from 1989 to 1992. He has received two National Intelligence Distinguished Service Medals for work in the intelligence community and two Distinguished Intelligence Medals for work in the CIA. President Bush gave him the Citizen's Medal for his work during *Desert Storm.*

John Mueller holds the Woody Hayes Chair of National Security Studies, Mershon Center, and is professor of Political Science, at Ohio State University. He is the author of *Overblown: How Politicians and the Terrorism Industry Inflate National Security Threats, and Why We Believe Them, War, Presidents and Public Opinion, Retreat from Doomsday: The Obsolescence of Major War,* and *The Remnants of War* among other books. Mueller is a member of the American Academy of Arts and Sciences.

Aris Pappas is Deputy Director of the Microsoft Institute for Advanced Technology in Governments. Prior to joining Microsoft, Mr. Pappas was co-founder and vice-president of Intelligence Enterprises, LLC, a consulting firm. His principal professional experience is 34 years of Federal service, six with the army and 28 with the Central Intelligence Agency, retiring as a member of the Senior Intelligence Service.

James P. Pfiffner is University Professor in the School of Public Policy at George Mason University. He has written or edited ten books on the presidency and American National Government, including *The Strategic Presidency: Hitting the Ground Running, The Modern Presidency,* and *The Character Factor: How We Judge Our Presidents.* His professional experience includes service in the Director's Office of the US Office of Personnel Management (1980–81), and he has been a member of the faculty at the University of California, Riverside and California State University, Fullerton. While serving with the 25th Infantry Division (1/8 Artillery) in 1970 he received the Army Commendation Medal for Valor in Vietnam and Cambodia.

Mark Phythian is Professor of Politics in the Department of Politics and International Relations at the University of Leicester. He has written widely on security and intelligence issues, including *Arming Iraq* (Northeastern University Press, 1997); *The Politics of British Arms Sales Since 1964* (Manchester University Press, 2000); *Intelligence in an Insecure World* (Polity, 2006, with Peter Gill), and *The Labour Party, War and International Relations 1945–2006* (Routledge, 2007).

Paul R. Pillar is on the faculty of the Security Studies Program at Georgetown University. He joined the Central Intelligence Agency in 1977 and he served as National Intelligence Officer for the Near East and South Asia from 2000 to 2005. He is the author of Negotiating Peace and Terrorism and US Foreign Policy. He served in Vietnam from 1972 to 1973 and earned a PhD at Princeton University.

Rodney Tiffen is Professor of Government and International Relations at the University of Sydney. His books include *How Australia Compares* (Cambridge University Press, 2004, with Ross Gittins); *Scandals: Media, Politics and Corruption in Contemporary Australia* (University of New South Wales Press, 1999); and *News and Power* (Allen & Unwin, 1989).

Jim Whitman is a senior lecturer in the Department of Peace Studies, Bradford University and general editor of the Palgrave series, *Global Issues*. His latest book is *The Limits of Global Governance* (Routledge, 2005).

Thomas Wolfe was a member of the RAND Corporation and served in "Team B" during the White House's competitive analysis exercise on intelligence about the Soviet Union in the 1970s.

1

Introduction: policymaking and intelligence on Iraq

James P. Pfiffner and Mark Phythian

It is already clear that the 2003 Iraq war represents a seminal event in the history of the twenty-first century, the consequences of which will continue to influence the nature of international politics for years to come. In a US context, the war and its aftermath are set to become at least as significant to twenty-first-century history as the Vietnam war (with which the Iraq war has come to be regularly compared) was to that of the twentieth.[1] Alongside the consequences of the war, the highly controversial decision to go to war in Iraq will be studied and debated well into the future.

This book is designed to help frame, facilitate, and inform these debates. The decision to go to war in Iraq offers an excellent case study through which we can analyze the nature of national security decision-making, the foreign policy roles of the President and Prime Minister, the roles of Congress and Parliament, the role and limits of intelligence, the management of public opinion, and the ethics of humanitarian military intervention. The case is unusual for such a contemporary event in that much official documentation is publicly available, allowing students to gain a nuanced understanding of both the process of going to war in Iraq and the making and implementation of national security policy in the US and UK.

Parallels between President Bush and Prime Minister Blair

At the outset it is useful to highlight a number of the most striking parallels and connections between the Bush administration in the US and the Blair government in the UK in making and sustaining the case for war in Iraq during 2002–3. Both leaders committed themselves to the probability of war with Iraq early in 2002, and each remained firmly committed despite broad international skepticism about the need for war. Blair's commitment to regime change was a direct response to post-September 11, 2001 (9/11) developments in the Bush administration's approach to the problem of Iraq. In both countries the decision to go to war drew on—or, at least, was taken in the context of—separate yet intersecting debates. In the US this context was provided by neoconservative intellectuals in or around the Bush administration, while in the UK the debate concerned the possibilities and limits of humanitarian military intervention.

The changing nature of executive leadership in the US and UK provides a further useful point of comparison. A marked trend in British politics over recent decades has been an increasing presidentialization of government. This has resulted in greater political control being centered in the prime minister himself and his personal entourage. This parallels a trend in the US over the past fifty years of centralized control of executive branch policymaking in the White House Office as opposed to the rest of the departments and agencies of the government.

Part of this trend in the US involved the marginalization of cabinet secretaries, even though they are appointed by the president because of their political loyalty and policy agreement with him. Younger and more politically attuned White House staffers came to dominate policymaking and wield the most power in presidential administrations. In the UK, the Cabinet had traditionally formed a collective deliberative body in which the prime minister was first among equals, and where policy emerged after informed consultation and debate, based on discussion of detailed position papers specially prepared for it. However, as various former members have attested, under Blair the Cabinet was shunted to the sidelines in policymaking in general, and national security policy in particular. It is not the case that Iraq rarely featured on the Cabinet agenda; rather that Cabinet was merely informed of developments and not involved as a policymaking body. Debate was not encouraged. For example, former Foreign Secretary Robin Cook, by this time demoted to the post of Leader of the House, recalled in his diaries a Cabinet meeting of February 28, 2002 at which Home Secretary David Blunkett, one of the most senior members of the Cabinet, and Cook asked for a Cabinet debate on Iraq. This was held the following week, when Cook recorded in his diaries: "A momentous event. A real discussion at Cabinet . . . For the first time I can recall in five years, Tony was out on a limb."[2] However, rather than seek to sum up the balance of a discussion that, on the basis of Cook's account, opposed the prime ministerial line on Iraq, Blair concluded the meeting by simply reiterating the rationale underpinning the existing approach. Moreover, leaks to newspapers over the next few days from sources close to the prime minister had the effect of undermining Cook's position and served as a disincentive for other Cabinet colleagues to continue their dissent.[3]

As Chapter 5 outlines, key decisions relating to Iraq were taken outside of Cabinet by a small group of (unelected) advisors operating within what amounted to a Prime Minister's Department in Downing Street, often in ad hoc meetings at which no minutes were taken. In the US, President Bush relied very heavily on Vice President Dick Cheney, National Security Advisor Condoleezza Rice, and Defense Secretary Donald Rumsfeld for advice on war. Secretary of State Colin Powell was sidelined by the White House staff and seen as not being a loyal team member, despite his being the only person at high levels in the Bush administration to have combat experience, in addition to his career in the military.

Experience and scholarship have agreed that an orderly policy process for decisionmaking, particularly about war, can help a leader get the most informed advice possible.[4] Experience has shown that it is important for leaders to listen to advice from several different, often conflicting, directions in order to be best informed when making crucial decisions. However, the Bush administration was different from most other recent administrations in its lack of a formal policy development process. In addition to the lack of orderly process, President Bush did not deliberate with his top advisors in any one meeting in which the pros and cons of going to war with Iraq were considered. His decisionmaking was seriatim and disjointed; his initial inclination to go to war went forward in a cascading fashion, without formal deliberations about whether going to war was a wise thing to do.[5] As former Director of the Central Intelligence Agency George Tenet wrote in his memoirs: "There was never a serious debate that I know of within the administration about the imminence of the Iraqi threat," nor even "a significant discussion" about options for continuing to contain Iraq.[6] In the UK case, as well as bypassing Cabinet as a consultative body, the small group of advisors around Prime Minister Blair operated independently of Foreign Office advice. A former diplomat who worked on Iraq, Carne Ross, has spoken of a "subtle and creeping politicisation of the diplomatic service, whereby in order to get promoted one has to show oneself as being sympathetic to, and identifying with, the views of Ministers—in particular the Prime Minister . . . Decision-making powers have become increasingly concentrated in No 10 rather than the Foreign Office, and the Foreign Office has become subsidiary to No 10."[7]

All of this means that in the cases of both Bush and Blair it is very difficult to identify the precise point at which they became committed to regime change in Iraq. For President Bush, the point seems to be somewhere around the time of the 2002 State of the Union address; for Prime Minister Blair shortly thereafter. By March, memoranda to and from

Downing Street staffers were referring to Blair's commitment to regime change, although his Cabinet remained unaware of this. Senior Cabinet members were aware by the summer of 2002, although those Cabinet members thought most likely to be resistant were kept in the dark well into the final months of 2002. Both men knew what they wanted, and their top aides worked to make this happen. Skeptics were shunted aside.

There were also clear parallels in the way in which intelligence was used to sell the case for war. As Chapters 12 and 13 argue, in the US, intelligence was used selectively to support the president's decision to go to war, and the intelligence was in some ways politicized. The Bush administration selectively leaked information to the press, which faithfully reported it with little skeptical analysis.[8] Intelligence findings were "cherry picked" to present to the public the most alarming allegations about Iraqi capabilities and intentions in order to support the drive to war. Systematically misleading implications were drawn by the top levels of the Bush administration about a purported link between Saddam and al Qaeda, and about Saddam's supposed nuclear capacity. Even after claims of either an Iraqi link to the events of 9/11 or more general Saddam–al Qaeda cooperation were conclusively rejected by official inquiries on both sides of the Atlantic, senior figures in the Bush and Blair administrations continued to refer or allude to them. They wanted to legitimize a war for which there was declining public support, despite their best efforts to manage public opinion. In both cases the Iraq war will dominate their historical legacies.

Similarly intelligence in the UK was presented to the public in a misleading way so as to generate support for Prime Minister Blair's decision to support the Bush administration's strategy of regime change. Intelligence was selectively leaked or "sexed up" in order to provide support for Blair's and Bush's charges about Saddam. The high water mark of this approach came with the publication in September 2002 of a dossier incorporating what turned out to be faulty intelligence on Iraq's weapons of mass destruction programs. This was prepared for publication by Downing Street and presented a suitably alarming portrayal of Iraqi capabilities and intent. Within eighteen months the intelligence underpinning all of the most alarming claims had been withdrawn by the foreign intelligence service, MI6, because it was unreliable.

After the war, several official investigations were conducted in both countries to determine why there had been such an enormous intelligence failure. In the US, the Senate Select Committee on Intelligence (SSCI), controlled by the Republicans, investigated and concluded that the intelligence process had failed and no inappropriate pressure had been placed on the intelligence community by the Bush administration. Subsequently, an independent commission, the Robb-Silberman Commission, was appointed by President Bush to examine the intelligence process leading up to the war. As with the SSCI report, the Commission found that the intelligence agencies had failed and that the Bush administration was innocent of any policy or analytic failures. Upon close reading, however, both reports provided considerable evidence that much of the intelligence failure was due to the way in which the intelligence was used by policy-makers, rather than to failures at the professional levels of the organizations comprising the intelligence community.

By July 2004 four separate UK investigations had considered the use of intelligence before the Iraq war. The first, by the parliamentary Foreign Affairs Committee, can be considered no more than a partial investigation because of the government's refusal to co-operate. A judicial inquiry conducted by Lord Hutton which considered the accuracy of claims contained in the September 2002 dossier, exonerated the government of any bad faith, although it subsequently transpired that it had not been informed of all relevant developments. The third inquiry, by the Intelligence and Security Committee—a quasi-parliamentary committee answerable to the prime minister and designed to provide a limited degree of oversight of the intelligence and security agencies—similarly absolved the government of bad faith, albeit in at times rather qualified language, although it emerged that it too had not had access to the full intelligence picture in carrying out its inquiry. Finally, the Butler inquiry was the most critical of the four, although it too exonerated any individual of responsibility for the failures it identified. In both countries, these inquiries suggested the inability of the politicians who undertook them to rise clearly above party political considerations where significant criticism of their party leader could have electoral consequences, or even bring about a change of government. With the exception of the Hutton inquiry in the UK, by their very nature all of these reports were the product of negotiation and compromise between committee or inquiry members.

The formal conclusions of these inquiries provided decisionmakers in the US and UK with an alibi for a course of action that proved disastrous for many Iraqis, leading to the deaths of between 70,000 and 80,000 by May 2007. The war also proved highly costly for the US and UK in financial and human terms, created an environment in which terrorism—both inside Iraq and more widely—flourished, and acted as a spur to suicide bombings in London. President John F. Kennedy had reflected in the wake of the 1961 Bay of Pigs debacle that victory has a hundred fathers, but defeat is an orphan. In the case of Iraq, decisionmakers sought to share the blame liberally, in particular by pinning it on the intelligence communities. Hence, in the US, the publication of George Tenet's memoirs was met by a White House spokesman's assurance that: "The president made the decision to remove Saddam Hussein for a number of reasons, mainly the National Intelligence Estimate on Iraq and Saddam Hussein's own actions, and only after a thorough and lengthy assessment of all available information as well as Congressional authorization."[9] Similarly, in the UK, the blame was heaped on the intelligence community, as when Prime Minister Blair told the 2004 Labour Party Conference, "the problem is, I can apologise for the information that turned out to be wrong, but I can't, sincerely at least, apologise for removing Saddam."[10] Trade and Industry Secretary Patricia Hewitt, a member of a Cabinet denied a full role in the decisionmaking process that led to war, repeated this formula, telling a television audience: "All of us who were involved in making an incredibly difficult decision are very sorry and do apologise for the fact that that information was wrong."[11] Similarly, the Lord Chancellor, Lord Falconer, told the *Today* radio programme that Blair "has made it absolutely clear that he is sorry about the sorts of issue—the information issue, the 45-minute issue—he is very sorry about that . . . We know the intelligence on which it was based is flawed and we are sorry about that."[12]

A further point of comparison concerns the roles of the respective legislatures, Congress and Parliament, in the war decision. Although President Bush maintained that he did not need the approval of Congress in order for him to attack Iraq, he knew that it would be useful politically if he did ask for their support. Many constitutional scholars, however, believed that he was required to go to Congress for authorization to go to war, because the Constitution vests the power to declare war in Congress.[13] In August 2002 the Bush administration argued that the 1991 resolution authorizing President George H. W. Bush to initiate the Gulf war extended to his son's initiating war with Iraq in 2002 or 2003. Although the president subsequently agreed to consult with members of Congress before going to war, he did not concede that he needed their approval or a formal declaration of war.

Bush was very skillful in the use of his political power in persuading Congress to grant him authority to take the country to war. The administration's public campaign heated up with Vice President Cheney's speech to the Veterans of Foreign Wars convention on August 26, 2002 (see excerpts in Appendix A). Cheney's strong speech argued that Saddam Hussein had chemical and biological weapons and was reconstituting his nuclear weapons capacity. Next, the administration leaked the purported evidence for Saddam's nuclear activity, claiming that a large shipment of aluminum tubes bound for Iraq was intended to be used as nuclear centrifuges.

On September 11, 2002, the first anniversary of the 9/11 attacks, President Bush gave a nationwide speech warning of the danger posed by Iraq. The next day in his address to the United Nations President Bush framed the issue as one of credibility for the UN and the need for its many resolutions to be enforced. Citing "flagrant violations" by Saddam Hussein, Bush declared that "we have been more than patient . . . The conduct of the Iraqi regime is a threat to the authority of the United Nations and a threat to peace." Arguing that the UN could not afford to become "irrelevant," he urged the passage of a tough resolution that would threaten Saddam with military action if he did not give up his weapons of mass destruction. "We cannot stand by and do nothing while dangers gather. We must stand up for our security and for the permanent rights and the hopes of mankind."[14]

On October 1, the National Intelligence Estimate (NIE) concerning Iraq (see Chapter 4 for a critique) was given to Congress, and it contained alarming assertions about Iraq's "weapons of mass destruction" (WMD) capacity. A White Paper containing the most disturbing claims of the NIE but none of the cautioning language or dissents was released to the public. In anticipation of the upcoming congressional vote on a resolution authorizing war with Iraq, the president made a speech to the nation from Cincinnati on 7 October 2002 in which he explained the need for the authorization to take military action. He outlined the capacity and intentions of Saddam Hussein in dire tones, and made his strongest case for war with Iraq (see excerpts in Appendix A). The president made the case that America was vulnerable to terrorist attack and that a hostile regime in Iraq might be willing to share its CBN (chemical, biological, nuclear) technology with terrorists. Thus the US had to act preemptively to prevent this from happening.

Not everyone agreed that the threat from Saddam was as immediate as the president argued. In a letter to SSCI chair Senator Bob Graham (D-Fl), CIA Director Tenet said that, in the judgment of the CIA, the probability of Saddam initiating an attack on the United States "in the foreseeable future, given the conditions we understand now, the likelihood I think would be low." But if faced with a "use or lose" situation, Saddam would likely use his weapons. "Baghdad for now appears to be drawing a line short of conducting terrorist attacks with conventional or C.B.W. [chemical and biological weapons] against the United States . . . Should Saddam conclude that a U.S.-led attack could no longer be deterred, he probably would become much less constrained in adopting terrorist actions."[15]

Critics of the administration's war plans argued that a US attack would likely precipitate the use of the chemical and biological weapons that the

US feared. They also felt that the negative consequences of a US invasion of Iraq would outweigh the benefits of stopping Saddam's efforts to obtain nuclear weapons and that Saddam could be contained. But President Bush's arguments were sufficient to persuade a majority of Congress to vote for an authorizing resolution.

The Democrats were in a difficult political situation. Many of them were skeptical of granting the president authority to take the country to war with Iraq, but they knew that he was persuasive with a narrow majority of the American public in arguing that war was necessary. In addition, congressional elections were coming up in the next month in which all of the House of Representatives was up for election and one third of the Senate. The Democrats did not want to run for reelection with their Republican opponents calling them 'soft' on Saddam and terrorism. Although some of the Democrats were truly convinced that war was necessary, others voted for the authorization for war because they wanted to defuse the war issue and campaign on domestic issues, in which the Democrats considered themselves to have an advantage.

Although there was a debate in Congress and statements by those supporting and opposing the resolution, there was never much doubt about the outcome, and the debate lacked the drama of the deliberation in 1991 over the Gulf War resolution. A number of Democrats voted for the resolution from fear that a negative vote could be used against them in the upcoming elections. The Democratic leadership, Majority Leader of the Senate Tom Daschle and House Minority Leader Richard Gephardt, voted for the measure. The resolution passed in the House by 296 to 133, with 6 Republicans and 126 Democrats (and one independent) voting against it. In the Senate the resolution passed 77 to 23, with 21 Democrats, one Republican, and one Independent voting against it. The president had managed to persuade former critics of war with Iraq, Senators Hagel, Lugar, and Kerry and Representative Richard Army to vote for the resolution.

The final resolution, which was passed by the House on October 10 and by the Senate on October 11, was very similar to the draft resolution proposed by the White House. After detailing Iraq's refusal to comply with UN resolutions on weapons inspections and noting that members of al Qaeda were in Iraq, the resolution stated: "The president is authorized to use the armed forces of the United States as he determines to be necessary and appropriate, in order to: (1) defend the national security of the United States against the continuing threat posed by Iraq; and (2) enforce all relevant United Nations Security Council resolutions regarding Iraq."[16]

Although it faces significant practical difficulties in making it felt, the US Congress enjoys far greater formal power over the decision to commit troops to war than does the UK Parliament. In the UK, the power to declare war is exercised by the prime minister under the terms of the Royal Prerogative—an arrangement dating back to the 1689 Bill of Rights. The Bill of Rights transferred many powers to Parliament, but the war power remained with the Crown. Because the power was handed down from monarch to prime minister, and because the prime minister wields this power on behalf of the Crown, there is no formal role for Parliament.

However, Labour Party backbenchers have been voicing anxieties about the implications of this position since at least the time of the 1982 Falklands war. At this time the only way in which they could register their opposition to imminent war was through the unsatisfactory procedural device of a vote on an adjournment motion, rather than a vote on a substantive motion.[17] Calls for Parliament to play a more substantive role grew in subsequent years, most notably in relation to the war over Kosovo. In the case of Iraq, Robin Cook, as Leader of the House, played a key role in persuading the government to grant Parliament a vote on the war, in which he was supported by Foreign Secretary Jack Straw. In part, Cook's argument was based on the fact that the US Congress was to vote on the war, so why not the UK Parliament? At this time—the latter part of 2002—the government's strategy was still to secure a specific UN Security Council resolution to legitimize the coming war, and substantive motions for parliamentary debate could be framed around support for the UN in enforcing Iraqi compliance with its resolutions. On this basis, a debate on a motion affirming the government's support for UN Security Council resolution 1441 on 25 November 2002 ended with 85, mainly Labour, Members of Parliament (MPs), approximately an eighth of all MPs, voting against the government.

The government's commitment to seeking a legitimizing vote in Parliament involved a manageable risk if the hoped-for UN Security Council resolution was forthcoming, but once it became clear it was not, MPs would be voting on whether to take Britain to war without a UN mandate. For a party within which support for the UN was a core principle of foreign policy, and which had played a role in the creation of the UN during the 1945 Attlee government, this was bound to prove highly divisive.[18] Hence, Labour MPs had to be convinced of the Iraqi threat, and here the flawed intelligence and exaggerations in threat presentation played a significant role in winning Parliament's support for the war. Still, in the final debate of March 18, 2003, where Parliament voted to commit British forces to war without UN authorization, 139 Labour MPs voted for an amendment to the motion stating that the case for war had still to be established—the largest rebellion by government backbenchers in

150 years.[19] If Blair had lost the vote he may well have had no choice but to do what his supporters told wavering Labour MPs he would do if he lost—that is, resign. Hence, although the flawed intelligence that underpinned the government's case for war may have had little significance in terms of the government's war decision, it was much more important in terms of the vital parliamentary vote and the future of Blair's prime ministership.

Nevertheless, the vote of March 18, 2003 set a precedent that it will prove difficult to move away from, establishing for Parliament a formal role in approving the deployment of British forces in war situations. Moreover, the government's manipulation of the case for war may well result in greater parliamentary skepticism in the future, and a determination not to get fooled again. However, as the history of the US Congress in relation to matters of war suggests, legislatures are poorly equipped to challenge the exercise of executive power in this area.

The structure of the book

The book is divided into five parts. The first examines the intellectual frameworks within which the case for war in Iraq was developed in the US and UK. In Chapter 2, John Dumbrell analyzes the neoconservative roots of the decision to go to war. He traces the evolution of neoconservative thinking on foreign and security policy issues, highlighting the complexity of, and potential contradictions within, neoconservative thought. By the 1990s the neocons had an influential base in the Project for a New American Century that called for military action to overthrow Saddam Hussein's regime. Signatories to this programme—including Donald Rumsfeld, Paul Wolfowitz, and John Bolton—would go on to secure important positions in the Bush administration, from which, post-9/11, they could make the case for the necessity of military action. However, the extent to which neoconservatives "captured" the Bush administration is still keenly debated, and Dumbrell cautions that, while they undoubtedly played an important role, their significance to the decision to go to war in Iraq can be overstated.

In the UK the Blair government presented the case for war in Iraq as being in part a continuation of the humanitarian military interventionism it had increasingly pursued since coming into office. In particular, in 1999 the Blair government had committed British forces to a war over Kosovo without UN approval, but within the framework of NATO. In Chapter 3, Jim Whitman analyzes the humanitarian intervention rationale that was developed in the context of the Kosovo campaign, Blair's presentation of it, and the case of Iraq. The question of whether Iraq represents a genuine case of humanitarian intervention remains highly controversial.[20] Whitman focuses on the essentially post-facto nature of this justification, emphasizes the damage the Iraq war has inflicted on the non-interventionist norm, considers the impact of the war on the authority of the UN, and the implications for future international order. In doing so, this chapter engages in important debates about the ethics, merits, risks and legality of humanitarian military intervention and, by extension, of the legality of the Iraq war itself.

The second part of the book looks at the parallel processes through which the Bush administration and Blair government constructed their cases for war, analyzing similarities and divergences in approach. Both faced considerable opposition which they sought to overcome, in part, by the public use of secret intelligence. In Chapter 4 James Pfiffner analyzes the arguments for war with Iraq put forward by President Bush and his top aides. He concludes that top administration members did not lie outright, but that they did systematically mislead the country about Saddam's nuclear capacity and the "link" between Saddam and al Qaeda. Pfiffner says that the intelligence on chemical and biological weapons in Iraq was outdated and exaggerated, but that most allied intelligence agencies agreed that Saddam had them, so the Bush administration cannot be faulted for agreeing with most other nations.

In Chapter 5, Mark Phythian analyzes the background to the Blair government's decision to go to war, focusing on the chronology underpinning the decision as revealed by official inquiries and leaked documents, and discussing the relationship between intelligence and policymaking in this case. He also considers the extent to which the increased presidentialization of British politics created the space in which the war decision was taken, and the failure of the Cabinet to adequately challenge the prime minister as he developed his pro-war case. The US and UK were not the only countries where the case for war proved controversial. In Australia, the government of John Howard strongly supported the Bush-Blair approach, and similarly engaged in a campaign to secure public support for its own military involvement. As Rodney Tiffen shows in Chapter 6, Australia enjoyed both the political luxuries and liabilities of being a junior ally. It did not have to take on the central responsibility for the conduct and outcome of the conflict. Nor did it have to make a military commitment on the same scale, or suffer as many casualties. Moreover, there was political benefit to be gained from proclaiming conformity with the country's two most traditionally important allies. On the other hand, it was captive to decisions made in Washington and London, which it was almost powerless to affect. It also relied on its two senior allies for most of its intelligence on the Middle East, and its policymaking was therefore to some extent dependent on the quality of information it was being supplied with. This chapter analyses this relationship over Iraq and the issues raised by Australia's reliance on the US and UK for intelligence.

In Chapter 7 public opinion expert John Mueller examines how the Bush administration tried to manage public opinion in support of its war policies. Although a small majority of Americans had favored going to war with Iraq since 2000 (support stayed within 5 points of 55 percent, except for short spikes right after 9/11 and after Colin Powell's speech to the UN), the administration was not able to improve those numbers as war approached. Once the war was underway and casualties increased with the rise of the insurgency, public support began to erode, and after several years solid majorities of the American public thought the war had been a mistake.

One of the most significant aspects of the war in Iraq was the scale of the intelligence failure leading up to it. The nature of intelligence failure is a keenly debated topic within the field of intelligence studies, but never before have students of intelligence had available to them so much primary documentation from so recent and significant a case from which they can analyze the issue. Parts III and IV provide a range of analyses that consider the loci of the intelligence failure over Iraq, the lessons for the intelligence communities, and the degree to which the decision to go to war in Iraq represented a policy rather than, or as well as, an intelligence failure. Richard Kerr, a former Deputy Director of Central Intelligence, along with several colleagues, conducted a post-mortem analysis on the intelligence process before the war in Iraq. In the unclassified analysis in Chapter 8, they conclude that the judgments of the intelligence community were "seriously flawed, misleading, and even wrong." Part of the reason for this was that the intelligence relied upon by the agencies was collected prior to 1998 and was not updated with more recent evidence. Ironically, they conclude that where the intelligence community was correct (about the absence of a link between Saddam and al Qaeda), the Bush administration applied pressure for changes. But where the intelligence community was wrong (about WMD), no pressure was applied because the intelligence supported the policy preferences of the administration.

In Chapter 9 intelligence scholar Robert Jervis takes a longer range and more detached view of the intelligence process in the US. Jervis argues that policymakers in all administrations say that they want better intelligence, but in fact they do not. Policymakers get frustrated with good intelligence analysis because it is often couched in careful terms and seldom presents clear and simple answers. He concludes that the usual response to intelligence failures is to reform the process, just as the US reorganized its intelligence community, but that these efforts are often futile because the fundamental problem is embodied in the different purposes of policymakers and intelligence professionals.

Intelligence scholar and former congressional intelligence staff member Loch Johnson in Chapter 10 looks at how Congress dealt with intelligence before the war. His analysis centers around why Congress, which is supposed to oversee the executive branch and hold it accountable for accomplishing the goals set out in legislation, failed to realize the faulty nature of the intelligence that the administration relied upon in taking the country to war. Johnson argues that lawmakers have varied and different approaches to the oversight of the intelligence community, and that while some take an appropriately skeptical but supportive stance toward the intelligence community, most others do not have the motivation to put their limited energy and time into intelligence oversight. Thus Congress as a whole failed to do its job with respect to the use of intelligence before the Iraq war.

In Chapter 11, Mark Phythian complements the analyses of US prewar intelligence failures contained in parts three and four by analysing what post-war inquiries have revealed about the nature of the failure in the UK case. The focus of the chapter is twofold—first, to consider the extent of and reasons for the UK intelligence failure over Iraq and, secondly, to assess the effectiveness of the different forms of inquiry into aspects of prewar intelligence in explaining how the UK came to go to war on what Robin Cook famously termed a "false prospectus."

In Chapter 12 James Pfiffner looks at the decisionmaking process of the Bush administration in the year before the war in Iraq. He argues that the process was minimal and that it was non-deliberative, sequential, and informal. He links the poor use of intelligence before the war to the faulty policy development process. President Bush failed to heed the advice of career professionals in the agencies of the government and relied instead on those close aides who agreed with him about Iraq. Thus the US went to war based on faulty intelligence and unprepared for the lengthy occupation after the initial combat phase was concluded.

Paul Pillar spent his career in the CIA and was the top intelligence official in the intelligence community responsible for the Near East and South Asia from 2000 to 2005. He was thus a major participant in the intelligence process from the career professional side during the time leading up to the Iraq war. That is why his criticisms of the Bush administration in Chapter 13 are so credible and important. Pillar charges the Bush administration with ignoring professional intelligence when it did not support its policy views, misusing intelligence in its attempt to build support for the war, and politicizing the intelligence process during the run-up to the war.

The volume concludes with Part V, which provides excerpts from a number of speeches and documents which are key to understanding the nature of national security decisionmaking and intelligence failure in this case and which are referred to in the preceding chapters.

Notes

1 See, for example, John Dumbrell and David Ryan (eds.), *Vietnam in Iraq: Tactics, Lessons, Legacies and Ghosts* (Abingdon: Routledge, 2007).
2 Robin Cook, *The Point of Departure* (London: Simon & Schuster, 2003), p. 115.
3 Ibid, pp. 120–1.
4 See, for example, John Burke and Fred Greenstein, *How Presidents Test Reality: Decisions on Vietnam, 1954 and 1965* (New York: Russell Sage Foundation, 1991); Alexander George, "The Case for Multiple Advocacy in Making Foreign Policy," *American Political Science Review*, Vol.66, No.3, 1972; and *Presidential Decisionmaking in Foreign Policy* (Boulder, CO: Westview Press, 1980).
5 See also, James P. Pfiffner, "The First MBA President: George W. Bush as Public Administrator," *Public Administration Review*, Jan/Feb. 2007, pp. 6–20.
6 See Scott Shane and Mark Mazzetti, "Ex-CIA Chief, in Book, Assails Cheney on Iraq," *New York Times*, Apr. 27, 2007.
7 Carne Ross: Minutes of Evidence, Foreign Affairs Committee, Nov. 8, 2006, www.publications.parliament.uk/pa/cm200607/cmselect/cmfaff/167/61108 05.htm. He went on to say that; "policy making in the run-up to the Iraq war was extremely poor, in that available alternatives to war were not properly considered, the presentation to the public of the intelligence on weapons of mass destruction was manipulated, and proper legal advice from the Foreign Office on the legality of the war was ignored." Ibid.
8 On this, see Chaim Kaufmann, "Threat Inflation and the Failure of the Marketplace of Ideas: The Selling of the Iraq War," *International Security*, Vol.29, No.1, Summer 2004, pp. 5–48.
9 Shane and Mazzetti, "Ex-CIA Chief."
10 Tony Blair's Speech to the Labour Party Conference, Sep. 28, 2004. at www.newsvote.bbc.co.uk/mpapps/pagetools/print/news.bbc.co.uk/1/hi/uk_politics/36.
11 BBC News, "Ministers 'Sorry' For Iraq Error", Oct. 8, 2004, at www.newsvote.bbc.co.uk/mpapps/pagetools/print/news.bbc.co.uk/1/hi/uk_politics/37.
12 *Today*, Radio 4, Oct. 13, 2004. Cited in *The Independent*, Oct. 14, 2004.
13 See for example, Louis Fisher, *Presidential War Power* (Lawrence, KS: University Press of Kansas, 1995); Harold Hongju Koh, *The National Security Constitution: Sharing Power After the Iran-Contra Affair* (New Haven, CT: Yale University Press, 1990).

14 President's Remarks to the Nation, Ellis Island, New York, Sep. 11, 2002, White House website.

15 CIA Letter to Senate on Baghdad's Intentions, Oct. 7, 2002. Reprinted on GlobalSecurity.org at: www.globalsecurity.org/wmd/library/news/iraq/2002/iraq-021007-cia01.htm.

16 Public Law 107-243-Oct. 16, 2002, Authorization for Use of Military Force Against Iraq Resolution of 2002. Available at: www.cspan.org/resources/pdf/hjres114.pdf.

17 See Cook, *The Point of Departure*, pp. 189–90 for a description of this device.

18 On this foreign policy tradition, see Mark Phythian, *The Labour Party, War and International Relations, 1945–2006* (Abingdon: Routledge, 2007).

19 Philip Cowley, *The Rebels: How Blair Mislaid His Majority* (London: Politico's, 2005), p. 123.

20 For example, Human Rights Watch's Kenneth Roth has argued that the invasion of Iraq failed to meet the test of a humanitarian intervention. Kenneth Roth, "War in Iraq: Not a Humanitarian Intervention," World Report 2004, www.hrw.org/wr2k4/3.htm. That it was a humanitarian invasion is argued in Thomas Cushman (ed.), *A Matter of Principle: Humanitarian Arguments for War in Iraq* (Berkeley, University of California Press, 2005).

Part I

Intellectual antecedents of the Iraq war

2

The neoconservative roots of the war in Iraq

John Dumbrell

The 2003 invasion of Iraq appeared, certainly on the surface of things, to exemplify and realize several of the fundamental tenets of neoconservative thought in the US. The Bush Doctrine of preemption, the tendency toward unilateralism and working via "coalitions of the willing," the willingness (even eagerness) to use and sustain American military power, the attendant moral certainty, the notion of using Iraqi regime change as the starting motor of a democratizing engine for the entire Middle East: locating such ideas and commitments in the columns of neoconservative-leaning journals, newspapers, and think tank reports is an easy task. The period between the terror attacks of September 11, 2001 and the onset of the Iraq war was, in Francis Fukuyama's phrase, "the neoconservative moment."[1] For Stefan Halper and Jonathan Clarke, there had occurred a neoconservative hijacking of US foreign policy. "In the tumultuous days following 9/11," wrote Halper and Clarke in 2004, "the neoconservatives were ready with a detailed, plausible blueprint for the nation's response."[2] Senator Joe Biden of Delaware, ranking Democrat on the Senate Foreign Relations Committee, declared in July 2003: "They [the neocons] seem to have captured the heart and mind of the President, and they're controlling the foreign policy agenda."[3]

This notion of post-9/11 neoconservative ascendancy is by no means unchallengeable. The fevered nature of international political discourse in the era of the Iraq invasion tended to militate against rational analysis. For many opponents of the invasion, the term "neocon" became little more than an insult, connoting extremism and conspiracy. The British writer Ian McEwan, whose 2005 novel *Saturday* was set on the day of the massive London anti-war march in February 2003, put the following words into the mouth of Daisy Perowne, a young protester against the policies of President George W. Bush: "You know very well, these extremists, the Neo-cons, have taken over America. Cheney, Rumsfeld, Wolfovitz [sic]. Iraq was always their pet project."[4]

The emotionalism exemplified in Daisy Perowne's outburst, reflecting the passions which affected even academic analysis of the Bush foreign policy, tended to ignore or conflate the complex and overlapping faction lines within the Bush administration. As will be made clear below, neoconservatism is a diverse intellectual movement; name-calling and "othering" of the neocons achieves little. As David Brooks, former journalist on the *Weekly Standard,* wrote in 2004, giving your foes "a collective name" makes meager analytic sense: "You get to feed off their villainy and luxuriate in your contrasting virtue".[5] The main purpose of this chapter is to provide a reasonably cool and rational account of the development of neoconservative views on US foreign policy, culminating in the decision to invade Iraq.

The neoconservative story: New York to Washington

American neoconservatism has been variously described as a movement, a persuasion, and a network. Its elite orientation, extreme intellectualism, and close-knit familialism have all attracted accusations of conspiracy, even of "unAmericanism." Populist New Righter Pat Buchanan declared in 1987 that "we are better off with these people as adversaries."[6] The Jewishness of some leading neoconservatives is well known, as is the Trotskyist past of first generation neocons, notably Irving Kristol. Joshua Muravchik, himself a former leftist, actually holds that Kristol was the only "major neocon figure" who had a "significant dalliance with Trotskyism."[7] Nevertheless, neoconservatism is frequently discussed almost as much in terms of its status as a deviant leftism as a feature of the American tradition of conservatism. The movement, if a movement it is, resembles a "clan" (as Anatol Lieven puts it) more than it does a "conspiracy." It has been made possible, to use Lieven's words once more, "by the American System's blurring of the lines among government, academia, the media and business."[8] The movement's intellectual output has been prodigious, belying notions of secrecy and conspiratorial intent. It has attracted Jewish and non-Jewish intellectuals, including prominent Roman Catholic thinkers and writers. The movement's ideas have not been Platonic constants, but rather have evolved and developed dialectically with the rhythms and cycles of history. Let us attempt a brief survey of the movement's historical development.

Most of the leading first generation neoconservatives, including Irving Kristol, Nathan Glazer and Daniel Bell, attended the City College of New York in the 1930s. Indeed, it is possible to trace the origins of the movement to one section of the CCNY canteen, where the young intellectuals debated varieties of Marxism. Disillusionment even with anti-Stalinist

Marxism led the group towards the project of creating an authentically American political philosophy, rooted in patriotic moral certainty and respect for free markets. As Francis Fukuyama later recalled, leading neocons traveled rightwards at their own individual pace: "Irving Kristol moved the farthest, Irving Howe the least, and [Daniel] Bell, [Nathan] Glazer, [Seymour Martin] Lipset and [Daniel Patrick] Moynihan ended up somewhere in between."[9] The new philosophy, initially located in the Democratic Party, was anti-communist and increasingly contemptuous of the social reforming ambitions of "high" American liberalism. In 2004, Fukuyama reminded his neoconservative associates that they had spent much of the latter part of the twentieth century warning against the kind of swift and ahistorical schemes of social transformation that were now being attempted in the Middle East: "If the United States cannot eliminate poverty or raise test scores in Washington DC, how does it expect to bring democracy to a part of the world that has stubbornly resisted it and is virulently anti-American to boot?"[10]

The intellectual lineage of neoconservatism snakes back to Plato. It certainly includes the work of Leo Strauss, University of Chicago philosopher and interpreter of canonical texts (including texts from the Islamic tradition). Milton Himmelfarb wrote that Strauss's work constituted "an invitation to join those privileged few who, having ascended from the (Platonic) cave, gaze upon the sun with unhooded eyes, while yet mindful of those others below, in the dark."[11] From Strauss and Straussianism, neoconservatism acquired the reputation for extreme elitism and for harboring somewhat ambivalent attitudes toward "those others below, in the dark." Strauss's own philosophical and literary exegesis emphasized the individual virtue of those who had managed to escape the darkness of the cave; it also focused on hidden meanings in canonical texts, especially those written under "tyrannical" regimes.[12]

By the 1960s and 1970s, young Straussian intellectuals became active in American academic, public and governmental life. If not exactly living in a Straussian "tyranny," they certainly felt themselves beleaguered by new, and profoundly uncongenial, strands within American liberalism: moral relativism, egalitarian anti-intellectualism and what were seen as the distasteful culture and practices of the anti-Vietnam war movement. To many self-consciously beleaguered neocons in the early 1970s, superpower détente was simply a euphemism for compromising with tyranny. The fact that it was being pursued by the "realist" Republican administration of Richard Nixon merely showed the distance which America's Grand Old Party needed to travel in order to achieve any kind of neoconservative authenticity. At best, détente was national self-deception, playing into the hands of Moscow; at worst, it was part of the indulgent self-hatred that had resulted from the failure of the US nerve in Vietnam. The neoconservative foreign policy hero of the 1970s was Democratic Senator and "defence hawk," Henry "Scoop" Jackson of Washington. Neocon intellectuals applauded Jackson's unblinking anti-Sovietism and excoriated President Jimmy Carter's efforts to substitute "human rights" for anti-communism as the integrative basis for US foreign relations.[13]

During the wilderness years—the Churchillian parallel is apt—the movement was sustained by magazine publication, and by family and personal connection. Domestic neoconservative themes were sounded in *The Public Interest*, international ones in *Commentary*. Also by the 1970s, the American Enterprise Institute, originally founded in 1943, was becoming the think tank of the right, with an increasingly neocon orientation. "Scoop" Jackson's Senate staff provided a temporary home for several important neocon politicos, including Elliott Abrams, Richard Perle and Frank Gaffney. On the executive side of government, Paul Wolfowitz—initially employed in Nixon's Arms Control and Disarmament Agency (ACDA), but moving to the Pentagon in the Carter years—became a seminal figure, encouraging and sponsoring young hawkish defense intellectuals.

Wolfowitz, later to become Donald Rumsfeld's deputy in George W. Bush's Defense Department, was a former pupil of Leo Strauss and, more importantly, for his future development, of rightist nuclear strategist and academic, Albert Wohlstetter. Wohlstetter's lines of argument, especially regarding the war-fighting potential of accurate missiles, themselves became neoconservative weapons to be hurled at détente and at the "realism" of Henry Kissinger. From 1973, Wolfowitz worked under Fred Iklé at ACDA, an agency which emerged in the second Nixon administration as a force which questioned and indeed opposed the building of détente and arms control. In 1976, under President Gerald Ford, Wolfowitz took part in the "Team B" exercise which investigated Soviet capabilities and intentions. He subsequently acknowledged the power of the "Team B" experience in causing him to look beyond consensus assumptions. At the Pentagon under Jimmy Carter, Wolfowitz became increasingly preoccupied with the politics of Middle Eastern oil. The 1979 Limited Contingency Study included a section, written by Dennis Ross under direction by Wolfowitz, on "the emerging Iraqi threat."[14]

The neoconservative story: Reagan to George W. Bush

As head of the State Department policy planning staff in the early 1980s, Paul Wolfowitz analyzed American options for the post-détente era. At this time, his main priority was China: essentially questioning the rationale of the Nixon/Kissinger opening. Wolfowitz's office, both in policy planning and after his 1982 promotion to the post of Assistant Secretary for East Asia and the Pacific, became a neocon outpost in a Reagan administration which tended to favour "pragmatic hawks" over intellectuals. Despite some traces of neocon enthusiasm in his policies and outlook—most clearly in Central America—President Reagan was not the ideological prisoner of the several hardline conservative intellectuals who comprised the anti-Carter Committee on the Present Danger in the late 1970s. Yet the neoconservative cause was nurtured in Reagan's Washington: by Wolfowitz and his associates, by Richard Perle and Fred Iklé at the Pentagon, by Elliott Abrams at State, and, most publicly of all, by Jeane Kirkpatrick, US Ambassador to the United Nations.

Kirkpatrick's appointment built on the tradition of extreme neoconservative skepticism about, and frustration with, the UN which had recently been demonstrated during Senator Moynihan's tenure as Ambassador to the UN under President Ford. Moynihan's UN memoir[15]—essentially an assault on the double standards, anti-Israeli and anti-American biases of the institution—had, by the early 1980s, become a classic recognition of how little could be achieved through indiscriminate international multilateralism. A former member of the Socialist Party of America and a Democrat until 1985, Kirkpatrick rapidly received Reagan's praise (as he put it) for removing from America's back the sign that said "Kick Me." Her major contribution to neoconservative thought was her 1979 *Commentary* article, "Dictatorships and Double Standards." The piece famously argued that non-communist autocracies at least had the potential to develop in a democratic direction; "totalitarian" communist states did not. The logic was clear: the US should look after its non-communist friends. Kirkpatrick's thinking pointed away from hasty, interventionist democracy-promotion. It represented strongly the realist strand in neoconservative thought, albeit a strand still rooted in moral certainty. Sentences from "Dictatorships and Double Standards" were quoted by commentators *in opposition* to the 2003 invasion of Iraq. "No idea holds greater sway in the mind of educated Americans than the belief that it is possible to democratize governments, anytime and anywhere, under any circumstances." Democracy, for Kirkpatrick, was an exceedingly slow-growing plant. She continued, writing nearly a quarter of a century before the post-invasion collapse of order in Iraq: "The speed with which armies collapse, bureaucracies abdicate, and social structures dissolve once the autocrat is removed frequently surprises American policymakers."[16]

Later neocon reverence for "Reaganism"—essentially for Reagan's values-oriented commitment to sustained American military primacy—was based on more than a degree of selective memory. In this respect it mirrored neocon worship of Winston Churchill, which tended to neglect the British leader's role as a post-1945 advocate of superpower proto-détente.[17] Reagan's "squeeze" strategy on the USSR, advocated by Richard Perle, was applied, at least in the non-military sphere, pragmatically and even half-heartedly. By the later 1980s, *Commentary* tended to represent a branch of American conservatism—implicitly or explicitly critical of Reagan—which felt that events were running ahead of American interests. The movement floundered as the Cold War expired.[18]

It fell to a new generation, led by William Kristol, son of Irving, and extending to controversialists such as Charles Krauthammer, to re-fashion neoconservatism for the new, Soviet-less era. The project began under Reagan; by the second term of President Clinton it had made extra-ordinary progress. The organizational practices of the "new" neocons echoed those of the founding generation. New journals, notably *The National Interest*—its publication in 1989 of Fukuyama's "end of history" ideas dragged an obscure magazine into the global sunshine—were generated. In 1995, the Rupert Murdoch-owned (and Rupert Murdoch-subsidized) *Weekly Standard* was launched as a somewhat downmarket and even, defying the Platonic elitism of neocon tradition, populist conduit for neoconservative ideas. By the later Clinton years, the "new" neoconservatism even had a postal address: 1150 Seventeenth Street, Washington DC—an office building which housed both the American Enterprise Institute and the *Weekly Standard*.[19] From his fifth floor office at 1150 Seventeenth, William Kristol coordinated the activities of an array of rightist lobbying associations. Among Kristol's organizational alphabet soup, one organization stood out in connection with evolving neocon ideas regarding Iraq: PNAC, the Project for a New American Century.

PNAC issued its founding Statement of Principles in 1997, though a letter, urging President Clinton to address the threat posed by Iraqi weapons of mass destruction, was sent under PNAC's auspices in July 1996. At one level, the Project for a New American Century was part of the "new" neo-conservative response to the end of the Cold War. Neoconservatism was now firmly a strand within the Republican party. Its adherents, in PNAC and well beyond, now argued the case for the "Reaganite" soul of the Grand Old Party. The immediate enemy was not so much Clinton and the Democrats, who actually were doing a reasonable job of keeping interna-tionalism at the centre of US foreign policy, but rather "new populist" or neo-isolationist Republicans.[20] Robert Kagan and William Kristol promoted a "neo-Reaganite foreign policy", committed to unrelenting American hegemony and contemptuous of notions of "overstretch."[21]

On the narrower issue of Iraq, PNAC's ideas were forged during the presidency of George Herbert Walker Bush. They proceeded from responses to the 1991 Gulf war, especially in connection with America's failure then to remove Saddam Hussein from power. Bush senior no more followed a neocon foreign policy than had Reagan. For a variety of reasons, contemporary neocons find it difficult to criticise either president. Yet, post-Cold War neoconservatism was actually defined in the space between Reagan's "utopianism"—notably his extraordinary attempt at the 1986 Reykjavik Summit to bargain away nuclear weapons altogether—and G. H. W. Bush's "pragmatic realism". Bushite pragmatism was seen as much in Bush senior's resolve to "avoid dancing on the Berlin Wall," as in the allowing of Saddam to remain safe in Baghdad two years later. The pragmatic realism of the 1991 decision to cease action in Iraq was defended in the memoirs of Colin Powell, the elder Bush and Brent Scowcroft. The US had no United Nations mandate to assault Baghdad; Muslim members of the coalition would oppose the move; removing Iraq's head would merely stimulate chaos, propelling Washington into an unpopular and unsustainable program of Vietnam-style nationbuilding. Powell was even prepared to acknowledge that Saddam had his limited virtues, as a secular strongman with whom Washington had done business in the past.[22] From a neocon perspective (though not all neoconservatives actually took this view), Colin Powell's line amounted to betrayal. In 1992, Joshua Muravchik attacked Bush's "foreign policy realism" in the pages of *New Republic*, the old leftwing journal which was now increasingly becoming a neoconservative platform. President G. H. W. Bush saw Saddam in Baghdad as capable of balancing Iran: "But," wrote Muravchik, "since both of these regimes remain bloodily repressive, internationally mischievous, and implacably hostile to America, just what is realistic about it?" Muravchik urged anyone who agreed with him to vote for Clinton in 1992. In 1996, Muravchik criticised the "balancing game," noting that "today the strongest criticism of Bush's action is not that he was too fast to resort to war but rather that he was too fast to end it."[23]

Neoconservatives publicly applauded the 1991 Gulf War as an effort to terminate "Vietnam syndrome" inhibitions on the use of American military power, and as a warning to the world. Muravchik declared in 1996: "The degree to which our decisive defeat of Iraq may have deterred others cannot be known."[24] No doubt the deterrent effect would have been stronger had Saddam been ousted successfully. The neoconservative role *within* the Bush administration, however, was rather more equivocal.

During the Bush (senior) presidential years, Paul Wolfowitz worked under Defense Secretary Richard Cheney as chief policy undersecretary.

Following the Iraqi invasion of Kuwait in August 1990, Wolfowitz and Lewis "Scooter" Libby, his contingency planning assistant, drew up plans directly to invade Iraq. The initiative emanated from Henry Rowen, from the Hoover Institution at Stanford University, who was then employed as another assistant to Wolfowitz. Under Cheney's overall direction, the plan, Operation Scorpion, was developed with no direct connection to the Joint Chiefs of Staff and certainly with no interagency input. The plan, which was eventually rejected by Colin Powell as chair of the Joint Chiefs, provided for the establishment of a US base in the western desert, within a hundred miles of Baghdad. The plan provided for the American forces to have the ability to destroy Scud missiles aimed at Israel. Despite the audacity of Operation Scorpion, Wolfowitz did not apparently oppose Powell's decision to leave Saddam in power in 1991; nor, indeed did Richard Cheney. In an essay on the future of Iraq published in 1997, Wolfowitz subscribed to the Bush-Scowcroft-Powell view on the Saddam ouster. Drawing a parallel with General Douglas MacArthur's "reckless" push to the Yalu river during the Korean war, Wolfowitz at that time acknowledged the possibility of the US being dragged into a "more or less permanent occupation of a country that could not govern itself, but where the rule of a foreign occupier would be increasingly resented".[25] In 1991, Wolfowitz and Libby were certainly in favour of inflicting the maximum *damage* on Saddam's forces. Along with Dennis Ross from the State Department, they also urged intervention, immediately following the 1991 ceasefire, on behalf of Shiite and Kurdish rebel forces who were being attacked by Saddam's helicopter gunships. In 1993, Wolfowitz wrote that the fate of the Shiites and Kurds "in no small part reflected a miscalculation by some of our military commanders that a rapid disengagement was essential to preserve the luster of victory, and to avoid getting stuck with postwar objectives that would prevent us from ever disengaging."[26]

The most celebrated emanation from Bush's office during this period was a more oblique reaction to the Gulf victory of 1991: the 1992 Defense Planning Guidance. This statement of post-Cold War purpose was designed to serve as a benchmark for US defense budgeting in the foreseeable future. The 1992 Guidance which was leaked to the press in April of that year was a draft, authored primarily by Zalmay Khalilzad (subsequently George W. Bush's post-invasion ambassador in Iraq and Afghanistan). Khalilzad, an Afghan-American with strong neocon links, portrayed future US policy as building on the opportunities created by the "two victories" in the Cold War and in the Gulf. America would not assume "responsibility for righting every wrong" in the world; it would "retain the pre-eminent responsibility for addressing selectively those wrongs which threaten not only our interests, but those of our allies and friends, or which could seriously unsettle international relations." Khalilzad listed the types of US interest which might be involved: "access to vital raw materials, primarily Persian Gulf oil; proliferation of weapons of mass destruction and ballistic missiles; threats to US citizens from terrorism or regional or local conflict; and threats to US society from narcotics trafficking." The document contained important implications for the future of the US commitment to multilateralism in the post-Gulf War era: "we should expect future coalitions to be *ad hoc* assemblies often not lasting beyond the crisis being confronted."[27]

The most controversial aspect of the leaked Guidance related to its "no rivals" section: a policy recommendation designed to deflect and "integrate" German and Japanese global ambitions. A revised version of the Guidance, written primarily by Lewis Libby, was accepted by Cheney. Libby's version was less abrasive: not only regarding Germany and Japan, but also in its willingness to concede the virtues of stable multilateralism. However, its general thrust—an integrated, doctrinally realist, global American hegemonism, rooted in the perpetual maintenance of US military primacy—was retained.

Whereas Bill Clinton became the object of extraordinary personal hatred for many Republican conservatives in the 1990s, neocons like Wolfowitz appreciated the force of his (and Secretary of State Madeleine Albright's) second term commitment to America as the world's "indispensable nation." The second Clinton administration even began to remilitarize, also yielding to Republican pressure to revive National Missile Defense. The 1999 action in Kosovo demonstrated the Democratic administration's willingness to take military action without UN sanction. Under Clinton, the US also bombed Iraq, with the UK as its only active ally, and was arguably also following a policy which embraced the goal of "regime change."[28] Despite all this, however, for most neocons, Clinton was too indecisive and too committed to working with the appeasing Europeans, not to mention being hopelessly on the "wrong" side in the culture wars.[29] Joshua Muravchik renounced his support for Clinton in 1993, citing the Balkans as his major complaint. In 1996, Muravchik was still bemoaning the failure to unseat Saddam in 1991: "The United States would have ousted Saddam, pulled together an interim governing coalition of Iraqi dissidents, supervised an open election, and still withdrawn within a year." Clinton had compounded Bush's errors.[30] In 1998, Wolfowitz attacked Clinton's Iraqi goals. The US should (according to Wolfowitz) begin real democracy-promotion and regime change, indicating its "willingness to recognise a provisional government of free Iraq" (essentially the Iraqi National Congress led by Ahmad Chalabi).[31]

A friend of Richard Perle since the 1980s, Ahmad Chalabi was to become increasingly central to the neocon strategy for Iraq. Chalabi opposed "solving" the problem of Iraq either through containing Saddam—the frequently stated Clinton idea of keeping the Iraqi dictator "in his box"—or by engineering some kind of internal putsch. Removing the dictator without dismantling his regime would merely subject the Iraqi nation to more agony, while doing nothing for the cause of Middle Eastern peace and security.[32] By 1997, Wolfowitz, now returned to academic life, was also advocating invasion. On 1 December 1997, the *Weekly Standard* published a piece by Wolfowitz and Khalilzad. Explaining their thinking on Saddam Hussein, it was entitled "Overthrow Him." On November 18, 1997, Wolfowitz wrote an article for the *Wall Street Journal* on "Rebuilding the anti-Saddam Coalition." Reflecting the view of the European alliance which derived from neocon interpretations of recent events in the Balkans, he argued that the allies could be "bounced" into supporting an invasion: "A willingness to act unilaterally can be the most effective way of securing effective collective action." His thoughts at this stage seemed to be running in the direction of America forcibly establishing a "liberated zone" in Southern Iraq, forming a platform from which to mount a war of liberation for the whole country.

The organizational expression of this new thinking on Iraq was William Kristol's Project for a New American Century. PNAC became part of the rightist assault on Clinton. It represented a conscious effort to align intellectual neoconservatism with more traditional Republican defence hawks: this new alignment, of course, was to prove crucial to the development of the Iraq invasion decisions of 2002–3. Donald Rumsfeld was a signatory to the 1996 letter to Clinton, urging "military action" in Iraq, in order to eliminate the "possibility that Iraq will be able to use or threaten to use weapons of mass destruction." Associated with PNAC's formal founding in 1997 were figures such as Wolfowitz, Libby, Kirkpatrick, Henry Rowen and Richard Perle. Francis Fukuyama was involved and, representing the older neocon generation, so was Norman Podhoretz. Also prepared to sign the founding PNAC document, however, were Rumsfeld, Dan Quayle, Jeb Bush and Richard Cheney. In January 1998, PNAC sent an open letter to the White House in advance of Clinton's State of the Union address. The letter argued that "we can no longer depend on our partners in the Gulf War coalition to continue to uphold the sanctions or to punish Saddam when he blocks or evades UN inspections." In the "near term," the US must demonstrate "a willingness to undertake military action." Clinton must embark on a clear strategy aimed "at the removal of Saddam Hussein from power."[33]

Neocon signatories included Bill Kristol, Wolfowitz, Khalilzad, Francis Fukuyama, John Bolton, Robert Kagan, and Richard Perle. Defense hawks were represented by Rumsfeld, though Cheney's signature was missing. Other signatories who were to serve in the George W. Bush administration included Richard Armitage, Paula Dobriansky, Peter Rodman, and Robert Zoellick.

By the end of the Clinton years, neoconservatism had been regenerated, primarily by Bill Kristol, as a force pressurizing US foreign policy. The revived movement spread its net widely; in 1999, PNAC urged Clinton to end his policy of "strategic ambiguity" for Taiwan. Yet, the movement had a very clear focus: regime change in Iraq. Important links and continuities had been established with more orthodox, defense-oriented conservatives. Though utterly opposed to the insular, occasionally anti-Jewish forces in the Grand Old Party represented by Pat Buchanan, the "new" neoconservatism was not entirely out of tune with the more general rightwing upsurge of the 1990s.

Neocons in the new century

The "new" neoconservatism was not merely a fan club for George W. Bush. Bill Kristol actually supported John McCain in the 2000 Republican primaries. Nevertheless various PNAC signatories— Armitage, Rumsfeld, Bolton, Abrams, Feith, Wolfowitz and Khalilzad were the most prominent—gained important positions in the Bush Pentagon, State Department or National Security Council staff. Cheney became Vice President, bringing Lewis Libby into his office. Neither Rumsfeld nor Cheney, however, were intellectual neocons on the Wolfowitz or Khalilzad model. Generally, the admistration neocons were second-level (as Richard Neustadt later argued) "junior ministers," much as they had been in the Reagan or Bush senior administrations.[34] Richard Armitage, though a PNAC signatory, was a strong supporter of Colin Powell, whose deputy he became. The 2001 Bush appointments signalled a more militarized foreign policy; they certainly did not signal a neocon takeover. The foreign policy of the first eight months of the administration were characterized by the rather narrow interests-based realism defended by National Security Advisor Condoleezza Rice during the election campaign.[35] Bush's willingness to reject treaties which seemed to impinge on US freedom of action pleased neocon commentators. The new foreign policy, however, also had, as was seen during the China spy plane crisis of April 2001, more than a hint of old-fashioned pragmatism. What changed this world—what changed the world—of course, was 9/11, an event which effectively solidified that alliance between neocon and "defense hawk" thinking which had been prefigured in PNAC. Before examining the course of events after 9/11, let us take stock of the neoconservative movement as it contemplated the new century.

Though, thanks largely to Bill Kristol, more organizationally coherent than the older movement, the "new" neoconservatism was far from intellectually united. In particular, it exhibited two sets of competing tensions: between optimism and pessimism, and between realism and moralistic idealism.

At one level, and certainly regarding their recommendations (under Clinton and under George W. Bush) for Iraq, the neocons were optimistic to the point of naivety. Recall Muravchik's comments, quoted above, about the possibility of achieving a democratic transition and removing US military forces from Iraq within a year. Wolfowitz in the 1990s clearly saw the problems faced by an occupying army which was also trying to build democracy. Yet, he tended to speak in terms of "trying to remove the shackles on democracy" in Iraq, as if some nascent democratic system were ready to sprout wings once Saddam was removed. Rather than the arrogance of "imposing" values, real arrogance, according to Wolfowitz, was to assume that democracy was an "American" rather than a universal good.[36] Optimistic democracy-promotion in neocon thought tends to find its own negation in the kind of cautious realism expressed in Kirkpatrick's "Dictatorships and Double Standards" article. It continually runs up against an underlying scepticism about the ability of the Platonic cave-dwellers actually to turn their faces to the light.

The realism/idealism tension in neocon thought is clear and widely recognized. For Chalmers Johnson, the movement was a combination of "the military imperialism of Theodore Roosevelt and the idealistic imperialism of Woodrow Wilson."[37] For Anatol Lieven, neoconservatism rests on the "selective use of 'democratization' with strategies based on ruthless 'Realism'".[38] Much early twenty-first-century ink has been spilled in the effort to capture the realism/idealism balance within neoconservatism. Charles Krauthammer, for example, distinguishes between "democratic realists," pro-democracy interventionists with a strong commitment to traditionally conceived national interests, and "democratic globalists," less cautious interventionists including moralistic liberals like Tony Blair as well as more idealist-oriented neocons.[39] Some commentators actually see neoconservatism as a branch of realism. It is certainly the case that some neocon policy formulations—one thinks of the 1992 Defense Guidance or even some of the essays in Kagan and Kristol's collection, *Present Dangers*[40]—were couched overwhelmingly in realist terms. For Gerard Alexander, neocons are simply "balance-of-threat realists."[41] Barely a month after 9/11, Richard Perle looked forward to a world transformed by regime change in both Afghanistan and Iraq: "Because having destroyed the Taliban, having destroyed Saddam's regime, the message to the others is, 'You're next'. Two words. Very efficient dipolomacy."[42] It would be hard to imagine a more clear expression of "balance-of-threat realism." Yet, Perle's 2004 statement of neoconservative aspiration (co-written with David Frum) went under the moralistic title, *An End to Evil*.[43] Foreign policy neoconservatism arguably came of age in its critique of the classical realism of Henry Kissinger. Post-Cold War neoconservatism also imbibed a version of liberal, neoKantian "democratic peace" theory: the view that international peace derives from international democratization.[44] In general, neoconservatism tends to accept the Jeffersonian view that American values and interests are one. Depending on the skill of individual thinkers, the realism/idealism puzzle is either a source of confusion or an occasion of transcendent Hegelian synthesis. In the case of the Iraq invasion, it was decidedly the former.

Early twenty-first-century foreign policy neoconservatism both reflected and encouraged the post-Cold War triumphalism which had been postponed during the uncertain, and relatively economically troubled years of the elder Bush and early Clinton. The end of the Cold War and the economic boom of the 1990s eventually ushered in a new age of American hegemony: the "unipolar moment" which US leaders must not squander. Around the turn of the century everything seemed to be going America's way. Not only had the Cold War ended in America's favor; the Japanese economy was apparently in deep trouble. The US was the only remaining superpower, with massive military, economic (especially now that the Reagan deficit had been eliminated), and "soft power" resources. John Bolton—dubbed by Chris Patten "the Pavarotti of the neo-conservatives"[45]—lost no opportunity in his role as US Ambassador to the UN to extol the view that America, the ultimate guarantor of the global future, should not succumb to the messy compromise that was collective decisionmaking. Turn of the century neoconservatism also famously toyed with the notion of benevolent empire. According to Kristol and Kagan in 2000, "it is precisely because American foreign policy is infused with an unusually high degree of morality that other nations find they have less to fear from its otherwise daunting power".[46]

George W. Bush: to Baghdad

Neoconservatives outside the administration tended to see 9/11 as a vindication of their pre-existing drive towards primacy, extended forward defence, unilateralism and globalism. At one level, the 9/11 terrorists had, in effect, made the case for American empire. Max Boot penned a piece in the *Weekly Standard* on October 15, 2001 entitled "The Case for American Empire." Robert Kaplan looked to earlier empires, including the British, for "helpful hints about how to run American foreign policy."[47] As the Bush administration made its post-9/11 decisions, it is certainly the case that talk of empire was in the air, and that the talk was led by neoconservative commentators and intellectuals. Charles Krauthammer wrote on September 21, 2001 that this was no time "for agonized relativism."[48] PNAC addressed yet another letter to the White House, urging the establishment of a "safe zone" in Iraq for opponents of Saddam. A "determined effort" must be made to remove Saddam: "Failure to undertake such an effort will constitute an early and perhaps decisive surrender in the war on international terrorism."[49]

Our knowledge of what transpired within the Bush administration in the period between 9/11 and the invasion of Iraq leans heavily on leaks, anonymous interviews and journalistic re-creations. Most accounts portray Paul Wolfowitz as pressing strongly and successfully for action in Iraq. This was scarcely surprising, given his (and Rumsfeld's) attitude towards Iraq *before* 9/11. The possibility of an attack on Iraq seems to have been discussed at a Bush National Security Council meeting as early as January 30, 2001. Iraq policy in this early period drifted, with different agencies going their separate ways.[50] Richard Clarke recalled Wolfowitz arguing at a deputies' meeting at the White House in April 2001 that action against Iraq would be a reasonable response to the al Qaeda threat. Clarke concluded that Wolfowitz still subscribed to the erroneous view that Iraq was behind the 1993 attack on the World Trade Center.[51]

Immediately after 9/11, according to Bob Woodward, at White House meetings on September 15, 2001, Wolfowitz argued that Iraq was "doable." Saddam's was "a brittle, oppressive regime that might break easily."[52] At this stage, Bush seems to have been skeptical, especially about being seen to use 9/11 as an excuse to settle old scores, including the 1993 Iraqi attempt to assassinate his father. The possibility of invading Iraq, however, even before attacking Afghanistan, was canvassed in this period, primarily by Rumsfeld, Wolfowitz, and Feith. Greg Newbold, operations officer for the Joint Chiefs of Staff, reported Douglas Feith as asking in the immediate aftermath of 9/11: "Why are you working on Afghanistan? You ought to be working on Iraq."[53] Following the terror attacks, Rumsfeld and Wolfowitz presided over the establishment of a special Pentagon intelligence unit, headed by Feith, to find evidence against Baghdad: either regarding links to al Qaeda or relating to Saddam's development of weapons of mass destruction. The ensuing politicization of intelligence, generally undertaken against the advice and working assumptions of the Central Intelligence Agency, became a vital part of the developing momentum for war. Formal, detailed planning for an attack on Iraq appears to have begun at the Pentagon in November 2001.[54] From then on it is difficult to disagree with Michael Clarke that US policy on Iraq was effectively "on tramlines."[55] The swift advances in Afghanistan led to enhanced confidence about the possibilities in Iraq. In June 2002, Bush announced the doctrine of pre-emption at West Point. The neocon attitude in the pre-invasion period was generally one of incautious optimism. Outside the administration, Kenneth Adelman, former ACDA head and sometime assistant to Rumsfeld, wrote in March 2002: "I believe demolishing Hussein's military power and liberating Iraq would be a cakewalk."[56]

As the conflict soured, leading neocons peeled off from the administration. Though clearly implicated in the failure to comprehend the difficulty of post-invasion Iraq, Paul Wolfowitz seems quickly to have come to the view that Rumsfeld was dodging the issue of post-invasion security. Though he originally forecast victory within seven days, he also foresaw the possibility of a prolonged insurgency by Baathists.[57] The neocons in and outside the administration to some degree deserved the contumely heaped upon them during the post-invasion conflict. Their evaluation of Chalabi was naive at best; the notion that the browbeaten Shia population of Southern Iraq would flock to the cause of returning exiles was absurd. Yet the entire administration was to blame, not just the neocons. Jay Garner's Office for Reconstruction and Humanitarian Assistance was a risible operation, while Paul Bremer's lumbering Coalition Provisional Authority committed bungle after bungle.[58] Francis Fukuyama wrote that the Bush Doctrine was "now in shambles."[59] Some neoconservatives simply blamed the ungrateful recipients of the liberation; Krauthammer intoned that "we have given the Iraqis a republic and they do not appear able to keep it."[60] For David Frum, the agony of Iraq was a victory for the pessimistic tendency within neoconservatism: "Paul Wolfowitz has lost. Sam Huntington has won."[61]

Conclusion

That neoconservatives in the administration, led by Wolfowitz, had an important role in moving Washington toward the invasion is not seriously in doubt. It is also reasonable to argue that neocon writing outside the administration was a significant factor in constructing the intellectual climate—broadly confident, unilateralist and wedded to regime change in Iraq—which nurtured the decision to invade. Was George W. Bush essentially following a neocon foreign policy? Max Boot addressed this question in early 2004 from a neocon perspective. He concluded that Bush's policies toward China, North Korea, Iran and even toward Israel-Palestine relations were certainly not neoconservative ones. However, the National Security Strategy document issued in September 2002, the document which provided the intellectual basis for invading Iraq "was a quintessentially neoconservative document." Its doctrines—US military primacy, democracy promotion, pre-emptive action to head off threat—were neocon doctrines.[62] All this, of course, does not mean that the influence of neoconservatism over the decision to invade Iraq has not been overstated. Various objections to viewing the decision to invade Iraq as a "neoconservative" one may be mounted.

The postulation of neoconservative ideas as a proximate source of policy—the decision to invade Iraq—raises profound philosophical questions which it is my intention to evade. International relations is studied and understood at many levels. The dominant paradigm is still a realist one, though most commentators would allow explanatory room, if not to unmediated ideas, at least to different *perceptions* of interest and to domestic popular and elite movements (such as American neoconservatism). More relevant to present discussion is the matter of nomenclature. So far in this chapter, I have used the term, "neoconservative", to refer primarily to the group of intellectuals, writers and academics—some of whom, like Wolfowitz, doubled as policymakers—who might reasonably trace their intellectual line back to figures such as Irving Kristol and Nathan Glazer, even arguably to Leo Strauss. Though spanning the generations, they were generally close friends and associates, though never a "conspiracy," with strong connections to publications such as *Commentary* and the *Weekly Standard*. Their thought, at least as far as foreign policy is concerned, was a mixture of anti-communism, democratic optimism, threats-based realism and, perhaps above all, a commitment to American exceptionalism. They tended to favor unilateral action, to be very skeptical of the worth of the United Nations, in favor of expansive use of US military power, committed generally to the interchangeability of American values and interests, even prepared at least to toy with the notion of openly promoting some form of American imperialism. Having fought something of a rearguard action against the fall in national confidence following the Vietnam war, they were buoyed up by the circumstances of the ending of the Cold War and by the upsurge in national confidence which attended the undisputed American hegemonism of the 1990s. Though generally taking a "conservative" line on domestic and defense issues, they were to some degree influenced by "liberal" notions, notably regarding free trade and post-Cold War democratic peace theory. 9/11, along with the 2002 successes in Afghanistan, constituted a step-change in the development of their agenda for Iraq.

The problem for the current analysis is that, according to the preceding definition, only a relatively few members of the George W. Bush administration fit the description. Most were practical, not intellectual, conservatives. When Richard Cheney was asked to respond to criticism from the *Weekly Standard*, he replied: "They have to sell magazines. We have to govern."[63] Various terms have been coined to describe the top people in the Bush foreign policy hierarchy: "traditional realists," "conservative nationalists," "offensive realists" (Cheney and Rumsfeld, possibly Condoleezza Rice), "defensive realists" (Powell), and so on. Stanley Renshon argues that Bush himself—a figure often strangely omitted from discussion of the policies developed in his own administration—is best seen as an "American nationalist." In 1999, Bush declared that "in defense of our nation, a president must be a clear-eyed realist." Unless the American leader "sets his own priorities, his priorities will be set by others."[64] What seems to happened following 9/11 is that there occurred a convergence between neoconservative positions on Iraq in particular, and on the kinds of priorities and policies detailed in the 2002 National Security Strategy in general, and the rather narrower, nationalist-conservative-realist positions of Cheney, Rumsfeld and Bush himself. This coalescence had already occurred to some degree in the 1990s—witness the range of signatures appended to the various PNAC letters—and had produced the phenomenon of the "Vulcan," a term used by James Mann to describe figures across the Republican board from Condoleezza Rice to Richard Armitage to Paul Wolfowitz.[65] The balance here is a fine one. Bush, Cheney and Rumsfeld were not suddenly "converted" to neoconservatism in 2001. If they were, the limits of that conversion soon became apparent, not least in terms of policy towards East Asia. Nevertheless, it is not unreasonable, given the history and extent of neocon lobbying in this connection, to describe the Iraq invasion, like the 2002 National Security Strategy as "neoconservative" in form and intent.

The final word of the preceding paragraph, of course, raises yet more problems. What *was* the intent behind the invasion? From a neocon perspective, it was the democratic transformation of the Middle East region, protecting American geopolitical interests and advancing American values. It was a move designed to shape the political context in a way which would deter enemies, provide for a dependable flow of oil, and also promote—at least in the long term—the security of Israel. It would be good for America and for the Middle East. In the nature of things, different actors view actions in different ways. The balance of motive varied across the administration. Decisional outputs, as a library of foreign policy texts argue, are mediated by bureaucratic politics. There is never an "essential" motive which finds its way from policy initiator—even if it is possible to identify such an initiator, and even in the unlikely circumstances that the initiator had a relatively simple motive—to policy. It is also clearly the case that the public defense of the invasion tended to focus primarily on the threat from weapons of mass destruction. Though he was speaking about the "monumental struggle between good and evil" soon after 9/11, President Bush tended to emphasize democracy promotion *per se*, notably in his 2005 State of the Union address, when it proved impossible to locate evidence of WMD in Iraq.[66] Various commentators have argued for a "forward defense" or "conservative nationalist" interpretation of the invasion.[67] Yet the invasion was intended, however unwisely or ill-advisedly, to convert a fascistic dictatorship into a democracy. Given their elitism and small numbers, neocons were unlikely ever to dominate even a fairly rightwing Republican administration. If their policy preferences were to be adopted, they would have to advance their ideas to sympathetic "American" or "conservative nationalists". That is exactly what they did.

Notes

1 Francis Fukuyama, "The Neoconservative Moment," *The National Interest*, 76, 2004, 57–68.

2 Stefan Halper and Jonathan Clarke, *America Alone: The Neoconservatives and the Global Order*, Cambridge, Cambridge University Press, 2004, 156, 138.

3 Ivo Daalder and James M. Lindsay, *America Unbound: The Bush Revolution in Foreign Policy*, Washington DC, Brookings Institution, 2003, 15.

4 Ian McEwan, *Saturday*, London, Cape, 2005, 190–1.

5 David Brooks, "The Neocon Cabal and other Fantasies," in Irwin Stelzer, ed., *Neoconservatism*, London, Atlantic Books, 2004, 39–42, 42.

6 Alan Crawford, *Thunder on the Right*, New York, Pantheon Books, 1980, 173.

7 Joshua Muravchik, "The Neoconservative Cabal," in Stelzer, ed., *Neoconservatism*, 241–58, 247.

8 Anatol Lieven, *America Right or Wrong: An Anatomy of American Nationalism*, London, HarperCollins, 2004, 152.

9 Francis Fukuyama, *After the Neocons: America at the Crossroads*, London, Profile, 2007, 16–17.

10 Fukuyama, "The Neoconservative Moment," 60.

11 Cited in John Micklethwait and Adrian Wooldridge, *The Right Nation: Why America is Different*, London, Penguin, 2005, 75. See also Anne Norton, *Leo Strauss and the Politics of American Empire*, New Haven, Yale University Press, 2004.

12 See Leo Strauss, *Persecution and the Art of Writing*, Chicago, University of Chicago Press, 1952.
13 See Joshua Muravchik, *The Uncertain Crusade: Jimmy Carter and the Dilemmas of Human Rights*, Lanham, Hamilton, 1986.
14 James Mann, *Rise of the Vulcans: The History of Bush's War Cabinet*, London, Penguin, 2004, 75–6, 81.
15 Daniel P. Moynihan, *A Dangerous Place*, New York, Secker & Warburg, 1975.
16 Jeane Kirkpatrick, "Dictatorship and Double Standards," *Commentary*, 68, 1979, 28–51, 41.
17 See Halper and Clarke, *America Alone*, 157–81; John Dumbrell, "Winston Churchill and American Foreign Relations: John F. Kennedy to George W. Bush," *Journal of Transatlantic Studies*, 3:1, 2005, 31–42; G. John Ikenberry, *Liberal Order and Imperial Ambition*, Cambridge, Polity, 2006, 239.
18 John Judis, "From Trotskyism to Anachronism," *Foreign Affairs*, 74:4, 1995, 123–9; John Ehrman, *The Rise of Neoconservatism: Intellectuals and Foreign Affairs, 1945–1994*, New Haven, Yale University Press, 1995.
19 See Micklethwait and Wooldridge, *The Right Nation*, 153–5.
20 See John Dumbrell, "Varieties of Post-Cold War American Isolationism," *Government and Opposition*, 34:1, 1999, 24–43.
21 William Kristol and Robert Kagan, "Towards a Neo-Reaganite Foreign Policy," *Foreign Affairs*, 75:4, 1996, 18–32.
22 George Bush and Brent Scowcroft, *A World Transformed*, New York, Knopf, 1998, 488; Colin Powell, *A Soldier's Way: An Autobiography*, London, Hutchinson, 1995, 271.
23 Joshua Muravchik, *The Imperative of American Leadership: A Challenge to Neo-isolationism*,Washington DC, American Enterprise Institute, 1996, 31, 155.
24 Muravchik, *The Imperative of American Leadership*, 156.
25 See Mann, *Rise of the Vulcans*, 187–8, Henry S. Rowen, "Inchon in the Desert," *The National Interest*, 40, 1995, 34–9.
26 Thomas E. Ricks, *Fiasco: The American Military Adventure in Iraq*, London, Allen Lane, 2006, 7.
27 Barton Gellman, "Keeping the US First," *Washington Post*, 11 March 1992.
28 See Scott Ritter, *Iraq Confidential: The Untold Story of America's Intelligence Conspiracy*, London, I. B. Tauris, 2005, 268–70.
29 See Mark Gerson, *The Neoconservative Vision: From the Cold War to the Culture Wars*, Lanham, Madison Books, 1997.
30 Muravchik, *The Imperative of American Leadership*, 182–3.
31 Halper and Clarke, *America Alone*, 101–2.
32 Mann, *Rise of the Vulcans*, 334.
33 "An Open Letter to President Clinton," in Micah L. Sifry and Christopher Cerf, eds., *The Iraq War Reader*, New York, Touchstone, 2003, 199–201.
34 Richard E. Neustadt, "Challenges Created by Contemporary Presidents," in George C. Edwards III and Philip J. Davies, eds., *New Challenges for the American Presidency*, New York, Pearson Longman, 2004, 12–22.

35 Condoleezza Rice, "Promoting the National Interest," *Foreign Affairs*, 79:1, 2001, 45–62.
36 Mark Bowden, "Wolfowitz: The Exit Interviews," *The Atlantic Monthly*, July/August 2005, 110–22, 115, 118.
37 Chalmers Johnson, *The Sorrows of Empire: Militarism, Secrecy and the End of the Republic*, London, Verso, 2006, 70.
38 Lieven, *America Right or Wrong*, 75.
39 Charles Krauthammer, "In Defense of Democratic Realism," *The National Interest*, 77, 2004, 15–25.
40 Robert Kagan and William Kristol, eds., *Present Dangers: Crisis and Opportunity in American Foreign and Defense Policy*, San Francisco, Encounter Books, 2000.
41 Gerard Alexander, "International Theory Meets World Politics," in Stanley A. Renshon, and Peter Suedfeld, eds., *The Bush Doctrine: Psychology and Strategy in the Age of Terrorism*, New York, Routledge, 2007, 39–64, 42.
42 Quoted in Thomas Powers, "Tomorrow the World," *New York Review of Books*, March 11, 2004, 4.
43 David Frum and Richard Perle, *An End to Evil: How to Win the War on Terror*, New York, Random House, 2004.
44 See Bruce Russett, *Grasping the Democratic Peace: Principles for a Post-Cold War World*, Princeton, Princeton University Press, 1993.
45 Chris Patten, *Not Quite the Diplomat*, London, Penguin, 2006, 252.
46 Robert Kagan and William Kristol, "Introduction," in Kagan and Kristol, eds., *Present Dangers*, 3–24, 22.
47 Robert Kaplan, *Warrior Politics: Why Leadership Demands a Pagan Ethos*, New York, Random House, 2002, 152.
48 Charles Krauthammer, "Visions of Moral Obtuseness," in Sifry and Cerf, eds., *The Iraq Reader*, 217–18.
49 "An Open Letter to President Bush," in Sifry and Cerf, eds., *The Iraq Reader*, 222–5, 223.
50 See Ron Suskind, *The Price of Loyalty: George W. Bush, the White House, and the Education of Paul O'Neill*, New York, Simon & Schuster, 2004, 70.
51 Richard A. Clarke, *Against All Enemies: Inside America's War on Terror*, London, Free Press, 2004, 231–2.
52 Bob Woodward, *Bush at War*, New York, Simon & Schuster, 2002, 83; see also Bob Woodward, *Plan of Attack*, New York, Simon & Schuster, 2004.
53 Michael Gordon and Bernard Trainor, *Cobra II: The Inside Story of the Invasion and Occupation of Iran*, London, Atlantic Books, 2007, 17.
54 Ricks, *Fiasco*, 32.
55 Michael Clarke, "The Diplomacy that led to the War in Iraq," in Paul Cornish, ed., *The Conflict in Iraq, 2003*, Basingstoke, Palgrave, 2004, 274–87, 283.
56 Ricks, *Fiasco*, 36.
57 Bob Woodward, *Bush at War, Part III: State of Denial*, New York, Simon & Schuster, 2006, 309.

58 See George Packer, *The Assassin's Gate: America in Iraq*, New York, Farrar, Straus, Giroux, 2005; Ali A. Allawi, *The Occupation of Iraq: Winning the War, Losing the Peace*, New Haven, Yale University Press, 2007.

59 *New York Times*, February 19, 2006.

60 *The Economist*, March 24, 2007, 27.

61 *Foreign Policy*, March/April 2007, "Who Wins in Iraq," 44. Huntington was a central figure in the 1970s "excess of democracy" debate, as well as in the later "clash of civilizations" debate. See Samuel P. Huntington, "The United States," in Michael J. Crozier, S. P. Huntington and Joji Watanuki, *The Crisis of Democracy*, New York, New York University Press, 1975, 105–201; Samuel P. Huntington, *The Clash of Civilizations and the Remaking of World Order*, New York, Simon & Schuster, 1996.

62 Max Boot, "Myths about Neoconservatism," in Stelzer, ed., *Neoconservatism*, 45–52, 46.

63 Adam Wolfson, "Conservatism and Neoconservatism," in Stelzer, ed., *Neoconservatism*, 213–33, 226.

64 Stanley A. Renshon, "The Bush Doctrine Considered," in Renshon and Suedfeld, eds., *The Bush Doctrine*, 1–37, 13.

65 Mann, *Rise of the Vulcans*, xv.

66 Halper and Clarke, *America Alone*, 156.

67 See Steven Hurst, "Myths of Neoconservatism: George W. Bush's 'Neoconservative' Foreign Policy Revisited," *International Politics*, 42:1, 2005, 75–96.

3

The origins of the British decision to go to war: Tony Blair, humanitarian intervention, and the "new doctrine of the international community"

Jim Whitman

Introduction: justifying the recourse to war

Ambivalence about war and its purposes is by no means a historical novelty—and nor are deeply felt and carefully articulated principles and codes concerning the conditions under which it can be justified, or limits to its conduct. This social, intellectual, and political history, an accumulation and continuous reconfiguration of values and beliefs tempered and shaped by the hard experience of violent conflict, has greatly conditioned "our received idea of war."[1] In our own time as in any other, we struggle to make ordered sense of the recent past (the first Gulf war; instances of genocide) and events on the periphery of living memory (both World Wars), against shared values and perceived threats. Of course, it is the prerogative of politicians to be selective about the past and to invoke particular experiences as "lessons." But in democratic states, the pressure of events also brings to public awareness deeper and more enduring considerations: normative expectations rooted in the human rights regime; the quality of interstate relations, bilaterally and within international institutions; the moral awfulness of politically driven human suffering on a large scale; an acute sensitivity to military casualties; and a calculation (if only at the gut level) of the costs and risks of deploying soldiers into dangerous situations.

For their part, politicians will routinely try to maximize their room for manoeuvre—at the very least so as not to be at the mercy of events, but also to pursue the particulars of a foreign policy agenda in uncertain and highly changeable arenas. The ability (both practical and political) to deploy armed force is clearly central to this enterprise. We can hardly be surprised, then, by political efforts to create or amplify an understanding of a nation's values, responsibilities, and vulnerabilities that facilitate planned or possible uses for armed forces. This task requires subtlety and good timing; a reliance on the effective use of potent memories, symbols and/or widely shared feelings and understandings; and the avoidance of offering a hostage to fortune—such as when in the UK, Robin Cook MP as Shadow Secretary of State for Foreign Affairs promised what became known as an "ethical foreign policy."[2]

The decision to send troops into volatile, dangerous situations carries a great deal of political and moral weight. Both find particularly strong expression in actions taken to defend a state's territorial integrity. But where the national interest is less immediate or obvious, it is unsurprising to note the emphasis given to moral duty. So it was that in 1996 when then-UK Secretary of State for Defence Michael Portillo, announcing Britain's willingness to send a contingent of troops to Zaire to ease the crisis there, pre-empted the question as to "why Britain should become involved in a place far from home where there was no vital national interest." His answer was "because Britain is a civilized nation. We can see that people are about to die in their thousands and we are one of the few nations on earth who have the military capability to help at least some of them."[3] Discerning what national interests might also have been at stake in this and subsequent instances when moral reasoning has been liberally applied is the stuff of foreign policy analysis, but this kind of public justification for the use of armed force also has considerably wider political meaning.

We can say with certainty that if military action is successful, the pronouncement of moral certitude and resolve combines wonderfully with success on the battlefield to great political effect—as it did for Mrs. Thatcher over the Falklands campaign; and if the practical outcome is more ambiguous, the assertion of moral rightness is a useful bulwark against the perception of political and/or strategic misjudgment. But the political meaning of moral justifications for the deployment of armed forces is much more significant than that: at present—and for the purpose of this discussion, in the UK in particular—moral justifications for military actions do not merely bolster the practical case for action against the strictures of international law and/or popular disquiet: they also facilitate the climate that makes such actions less uniquely challenging—and eventually, unexceptional. This is important because although all states try to extend their power without significant constraint, it is the most powerful that have the most to gain by maintaining a law-based status quo. For this reason, their justifications for individual acts of law-breaking are usually calibrated so that they do not appear to offer a fundamental challenge to the rule of law more generally; and the relief of gross human suffering can be quite compelling in this regard. One can even see this in the 2002 US National Security Strategy – the so-called "Bush Doctrine" of pre-emptive self- defense—which contains the assertion that "nations should not use pre-emption as a pretext for aggression."[4] One might also note, however, the assurance that when in the future the US acts pre-emptively, "the reasons for our actions will be clear, the force measured and the cause just."[5]

Leaving aside the particulars of the Just War tradition,[6] the appearance of "just cause" in political rhetoric has always been used to forestall or quell dissent, its political utility in the current era being that it blurs the distinctions and/or the relative importance between what is politically expedient, morally right and legally sanctioned. In this regard, what is notable about justifications for the UK's participation in the invasion of Iraq in 2003 is the way in which moral and prudential reasoning were freely mixed, both before the fact and afterward.

Humanitarian intervention as a legitimating construct

Righteous interventions (however credible) are not a late-twentieth-century phenomenon. Even before the advent of the modern state system and codified international law, military action was taken to rescue, defend, or protect persecuted peoples in other polities; and even to "wage war against war."[7] If the Just War tradition has long provided or at least informed a generally acknowledged normative framework for the exercise of military power,[8] it is international law that informs and constrains states today. The legal foundations of the international system are not without ambiguity, but international law in the form of the United Nations Charter does recognize and forbid intrusions into the sovereign integrity of states. Yet a heartfelt belief that military force can and should at least sometimes be deployed to defend or protect the weak has long persisted, the strictures of current international law notwithstanding. So it was that the British economic historian and Labour Party activist R. H. Tawney famously asserted, "Either war is a crusade or it is a crime." "Crime" in Tawney's sense was a moral outrage, not a violation of law. In our own time, since the advent of article 2(4) of the UN Charter, military intervention for professed humanitarian reasons that is not sanctioned by the UN Security Council is at least nominally a crusade (the assertion of overwhelming moral necessity) *and* a crime—that is, a violation of international law. Whether in specific instances a declared humanitarian intervention undertaken by one or more states can be justified has come to form an important literature shared between International Relations and International Law.[9] It has also become an important dynamic in practical international relations as clearly indicated by UK Prime Minister Tony Blair's pronouncement of a "new doctrine of the international community," discussed below.

The crux of the humanitarian intervention debate is most often depicted as a tension between moral and legal imperatives—here succinctly depicted by no less than former UN Secretary-General Kofi Annan, who was writing in the aftermath of the unsanctioned NATO intervention on behalf of the Kosovo Albanians.[10] First, the moral imperative:

> To those for whom the greatest threat to the future of international order is the use of force in the absence of a Security Council mandate, one might say: leave Kosovo aside for a moment, and think about Rwanda. Imagine for one moment that, in those dark days and hours leading up to the genocide, there had been a coalition of states ready and willing to act in defense of the Tutsi population, but the council had refused or delayed giving the green light. Should such a coalition then have stood idly by while the horror unfolded?[11]

The other less frequently quoted passage from Annan's article concerns the legal meaning of unsanctioned humanitarian interventions:

> To those for whom the Kosovo action heralded a new era when states and groups of states can take military action outside the established mechanisms for enforcing international law, one might equally ask: Is there not a danger of such interventions undermining the imperfect, yet resilient, security system created after the second world war, and of setting dangerous precedents for future interventions without a clear criterion to decide who might invoke these precedents and in what circumstances?[12]

Taken together, these two passages are a useful but partial characterization because they abstract the moral and legal substance of humanitarian intervention from the political interests of states. Were the government of any state subject to moral agonies over whether to rescue the beleaguered or to obey the law, we would not have had a strongly argued case for the Kosovo Albanians but embarrassed silence over the genocide in Rwanda—itself merely one of many cases more egregious than Kosovo. The professed humanitarian interventions of states do not make sense on the basis of human suffering alone; and the apparent inconsistency dissolves once state interests are factored in.

Because states do not act on the basis of moral impulses alone, and because the dispatch of troops into dangerous and volatile environments is both morally consequential and politically risky, political interests are always key. This is not to deny the capacity of political leaders for moral sympathy or to preclude genuine humanitarian impulses informing a decision to intervene, but these matters are neither necessary nor sufficient for a declared humanitarian intervention. At the same time, the legal prohibition against intervention cannot lightly be dismissed, so when humanitarian need and national interests coincide (as they must in these cases), publicly aired moral reasoning becomes very important as a legitimating device for illegal acts, the motive force for which will be mixed, at best. But the moral reasoning that at least nominally supports the determination to save considerable numbers of human lives can elide into wider, "values-based" lines of argumentation—that is, momentous decisions simplified to a form of moral scales, with tyranny, repression, aggression, and territorial ambition on one side; and disinterested, internationalist, humane ideals on the other. These kinds of characterizations can be deployed in quite compelling ways, particularly when politically driven human suffering becomes a prominent news item. At other times, the accommodation and even support of quite reprehensible rulers and regimes (Saddam Hussein being a particularly striking example) takes place in a political world that is messier and less Manichean—when it is visible at all.

The danger that accompanies strong advocacy of humanitarian intervention as a right of states or as customary international law is not only that it runs the risk of making conformity to the non-interventionist provisions of the UN Charter *à la carte*, but that it creates a climate in which the same quality of moral imperative can readily be directed to other purposes: for establishing democracy, ushering in human rights, or—as we have now seen—eliminating weapons of mass destruction, or the capacity to make them. The license afforded by claims of a right of humanitarian intervention goes some way to enabling states to intervene for a variety purposes, all of them "moral," "humane" (covering both good intentions before the fact and the minimisation of civilian casualties), and in highly resonant yet unspecified ways, "just," even though illegal. Tony Blair defended the rightness of the 1999 NATO incursion into Kosovo with the assertion, "This is a just war, based not on any territorial claims, but on values."[13] That these values were pursued by means of high-altitude bombing is in the longer run less important than the fact that the intervention met a considerable degree of international approval. The Independent International Commission on Kosovo, for example, judged the intervention to be "illegal but legitimate."[14] This conclusion and its implications are certainly arguable,[15] but the context of Blair's remarks is of greater significance, signaling a worrisome extension of the highly contentious right of humanitarian intervention, to a more generalized conception of "just" war—much as though Tawney's logic had been turned against itself: If war is a crusade, it can't be a crime.

"The new doctrine of the international community"

Even as the bombing of Serbia was under way, Tony Blair made a high-profile and much-publicized speech to the Chicago Economic Club in which he unveiled his "doctrine of the international community" (see Appendix C). The speech is much more wide-ranging than is generally appreciated; and surprisingly, rather lacking in doctrinal specifics. It is nevertheless important for signaling, and indeed urging a fundamental change in the attitude of powerful states toward growing interdependence fueled by a variety of globalizing forces.

The speech was framed by events then taking place in Kosovo but was not specifically devoted to it. Instead, Blair shrewdly linked past and present by rehearsing the appeasement of the 1930s: a "never again!" tone is invoked, after which Milosevic and Saddam Hussein are explicitly linked. He also linked military security with broader notions of international security by warning his American audience, "never fall again for the doctrine of isolationism." He told them that "We are all internationalists now, whether we like it or not"—and it is this that comprises the framework of his "new doctrine of the international community":

> Today the impulse towards interdependence is immeasurably greater. We are witnessing the beginnings of a new doctrine of the international community. By this I mean the explicit recognition that today more than ever before, we are mutually dependent, that national interest is to a significant extent governed by international collaboration and that we need a clear and coherent debate as to the direction this doctrine takes us in each field of international endeavour. Just as within domestic politics, the notion of community—the belief that partnership and co-operation are essential to self-interest—is coming into is own; so it needs to find its international echo. Global financial markets, the global environment, global security and disarmament issues: none of these can be solved without international co-operation.[16]

The list of thematic issues that require international collaboration was in itself quite unremarkable, even in 1999; more importantly, this expression of contemporary verities hardly counts as a "doctrine" in any meaningful sense. And notably, in the six examples that follow, the case for reform is made: for global finance; free trade; the UN; NATO; the global environment; and third world debt. Humanitarian intervention does not receive a mention.

Perhaps what is most telling in the Chicago speech is Blair's list of the five conditions which should help the government to determine when and whether to intervene. Although he himself said that these were not exhaustive, they are still notable for what they leave out. In summary, they are as follows: Are we sure of our case? Have we exhausted the diplomatic options? Can military means achieve the desired political outcomes? Are we prepared for the long term? Finally, do we have national interests involved? The list does not differ in any significant particular from a rational calculation of whether a nation should fight a war for directly self-interested reasons as opposed to professed humanitarian ones. What nation would act differently —now or in the past? Moreover, there is no mention of the United Nations, of article 2(4) or the role of international law more generally. What is revealing about this list is that it strips back the principle of "overwhelming humanitarian necessity" which is the *sine qua non* of humanitarian intervention. Blair himself is quite clear that states are not and cannot be altruistic. Their impulses to humanitarian action are inspired by a more familiar calculation of national interests, or at least tempered by them—as his conditions make plain. Humanitarian need in distant lands never overwhelms national interest; instead, when the two coincide, the humanitarian goals are deployed to overwhelm international law—and possibly to win public support.

Yet the invocation of humanitarianism has more than instrumental use. Its repeated (if highly selective) use also helps to create a normative expectation at variance with codified law. What gives law its force is not the means or willingness to enforce it on a regular basis, but a normative expectation that it will routinely be adhered to. This holds particularly for international law, which has remarkably little in the way of enforcement provisions. Article 2(4) of the UN Charter, which is the foundation of the post-World War II international order, is a particularly sensitive instrument—as was made plain in the three pre-Kosovo "classic" instances of humanitarian intervention: India in Bangladesh; Vietnam in Cambodia; and Tanzania in Uganda.[17] In each of these cases, the intervening states were at pains to offer a justification for intervention, offering a signal to the international community that although their actions were not in strict conformity with the law, nor were they offering a direct challenge to it. The credibility of these rationales was perhaps less important than the fact of them. The normative tenor of international law has sufficient resilience to be able to accommodate actions which in their effects honour of the spirit of the law even though they flout its letter—at least up to a point. More than thirty years ago, Thomas Franck and Nigel Rodley outlined the legal-political setting in the following terms: "[T]here are virtually no penalties presently inflicted, or likely to be inflicted, by the international system on states which engage, or might engage, in disinterested, neutral, and effective interventions that achieve limited objectives generally perceived as desirable in specific, adequately proven circumstances."[18] The difficulty is that there is virtually no burden of proof on states professing humanitarian intent—or now, high moral principle; and that what is "generally seen to be desirable" is highly malleable, particularly if international law can easily be suspended.

The largest part of Blair's post-facto justification for the bombing of Serbia (which was well advanced at the time of his Chicago speech) comprised moral outrage on behalf of suffering Kosovars, and principle that carefully skipped around any mention of international law—bar the discussion of international trade, where Blair's listeners were reminded that "[The] international system [has to be] based on rules. That means accepting the judgements of international organisations even when you do not like them." Of course, humanitarian intervention has long been held by its advocates to be both an exceptional occurrence and the exception to the rule. In response, one might ask what happened to those exceptional conditions and to the rule of law prior to the invasion of Iraq in 2003. Part of the answer to that question can be found in the expansion of the compass of political morality and its quite explicit linkage to self interest—itself now widened in the form of the "new doctrine of the international community." Unlike the Cold War period, said Blair, "Now our actions are guided by a more subtle blend of mutual self-interest and moral purpose in defending the values we cherish. In the end, vales and interests merge." The second sentence might be unremarkable coming from certain human rights quarters,[19] but from a seasoned politician it is rather more troubling. It is precisely this "subtle blend" which has long troubled those flagging up the disquieting implications of an asserted "right" of humanitarian intervention. A case in point was the 1996 US/UK extension of the aerial exclusion zone in Iraq:

> As time progressed, the credibility of the argument that the aerial exclusion zones were strictly necessary to meet an urgent and ongoing humanitarian emergency eroded. Instead, it appeared that the zones were also used to keep Iraq "in its box" and constrain its freedom of action in the region. This suspicion turned into certainty when, on September 3, 1996, the southern aerial exclusion zone was moved northwards, from the 32nd to the 33rd parallel. This action, along with an attack against Iraq involving 44 cruise missiles, was triggered by internal fighting among Kurdish factions in the north, and the intervention of Iraqi troops on the side of one of them, at its own request. Even if this Iraqi operation could have had humanitarian implications, it was not clear how the extension of the aerial exclusion zone in the south could improve the situation of the Kurds in the north. In consequence, the humanitarian veneer which had covered the aerial exclusion zones was peeled off. It appeared that the worst fears of the opponents of a right of humanitarian "intervention" in international law were being fulfilled: the doctrine appeared to be abused by powerful states as a cover for power politics.[20]

The bombardment of Iraq in September 1996 was but one of a number taken against that country between the end of the first Gulf War and the invasion of 2003—all without explicit Security Council authorization and also blatantly outside of a humanitarian intervention rationale. Indeed, what was to prove a forerunner for the US–UK rationale for the invasion of Iraq—that previous Security Council resolutions gave them license to do so – was first deployed a decade earlier:

> in January 1993, while mounting air strikes against air-defence sites which threatened coalition aircraft patrolling no-fly zones, the US also hit an alleged Iraqi nuclear facility on the outskirts of Baghdad. Washington argues that this action was triggered by Iraq's failure to comply with the terms of resolution 687 and was undertaken "to back up UN Security Council resolutions against Iraq developing weapons of mass destruction." This element of the operation did not even commend itself to members of the coalition that had participated in the rest of the operation; France expressly dissociated itself.[21]

After the September 1996 bombing, the largest and most sustained military campaign against Iraq prior to the 2003 was commenced under the name of *Desert Fox*.[22] From December 16, 1998, the US and the UK launched aerial assaults that continued throughout much of 1999, in the middle of which "the new doctrine of the international community" was unveiled. It is therefore plain that Blair's speech was not so much a catalyst as a culmination; and the context to the speech was not the air assaults on Serbia or Iraq themselves, but the rationale offered for them.

The invasion of Iraq: interventionist preludes and their rationales

It was with the troublesome regime of Saddam Hussein that US and UK interventionist rationales gradually shed declared humanitarianism in favor of appeals to national, regional, and international security. Neither country directly eschewed international law nor the United Nations, since Security Council sanction for such acts is powerfully legitimating— hence their repeated defence that they were acting to uphold the will of the Security Council, even though these claims were without legal foundation.[23]

As the September 1996 bombing got under way, President Clinton assured the world: "Our objectives there are limited, but our interests are clear, to demonstrate once again that reckless acts have consequences, to reduce Saddam's ability to strike out again at his neighbors, to increase America's ability to prevent future acts of violence"[24] As *Desert Fox* got under way in 1998, President Clinton explained, "[I]n halting our air strikes in November, I gave Saddam a chance, not a license. If we turn our backs on his defiance, the credibility of US power as a check against Saddam will be destroyed"[25]—a motivating factor consonant with that offered by then-UK Foreign Secretary Robin Cook for the declared humanitarian intervention in Kosovo:

> I am well aware that one should not commit servicemen to take the risk of military action unless our national interest is engaged. I firmly believe that upholding international law is in our national interest. Our national security depends on NATO. NATO now has a common border with Serbia as a result of the expansion to embrace Hungary and other countries of central Europe. Our borders cannot remain stable while such violence is conducted on the other side of the fence. NATO was the guarantor of the October agreement. What credibility would NATO be left with if we allowed that agreement to be trampled on comprehensively by President Milosevic and did not stir to stop him?[26]

Speaking for the disposition of both the US and UK over the decision to launch *Desert Fox*, Clinton referred to previous UN resolutions, but the orientation is plainly unilateralist: "I made it very clear at that time what unconditional cooperation meant, based on existing UN resolutions and Iraq's own commitments. And along with Prime Minister Blair of Great Britain, I made it equally clear that if Saddam failed to cooperate fully, we would be prepared to act without delay, diplomacy or warning." He added darkly, "The best way to end that threat once and for all is with a new Iraqi government—a government ready to live in peace with its neighbors, a government that respects the rights of its people."[27]

Even as the interventions in Iraq shed their humanitarian cover and increased in military intensity (with a notable widening of targets well beyond WMD research and manufacturing infrastructure), neither the US nor the UK turned their backs on interventions that did evince humanitarian objectives, albeit with national interests still evident. The UN-sanctioned intervention in Haiti by the United States (narrowly averted by the last-minute diplomacy of Jimmy Carter) eventually led to the deployment of more than 21,000 US soldiers there under *Operation Restore Democracy* and an eventual and successful handover to the UN Mission in Haiti. Likewise, the UK intervention in Sierra Leone (not sanctioned by the UN but undertaken on the basis of protecting British nationals in Freetown) is widely regarded as having been honourably motivated and competently executed:

> On May 7, the UK Ministry of Defence announced that it was sending a battalion of paratroopers and five warships to protect British nationals. [. . .] Freetown might have fallen to the RUF without the deployment of more than 1,000 British troops. In fact, the British force kept UNAMSIL

from totally disintegrating. According to a UN official, "They stiffened the spines of everyone around by coming in, taking charge and simply stating that the RUF would not be allowed to succeed." By securing the airport, they ensured the safe departure of expatriates, enabled UNAMSIL troops to be redeployed elsewhere in Freetown, and facilitated the arrival of thousands of additional peacekeepers. British forces also provided training to the Sierra Leone armed forces.[28]

It would be perverse not to recognize these interventions as generally beneficent, even though the arrival of UK paratroopers in Sierra Leone was not UN-authorized. But they took place in an international ethos in which interventions of all kinds were becoming less exceptional, a trend led by the US and the UK—as we have seen, most notably and consistently in Iraq, but also elsewhere. In 1998, under the name *Operation Infinite Reach*, the US launched air strikes against suspected terrorist operations in Sudan and Afghanistan; deployed Predator attack drones in Yemen (2002) and Pakistan (2006); and most recently (in 2007) conducted an aerial bombardment in Somalia against a suspected al Qaeda operative. For its part, the UK has engaged in five interventions since 1997; and according to the UK government's own figures, it spent £1.3 billion on military interventions in 2002–3 alone.[29]

One would not expect political justifications for these and other acts to evince anything other than the claim that they are "just" and that they are of a piece with national values and—as Tony Blair would have it, with the new doctrine of the international community. But what gave shape, substance and enormous momentum to the "doctrine" was the post-9/11 "war on terror." The "war on terror" has not supplanted broadly humanitarian rationales for intervention but has complemented them in two important ways. First, like "humanitarian intervention," the term is to a considerable degree self-validating: one cannot easily oppose the "war on terror" without attracting widespread political opprobrium. Legally and politically dubious actions taken under that rubric still enjoy a measure of cushioning that the moral awfulness of terrorism provides. Second, in terms of declared intention, what can be classed as "terrorist" is every bit as open-ended and expansive as what can be classed as "humanitarian." In combination, there are few interventionist acts below the level of outright war that cannot be justified in terms of one or the other—or both.

With the commencement of the unquestionably illegal Iraq war, an important threshold was crossed. What is coming to count as the kinds of values that can be made to stand above or outside the compass of international law has now been expanded from fundamental humanitarianism to subtle and not so subtle blends with the more familiar concerns of international politics: regional security; forcible democratization; WMD capacity; and terrorism. Perhaps the much-heralded "new world order" of 1990 was not misnamed but mistimed. If so, its advent was the invasion of Iraq; and unlike its forbearer, it has little to recommend it.

The invasion of Iraq and the retrospective uses of declared humanitarian motives

Humanitarian rationales did not feature prominently in the run-up to the invasion of Iraq in 2003; however, the non-interventionist norm in international politics was certainly loosened by appeals to a widening span of humanitarian purpose and outcomes. We can see a trajectory from political and legal claims made on behalf of "humanitarian intervention" to more generalized appeals based on less extreme forms of human suffering, to the more recent appeals to a non-specific "war on terror." Now, the possibility of preventive war (extending to the tense relations between Iran and Israel) is openly discussed—and furthermore enshrined in the "Bush Doctrine." This drift away from a law-based international order to a forced-based order has been visible for some years: for example, US Secretary of State Madeleine Albright, speaking on the US–UK bombing of Iraq on 16 December 1998 offered a rationale that can only be described as a defence of preventive war:

> We are now dealing with a threat, I think, that is probably harder for some to understand, because it is a threat of the future rather than a present threat or a present act, such as a border crossing, a border aggression. Here . . . we are concerned about the threat posed by Saddam Hussein's ability to have, develop, deploy WMD and the threat he poses to the neighbors, to the stability of the Middle East and therefore ultimately to ourselves.[30]

It is perhaps not altogether surprising to find that these various means of justifying non-sanctioned intervention culminated in the case of Iraq, since full-scale war and occupation is of a different order from short-term incursions with at least a credible humanitarian purpose, or from cruise missile or Predator strikes. The focus here is not on what might have been the true motive forces of the UK and US governments for the war, although this remains a vital matter of democratic accountability, since the supposed al Qaeda–Saddam Hussein links and an advanced state of Iraqi WMD capacity were both comprehensively invalidated after the fact.[31]

The rupture with the non-interventionist order of international politics is only partly a matter of scale, or of the standing of the UK and the US. The cynical manipulation of international law by way of arguing that they were preparing to act to uphold the will of the Security Council was in this case put to the test. There was no ambiguity about the outcome of this extraordinary political gamble, even though a vote was never formally taken. (The voting procedure in the UN Security Council is essentially political theatre; and the UK and US ceased their efforts knowing that they had failed to secure a majority.) The US–UK invasion of Iraq had no more legality than Saddam Hussein's invasion of Kuwait in 1990. Two permanent members of the UN Security Council saw fit to act in defiance of what can fairly be described as the principal purpose of the United Nations at its founding. Yet more than two years after the invasion, the UK Foreign Secretary felt able to state, "On the foundation of our alliance with the United States and membership of the European Union, it is the United Nations which is at the heart of how we achieve [our] active and engaged foreign policy."[32]

As Iraq continues to deteriorate, post-facto ethical justifications— freeing the Iraqi people from tyranny, bringing democracy to the country, reversing its appalling human rights record—have come much to the fore. As the UK Foreign Secretary now describes matters, "We are in Iraq for one reason and one reason only—to help the elected Iraqi government build a secure, democratic and stable nation—and we can and will only remain with their consent."[33] (The embarrassments of both UK and US dalliance with Saddam Hussein's regime from the time of the Iraq–Iran war and even after the gassing of the Kurds are conveniently fenced off from an understanding of that event as a specimen case for why regime change was necessary.) No doubt the emphasis in justifications will shift according to prevailing conditions; and several can be advanced at once, as did George Bush, speaking on the first anniversary of the invasion: "One year ago, military forces of a strong coalition entered Iraq to enforce United Nations demands, to defend our security, and to liberate that country from the rule of a tyrant. For Iraq, it was a day of deliverance."[34]

Conclusion

The broader and longer-term meaning of the invasion of Iraq is the deliberate merging of values and interests, together with a determination to be able to secure them without the inconveniences of international law. This is most succinctly expressed by Tony Blair in a speech made in March 2004, in which he traces the evolution of his thinking from his Chicago speech five years earlier. The change was prefigured, but it is nevertheless marked:

> It may well be that under international law as presently constituted, a regime can systematically brutalise and oppress its people and there is nothing anyone can do, when dialogue, diplomacy and even sanctions fail,

unless it comes within the definition of a humanitarian catastrophe (though the 300,000 remains in mass graves already found in Iraq might be thought by some to be something of a catastrophe). This may be the law, but should it be?[35]

The clear suggestion that the UK or some other state had or might have faced something of a dilemma on this point is familiar enough to anyone versed in the "humanitarian intervention" literature. One wonders whether it is the strictures of international law that prevent a robust response to the continuing humanitarian crisis in Darfur, by the UK or any other country with them capacity do so? More strikingly, this depiction also offers a post-facto humanitarian endorsement for what at the time was not presented as humanitarian at all.

There then follows a return to the interdependence theme which was at the heart of the Chicago speech:

We know now, if we didn't before, that our own self interest is ultimately bound up with the fate of other nations. The doctrine of international community is no longer a vision of idealism. It is a practical recognition that just as within a country, citizens who are free, well educated and prosperous tend to be responsible, to feel solidarity with a society in which they have a stake; so do nations that are free, democratic and benefiting from economic progress, tend to be stable and solid partners in the advance of humankind. The best defence of our security lies in the spread of our values.[36]

"But," cautions Blair,

we cannot advance these values except within a framework that recognises their universality. If it is a global threat, it needs a global response, based on global rules.[37]

Blair's listeners are not told what these "global rules" might comprise; whether they are international law—and if not, how they might relate to it; whether universal values can be as readily agreed and sustained as summoned up; and how, if the non-interventionist law is removed or amended, international life will give way to uniform "global responses."[38] The only sense in which this prescription is practical politics is as a form of enabled Wilsonianism: the unfettered ability to "make the world safe for democracy."

The end of this speech contains the following, remarkable assertion— a fusion of the right to preventive war (as was the invasion of Iraq), together with an unfettered right of humanitarian intervention:

If we are threatened, we have a right to act. And we do not accept in a community that others have a right to oppress and brutalise their people. We value the freedom and dignity of the human race and each individual in it.[39]

We can now see that strong advocacy for humanitarian intervention as a right of states weakens not only Article 2(4) of the UN charter; it also weakens the more general viability of the rule of law. Weakened legal strictures then make it easier to act in interventionist ways that could not plausibly be construed as humanitarian, although humanitarianism can be invoked, even if retrospectively—a form of speaking power to truth. Worse still, what appears to be beyond Blair's reckoning is what kind of international order could be expected if the UK's "right to act" as he has characterised it were similarly espoused and pursued by other states—and even by non-state groups.[40] This is a tawdry and worrying juncture for the important debates about how we might go about genuine humanitarian rescue for beleaguered populations without undermining the legal foundations of international order. It is a debate that should be approached with a degree of appropriate humility, especially in view of our political and practical failings in so many cases. Instead, it has now been linked to overtly unilateralist impulses, manifestly non-legal and potentially highly destabilising. That thinking of this kind could take shape even as the carnage in Iraq continues is scarcely credible.

Notes

1 W. B. Gallie, *Understanding War* (London: Routledge, 1991).
2 Nicholas J. Wheeler and Tim Dunne, "Moral Britannia? Evaluating the Ethical Dimension in Labour's Foreign Policy," The Foreign Policy Centre, April 2004, available at: www.isn.ethz.ch/pubs/ph/details.cfm?q51=moral+britannia&v21=93130&ord51=Title&lng=en&id=23012.
3 Hansard, Nov. 14 , 1996, available at: www.publications.parliament.uk/pa/cm199697/cmhansrd/vo961114/debtext/61114–05.htm.
4 White House, *The National Security Strategy of the United States of America* (2002), available at: www.whitehouse.gov/nsc/nss.html, p. 15.
5 Ibid, p. 16.
6 Oliver O'Donovan, *The Just War Revisited* (Cambridge: Cambridge University Press, 2003).
7 Gabriella Rosner, *The United Nations Emergency Force* (New York: Columbia University Press, 1963), p. 207.
8 Michael Walzer, *Just And Unjust Wars: A Moral Argument With Historical Illustrations* (New York: Basic Books, 4th edition, 2006).
9 J. L. Holzgrefe and Robert O. Keohane (eds.), *Humanitarian Intervention* (Cambridge: Cambridge University Press, 2003); Nicholas J. Wheeler, *Saving Strangers: Humanitarian Intervention in International Society* (Oxford: Oxford University Press, 2000).
10 Kofi A. Annan, "Two Concepts of Sovereignty," *The Economist* (September 18, 1999), available at: www.un.org/News/ossg/sg/stories/kaecon.html.
11 Ibid.

12 Ibid.

13 Tony Blair, "Doctrine of the International Community," speech to the Chicago Economic Club, April 22, 1999, available at: www.number-10.gov.uk/output/Page1297.asp.

14 Independent International Commission on Kosovo, *Kosovo Report: Conflict, International Response, Lessons Learned* (Oxford: Oxford University Press, 2001), p. 4.

15 Jim Whitman, "After Kosovo: The Risks and Deficiencies of Unsanctioned Humanitarian Intervention," *Journal of Humanitarian Assistance*, www.jha.ac/articles/a062.htm (posted September 28, 2000).

16 Blair, "Doctrine."

17 Wheeler, *Saving Strangers*.

18 Thomas M. Franck and Nigel S. Rodley, "After Bangladesh: The Law of Humanitarian Intervention by Military Force," *American Journal of International Law* 67 (1973), p. 305.

19 William F. Schultz, *In Our Own Best Interests: How Defending Human Rights Benefits Us All* (Boston: Beacon Press, 2001).

20 Marc Weller, "The US, Iraq and the Use of Force in a Unipolar World," *Survival*, Vol.41, No.4 (Jan. 1999), p. 95.

21 Ibid, pp. 88–9.

22 Tim Youngs and Martin Oakes, "Iraq: 'Desert Fox' and Policy Developments," Research Paper 99/13, International Affairs and Defence Section, House of Commons Library (10 February 1999). Available at: www.parliament.uk/commons/lib/research/p99/rp99–013.pdf.

23 Weller, "The US, Iraq and the Use of Force in a Unipolar World."

24 Bill Clinton, Remarks to the National Guard Association of the United States, 3 September 1996, available at: www.presidency.ucsb.edu/ws/index.php?pid=53281. Note how Blair's assurance over Kosovo less than three years later—"a just war, based not on any territorial claims, but on values"—is of a similar cast.

25 Bill Clinton, Oval Office Address, "We Must Be Prepared to Use Force Again," Wednesday, December 16, 1998, available at: www.washingtonpost.com/wp-srv/politics/special/clinton/stories/clintontext121698.htm.

26 Robin Cook, "Kosovo and the Modern Europe," speech at the Lord Mayor's Easter Banquet, April 14, 1999.

27 Clinton, "We Must be Prepared to Use Force Again."

28 The International Development Research Centre (IDRC) (2007), "Five Interventions After the Cold War," available at: www.idrc.ca/en/ev-62203–201–1–DO_TOPIC.html.

29 UK Cabinet Office (undated), "Enhancing Britain's Place in the World," available   at: www.cabinetoffice.gov.uk/strategy/downloads/files/sa_wfs_extract.pdf.

30 Cited in Weller, "The US, Iraq and the Use of Force," p. 87.

31 US Senate (109th Congress, 2nd session), Report of the Select Committee on Intelligence, "Postwar Findings About Iraq's WMD Programs and Links to

Terrorism and How They Compare with Prewar Assessments" (September 8, 2006). Available at: www.fas.org/irp/congress/2006_rpt/srpt109–331.pdf; House of Commons, "Review of Intelligence on Weapons of Mass Destruction," report of a Committee of Privy Counsellors, Lord Butler, Chairman (July 14, 2004). Available at: www.butlerreview.org.uk/report/report.pdf.

32 Jack Straw, "We Are in Iraq to Bring bout Democracy," speech by Foreign Secretary Jack Straw to the Labour Party Conference, September 28, 2005, available at: www.labour.org.uk/index.php?id=news2005&ux_news%5Bid %5D=ac05js&cHash=6cd4f7cecf.

33 Ibid.

34 White House, "President Bush Reaffirms Resolve to War on Terror, Iraq and Afghanistan," March 19, 2004, available at: www.whitehouse.gov/news/releases/2004/03/20040319–3.html

35 Tony Blair, Speech given by the Prime Minister in Sedgefield, March 5, 2004, available at: www.politics.guardian.co.uk/iraq/story/0,12956,1162991,00.html.

36 Ibid.

37 Ibid.

38 Thomas M. Franck, "Who Killed Article 2(4)? Or: Changing Norms Governing the Use of Force by States," *American Journal of International Law* 64 (1970), pp. 809–10.

39 Blair, Sedgefield speech.

40 Jim Whitman, "Humanitarian Intervention in an Era of Pre-emptive Self-Defence," *Security Dialogue*, Vol.36, No.3 (2005), pp. 259–74.

Part II

The public case for war

4

Did President Bush mislead the country in his arguments for war with Iraq?

James P. Pfiffner

President Bush was accused by some in the popular press of lying in his arguments for taking the US to war with Iraq in 2003. But in order to make judgments about the accuracy of the president's statements, the claims must be analyzed separately. This chapter examines several sets of statements by President Bush and his administration: first, about the implication that there was a link between Saddam Hussein, al Qaeda, and the terrorist attacks of 9/11; second, about Iraq's nuclear weapons capacity; and third; about Saddam's chemical and biological weapons and his ability to deliver them. The possibility that the intelligence process was politicized is also examined.

Although the record at this early date is far from complete, the chapter concludes that from publicly available evidence, the president misled the country in implying that there was a connection between Saddam and 9/11. The administration's claims about Iraq's nuclear capacity were based on dubious evidence that was presented in a misleading manner. Claims about chemical and biological weapons were based on legitimate evidence that was widely accepted internationally, despite the failure to find the weapons by late 2003. Claims of Saddam's ability to deliver these weapons, however, were exaggerated. Finally, there was circumstantial and inconclusive evidence that in 2002 the intelligence community may have been under unusual pressure to support the administration's goals.

A link between Saddam Hussein, al Qaeda, and 9/11

Two days after the terrorist attacks of September 11, 2001, a Time/CNN poll found that 78 percent of respondents thought that Saddam Hussein was involved with the attacks on the twin trade towers in New York and the Pentagon in Washington.[1] From that time to the beginning of the war and into the summer of 2003, the President Bush and his administration strongly implied that there was a link between Saddam and the al Qaeda hijackers, despite Ossama bin Laden's contempt for Saddam as the head of a secular state.[2] Although Bush probably knew that the evidence was quite sketchy at best, he used the implied link to bolster support for war with Iraq in Congress before the authorizing resolution and more generally with the American public before and after the war.

In early October 2002 President Bush was trying to convince Congress to pass a resolution to give him unilateral authority to go to war with Iraq. In a major address to the nation on October 7th he said "We know that Iraq and al Qaeda have had high-level contacts that go back a decade . . . We've learned that Iraq has trained al Qaeda members in bomb-making and poisons and deadly gasses." He also said that a "very senior al Qaeda leader" received medical treatment in Baghdad. In the same speech the president closely connected the need to attack Iraq with the 9/11 attacks: "Some citizens wonder, 'after 11 years of living with this [Saddam Hussein] problem, why do we need to confront it now?' And there's a justification. We have experienced the horror of September the 11." Thus the terrorist attacks of 9/11 were a major reason for attacking Iraq.

Vice President Cheney said on "Meet the Press" in late 2001 that a meeting between Mohamed Atta and an Iraqi official in Prague in 2000 was "pretty well confirmed."[3] On September 27, 2002 Secretary of Defense Donald Rumsfeld argued that the link between Saddam and al Qaeda was "bulletproof."[4] National Security advisor Condoleezza Rice said on September 25, 2002, "There clearly are contacts between Al Qaeda and Iraq . . . There clearly is testimony that some of the contacts have been important contacts and that there's a relationship there."[5]

The problem was that evidence for a connection between Saddam and al Qaeda was never very solid. The administration based part of its argument on a claim that 9/11 leader Mohamed Atta met with an Iraqi official in Prague in April 2000. An investigation by the FBI, however, concluded that there was no convincing evidence that Atta was in Prague at the time of the meeting and the CIA was doubtful about any meeting of Atta and an Iraqi official.[6] A congressional report said that "The CIA has been unable to establish that [Atta] left the United States or entered Europe in April [2000] under his other name or any known alias."[7]

The "very senior al Qaeda leader" to whom Bush referred was Abu Mussab Zarqawi, a Jordanian who was not in al Qaeda, though he was a terrorist and had had contacts with al Qaeda.[8] A UN terrorism committee did not find any link between al Qaeda and Saddam. According to the chief investigator, Michael Chandler, "Nothing has come to our notice that would indicate links between Iraq and al-Qaeda."[9] But even if there was some evidence that al Qaeda members had been in Iraq at some time, it would not constitute proof that Iraq was connected to the terrorist attacks of 9/11.

Despite the lack of solid evidence, President Bush continued to connect the war in Iraq with al Qaeda and 9/11. In his victory speech on May 1, 2003 on an aircraft carrier off the coast of California, he said: "The battle of Iraq is one victory in a war on terror that began on September the 11, 2001. We've removed an ally of al Qaeda, and cut off a source of terrorist funding . . . With those attacks [of 9/11], the terrorists and their supporters declared war on the United States. And war is what they got."[10]

On September 7, 2003 in his speech announcing the administration's request for an additional $87 billion for the occupation of Iraq, President Bush continued to connect Iraq and 9/11.

> Nearly two years ago, following deadly attacks on our country, we began a systematic campaign against terrorism . . . And we acted in Iraq, where the former regime sponsored terror . . . And for America, there will be no going back to the era before September the 11th, 2001, to false comfort in a dangerous world . . . We are fighting that enemy in Iraq and Afghanistan today so that we do not meet him again on our own streets, in our own cities.[11]

The implication was still that there was a link between al Qaeda and Iraq. In a defense of the administration's policies in Iraq on September 14, 2003 Vice President Cheney said: "If we're successful in Iraq . . . then we will have struck a major blow right at the heart of the base, if you will, the geographic base of the terrorists who had us under assault now for many years, but most especially on 9/11."[12]

But on September 18 President Bush conceded: "No, we've had no evidence that Saddam Hussein was involved with September the 11th."[13] He gave no explanation at to why the previously implied connection was abandoned.

How can we judge this systematic pattern of implication and the sudden reversal by the president? It is difficult to show that there was an outright lie in the president's rhetoric, because his use of language was too careful. Some of the statements by Bush might have been based on claims that he thought were true when he implied the connection between Saddam and 9/11. The problem is that as it became clear that the evidence was dubious, the president continued to imply that the connection was real. But as time went by, there was enough coverage in the press of the failure of intelligence agencies to substantiate the claim, that the president could not credibly claim ignorance. The careful phrasing of administration statements implying a link between Saddam and 9/11 suggests that they knew there was no compelling evidence. If there was, they would have made an outright claim for the link, and the argument for war would have been much easier to make.

President Bush did exploit and encourage the general public belief that Saddam was connected to the attacks of 9/11, and his strong implications served his purpose of achieving public support for war with Iraq. Though we might not be able to conclude that the president lied directly about the connection, he did encourage and further the mistaken public belief because it supported his policy goals. We can conclude that his statements were misleading and deceptive, though not outright lies.

Nuclear weapons in Iraq

In 2002 President Bush and his administration made a number of claims about Saddam Hussein's potential nuclear capacity, allegations that culminated in a statement in the president's State of the Union speech on January 29, 2003. Throughout the build-up to the war with Iraq, the administration consistently conflated biological, chemical, and nuclear weapons as "weapons of mass destruction" (WMD). As horrible as chemical and biological weapons are, they pale in comparison with the potential destructiveness of nuclear weapons. As Kenneth M. Pollack, a proponent of war with Iraq put it, "A successful attack with VX could kill thousands; with a BW agent, tens of thousands; and with a nuclear weapon, hundreds of thousands or even millions." In addition, chemical and biological weapons are difficult to maintain and deliver effectively.[14]

The claim that Saddam Hussein had reconstituted his nuclear weapons program and was potentially "less than a year" away from possessing nuclear weapons was a powerful argument that deposing Saddam Hussein was important for US national security. Even those who thought that Saddam could be deterred from using chemical and biological weapons (as he had been in 1991) might be persuaded that an attack was necessary if they were convinced that Saddam was closing in on a nuclear weapons capability.[15] Thus the claim of Saddam's nuclear capacity was one of the strongest arguments that President Bush could make for war with Iraq.

In his speech on August 26, 2002 laying out the administration's argument for war with Iraq, Vice President Cheney said, "Many of us are convinced that Saddam will acquire nuclear weapons fairly soon . . . There is no doubt he is amassing [WMD] to use against our friends, against our allies, and against us."[16] Condoleezza Rice said in September 2002, "There will always be some uncertainty about how quickly [Saddam] can acquire nuclear weapons. But we don't want the smoking gun to be a mushroom cloud."[17]

On September 7, 2002 at Camp David President Bush told reporters on the issue of Iraqi nuclear capacity, "I would remind you that when the inspectors first went into Iraq and were denied, finally denied access, a report came out of the Atomic—the IAEA—that they were six months away from developing a weapon. I don't know what more evidence we need."[18] The International Atomic Energy Agency (IAEA) report did say that in 1991 Iraq had been six to twenty-four months away from the capacity to produce a nuclear bomb, but that capacity had been destroyed by UN inspectors before 1998. When the inspectors left Iraq in 1998, the report said: "Based on all credible information to date, the IAEA has found no indication of Iraq having achieved its program goal of producing nuclear weapons or of Iraq having retained a physical capability for the production of weapon-usable nuclear material or having clandestinely obtained such material."[19] It is possible, though unlikely, that the president was consciously misleading the press in order to present a strong case for going to war with Iraq. More likely, it was mere confusion, but if so, it was confusion about a crucial element in the decision of going to war.

Before the president's campaign to convince Congress of the necessity of war with Iraq, the White House asked the CIA to prepare a National Intelligence Estimate (NIE) on Iraq. According to the CIA, "A National Intelligence Estimate is the most authoritative written judgment concerning a national security issue prepared by the Director of Central Intelligence . . . NIEs are addressed to the highest level of policy making—up to and including the President."[20]

The NIE of early October 2002 stated:

> How quickly Iraq will obtain its first nuclear weapon depends on when it acquires sufficient weapons-grade fissile material.
> If Baghdad acquires sufficient fissile material from abroad it could made a nuclear weapon within several months to a year.
> Without such material from abroad, Iraq probably would not be able to make a weapon until 2007 to 2009.[21]

The NIE was used as a basis for President Bush's speech in Cincinnati on October 7, 2002 to convince Congress to give him the authority to go to war with Iraq and convince the nation of the immediacy of the threat from Saddam Hussein. In the speech President Bush said:

> We agree that the Iraqi dictator must not be permitted to threaten America and the world with horrible poisons and diseases and gasses and atomic weapons . . . The evidence indicates that Iraq is reconstituting its nuclear weapons program . . . Satellite photographs reveal that Iraq is rebuilding facilities at sites that have been part of his nuclear program in the past . . . *he could have a nuclear weapon in less than a year* . . . Facing clear evidence of peril, we cannot wait for the final proof, the smoking gun that could come in the form of a mushroom cloud. (emphasis added)

On January 23 Deputy Secretary of Defense Paul Wolfowitz said: "Disarming Iraq and the war on terror are not merely related. Disarming Iraq of its chemical and biological weapons and dismantling its nuclear weapons program is a crucial part of winning the war on terror."[22]

Then in his State of the Union Speech on January 28, 2003, President Bush said the 16 words that would become the center of controversy: "The British Government has learned that Saddam Hussein recently sought significant quantities of uranium from Africa." Immediately before the war, on March 16, Vice President Cheney declared: "We know [Saddam Hussein] has been absolutely devoted to trying to acquire nuclear weapons. And we believe he has, in fact, reconstituted nuclear weapons."[23] Then on March 17, on the eve of the war, President Bush said: "Using chemical, biological or, one day, nuclear weapons obtained with the help of Iraq, the terrorists could fulfill their stated ambitions . . ."[24]

The problem with this series of statements was that the evidence upon which the president's claims were based turned out to be questionable. Two claims of evidence for Saddam's nuclear capacity that the administration relied upon were of dubious authenticity: the claim that Iraq sought uranium oxide, "yellowcake," from Niger and that aluminum tubes shipped to Iraq were intended to be used as centrifuges to create the fissile material necessary for a nuclear bomb. Each of these claims will be examined separately.

The Niger claim

The claim in the 2003 State of the Union address that the British had learned about an attempt by Iraq to procure nuclear material from Iraq was based in part on a British intelligence report in September 2002 that Iraq was seeking yellowcake from Niger. The administration was going to use the claim in the president's October 7 speech, and one draft of the speech said, "The [Iraqi] regime has been caught attempting to purchase substantial amounts of uranium oxide from sources in Africa."[25] CIA Director George Tenet had warned the British that the Niger claim published in their September 24 dossier was probably not true, but they used it anyway. Before the president's speech, on October 5 and 6 Deputy National Security Advisor Stephen Hadley received two memoranda from the CIA expressing the CIA's reservations about the Niger claim. In addition, Tenet personally called Hadley and told him that the claim was not sound. Tenet was successful in convincing White House to delete the claim from the president's speech.[26]

The report about Niger and yellowcake may have originated in several letters obtained by Italian intelligence sources. On October 11, 2002 Italian journalist Elisabetta Burba gave copies of the Niger letters to the

US Embassy in Rome. In response to the question of why she did not publish the letters herself, she said "The story seemed fake to me . . . I realized that this could be a worldwide scoop, but that's exactly why I was very worried. If it turned out to be a hoax, and I published it, it would have ended my career."[27] The letters were distributed to US intelligence agencies with caveat that they were of "dubious authenticity."

The CIA was doubtful about the Niger claim because after the reports arose, the Vice President's office requested that the CIA investigate the claim. So in February 2002 the CIA sent former ambassador Joseph Wilson to Niger to investigate the question. Wilson had been a career foreign service officer, was appointed ambassador by George H. W. Bush, and had served as a diplomat in Niger's capital (Niamey) in the 1970s. He met with the US ambassador to Niger who had herself "debunked" in reports to Washington the rumors of Iraqi attempts to buy yellowcake in Niger. After his investigation, Wilson concluded that the rumored efforts were not true and reported this back to the CIA.[28] In addition, on February 24 General Carlton W. Fulford, Jr. and the US ambassador to Niger visited Niger's president and reported to the State and Defense Departments that the supply of uranium ore was secure. He said he was "assured" that the yellowcake was being kept secure by the French consortium that controlled it.[29]

Despite these reports, the NIE of October 2002 stated "A foreign government service reported that as of early 2001, Niger planned to send several tons of 'pure uranium' (probably yellowcake) to Iraq. As of early 2001, Niger and Iraq reportedly were still working out arrangements for this deal, which could be for up to 500 tons of yellowcake. We do not know the status of this arrangement."[30] In an annex to the NIE, however, the State Department's Bureau of Intelligence and Research concluded: "Finally, the claims of Iraqi pursuit of natural uranium in Africa are, in INR's assessment, highly dubious."[31]

The US gave copies of the Niger-related documents (12 pages) to International Atomic Energy Agency (IAEA) Director, General Mohamed ElBaradei.[32] After a search through Google, Jacques Baute, head of the IAEA inspection section, found that the letterhead of one letter was from the military government that had been replaced before the 1999 date on the letter, and the signature on the letter indicated the name of a foreign ministry official who had left the position in 1989.[33] The forgery was made public on March 7, 2003 by Mohamed ElBaradei who reported the findings to the UN Security Council.[34]

Given that the basis for the claim for the Niger yellowcake was known by the CIA to be dubious, how did the claim make it into the president's State of the Union address?[35] When the State of the Union speech was being prepared, NSC official Robert Joseph faxed a paragraph on uranium from Niger to CIA official Alan Foley. Foley told Joseph that the reference to Niger should be taken out. Joseph insisted that a reference remain in the speech, so they compromised: Niger was changed to Africa; they did not include any specific quantity; and the source was attributed to the British rather than to US intelligence.[36] Thus there was high level doubt about the wisdom of including the dubious claim about Niger in the president's State of the Union message, particularly since the same claim had been deleted from the president's October 7, 2002 speech in Cincinnati.

Although knowledge of the forged letters was made public in February 2003, the sentence did not arouse public controversy until, it in the wake of the US war with Iraq, no evidence of weapons of mass destruction, much less nuclear weapons, could be found. In explaining why the president might not have known that the claim was not accurate, a high-level White House official said, "The president of the United States is not a fact-checker,"[37] This type of response trivializes the role of the president. The issue was not a minor detail; it was a question of a potential nuclear threat to the United States and the possibility of going to war. The president has an obligation to get the facts as right as they can be in such situations.

National Security Advisor Condoleezza Rice minimized the problem by saying: "It is 16 words, and it has become an enormously overblown issue."[38] She denied that any doubts were evident to her or the president. On July 11, 2003 she said: "All that I can tell you is that if there were doubts about the underlying intelligence on the NIE, those doubts were not communicated to the president. The only thing that was there in the NIE was a kind of a standard INR footnote, which is kind of 59 pages away from the bulk of the NIE . . . So if there was a concern about the underlying intelligence there, the president was unaware of that concern and as was I." Even though the State Department's INR dissent was placed toward the end of the document, the "Key Judgments" section near the front called attention to the "INR alternative view at the end of these Key Judgments."[39]

If what Rice said was true, it would mean that on the crucial issue of Iraqi nuclear weapons: she was not aware that the CIA sent two memos and director Tenet called her deputy in order to get the Niger claim out of the President's October 7 speech; she was not aware that the State Department had serious reservations about the claim; she was not aware that the CIA had sent, at the vice president's request, Joseph Wilson to Niger to investigate the claim; and she was not aware that Robert Joseph negotiated with the CIA a change in wording in the State of the Union speech. If, as Rice said, no one communicated any of these reservations about something as crucial as nuclear weapons in Iraq to the president, the president was not being well served. Even though the president and his national security advisor are deluged with intelligence information, and the State of the Union preparation is an elaborate process, the stakes on this particular issue could not have been much higher: Iraq with a possible nuclear weapon and taking the nation to war.

After intensive press inquiry about how the sentence got into the State of the Union, on July 11, 2003 CIA Director George Tenet took responsibility for the inclusion of the inaccurate sentence. "I am responsible for the approval process in my agency. And . . . the President had every reason to believe that the text presented to him was sound. These 16 words should never have been included in the text written for the President."[40] Later, on July 21 Rice's deputy, Stephen Hadley, said that he was at fault for the reference to uranium because he had been the one whom Tenet had called to get it removed from the October 7 speech. "I should have recalled [the issue] at the time of the State of the Union address . . . If I had done so, it would have avoided the entire current controversy."[41] Finally, on July 30 the president said, "I take personal responsibility for everything I say, of course. I also take responsibility for making decisions on war and peace. And I analyzed a thorough body of intelligence, got solid, sound intelligence that led me to come to the conclusion that it was necessary to remove Saddam Hussein from power."[42]

In the summer of 2003 the administration argued that the president's words were technically truthful because he referred to British intelligence as the source of the conclusion about the Niger connection. Condoleezza Rice said, "The statement that he made was indeed accurate. The British government did say that." Donald Rumsfeld said, "It turns out that it's technically correct what the president said, that the U.K. does—did say that—and still says that."[43] The legalistic parsing of the president's words was reminiscent of President Clinton's statement about the meaning of the word "is." But President Bush's statement was not literally or technically true. He did not say that the British "claimed" or "asserted" or "said" or "stated" that Saddam had sought yellowcake from Africa. He said that they "learned" of it. Is it possible to learn something that is false? The president clearly indicated by his use of the word "learned" rather than another word, that he believed the statement to be true.[44]

The aluminum tubes

In addition to the Niger yellowcake claim, the administration also adduced as evidence for Iraq's reconstituting its nuclear program reports of large numbers of aluminum tubes purchased by Iraq. President Bush said in his September 12 speech to the United Nations: "Iraq has made several attempts to buy high-strength aluminum tubes used to enrich uranium for a nuclear weapon. Should Iraq acquire fissile material, it would be able to build a nuclear weapon within a year."[45] Condoleezza Rice also said in September "We do know that there have been shipments going . . . into Iraq, for instance, of aluminum tubes that really are only suited for nuclear weapons programs, centrifuge programs."[46]

The evidence of the aluminum tubes was also featured in the NIE issued in early October which played an important role in convincing members of Congress to vote for the resolution giving the President the authority to take the United States to war with Iraq. The NIE stated:

> Most agencies believe that Saddam's personal interest in and Iraq's aggressive attempts to obtain high-strength aluminum tubes for centrifuge rotors . . . provide compelling evidence that Saddam is reconstituting a uranium enrichment effort for Baghdad's nuclear weapons program. (DOE agrees that reconstitution of the nuclear program is underway but assesses that the tubes probably are not part of the program.) . . .
>
> All agencies agree that about 25,000 centrifuges based on tubes of the size Iraq is trying to acquire would be capable of producing approximately two weapons' worth of highly enriched uranium per year.[47]

The State Department's Bureau of Intelligence and Research (INR), however, dissented from the argument of the rest of the NIE:

> In INR's view Iraq's efforts to acquire aluminum tubes is central to the argument that Baghdad is reconstituting its nuclear weapons program, but INR is not persuaded that the tubes in question are intended for use as centrifuge rotors. INR accepts the judgment of technical experts at the US Department of Energy (DOE) who have concluded that the tubes Iraq seeks to acquire are poorly suited for use in gas centrifuges to be used for uranium enrichment and finds unpersuasive the arguments advanced by others to make the case that they are intended for that purpose. INR considers it far more likely that the tubes are intended for another purpose, most likely the production of artillery rockets.[48]

The State Department's skepticism was based on a number of factors that made claiming the aluminum tubes as evidence of Iraq's attempt to obtain a nuclear capacity questionable.

The physical characteristics of the tubes matched closely the dimensions of aluminum tubes used in Medusa Rockets, but did not track closely with the dimensions of centrifuge rotors:

1 The tubes were narrower and longer (910mm. versus 500–600mm) for a centrifuge rotor. The Medusa Rocket fuselage is 910mm in length.

2 They were made of aluminum, which since the 1950s had not been used for centrifuge rotors.
3 The tubes had an anodized coating which was right for rocket tubes but would have to be removed for use as centrifuges for nuclear material.
4 The diameter of the tubes was 81 millimeters, the same as would be used for a Medusa Rocket, but the usual diameter for gas centrifuges was 145 mm.
5 The thickness of the tubes was 3mm, while the thickness of a centrifuge rotor is .5mm.[49]

One of the foremost living experts on centrifuge physics, Houston G. Wood III, who founded the Oak Ridge National Laboratory centrifuge physics department (run by the Department of Energy) said, "[I]t would have been extremely difficult to make these tubes into centrifuges. It stretches the imagination to come up with a way. I do not know any real centrifuge experts that feel differently."[50] The director of the inspections unit for the IAEA, Jacques Baute, convened a team of experts (two from England, two Americans, and one from Germany) who examined the available evidence from Iraqi front companies and military facilities and concluded that "all evidence points to that this is for the rockets."[51]

Nuclear weapons summary

There is no doubt that Iraq sought nuclear weapons in the 1970s and 1980s. In 1976 Iraq bought a nuclear reactor from France that it assembled at Osiraq, but just before it was to come on line in 1981 the Israelis launched an air attack that destroyed it. By the Gulf war in 1991 Iraq had made great progress in its nuclear program, lacking only fissile material necessary for nuclear bombs. After the war, however, UN inspectors destroyed most, if not all, of the physical capacity to construct nuclear bombs, though engineers and scientists remained in Iraq.[52]

In addition to the destruction of weapons by the UN inspectors before they left in 1998, the economic sanctions severely limited the materials that could be brought into the country for potential use for WMD. US enforcement of the no-fly zones also limited what the Iraqis could do, and satellite surveillance was used extensively to monitor the country. The effectiveness of the UN inspectors before 1998, and the sanctions and the no-fly zones after 1998 was reflected in remarks by Colin Powell when he visited Egypt on 24 February 2001:

> the sanctions exist—not for the purpose of hurting the Iraqi people, but for the purpose of keeping in check Saddam Hussein's ambitions toward developing weapons of mass destruction . . . And frankly they have worked. He has not developed any significant capability with respect to weapons of

mass destruction. He is unable to project conventional power against his neighbors. [53]

But in spite of the lack of evidence, some US intelligence agencies concluded that Saddam's nuclear program had been reconstituted.

The NIE of October 2002 stated that "in the view of most agencies, Baghdad is reconstituting its nuclear weapons program."[54] It also said, "if left unchecked, it probably will have a nuclear weapon during this decade. (See INR alternative view at the end of these Key Judgments.)"[55] The alternative view of the State Department Assistant Secretary for Intelligence and Research (INR) was enclosed in a lined box around the type and stated that in its judgment, Saddam wanted nuclear weapons and was pursuing "at least a limited effort" to acquire them,

> The activities we have detected do not, however, add up to a compelling case that Iraq is currently pursuing what INR would consider to be an integrated and comprehensive approach to acquire nuclear weapons. . . .INR is unwilling to speculate that such an effort began soon after the departure of UN inspectors or to project a timeline for the completion of activities it does not now see happening.[56]

Greg Thielmann, former director of the State Department Bureau of Intelligence and Research's program on strategic proliferation and military affairs said: "During the time that I was office director, 2000–2002, we never assessed that there was good evidence that Iraq was reconstituting or getting really serious about its nuclear weapons program."[57]

In his report to Congress, David Kay told Congress that Iraq's nuclear program was in "the very most rudimentary" state, "It clearly does not look like a massive, resurgent program, based on what we discovered."[58] According to Kay's report, Iraqi scientists said that Hussein "remained firmly committee to acquiring nuclear weapons" and "would have resumed nuclear weapons development at some future point." But "to date we have not uncovered evidence that Iraq undertook significant post-1998 steps to actually build nuclear weapons or produce fissile material."[59]

If the administration had compelling evidence that Saddam was reconstituting its nuclear capacity, why did it rely on the two dubious claims analyzed above. And if the United States knew of the efforts, why were the UN inspectors unable to find any evidence before the war or US forces able to find any evidence after the war? In September 2003 the ranking majority and minority members of the House Select Committee on Intelligence concluded that the administration did not have any compelling evidence that it could not make public that supported its claims about Iraq's WMD programs. "The absence of proof that chemical and biological weapons and their related development programs had been destroyed was considered proof that they continued to exist. . . .We have not found any information in the assessments that are still classified that was any more definitive."[60]

Chemical and biological weapons, UAVs, and intelligence

The Bush administration claimed with some certainty that Iraq possessed chemical and biological weapons as well as unpiloted aerial vehicles (UAVs) that were capable of delivering them. This section takes up these claims as well as the question of whether the intelligence process was politicized by the administration. That is, was there pressure on intelligence agencies to produce reports that supported the administration's policy goals rather than reports that reflected the best intelligence judgment of the analysts.

Chemical and biological weapons

That Iraq had chemical and biological weapons in the 1980s is certain, in part because some of the materials came from the United States and because Saddam used chemical weapons against Iran and against the Kurds in northern Iraq. Thus it was surprising that little evidence of these programs was found by US troops in the aftermath of the war, especially since the United States devoted considerable manpower and expertise to the effort to discover them.[61]

Although Iraq purchased most of its chemical and biological weapons materials from Europe and a few other regions, significant materials came from the United States in the 1980s. When it began to look like Iran might be able to defeat Iraq in the war Iraq had initiated in September 1980, the United States moved to open diplomatic relations with Iraq and in February 1982 removed it from the list of terrorist countries that US companies could not trade with. Despite reports that the Iraqis were using chemical warfare weapons against the Iranians, the Reagan administration moved aggressively to support Iraq, sending Donald Rumsfeld as a special envoy to meet with Saddam Hussein in December 1983.[62]

The United States supported Iraq during the war in a number of ways, including economic aid in Commodity Credit Corporation guarantees of more than $1 billion from 1983 to 1987 and regular intelligence help that reached the liaison level of relationship between the two countries' intelligence agencies.[63] But more importantly the United States encouraged its allies, particularly France and Germany, to allow sale of weapons to Iraq, where Iraq got much of its chemical and biological weapons capacity.[64]

The Reagan administration also, through policy changes in the Departments of State and Commerce, allowed US companies to export dual-use materials (such as chemical precursors to weapons and steel tubes for artillery) to Iraq, which were expected to be used for its biological and chemical programs. Biological agents sold to Iraq from the United States during this period included several strains of anthrax and bubonic plague. Despite the killing of 200,000 Kurds with chemical weapons and high explosives from 1987 to 1989 and the destruction of the Kurdish town of Halabja on March 15, 1988, the United States did not stop US companies from continuing to sell insecticides and other chemical components of chemical weapons to Iraq. In 1988 Iraq purchased $1.5 million worth of pesticides from Dow Chemical.[65] The United States benefited from its support of Iraq by being allowed to purchase Iraqi oil at lower than world market prices.[66]

Saddam's chemical and biological warfare capacity formed much of the basis for the Bush administration's argument that Saddam's weapons of mass destruction were a threat to the United States. Often the president's remarks were modified by words such as likely or possible, but sometimes his words and those of other administration officials were more categorical. President Bush said on September 26, 2002 that "the Iraqi regime possesses biological and chemical weapons. The Iraqi regime is building the facilities necessary to make more biological and chemical weapons."[67]

A report by the Defense Intelligence Agency (DIA) from September 2002, however, voiced some skepticism about the recent status of Iraq's chemical and biological production capacity. The report stated, "A substantial amount of Iraq's chemical warfare agents, precursors, munitions, and production equipment were destroyed between 1991 and 1998 as a result of Operation Desert Storm and UNSCOM [United Nations Special Commission] actions. There is no reliable information on whether Iraq is producing and stockpiling chemical weapons, or where Iraq has—or will—establish its chemical warfare agent production facilities."[68]

When the president was in Krakow, Poland on May 30, 2003 he announced that US troops had discovered firm evidence of biological weapons labs when they found two trailers that seemed to have been used for biological weapons production. The president said, "But for those who say we haven't found the banned manufacturing devices or banned weapons, they're wrong. We found them."[69] The CIA, however, found no pathogens in the trailers, and some US defense scientists felt that there was a rush to conclude that the trailers were mobile germ warfare labs. William C. Patrick III a former senior official in US germ warfare programs said that a key component, the capacity for steam sterilization, was missing from the trailers. Another senior US analyst said, "I have no great confidence that it's a fermenter."[70] In addition, a majority of the engineering team of the Defense Intelligence Agency came to the conclusion that the trailers were not for making weapons but rather for producing hydrogen, probably for balloons.[71]

The most serious questions about the administration's claims were raised when US forces were not able to find evidence of Iraq's chemical and biological weapons after the war, despite the diligent searching of US military forces and the 1200 member Iraq Survey Group headed by David Kay.[72] Kay reported that with respect to chemical weapons. "Iraq's large-scale capability to develop, produce, and fill new CW munitions was reduced—if not entirely destroyed—during Operations Desert Storm and Desert Fox, 13 years of UN sanctions and UN inspections." With respect to biological weapons the Iraq Survey Group found evidence of various "biological warfare activities" and one "vial of live C. Botulinum Okra B. From which a biological agent can be produced." But they found no biological weapons. With respect to the two trailers, Kay reported "We have not yet been able to corroborate the existence of a mobile BW production effort."[73]

Most experts were perplexed at the inability of the Iraq Survey Group to find the chemical and biological weapons that were expected to be found. After the war, many Iraqi scientists denied that they existed, and no evidence was found that they did. It is possible that Saddam cleverly hid them or destroyed them. It is also possible that before the war Saddam's scientists exaggerated their success in producing such weapons because they were afraid to tell him the truth if they had failed to produce them.[74]

Unpiloted aerial vehicles (UAVs)

One of the keys to broad public support for an invasion of Iraq was the fear that the US mainland could be attacked. Thus the possibility of unmanned, drone airplanes armed with chemical or biological weapons could provoke serious concern. President Bush brought up in his October 7 speech in Cincinnati Iraq's potential to deliver chemical and biological weapons that could threaten the United States and its allies. "We have also discovered through intelligence that Iraq has a growing fleet of manned and unmanned aerial vehicles that could be used to disperse chemical or biological weapons across broad areas . . . We are concerned that Iraq is exploring ways of using these UAVs *for missions targeting the United States*" (emphasis added). This claim was based in part on the NIE's conclusion that "Baghdad . . . is working with unmanned aerial vehicles (UAVs), which allow for a more lethal means to deliver biological and, less likely, chemical warfare agents."[75] The NIE later stated, "Baghdad's UAVs could threaten Iraq's neighbors, US forces in the Persian Gulf, *and if brought close to, or into, the United States, the U.S. Homeland.*"[76]

Several lines below that statement, however, the Air Force voiced its disagreement: "The Director, Intelligence, Surveillance, and Reconnaissance, US Air Force, does not agree that Iraq is developing UAVs primarily intended to be delivery platforms for chemical and biological warfare (CBW) agents. The small size of Iraq's new UAV strongly suggests a primary role of reconnaissance, although CBW delivery is an inherent capability."[77] President Bush seemed to be relying on the NIE conclusion in his statements about the danger to the United States from Iraqi unmanned aerial vehicles, and the thought of planes spraying chemical or biological agents in the United States brought back visions of the 9/11 terrorists seeking training on crop dusting planes. But his advisors seemed to give little weight to the considered judgment of the, the United States Air Force, in coming to the conclusion that UAVs were likely threats to the homeland.

As it turned out after the war, the Air Force seemed to be correct. After examining the captured UAVs in Iraq, Robert S. Boyd, the senior intelligence analyst of the Air Force, explained why the Air Force voiced its dissent from the NIE of October 2002. He said that the aircraft that Iraq was using had wingspans of 12 to 16 feet and that they were not configured to carry chemical or biological warfare agents. "What we were thinking was: Why would you [the Iraqis] purposefully design a vehicle to be an inefficient delivery means? . . . Wouldn't it make more sense that they were purposefully designing it to be a decent reconnaissance UAV? . . . Everything we discovered strengthened our conviction that the UVVs were to be used for reconnaissance."[78]

Politicizing intelligence

One possible explanation for the administration's inaccurate claims about Iraq's WMD was that the intelligence-gathering capacities of the government were subject to pressure to suit their analyses to the policy goals of the administration. Allegations centered around the vice president's visits to CIA headquarters, the creation of the Office of Special Plans in Office of the Secretary of Defense, and the use of the Defense Policy Board.

Richard Cheney and his aide Scooter Libby made a number of personal visits the CIA Langley headquarters to question the CIA judgment that Iraq did not pose as immediate a threat as the administration was arguing it did. While it is appropriate for the vice president and other

high administration officials to ask tough questions and challenge intelligence agencies with hard questions, and it is understandable that career
civil servants may see this as pressure; the interventions in the intelligence
process seemed to be different in 2002 with respect to Iraq. These visits
were perceived by some CIA veterans as political pressure for the agency
to come to the conclusions that the administration wanted.[79] Ray
McGovern who had been a CIA analyst from 1964 to 1990 and had
briefed Vice President George H. W. Bush in the 1980s said, "During my
27-year career at the Central Intelligence Agency, no vice president ever
came to us for a working visit."[80]

In addition to close attention from the vice president, CIA analysis was
also treated with suspicion in the Department of Defense because the CIA
was not coming to the conclusions about Iraq's WMD capabilities as the
Secretary and undersecretary of Defense expected. A number of CIA analysts perceived this as pressure.[81] In the Pentagon, according to a former
official who attended the meetings, "They were the browbeaters. In interagency meetings Wolfowitz treated the analysts' work with contempt."[82]
From the perspective of some CIA veterans, the administration was
undermining the objectivity and professionalism of the intelligence
process. Former DIA analyst and specialist on Iraq, Patrick Lang, characterized the administration's efforts to influence intelligence as not professional. "What we have here is advocacy, not intelligence work."[83] One
senior State Department analyst told a congressional committee that he
felt pressured by the administration to shift his analysis to be more
certain about the evidence on Iraq's activities. Other analysts told the
Senate Intelligence Committee that the administration was disclosing
only the worst case scenario aspects of intelligence reports and not accurately representing the work of the professional analysts.[84]

One response of Secretary Rumsfeld to his dissatisfaction with the
analysis of the CIA was to create an Office of Special Plans headed by
Undersecretary of Defense William Luti to do intelligence analysis and
bring a different perspective than the DIA and the CIA.[85] One important
difference in their analysis was the weight they gave to claims provided
by the Iraqi National Congress and its leader Ahmad Chalabi about
Saddam's WMD. The CIA had discounted these same claims because the
exiles had a stake in the outcome of US policy and thus the CIA did not
consider them as credible as the Office of Special Plans judged them to
be.[86] According to W. Patrick Lang who was the head of Middle East
intelligence for the DIA, "The DIA has been intimidated and beaten to a
pulp. And there's no guts at all in the CIA."[87]

Another tactic Secretary Rumsfeld used to circumvent the established
professional intelligence apparatus of the executive branch was his

reliance on the Defense Policy Board. The DPB was chaired by Richard Perle, a hawk on Iraq and former member of the Reagan administration. In Perle's judgment, the CIA's judgment about Iraq "isn't worth the paper it is written on."[88] The Board also contained other high visibility hawks on Iraq, such as James Woolsey and Newt Gingrich, as well as a range of other former defense officials not necessarily committed to war with Iraq. It is interesting that this board of outside advisors played a much more highly visible role in supporting the administration's war plans than the traditional outside advisory board to the president, the President's Foreign Intelligence Advisory Board. Perhaps that was because the PFIAB was chaired by Brent Scowcroft, national security advisor to President George H. W. Bush and critic of war with Iraq.

While all executive branch agencies should take their guidance from the president and his appointees, it is dangerous for a presidential administration to pressure intelligence agencies to distort their professional judgments in order to support an administration's short-term policy goals. Once intelligence is politicized, it becomes more difficult for a president to distinguish the professionals' best judgment from what they think that he wants to hear. Such a situation is dangerous for the American presidency. While evidence of undue pressure from the administration is inconclusive and circumstantial at this time, insofar as the Bush administration put pressure on US intelligence agencies to suit their analyses to its policy goals, it jeopardized its own best sources of intelligence.

Conclusion

Possible justifications for war with Iraq ranged from the idealistic goal of bringing democracy to Iraqis and the humanitarian desire to rid them of a tyrant to geostrategic concerns about the future of the Middle East. That Saddam was a vicious tyrant who tortured his political enemies, gassed his own people, and invaded other countries was known long before the Bush administration decided to go to war to depose him. But the most compelling arguments to the American people were the arguments that the national security of the United States was at risk. Thus the claims that Saddam's WMD posed a direct threat were most effective in sustaining political support for war.

In an interview, Deputy Secretary of Defense Paul Wolfowitz implied that the WMD argument was not necessarily the most important for policymakers. "For bureaucratic reasons we settled on one issue, weapons of mass destruction, because it was the one reason everyone could agree on."[89] On the other hand, in a discussion with the editors of the

New York Times, Colin Powell implied that the claimed WMD were central to his own support of the war. "Asked whether Americans would have supported this war if weapons of mass destruction had not been at issue, Mr. Powell said the question was too hypothetical to answer. Asked if he, personally, would have supported it, he smiled, thrust his hand out and said, 'It was good to meet you.' "[90]

In the judgment of Ivo Daalder and James Lindsay, the imminent threat to the United States was crucial to President Bush's argument for war with Iraq. "Bush's ex post facto justification for the war—that the Iraqi people are much better off without Saddam—ignores the basic but highly salient fact that there would not have been a war without his argument that Iraq's weapons of mass destruction posed an unacceptable threat that was both immediate and serious."[91] In focusing on WMD as the main reason for war and arguing that there was an imminent threat to the United States, President Bush left himself open to the doubts expressed by Senator Carl Levin (D-MI), when he said that the issue "is about whether administration officials made a conscious and very troubling decision to create a false impression about the gravity and imminence of the threat that Iraq posed to America."[92]

The administration's inference that Saddam Hussein was continuing his previous weapons programs was not an unreasonable conclusion, one that was shared by intelligence agencies in other countries. The problem was that there was little evidence to support their conclusion, and they used claims of dubious validity to make their case to the American people. There is no doubt that Saddam Hussein had significant conventional warfare capacity and was developing missiles and other weapons systems that violated UN resolutions. But the focus of this chapter has been on the Bush administration's arguments that Saddam's WMD presented an imminent threat to the United States.

This chapter has addressed the question of the accuracy of some of the claims in the arguments that the Bush administration used in favor of war with Iraq. While President Bush made few untrue statements in his arguments for the war, the real problem was his broader claims.[93]

1 His series of statements connecting Saddam to the atrocities of 9/11 created a false impression that the administration had evidence of a connection between Saddam and the 9/11 terrorist attacks.
2 His pattern of statements about Saddam Hussein's nuclear capacity were also systematically misleading.
3 His claims about Iraq's chemical and biological capacity were shared by many, including allied intelligence agencies, UN inspectors, and the Clinton administration. Bush cannot be fairly blamed for using such

widely accepted claims, even though little evidence of the weapons were found in Iraq after the war.

4 His claims about the possible use of Iraqi UAVs to deliver chemical and biological weapons to the US homeland were made despite the best judgment of the US Air Force.

Should the president be held responsible for what he said during the course of his argument that war with Iraq was necessary? It is true that much of what the president said about nuclear weapons was supported by the NIE of October 2002. But it is also true that there were serious caveats in the NIE that called into question the certainty of the conclusions the president expressed. Although it is too soon to come to firm historical judgments, the publicly available evidence so far seems to support the following conclusions:

- To the extent that the president himself understood that there were serious doubts about Saddam's connections to 9/11, he is responsible for playing upon fears of the American public and encouraging the desire for revenge in order to build support for a war with Iraq.

- To the extent that the president was aware of serious doubts about Saddam's nuclear capacity, he failed to present a balanced or accurate view to Congress and the American people. He himself may have been convinced of the rightness of his cause, but that did not justify misleading the country by the certainty of his assertions about Saddam's nuclear capacity in his campaign to create political support for the war. To the extent that the serious doubts about Iraq's nuclear capacity were not presented to the president, he was poorly served by his staff and advisors.

- To the extent that the president's immediate advisors reported to him only the evidence and analysis that supported his own predilection to attack Iraq, the president was not well served. It is the president's responsibility to create an atmosphere in which the White House staff and cabinet officers give the president all of the relevant evidence to help him make an informed decision. If they bend their advice to suit his preconceptions, they are not serving his best interests nor the country's.

- Although evidence is circumstantial and inconclusive, to the extent that the intelligence process was politicized and distorted in order to produce conclusions with insufficient evidence, the presidency may be vulnerable to future distortions and the capacity of the intelligence community to produce objective analysis in the future may have been undermined.

The issue here is not whether the war with Iraq was wise; whether it was a wise war will become clear only with the passage of years. At issue here is a matter of democratic leadership. Citizens must trust the president because they do not have all of the information that he has. If the president misrepresents the nature of crucial information, he undermines the democratic bonds between citizens and president upon which this polity is based. Insofar as President Bush misled the Congress and the citizenry, either from deliberate misstatements or through creating an atmosphere in which he was not well informed by his advisors, he undermined the crucial trust upon which the nation depends.

Notes

Acknowledgements: A number of friends and colleagues made helpful comments on an earlier version of this chapter, though none of them should be associated with my conclusions, with which not all of them agreed. I would like to thank the following people: David Armor, Douglas Brook, Robert Dudley, Frank Fukuyama, Jack Goldstone, Nguyen Hung, Don Kash, Arnauld Nikogosian, Patrick Pfiffner, Russell Riley, Colleen Shogan and Clyde Wilcox.

1 Dana Milbank and Claudia Deane, "Hussein Link to 9/11 Lingers in Many Minds," *Washington Post* (September 6, 2003), p. 1.
2 In a tape urging Muslims to fight against the United States, Osama bin Laden said that the fighting should be for God, not for "pagan regimes in all the Arab countries, including Iraq . . . Socialists are infidels wherever they are, either in Baghdad or Aden." Transcript posted on www.indybay.org, accessed April 10, 2003. See also Louis Fisher, "Deciding on War Against Iraq: Institutional Failures," *Political Science Quarterly*, September 2003.
3 Milbank and Deane, "Hussein Link," p. 1.
4 Eric Schmitt, "Rumsfeld Says US Has 'Bulletproof' Evidence of Iraq's Links to Al Qaeda," *New York Times* (September 28, 2002).
5 John B. Judis and Spencer Ackerman, "The Selling of the Iraq War," *The New Republic* (June 30, 2003), online version, no page numbers: www.tnr.com, accessed June 30, 2003.
6 Dana Milbank and Walter Pincus, "Cheney Defends US Actions In Bid to Revive Public Support," *Washington Post* (September 15, 2003), p. 1, A19.
7 Milbank and Deane, "Hussein Link."
8 Walter Pinkus, "Report Casts Doubt on Iraq-Al Qaeda Connection," *Washington Post* (June 22, 2003), p. 1, A19. For a detailed analysis of German police records that undercut the link between Zarqawi and al Qaeda, see Michael Isikoff, "Distorted Intelligence?", *Newsweek* (June 25, 2003), online version.
9 Associated Press, "UN Panel Finds No Evidence to Link Iraq, Al-Qaeda," online version June 26, 2003; www.truthout.org.

10 Quoted in Milbank and Deane, "Hussein Link."

11 The president's speech was printed in the *New York Times* (September 8, 2003), p. A10.

12 Milbank and Pincus, "Cheney Defends US Actions."

13 Dana Milbank, "Bush Disavows Hussein–Sept. 11 Link," *Washington Post* (September 18, 2003), p. A18; David E. Sanger, "Bush Reports No Evidence of Hussein Tie to 9/11," *New York Times* (September 18, 2003), p. A18.

14 Kennth M. Pollack, *The Threatening Storm* (New York: Random House, 2002), p. 179. According to Pollack, "It is actually quite difficult to use chemical or biological weapons to kill large numbers of people. The agents have to be properly prepared in a form that remains airborne for some time and can be disseminated in the right dosages to actually kill people. Atmospheric conditions have to be just right, or the agent may be dissipated or destroyed. The attackers have to know when and where to disseminate the agent and to do it in a way that will actually allow it to have its maximum effect. The agent also has to be stored properly so that it does not lose its potency before it can be used. For all of these reasons, previous terrorist attacks using CW and BW have not killed very many people. In fact, on just about every occasion when terrorists did employ WMD, they undoubtedly would have killed far more people if they had employed conventional explosives instead." Ibid.

15 For an analysis that Saddam was deterred from using chemical and biological weapons in the 1991 Gulf war, see Pollack, *The Threatening Storm*, p. 243.

16 Remarks by the Vice President to the Veterans of Foreign Wars 103rd National Convention," White House website (August 26, 2002).

17 Judis and Ackerman, "The Selling of the Iraq War," p. 6; Dana Milbank and Mike Allen, "Iraq Flap Shakes Rice's Image," *Washington Post* (July 27, 2003), p. 1, A18.

18 Dana Milbank, "For Bush Facts Are Malleable," *Washington Post* (October 22, 2003), p. 1, A22.

19 Ibid.

20 Steven Mufson, "Forget WMD. What's an NIE?", *Washington Post* (July 20, 2003), p. B3.

21 Central Intelligence Agency, *Key Judgments* [from October 2002 NIE]: *Iraq's Continuing Programs for Weapons of Mass Destruction*. Declassified excerpts published on the CIA website: www.odci.gov/nic/pubs/research, accessed Oct. 10, 2003, pp. 5–6.

22 Barton Gellman and Walter Pincus, "Depiction of Threat Outgrew Supporting Evidence," *Washington Post* (August 10, 2003), p. 1, A9.

23 Ibid. Cheney retracted his statement on September 14, 2003 on Meet the Press when he said, "Yeah. I did misspeak. I said repeatedly during the show weapons capability. We never had any evidence that he had acquired a nuclear weapon." But the real claim was that Saddam had reconstituted his nuclear program rather than that he had workable weapons. Cheney was quoted in

a letter to the vice president from Representatives Dennis Kucinich, Carolyn Maloney, and Bernie Sanders, published on website truthout.org (September 17, 2003).

24 Gellman and Pincus, "Depiction of Threat."

25 Walter Pincus, "Bush Team Kept Airing Iraq Allegation," *Washington Post* (August 8, 2002), p. A10.

26 Associated Press, "White House Official Apologizes for Role in Uranium Claim," *New York Times* (July 22, 2003), www.nytimes.com (accessed July 22, 2003).

27 Dana Priest, "Uranium Claim Was Known for Months to Be Weak," *Washington Post* (July 20, 2003), p. A22. Dana Priest and Dana Milbank, "President Defends Allegation On Iraq," *Washington Post* (July 15, 2003), p. 1, A11. Walter Pincus and Dana Priest," US Had Uranium Papers Earlier," *Washington Post* (July 18, 2003), p. 1, A12.

28 Though Wilson strongly supported the 1991 Gulf war, he was critical of the Bush administration's claims about Iraq's WMD in 2003. After the public account of his mission to Niger journalist Robert Novak reported that "two senior Administration officials" told him that Wilson's wife was a CIA agent, and he revealed her name in his column. Mrs. Wilson had been a CIA non-covered agent; that is, her claimed cover was not as a US government official but as a private business person. Exposure of her identity potentially jeopardized all of her previous contacts throughout the world and any operations in which she was involved. In September 2003 CIA Director Tenet asked the Justice Department to investigate the disclosure of the secret agent's identity. Mike Allen and Dana Priest, "Bush Administration Is Focus of Inquiry," *Washington Post* (September 28, 2003), p. 1, A1. See: Joseph C. Wilson IV. "What I Didn't Find in Africa," *New York Times*. July 6, 2003, *New York Times* website.

29 Dana Priest and Dana Milbank, "President Defends Allegation On Iraq," *Washington Post* (July 15, 2003), p. 1, A11.

30 Central Intelligence Agency, *Key Judgments*, p. 25.

31 Ibid, p. 84.

32 Pincus and Priest, "US Had Uranium Papers Earlier."

33 Michael Isikoff and Evan Thomas, "Follow the Yellowcake Road," *Newsweek* (July 28, 2003), pp. 23–5. Also Dana Priest, "Uranium Claim Was Known for Months to Be Weak," *Washington Post* (July 20, 2003), p. A22. Priest and Milbank, "President Defends Allegation On Iraq"; Pincus and Priest, "US Had Uranium Papers Earlier"; Judis and Ackerman, "The Selling of the Iraq War", p. 10.

34 Dana Priest and Karen DeYoung, "CIA Questioned Documents Linking Iraq, Uranium Ore," *Washington Post* (March 22, 2003), p. A30; and Seymour M. Hersh, "Who Lied to Whom?" *New Yorker* (March 31, 2003), pp. 41–3.

35 The administration also used the Niger claim in a number of other forums before the State of the Union speech, for example in reports to Congress and

in speeches by Paul Wolfowitz and Donald Rumsfeld. See, Pincus, "Bush Team Kept Airing Iraq Allegation." See also Condoleezza Rice, "Why We Know Iraq is Lying," *New York Times* (January 23, 2003), on White House website.

36 Matthew Cooper, "Pinning the Line on the Man," *Time* (July 28, 2003), p. 31. See also, Pincus and Priest, "US Had Uranium Papers Earlier."

37 Dana Milbank and Dana Priest, "Warning in Iraq Report Unread," *Washington Post* (July 19, 2003), p. 1, A13.

38 Dana Milbank, "Intelligence Dispute Festers as Iraq Victory Recedes," *Washington Post* (July 17, 2003), p. A15.

39 Mufson, "Forget WMD. What's an NIE?" See also, Priest and Milbank, "President Defends Allegation On Iraq"; Milbank and Allen, "Iraq Flap Shakes Rices Image"; Central Intelligence Agency, *Key Judgments*, p. 5.

40 Michael Duffy and James Carney, "A Question of Trust," *Time* (July 21, 2003), pp. 23–6.

41 Associated Press, "White House Official Apologizes for Role in Uranium Claim," *New York Times* (July 22, 2003), *New York Times* website, no page number, accessed July 22, 2003.

42 Richard W. Stevenson, "Bush Denies Claim He Oversold Case for War," *New York Times* (July 31, 2003), *New York Times* website, no page number, accessed July 31, 2003.

43 James Risen, "Bush Aides New Say Claim on Uranium Was Accurate," *New York Times* (July 14, 2003), no page, www.nytimes.com.

44 Michael Kinsley, "Or More Lies From the Usual Suspects," *Washington Post*, July 16, 2003, p. A23.

45 President Bush's Address to UN, printed in the *New York Times* (September 13, 2003), p. A31.

46 Gellman and Pincus, "Depiction of Threat Outgrew Supporting Evidence." In an interview an intelligence analyst who had taken part in the internal debate over the aluminum tubes issue said, "You had senior American officials like Condoleezza Rice saying the only use of this aluminum really is uranium centrifuges. She said that on television. And that's just a lie." Quoted in Judis and Ackerman, "The Selling of the Iraq War," p. 7.

47 Central Intelligence Agency, *Key Judgments*, p. 6.

48 Ibid, p. 9.

49 Gellman and Pincus, "Depiction of Threat Outgrew Supporting Evidence."

50 Ibid.

51 Judis and Ackerman, "The Selling of the Iraq War," p. 10.

52 Pollack, *The Threatening Storm*, pp. 169–75.

53 From Press Release: US State Department, "Colin Powell Remarks With Egypt FM February 24, 01," published on www.scoop.co.nz (accessed September 25, 2003).

54 Central Intelligence Agency, *Key Judgments*, p. 5

55 Ibid (both quotes).

56 Ibid, pp. 8–9.

57 Judis and Ackerman, "The Selling of the Iraq War."

58 Dana Priest and Walter Pincus, "Search in Iraq Finds No Banned Weapons," *Washington Post* (October 3, 2003), p. 1.

59 David Kay, Unclassified Statement of the Iraq Survey Group to the House Permanent Select Committee on Intelligence and the House Committee on Appropriations, Subcommittee on Defense and the Senate Select Committee on Intelligence, October 2, 2003, p. 7. The text of the statement was published by CNN.com, www.cnn.allpolitics. Accessed October 10, 2003. The page number refers to the CNN version.

60 The letter to CIA Director Tenet was quoted by Dana Priest, "House Probers Conclude Iraq War Data Was Weak," *Washington Post* (September 28, 2003), p. 1, A9.

61 Judith Miller, "A Chronicle of Confusion in the US Hunt for Hussein's Chemical and Germ Weapons," *New York Times* (July 20, 2003), p. 12.

62 Michael Dobbs, "US Had Key Role in Iraq Buildup," *Washington Post* (December 30, 2002), p. 1, A12.

63 Pollack, *The Threatening Storm*, pp. 18–19.

64 For data on where Iraq purchased much of the ingredients, equipment, and munitions for its chemical weapons program, see Gary Milhollin and Kelly Motz, "The Means to Make the Poisons Came From the West," *New York Times* (April 13, 2003), p. wk5.

65 Pollack, *The Threatening Storm*, pp. 20–1, 170; Dobbs, "US Had Key Role in Iraq Buildup," p. A12.

66 Pollack, *The Threatening Storm*, p. 21.

67 Dana Priest and Walter Pincus, "Bush Certainty on Iraq Arms Went Beyond Analyst's Views," *Washington Post* (June 7, 2003), p. 1, A17.

68 Judis and Ackerman, "The Selling of the Iraq War: The First Casualty", pp. 3–4. Priest and Pincus, "Bush Certainty on Iraq Arms Went Beyond Analyst's Views."

69 Mike Allen, "Bush: 'We Found' Banned Weapons," *Washington Post* (May 31, 2003), p. 1.

70 Judith Miller and William J. Broad, "Some Analysts Of Iraq Trailers Reject Germ Use," *New York Times* (June 8, 2003), p. 1, B14.

71 Douglas Jehl, "Iraqi Trailers Said to Make Hydrogen, Not Biological Arms," *New York Times* (August 9, 2003).

72 Walter Pincus and Dana Priest, "Iraq Weapons Report Won't Be Conclusive," *Washington Post* (September 25, 2003), p. 1, A24.

73 Kay, Unclassified Statement of the Iraq Survey Group, pp. 4–6 for the quotes.

74 Francis Fukuyama, "The Real Intelligence Failure?", *Wall Street Journal.* August 5, 2003.

75 Central Intelligence Agency, *Key Judgments*, p. 5.

76 Ibid, p. 7.

77 Ibid.

78 Bradley Graham, "Air Force Analysts Feel Vindicated on Iraqi Drones," *Washington Post* (September 26, 2003), p. A23. See also Dafna Linzer and

John J. Lumpkin, "Experts Doubt US Claim on Iraqi Drones," Associated Press (August 24, 2003), online version, www.truthout.org.

79 Judis and Ackerman, "The Selling of the Iraq War," p. 5.

80 Ray McGovern, "Cheney and the CIA: Not Business As Usual," (June 27, 2003), truthout.org website.

81 James Risen, "CIA Aides Feel Pressure In Preparing Iraqi Reports," *New York Times* (March 23, 2003), p. B10.

82 Walter Pincus and Dana Priest, "Some Iraq Analysts Felt Pressure from Cheney Visits," *Washington Post* (June 5, 2003), p. 1.

83 Bruce B. Auster, Mark Mazzetti, and Edward T. Pound, "Truth and Consequences," *US News and World Report* (June 9, 2003), p. 17.

84 James Risen and Douglas Jehl, "Expert Said to Tell Legislators He Was Pressured to Distort Some Evidence," *New York Times* (June 25, 2003), no page number, *New York Times* website.

85 Judis and Ackerman, "The Selling of the Iraq War," p. 5.

86 See Seymour M. Hersh, "Selective Intelligence," *New Yorker* (May 12, 2003), pp. 44–51.

87 Ibid, p. 44.

88 Judis and Ackerman, "The Selling of the Iraq War," p. 5.

89 Sam Tanenhaus, "Bush's Brain Trust," *Vanity Fair* (July 2003), p. 169.

90 Editorial in the *New York Times*, "The Failure to Find Iraqi Weapons," (September 26, 2003), p. A24.

91 Ivo H. Daalder and James M. Lindsay. 2003. *American Unbound: The Bush Revolution in Foreign Policy* (Washington: Brookings, 2003), p. 167.

92 Dana Milbank, "White House Didn't Gain CIA Nod for Claim," *Washington Post* (July 20, 2003), p. 1, A21.

93 President Bush said on July 14, 2003 in response to questions about Iraq's WMD, "And we gave him a chance to allow the inspectors in, and he wouldn't let them in. And, therefore, after a reasonable request, we decided to remove him." (Quoted by Jonathan S. Landay, "Controversy Over Iraq: The President Pushes Back," *Detroit Free Press* (July 15, 2003), article published on www.freep.com). In fact Saddam did allow UN inspectors to come into Iraq, and they had virtually free rein to search the country. When they failed to find WMD the administration criticized them, and they withdrew in anticipation of a military attack by the United States. Mentioned previously in this chapter were the president's claims that WMD had been found in the two trailers in Iraq and that the IAEA had said that Saddam was within six months of producing a nuclear weapon. Each of these inaccurate statements was more likely due to confusion than an attempt to lie.

5

The British road to war: decisionmaking, intelligence, and the case for war in Iraq

Mark Phythian

This chapter charts the basis and evolution of a decision that is set to define the ten-year premiership of Tony Blair; the decision to go to war in Iraq. It begins by focusing on the institutional context within which the decision was taken, paying particular attention to the ongoing presidentialization of British politics and consequent downgrading of Cabinet as a decisionmaking body. This process created the political space in which the decision could be taken. It goes on to consider the timing, nature, and presentation of the decision, and the relationship between decisionmaking and intelligence in this case. It suggests that, as in the US case discussed by James Pfiffner in Chapter 4, political leaders ultimately misled the public by exaggerating the threat posed by Iraq. This was also the public's perception. In the 2005 general election the Labour Party's parliamentary majority was reduced by almost a hundred seats, while post-2003 opinion polls reflected a collapse of trust in Blair personally,[1] a collapse that cannot be understood without reference to the decision to go to war in Iraq.

The institutional context of the decision

Key to understanding the decisionmaking environment within which the war choice was made, and which helped facilitate it, is an appreciation of a trend that pre-dated Tony Blair's premiership, but which was accelerated during it; namely, the presidentialization of British politics.[2] In effect, under Blair a Prime Minister's Department came to operate out of 10 Downing Street, staffed by unelected advisors, at times in apparent opposition to the departments of state. In addition, Blair created his own prime ministerial diplomatic network, going further, in Anthony Sampson's words, "than any Prime Minister since Churchill in overriding and by-passing the advice of the Foreign Office."[3] The dominance of Downing Street in this regard is reflected in the recollection of former Ambassador to the US, Sir Christopher Meyer, that, "between 9/11 and the day I retired at the end of February 2003 I had not a single substantive policy discussion on the secure phone with the Foreign Office. This was in contrast to the many contacts and discussions with No 10."[4] Blair's first Foreign Secretary, Robin Cook, initially fought an internal guerrilla campaign to retain control of foreign policy and resist pressure from Downing Street—for example, in relation to arms export policy[5]— but his authority was undermined by developments in his personal life.[6] Post-9/11, as Blair came to centralize foreign policymaking in Downing Street to a still greater extent, Cook's successor, Jack Straw, cut such an anonymous figure that in January 2002 the *Guardian* newspaper printed a full-page photograph of him with the headline, "Have you seen this man?."[7] A year later, Father of the House, Tam Dalyell, was complaining: "We all know that Sir David Manning, Mr. Blair's foreign policy adviser, is the real Foreign Secretary."[8]

Blair's presidential position was further strengthened by a number of other factors, such his large parliamentary majority, his personal authority stemming from election victories in 1997 and 2001, and by the absence of an effective Opposition. This presidentialism helps explain Blair's increased interest in foreign policy during his second term. Foreign policy was an area where his exposure was severely limited prior to 1997, and about which he had shown scant interest as a backbencher. However, it was here that he found he could act with a freedom that his and Chancellor Gordon Brown's caution had made near impossible in domestic affairs. As early as 1999 spin doctor Lance Price noted in his diary that: "There's a feeling about the place that TB is losing touch with ordinary people and what matters to them. He seems almost bored with the ordinary stuff and interested only in all the foreign leaders, Clinton, wars, etc."[9]

This approach to governance also had significant implications for the role of the Cabinet in decisionmaking regarding Iraq during 2002–3. Where the consent of particular ministers was required, it was sought in informal discussions away from the full Cabinet, what came to be termed Blair's "sofa diplomacy." It is this alternative source of advice and bypassing of Cabinet government that Secretary of State for International Development Clare Short highlighted in her 2003 resignation speech:

> In the second term, the problem is centralisation of power into the hands of the Prime Minister and an increasingly small number of advisers who make decisions in private without proper discussion. It is increasingly clear that the Cabinet has become . . . a dignified part of the constitution, joining the Privy Council. There is no real collective, just diktats in favour of increasingly badly thought through policy initiatives that come from on high.

The consequences of this are serious. Expertise in our system lies in departments. Those who dictate from the centre do not have full access to this expertise and they do not consult. This leads to bad policy . . . Thus we have the powers of a presidential-type system with the automatic majority of a parliamentary system.[10]

Other MPs echoed Short's concern at the implications of an increasingly presidential style of leadership in a British parliamentary system that did not offer the checks and balances built into the US system of government.[11] Moreover, her concern at the downgrading of the Cabinet as a forum for decisionmaking was shared by other Cabinet colleagues. On March 7, 2002 what Robin Cook described as, "the last meeting of the Cabinet at which a large number of ministers spoke up against the war,"[12] took place. Cook noted in his diary:

I am told, not that I have witnessed it, that in the old days Prime Ministers would sum up the balance of view in the discussion. This would be simple in the present case as all contributions pointed in one direction. However, Tony does not regard the Cabinet as a place for decisions. Normally he avoids having discussions in Cabinet until decisions are taken and announced to it. Tony appeared totally unfazed that on this occasion the balance of discussion pointed strongly in the reverse direction of his intentions. Rather than attempt to sum up the discussion of this supreme body of collective government, he responded as if he was replying to a question and answer session from a party branch. . ."I tell you that we must steer close to America. If we don't we will lose our influence to shape what they do. That is understood in Europe. I have spoken to both Jospin and Schroder, and they both understand that we cannot oppose the Americans."[13]

The publication of former Home Secretary David Blunkett's diaries offered further confirmation of the picture provided by Cook and Short.[14] In February 2002 Blunkett (at the time Home Secretary) felt he had 'blotted his copybook" merely by raising the question of Iraq. At a Cabinet meeting a month later, he described Straw and Defence Secretary Geoff Hoon as having, "clearly got the message to be gung ho" although everyone else was, "drawing the conclusion that we needed to go into depth with this." "Look," Blair reassured the Cabinet, "the management hasn't lost its marbles. We do know these things. We are not going to rush in." It seems from Blunkett's account that by March 2003 the Cabinet saw its role as being to support Blair uncritically, and that those who did not were regarded as having "burnt their boats." Even though Britain was on the verge of engaging in its most divisive war since Suez, against the prospect of which millions had marched in protest, Blunkett felt that: "It was important to be really supportive of Tony at Cabinet, and when I saw him privately afterwards he was very grateful."[15]

The Butler review of prewar intelligence on Iraqi weapons of mass destruction (WMD)[16] was critical of Blair's approach to Cabinet government, concluding that:

> Without papers circulated in advance, it remains possible but is obviously much more difficult for members of the Cabinet outside the small circle directly involved to bring their political judgement and experience to bear on the major decisions for which the Cabinet as a whole must carry responsibility. The absence of papers on the Cabinet agenda so that Ministers could obtain briefings in advance from the Cabinet Office, their own departments or from the intelligence agencies plainly reduced their ability to prepare properly for such discussions, while the changes to key posts at the head of the Cabinet Secretariat lessened the support of the machinery of government for the collective responsibility of the Cabinet in the vital matter of war and peace.[17]

This presidentialism, then, created the space within which the decision to join the US in a war to remove Saddam Hussein from power was taken. The decision itself was rooted in the fact that Blair was very much a conviction politician (as Roy Jenkins once quipped, Blair; "far from lacking conviction, has almost too much, particularly when dealing with the world beyond Britain"[18]), who tends to be described as being, for example, "more of an instinctive politician than an intellectual politician" and one who, "relies heavily on his intuition" and "does not have a vast store-house of political or policy knowledge."[19] His lack of expertise in foreign affairs would have heightened the need for him to rely on his intuition.[20] One thing Blair quickly became convinced of was the threat posed by Saddam Hussein. In late 1997 Liberal Democrat leader Paddy Ashdown noted in his diary a conversation with Blair which covered Iraq in which Blair told him: "I have now seen some of the stuff on this. It really is pretty scary. He is very close to some appalling weapons of mass destruction. I don't understand why the French and others don't understand this. We cannot let him get away with it."[21] For some this is proof that Blair's approach to Iraq was a constant, but this is not the case. In December 1998, at the time of the Desert Fox military strikes on Iraq, Blair offered the following view:

> Is it a specific objective to remove Saddam Hussein? The answer is: it cannot be. No one would be better pleased if his evil regime disappeared as a direct or indirect result of our action, but our military objectives are precisely those that we have set out. Even if there were legal authority to do so, removing Saddam through military action would require the insertion of ground troops on a massive scale—hundreds of thousands, as the British Chief of the Defence Staff, Sir Charles Guthrie, made clear this morning. Even then, there would be no guarantee of success. I cannot make that commitment responsibly.[22]

Making the decision

How did Blair come to abandon this prudence just a few years later? One part of the explanation must lie in Blair's experience as a war leader over Kosovo, but overwhelmingly it is to be found in New Labour's attitude to the US.[23] On coming to power in 1997, the links between the US Democrats and New Labour were strong, with the Clinton administration providing something of a model for New Labour, and Blair's closeness to President Clinton reinforcing his own sense of presidentialism.[24] A year after the events of 9/11, Blair would tell the House of Commons: "I believed this before I became Prime Minister, but I believe it even more strongly—in fact, very strongly; it is an article of faith with me—that the American relationship and our ability to partner America in these difficult issues is of fundamental importance, not just to this country but to the wider world."[25]

Hence, transferring his loyalty from Clinton to the Republican Bush administration was not difficult for Blair, as it might have been for some more steeped in the Labour Party's traditions, and was consistent with the advice offered by Clinton to, "get as close to George Bush as you have been to me," and similar advice from closer to home, from people such as former Labour leader Neil Kinnock.[26] It was here, in the immediate aftermath of the 9/11 attacks, that the origins of the 2003 war lay. Terrorism expert Richard Clarke has claimed that the Bush administration entered office "with Iraq on its agenda," and that Bush and his inner circle, a number of whom had advocated the removal of Saddam during the Clinton Administration, "must have known there was no 'imminent threat' to the US," despite their clear public message to the contrary.[27] The attacks of 9/11 lent greater urgency to an existing preference. That very afternoon Defense Secretary Donald Rumsfeld told General Richard Myers to find; "[b]est info fast. . .judge whether good enough to hit S.H. @ same time—not only U.B.L."[28] In the immediate aftermath Bush asked Richard Clarke three times to find a link between Saddam and the 9/11 attacks, even though Clarke told him that the intelligence community thought that al Qaeda was behind them.[29]

In the wake of the attacks Tony Blair visited Washington, where he was made aware of the current within the Bush Administration in favour of extending the "war on terror" to Iraq once operations in Afghanistan were complete. As Ambassador Meyer recalled: "Rumours were already flying that Bush would use 9/11 as a pretext to attack Iraq. On the one hand, Blair came with a very strong message—don't get distracted; the priorities were al-Qaeda, Afghanistan, the Taliban. Bush said, 'I agree with you, Tony. We must deal with this first. But when we have dealt with Afghanistan, we must come back to Iraq.'"[30]

This US commitment to removing Saddam was signaled publicly in President Bush's January 29, 2002 State of the Union address, in which he announced the existence of an "axis of evil" comprising Iraq, Iran, and North Korea. "What we have found in Afghanistan," Bush explained, "confirms that, far from ending there, our war against terror is only beginning . . . I will not wait on events, while dangers gather. I will not stand by as peril draws closer. The United States of America will not permit the world's most dangerous regimes to threaten us with the world's most destructive weapons."[31]

Two months later, in March 2002, Blair would undertake a visit to Bush in Texas, at which his initial commitment to support the US approach to Iraq was reportedly extended.[32] Given this, it is worth considering the state of the government's understanding of the situation in Iraq and options available. As the Butler Report shows, two options were considered to exist for achieving Iraqi disarmament at this time; first, a strengthening of containment and, secondly, enforced regime change. Ministers were informed that, "regime change of itself had no basis in international law; and that any offensive military action against Iraq could only be justified if Iraq were to be held in breach of its disarmament obligations."[33] They were also told that for the entire United Nations Security Council (UNSC) to take this view, "proof would need to be incontrovertible and of large-scale activity."[34] Hence, Ministers knew in March 2002 that the justification for regime change had to lie in the threat posed by an active and imminently deliverable Iraqi weapons program. However, they were also told that "current intelligence is insufficiently robust to meet this criterion," and hence there was at that time no legal justification for an invasion.[35] Furthermore, the best advice available to the British government was that containment was essentially working, that the Iraqi nuclear program was effectively frozen, and that while there were indications of a continuation of chemical and biological weapons programs, the circumstances in which Saddam could use WMD were restricted to those where his regime was threatened. At the same time, though, ministers were also informed that the US had lost confidence in containment and that the Bush administration believed that the legal basis for an attack already existed.

A week after the March 7th Cabinet meeting described by Cook, and following a trip to London by US Vice-President Dick Cheney, Blair dispatched foreign policy advisor David Manning to Washington, in advance of his own US visit. Manning's report on a dinner with National Security Advisor Condoleezza Rice clearly suggests that Blair had already, by mid-March 2002, offered his government's support to the

Bush Administration in its regime change strategy, even though his own Cabinet knew nothing of this:

> We spent a long time at dinner on Iraq. It is clear that Bush is grateful for your support and has registered that you are getting flak. I said that you would not budge in your support for regime change but you had to manage a press, a Parliament and a public opinion that was very different than any-thing in the States. And you would not budge on your insistence that, if we pursued regime change, it must be very carefully done and produce the right result. Failure was not an option. Condi's enthusiasm for regime change is undimmed. But there were some signs, since we last spoke, of greater awareness of the practical difficulties and political risks.[36]

Three days later, on March 17, Paul Wolfowitz, Rumsfeld's deputy, lunched with Ambassador Meyer at the British Embassy in Washington, which provided an opportunity for Meyer to reinforce Blair's support for regime change in advance of the Texas visit. "I opened by sticking very closely to the script that you used with Condi Rice," Meyer reported. "We backed regime change, but the plan had to be clever and failure was not an option. It would be a tough sell for us domestically and probably tougher elsewhere in Europe."[37]

Outside Downing Street and the British Embassy, however, concerns about the manner in which Blair was aligning Britain so closely to the Bush administration over Iraq policy were being voiced from within the Labour Party, Blair's own Cabinet (where, in addition to those voiced by Cook, Short, and Blunkett, Secretary of State for Trade and Industry Patricia Hewitt also voiced concerns), and the Foreign Office. From there, on March 2, Straw's policy director, Peter Ricketts, summarized his concerns. The first lay in the nature of the threat posed by Iraq. "The truth," explained Ricketts, "is that what has changed is not the pace of Saddam Hussein's WMD programmes, but our tolerance of them post-11 September."[38] Already the government was working on what would emerge, in an attempt to convince British public opinion of the necessity of war, as the September 2002 Downing Street dossier, but Ricketts warned Straw that more work was needed on it, and that, "even the best survey of Iraq's WMD programmes will not show much advance in recent years on the nuclear, missile or CW/BW fronts."[39] Getting public opinion to accept the imminence of the threat from Iraq would be prob-lematic, especially given that other proliferators, such as Iran, were thought to be closer to achieving a nuclear capability.

Straw summarized these concerns in a memo sent to Blair less than two weeks before his US visit, clearly warning the Prime Minister that he risked splitting the parliamentary Labour Party (PLP) if he supported the Bush administration's policy of regime change:

The rewards from your visit to Crawford will be few. The risks are high, both for you and for the Government. I judge that there is at present no majority inside the PLP for any military action against Iraq (alongside a greater readiness in the PLP to surface their concerns). Colleagues know that Saddam and the Iraqi regime are bad. Making that case is easy. But we have a long way to go to convince them as to:
(a) the scale of the threat from Iraq and why this has got worse recently;
(b) what distinguishes the Iraqi threat from that of eg Iran and North Korea so as to justify military action;
(c) the justification for any military action in terms of international law; and
(d) whether the consequence of military action really would be a compliant, law abiding replacement government.[40]

Straw confirmed that from intelligence to date it was, "hard to glean whether the threat from Iraq is so significantly different from that of Iran and North Korea as to justify military action," and pointed to the Foreign Office view that if the 9/11 attacks had not occurred it was doubtful whether the US would be considering an attack on Iraq. After all, the threat from Iraq had not worsened as a result of 9/11, and there was no link between Osama bin Laden and Iraq, although members of the Bush administration continued to allude to one. Straw then turned to the tactical approach that would have to be adopted in order to keep Labour Party and public opinion on side:

I know there are those who say that an attack on Iraq would be justified whether or not weapons inspectors were readmitted. But I believe that a demand for the unfettered readmission of weapons inspectors is essential, in terms of public explanation, and in terms of legal sanction for any subsequent military action.
Legally there are two potential elephant traps:
(i) regime change per se is no justification for military action; it could form part of the method of any strategy, but not a goal. Of course, we may want credibly to assert that regime change is an essential part of the strategy by which we have to achieve our ends—that of the elimination of Iraq's WMD capacity: but the latter has to be the goal;
(ii) on whether any military action would require a fresh UNSC mandate (Desert Fox did not). The US are likely to oppose any idea of a fresh mandate. On the other side, the weight of legal advice here is that a fresh mandate may well be required. There is no doubt that a new UNSCR would transform the climate in the PLP. Whilst that (a new mandate) is very unlikely, given the US's position, a draft resolution against military action with 13 in favour (or handsitting) and two vetoes against could play very badly here.[41]

This was the background to Blair's April 5 to 7 visit to Bush in Crawford, Texas. Whilst there he delivered a major foreign policy speech at the

George Bush Senior Presidential Library, intended as an updating of his 1999 "Doctrine of the International Community" speech delivered in Chicago. Blair ended this by making a public commitment that was both unnecessary and imprudent, and which served to tie his government to a course of action from which it could not easily disentangle itself thereafter. Moreover, it was emblematic of his presidential style. There was clearly no Cabinet agreement for such a wide-ranging statement of support—indeed, as Robin Cook noted of the Cabinet meeting of a month earlier, "a large number of ministers spoke up against the war."[42] Nevertheless, Blair informed his Texas audience that:

> we don't shirk our responsibility. It means that when America is fighting for those values, then, however tough, we fight with her. No grandstanding, no offering implausible but impractical advice from the comfort of the touchline, no wishing away the hard not the easy choices on terrorism and WMD, or making peace in the Middle East, but working together, side by side. That is the only route I know to a stable world based on prosperity and justice for all, where freedom liberates the lives of every citizen in every corner of the globe. If the world makes the right choices now—at this time of destiny—we will get there. And Britain will be at America's side in doing it. [43]

Hence, by mid-April 2002 Blair had committed his government to support the US both in secret and in public. The weakness of the case against Iraq was no barrier, but it was something of which Blair was clearly aware. On July 23, Blair met with senior Cabinet colleagues and senior officials to discuss Iraq. Here, Sir Richard Dearlove, head of MI6, reported on his recent discussions in Washington, where:

> There was a perceptible shift in attitude. Military action was now seen as inevitable. Bush wanted to remove Saddam, through military action, justified by the conjunction of terrorism and WMD. But the intelligence and facts were being fixed around the policy. The NSC [National Security Council] had no patience with the UN route, and no enthusiasm for publishing material on the Iraqi regime's record. There was little discussion in Washington of the aftermath after military action.[44]

Defense Secretary Hoon told the meeting that the US had already begun "spikes of activity" and that the most likely timing for US military action to begin was during January 2003. Straw agreed that it, "seemed clear that Bush had made up his mind to take military action," but again warned that, "the case was thin. Saddam was not threatening his neighbours, and his WMD capability was less than that of Libya, North Korea or Iran."[45] Straw also conveyed his department's advice that it would be prudent to insist that Iraq allow weapons inspectors to re-enter the country, not so as to eliminate any WMD uncovered or enable them to declare that Iraq possessed none (post-9/11, any solution that left Saddam in power was clearly unacceptable—as Blair would tell the meeting, "regime change and WMD were linked in the sense that it was the regime that was producing the WMD"[46]), but because this, "would also help with the legal justification for the use of force."[47]

This was especially important because, as the Attorney-General, Lord Goldsmith, told the meeting, "the desire for regime change was not a legal base for military action." There were only three possible legal bases for an attack on Iraq—self-defense, humanitarian intervention, or UNSC authorization based on Iraqi non-compliance with UNSC resolutions. The first two could not apply, so the only route that could confer legality on an attack involved Iraq's continued breach of UNSC resolutions. Moreover, he warned, relying for authority on UNSC resolutions passed years earlier "would be difficult."

The questions about the case and the qualified intelligence concerning the threat posed by Iraq were of less importance to Blair than being seen to perform the role of key US ally. When he flew to Camp David to meet Bush in early September 2002, according to Bob Woodward's account:

> Bush looked Blair in the eye. "Saddam Hussein is a threat. And we must work together to deal with this threat, and the world will be better off without him." Bush recalled that he was "probing" and "pushing" the Prime Minister. He said it might require—would probably entail—war. Blair might have to send British troops. "I'm with you," the Prime Minister replied, looking Bush back in the eye, pledging flat out to commit British military forces if necessary, the critical promise Bush had been seeking.[48]

Still, most of Blair's Cabinet were unaware of this, and Blair was unwilling to confide in them. For example, Clare Short's diary entry of September 9, 2002 records Blair assuring her that no final decisions had been taken, and so there was no need to discuss Iraq in Cabinet, only for Short to find out from Gordon Brown later that day that Blair had asked for 20,000 British troops to be made available for the Gulf.[49]

Selling the decision

Having determined that Britain would support the US in a war to remove Saddam Hussein, the Blair inner sanctum had to sell the war to the British public. The focal point of this effort would be the September 2002 publication by Downing Street of a dossier based on intelligence material detailing the threat from Iraq's WMD. When Tony Blair came to give evidence to the post-war Hutton inquiry (see Chapter 1 of this book), the documents that contribute much to understanding the March–September 2002 dynamic, cited above, were still to be leaked. Moreover, the Hutton inquiry did not have access to intelligence material. In the context of this information advantage, Blair explained the emergence of the September 2002 dossier thus: "What changed was really two things which came together. First of all, there was a tremendous amount of information and evidence coming across my desk as to the weapons of mass destruction and the programmes associated with it that Saddam had . . . There was also a renewed sense of urgency, again, in the way that this was being publicly debated . . . Why did we say it was a big problem? Because of the intelligence. And the people were naturally saying: produce that intelligence then." And again later: "So, in a sense, the 24th September dossier was an unusual—the whole business was unusual, but it was in response to an unusual set of circumstances. We were saying this issue had to be returned to by the international community and dealt with. Why were we saying this? Because of the intelligence."[50] However, as the subsequent Butler inquiry was to reveal, this was somewhat misleading.

In light of the chronology outlined above, it is no coincidence that, from the time of the Crawford meeting, the frequency of Blair's references to the threat posed by Iraq increased and the language used became more emphatic—more so than warranted by the intelligence. Selling the decision involved exaggerating the threat.[51] For example, on April 3, 2002, Blair told NBC News: "We know that he has stockpiles of major amounts of chemical and biological weapons, we know that he is trying to acquire nuclear capability, we know that he is trying to develop ballistic missile capability of a greater range."[52] The following week, he told the House of Commons that; "there is no doubt at all that the development of weapons of mass destruction by Saddam Hussein poses a severe threat not just to the region, but to the wider world . . . He is a threat to his own people and to the region and, if allowed to develop these weapons, a threat to us also."[53] Yet, as the Butler report would reveal, the most current Joint Intelligence Committee (JIC) assessment at that time, from March 15, 2002, told a somewhat different story:

> Intelligence on Iraq's weapons of mass destruction (WMD) and ballistic missile programmes is sporadic and patchy . . . From the evidence available to us, we believe Iraq retains some production equipment, and some small stocks of CW agent precursors, and may have hidden small quantities of agents and weapons. . .There is no intelligence on any BW agent production facilities but one source indicates that Iraq may have developed mobile production facilities.[54]

Carne Ross, who served as First Secretary to the UK Mission to the UN from December 1997 until June 2002, where he was responsible for Iraq policy, told the Butler inquiry:

I read the available UK and US intelligence on Iraq every working day for the four and a half years of my posting. This daily briefing would often comprise a thick folder of material, both humint and sigint . . . During my posting, at no time did HMG assess that Iraq's WMD (or any other capability) posed a threat to the UK or its interests. On the contrary, it was the commonly-held view among the officials dealing with Iraq that any threat had been effectively contained . . . There was moreover no intelligence or assessment during my time in the job that Iraq had any intention to launch an attack against its neighbours or the UK or US. I had many conversations with diplomats representing Iraq's neighbours. With the exception of the Israelis, none expressed any concern that they might be attacked. Instead, their concern was that sanctions, which they and we viewed as an effective means to contain Iraq, were being delegitimised by evidence of their damaging humanitarian effect.

I quizzed my colleagues in the FCO and MOD working on Iraq on several occasions about the threat assessment in the run-up to the war. None told me that any new evidence had emerged to change our assessment; what had changed was the government's determination to present available evidence in a different light. I discussed this at some length with David Kelly in late 2002, who agreed that the Number 10 WMD dossier was overstated.[55]

In his Foreword to the September 2002 Downing Street dossier and in his presentation of this to the House of Commons—recalling Parliament a day early in order to heighten the sense of threat—Blair's message was almost the opposite of this. He emphasized that Iraq's "WMD programme is active, detailed and growing. The policy of containment is not working. The WMD programme is not shut down. It is up and running."[56] In his Foreword to the dossier, Blair claimed that the, "picture presented to me by the JIC in recent months has become more not less worrying," and wrote of Iraq's WMD programs constituting, "a current and serious threat to the UK national interest."[57]

In contrast to this public presentation, however, contemporaneous internal Downing Street emails released to the Hutton inquiry show that the available intelligence was a problem in the early stages of drafting the dossier. A September 11th email from Downing Street advisor Philip Bassett to Daniel Pruce and Alastair Campbell made this clear: "Very long way to go I think. Think we're in a lot of trouble with this as it stands."[58] The same day an email sent out to the intelligence community appealed for additional intelligence: "No. 10 through the Chairman want the document to be as strong as possible within the bounds of available intelligence. This is therefore a last (!) call for any items of intelligence that agencies think can and should be included. Responses needed by 12.00 tomorrow." Dr. Brian Jones, at the time head of the Nuclear,

Biological, Chemical Technical Intelligence branch of the Defence Intelligence Staff (DIS), has stated that he "couldn't relate" to Blair's evidence to Hutton on the volume of intelligence passing across the prime ministerial desk, commenting that, "no one on my staff had any visibility of large quantities of intelligence," and recalled his reaction on being told that Downing Street was intent on producing the dossier as being that it, "would be a considerable challenge because of the relatively sparse nature of the intelligence available on Iraq's weapons of mass destruction."[59]

That the intelligence services owned the text of the dossier was, of course, crucial to its credibility. However, questions remain unanswered about the authorship of the earliest drafts.[60] Moreover, a trail of emails and memos to and from Downing Street staffers show that they were unhappy with what they called the "Scarlett version" of the dossier, that initially approved by JIC Chairman John Scarlett, and were discussing amendments that would have the effect of heightening the sense of threat. The Hutton inquiry revealed a rich seam of email traffic as the drafting process neared its end. In a September 10th email from Daniel Pruce to Mark Matthews, Pruce advises "we make a number of statements about Saddam's intentions/attitudes. Can we insert a few quotes from speeches he has made which, even if they are not specific, demonstrate that he is a bad man with a general hostility towards his neighbours and the West? . . . much of the evidence we have is largely circumstantial so we need to convey to our readers that the cumulation of these facts demonstrates an intent on Saddam's part—the more they can be led to this conclusion themselves rather than have to accept judgements from us, the better." These coexisted with more despairing emails such as this sent to Alastair Campbell by Philip Bassett a day earlier: "Needs much more weight, writing, detail, and we need to find a way to get over this a) by having <u>better</u> intelligence material, b) by having <u>more</u> material (and better flagged-up), and c) more <u>convincing</u> material."

The common thread running through these exchanges is the need to demonstrate Saddam's malign intent, ideally toward the UK. Hence, on September 11, Daniel Pruce emailed Alastair Campbell: "I think we need to personalise the dossier onto Saddam as much as possible—for example by replacing references to Iraq with references to Saddam. In a similar vein I think we need a device to convey that he is a bad and unstable man . . . a few quotes from Saddam to demonstrate his aggressive intent and hatred of his neighbours and the West would help too." The same day Tom Kelly emailed Alastair Campbell, commenting on the current draft and again emphasizing the importance of demonstrating intent: "This does have some new elements to play with, but there is one central weakness—we do not differentiate enough between capacity and intent. We know that he is a bad man and has done bad things in the past. We know he is trying to get WMD—and this shows those attempts are intensifying. But can we show why we think he intends to use them aggressively, rather than in self-defence. We need that to counter the argument that Saddam is bad, but not mad . . . The key must be to show that Saddam has the capacity, and is intent on using it in ways that threaten world stability, and that our ability to stop him is increasingly threatened."

The bid to show "intent," and hence imply imminence, involved moving beyond a position supported by the available intelligence. As John Morrison, a former Deputy Chief of Defence Intelligence, put it: "In moving from what the dossier said Saddam had, which was a capability possibly, to asserting that Iraq presented a threat, then the Prime Minister was going way beyond anything any professional analyst would have agreed."[61] In Hans Blix's characterization, exclamation marks where inserted where there should have been question marks.

Within the dossier the "45-minutes claim"—that Iraqi chemical and biological weapons could be deployed within 45 minutes of an order being given—represented the threat headline. It was a claim that appeared in three separate parts of the dossier—in the main body, the executive summary, and Blair's Foreword. Its appearance in Blair's Foreword could reasonably have been interpreted as reflecting both intelligence and governmental confidence in the reliability of this evidence. Yet, in the parliamentary debate on the Hutton Report, Blair surprised observers by saying that he was unaware that the claim referred only to battlefield munitions. Robin Cook pronounced himself "astonished" by this[62]—while merely Leader of the House, JIC chairman John Scarlett had provided Cook with this very information. There was no indication anywhere in the dossier that the claim was intended to refer solely to battlefield munitions, and when newspapers ran alarmist front-page stories on the Iraqi threat to Cyprus, no one from government moved to correct their interpretation. The dossier had been about threat creation. Through the 45-minutes claim it had succeeded. The Butler Report criticized both its inclusion in this form and its repetition. Moreover, it revealed that "the validity of the intelligence report on which the 45-minute claim was based has come into question."[63] In fact it was false, and in October 2004 Jack Straw announced that it had been formally withdrawn.[64]

Conclusion

Notwithstanding his public statements from April to September 2002, the claims made in the September 2002 dossier, his threat presentation on the eve of war, and his explanation of the war's origins as lying in intelligence to the Hutton inquiry, Blair was subsequently obliged to shift his ground. Unlike the Hutton inquiry, the Butler inquiry had access to intelligence material. Counter to the impression given by Blair, but consistent with the assessments contained in leaked documents, the Butler report concluded that: "The Government's conclusion in the spring of 2002 that stronger action (although not necessarily military action) needed to be taken to enforce Iraqi disarmament was not based on any new development in the current intelligence picture on Iraq."[65] Moreover, in his evidence to the inquiry Blair was obliged to agree with, "the view expressed at the time that what had changed was not the pace of Iraq's prohibited weapons programmes, which had not been dramatically stepped up, but tolerance of them following the attacks of September 11 2001." Damningly, and contradicting the picture presented by Blair in Parliament and in the dossier in September 2002, the report concluded that, "there was no recent intelligence that would have given rise to a conclusion that Iraq was of more immediate concern than the activities of some other countries."[66] However, as Robin Cook argued: "Downing Street did not worry that the intelligence was thin and inferential or that the sources were second-hand and unreliable, because intelligence did not play a big part in the real reason why we went to war."[67] Ironically, while intelligence was central to Downing Street's strategy for selling the war, it was not central to the actual war decision.

Had the Downing Street dossier and subsequent statements contained the appropriate qualifying statements, recognized the limits of intelligence, and presented the more nuanced picture that the evidence justified, then the sense of threat would have been correspondingly reduced, and so too would the chances of the Prime Minister carrying the pivotal House of Commons vote in advance of the war. Robin Cook subsequently argued that, "it is embarrassingly clear that Parliament was misled into voting for war on the basis of unreliable sources and overheated analysis, producing between them false intelligence."[68] As former Deputy Chief of Defence Intelligence John Morrison has suggested, intelligence was used as a "public relations tool."[69] Moreover, it was a tool which was also used to sway votes on the UNSC. In November 2004, Foreign Office Minister Denis McShane informed Labour MP Llew Smith that the dossier had been distributed to UN members in advance of their November 2002 vote on Resolution 1441.[70]

Exaggeration was not the only form of deception deployed in selling the war to public and Parliament. It was joined by omission. The 1995 defection to Jordan of Saddam Hussein's son-in-law, Hussein Kamel, facilitated a better understanding of Iraq's biological weapons program, and was repeatedly referred to by Blair in making the case for war.[71] However, at no point did he reveal that Hussein Kamel had claimed, accurately as it turned out, that the biological weapons program was shut down after the 1991 Gulf war, a fact reported at the time of the defection by the JIC.[72] Misrepresentation of the firmness of the intelligence base was another form of deception,[73] as was misrepresentation of the position of France in relation to a further UNSC resolution specifically authorizing the use of force against Iraq.[74]

The drift to war with Iraq during 2002–3 represents a collective failure of Cabinet, arguably, alongside the Conservative Cabinet's failure to check Eden over the Suez collusion, the gravest of the modern era.[75] As Peter Hennessy has observed; "if the full Cabinet will not take on a dominant Prime Minister in full cry—even in the last days before hostilities begin— there is no other part of the system of government that can compensate for such supineness."[76] Robin Cook was the only senior Cabinet figure to resign over the impending war with Iraq, alongside two junior ministers, John Denham and Lord Hunt. Another senior Cabinet figure critical of the drift to war, International Development Secretary Clare Short, chose not to, unaware in advance of Cook's intention to resign.[77] When she did resign in May 2003, the impact of her resignation was much blunted. Foreign Secretary Jack Straw's position seems to have been ambivalent. In December 2002 he had told a journalist that the odds against war were 60:40. In March 2003, on the eve of war, he wrote a personal minute to Blair suggesting the Prime Minister consider alternatives to immediate war.[78] At the same time, a man who had warned that the case for war was "thin" in July 2002 was, by December, publicly suggesting that Iraq "probably" possessed nuclear weapons.[79] If those Cabinet members who had serious misgivings about the impending war had acted in a coordinated fashion, the parliamentary vote of March 18, 2003, authorizing the use of military force, would have taken place in a much changed environment and could have resulted in the resignation of the Prime Minister, rather than British involvement in the war that followed.[80]

Notes

1 In an opinion poll commissioned to mark the tenth anniversary of his premiership, only 22 percent thought Blair could be trusted, contrasting with 63 percent in 1997. Anthony King, "Mediocre or Worse: Voters Give Their Verdict on Blair's Legacy," *Daily Telegraph*, Apr. 30, 2007.
2 The key indicators of presidentialization have been summarized by Ludger Helms as follows: a significant increase in the impact of the leader in determining the outcome of elections; increased prime ministerial involvement in

international summitry; decreasing prime ministerial involvement in the business of Parliament (making speeches, voting); modest knowledge of and experience in government on the part of prime minister and Cabinet; the growing importance of extra-parliamentary media strategies; increased concentration of resources in the "center" in, for example, a prime minister's office; a weakening of collective (Cabinet) government; the transfer of political and policy initiatives from departments to the centre; a notable detachment of prime minister from government; a growing detachment of government from the judiciary. Ludger Helms, "The Presidentialisation of Political Leadership: British Notions and German Observations," *The Political Quarterly*, Vol.76, No.3 Jul–Sep. 2005, pp. 430–8.

3 Anthony Sampson, "Hijacked by that Mob at No.10," *Observer*, Jun. 8, 2003.

4 Christopher Meyer, *DC Confidential* (London, Weidenfeld & Nicolson, 2005), p. 190.

5 See, Mark Phythian, *The Politics of British Arms Sales Since 1964* (Manchester, Manchester University Press, 2000), Ch.8.

6 See, for example, Julia Langdon, "Labour's Falling Star", *Independent*, Sep. 26, 1998. His estranged wife's memoir, Margaret Cook, *A Slight and Delicate Creature: The Memoirs of Margaret Cook* (London, Weidenfeld & Nicolson, 1999), didn't help matters.

7 Nicholas Watt, "The Lost Straw," *Guardian*, Jan. 4, 2002.

8 Paul Gilfeather, "Blair Knifes 'Extremely Stupid' Jack Straw" *Daily Mirror*, Jan. 9, 2003.

9 Lance Price, *The Spin Doctor's Diary: Inside Number 10 With New Labour* (London, Hodder & Stoughton, 2005), p. 69.

10 Clare Short, *An Honourable Deception? New Labour, Iraq, and the Misuse of Power* (London, The Free Press, 2004), pp. 220–1.

11 Paul Waugh, "Influential MPs Back Criticisms of Presidential Powers Without Accountability'," *Independent*, May 14, 2003.

12 Robin Cook, *The Point of Departure* (London, Simon & Schuster, 2003), p. 116.

13 Ibid, pp. 115–16.

14 Additionally, Lance Price records sitting in on a Cabinet meeting in October 1999: "TB said at the beginning that he hoped they would be able to have a good discussion and when somebody made an aside about making a decision he said, 'Oh, I don't think we should go that far.' His disarming manner allows him to get away with murder like that." Price, *The Spin Doctor's Diary*, p. 156.

15 David Blunkett, *The Blunkett Tapes: My Life in the Bear Pit* (London, Bloomsbury, 2006), pp. 355, 359, 460.

16 This is discussed in detail in Chapter 11.

17 Lord Butler, *Review of Intelligence on Weapons of Mass Destruction: Report of a Committee of Privy Counsellors*, HC898 (London, The Stationery Office, July 2004), para.610.

18 Cited in Peter Riddell, *Hug Them Close: Blair, Clinton, Bush and the "Special Relationship"* (London, Politico's, 2003), p. 8.

19 Ibid, pp. 4–5.

20 On the impact of Blair's personality on the war decision, see Stephen Benedict Dyson, "Personality and Foreign Policy: Tony Blair's Iraq Decisions," *Foreign Policy Analysis*, Vol.2, No.3, Jul. 2006, pp. 289–306. Dyson finds that Blair exhibited a high belief in his ability to control events, low conceptual complexity, and a high need for power. See also, Mark Phythian, *The Labour Party, War and International Relations, 1945–2006* (London, Routledge, 2007), Ch.8.

21 Paddy Ashdown, *The Ashdown Diaries, Volume 2: 1997–1999* (London, Allen Lane, 2001), entry for Nov. 15, 1997, p. 127.

22 Hansard, Dec. 17, 1998, col.1101.

23 On this, see Riddell, *Hug Them Close*; Anthony Seldon, *Blair* (London, The Free Press, 2004), esp. Chs. 11, 26; James Naughtie, *The Accidental American: Tony Blair and the Presidency* (London, Macmillan, 2004); John Dumbrell, *A Special Relationship: Anglo-American Relations From the Cold War to Iraq* (Basingstoke, Palgrave Macmillan, 2nd ed. 2006).

24 Blair was so taken by the trappings of power enjoyed by US presidents that on returning from his first official visit to Washington, DC, in 1998, talks were reportedly held on acquiring a "Blairforce One" jet and moving the prime ministerial residence from the relatively cramped quarters of 10 Downing Street to the more presidential Dover House nearby. Simon Jenkins, "We Ain't Seen Nothing Yet", *Sunday Times*, Jul. 4, 2004. At the time journalist Alan Watkins noted how: "Mr. Clinton's attraction for Mr. Blair is that it allows him to cavort on the international stage, now getting into aeroplanes, now getting out of them, appearing before us as a person of consequence and power." Alan Watkins, "Worse Than a Crime, It Was a Blunder", *Independent on Sunday*, Feb. 8 1998.

25 Hansard, Sep. 24, 2002 col.21.

26 Riddell, p. 2; Interview with Lord Kinnock, Feb. 22, 2007.

27 Richard A. Clarke, *Against All Enemies* (New York, Free Press, 2004), pp. 264, 268. On this pre-history, see also James Mann, *Rise of the Vulcans: The History of Bush's War Cabinet* (New York, Viking, 2004).

28 Andrew Cockburn, *Rumsfeld: His Rise, Fall, and Catastrophic Legacy* (New York, Scribner, 2007), p. 9.

29 Clarke, *Against All Enemies*, p. 32.

30 Bryan Burrough, Evgenia Peretz, David Rose, and David Wise, "The Path to War," *Vanity Fair*, May 2004, p. 110.

31 George W. Bush, State of the Union Address, Jan. 29, 2002. www.whitehouse.gov/news/releases/2002/01/20020129–11.html. Last accessed Mar. 5, 2007.

32 See, for example, John Kampfner, *Blair's Wars* (London, The Free Press, revised ed. 2004), p. 168.

33 Butler Report, para.266.

34 Ibid, para.267.

35 Ibid.

36 "Your Trip to the US." Memo from David Manning to Tony Blair, Mar. 14, 2002. www.downingstreetmemo.com/docs/manning.pdf. Last accessed Jan. 5, 2007.

37 Memo from Christopher Meyer to Sir David Manning, Mar. 18, 2002. www.downingstreetmemo.com/docs/meyermemo.pdf. Last accessed Jan. 5, 2007.

38 "IRAQ: Advice for the Prime Minister". Memo from P. F. Ricketts to Jack Straw, Mar. 22, 2002. www.downingstreetmemo.com/docs/ricketts.pdf. Last accessed Jan. 5, 2007.

39 Ibid.

40 "Crawford/Iraq." Memo from Jack Straw to Tony Blair, Mar. 25, 2002. www.downingstreetmemo.com/docs/straw.pdf. Last accessed Jan. 5, 2007.

41 Ibid.

42 See note 11, above.

43 Prime Minister's speech at the George Bush Senior Presidential Library, Apr. 7, 2002. www.pm.gov.uk/output/Page1712.asp. Last accessed, Jan. 5, 2007.

44 "Iraq: Prime Minister's Meeting, Jul." Memo from Matthew Rycroft to David Manning, Jul. 23, 2002. www.downingstreetmemo.com/memos.html #originalmemo. Last accessed Jan. 5, 2007.

45 Ibid.

46 Ibid.

47 Ibid.

48 Bob Woodward, *Plan of Attack* (London, Simon & Schuster, 2004), p. 178.

49 B. Burrough, E. Peretz, D. Rose, and D. Wise, "The Path to War," *Vanity Fair*, May 2004, p. 172.

50 Hutton Inquiry, Evidence of Tony Blair, Aug. 28 2003. www.the-hutton-inquiry.org.uk/content/transcripts/hearing-trans22.htm. Last accessed Mar. 26, 2007.

51 In addition to the examples given below, see Alan Doig and Mark Phythian, "The National Interest and Politics of Threat Exaggeration: The Blair Government's Case for War Against Iraq," *The Political Quarterly*, Vol.76, No.3, Jul.–Sep. 2005, pp. 368–76.

52 www.number-10.gov.uk/output/Page1709.asp.

53 Hansard, Apr. 10, 2002, cols. 11, 23.

54 Butler Report, Annex B, pp. 164, 167, 168–9.

55 Carne Ross, Supplementary Evidence submitted to the Foreign Affairs Committee Dec. 2006 (originally drafted for the Butler Inquiry, Jun. 9, 2004. www.publications.parliament.uk/pa/cm200607/cmselect/cmfaff/167/61108 10.htm. Last accessed Apr. 5, 2007.

56 Hansard, Sep. 24, 2002, col. 3.

57 *Iraq's Weapons of Mass Destruction: The Assessment of the British Government*. www.number-10.gov.uk/output/Page284.asp. Last Accessed Apr. 5, 2007.

58 The emails quoted from here are either reproduced on the Hutton Inquiry website, or discussed in evidence given there. www.the-hutton-inquiry.org.uk/content/evidence.htm#full. Last accessed, Mar. 26, 2007. On the role of Alastair Campbell generally, and more specifically in the creation of the dossier, see Peter Oborne and Simon Walters, *Alastair Campbell* (London, Aurum Press, 2004), esp. Ch. 15.

59 *Panorama*, "A Failure of Intelligence", BBC1, Jul. 11, 2004.

60 Martin Bright, "Iraq: The New Cover-up," *New Statesman*, Nov. 13, 2006, pp. 12–16.

61 *Panorama*, "A Failure of Intelligence."

62 Robin Cook, "Blair and Scarlett Told Me Iraq Had No Usable Weapons," *Guardian*, July 12, 2004.

63 Butler Report, p. 127, para. 512.

64 Marie Woolf, "The 45-Minute Claim Was False," *Independent*, October 13, 2004. This is discussed in greater detail in Chapter 11.

65 Ibid, para.427.

66 Ibid.

67 Robin Cook, "The Die Was Cast: The Dossiers Were Irrelevant", *Independent on Sunday*, Jul. 18, 2004.

68 Robin Cook, "Britain's Worst Intelligence Failure, and Lord Butler Says No One is to Blame," *Independent*, Jul. 15, 2004.

69 Richard Norton-Taylor and Michael White, "Blair Misused Intelligence, Says Ex-Spy Officer," *Guardian*, Oct. 29, 2004.

70 Letters, *Independent*, Nov. 12, 2004.

71 See, for example, Tony Blair, "My Christian Conscience is Clear Over War," *Independent on Sunday*, Mar. 2, 2003.

72 Butler Report, para.177.

73 For example, in his House of Commons speech presenting the Iraq dossier, Blair said: "I am aware, of course, that people will have to take elements of this on the good faith of our intelligence services, but this is what they are telling me, the British Prime Minister, and my senior colleagues. The intelligence picture that they paint is one accumulated over the last four years. It is extensive, detailed and authoritative." Hansard, Sep. 24, 2002, col. 3.

74 See Kampfner, *Blair's Wars*, pp. 286–9.

75 Peter Hennessy, *Having It So Good: Britain in the Fifties* (London, Allen Lane, 2006), p. 437.

76 Peter Hennessy, "Informality and Circumscription: The Blair Style of Government in War and Peace," *The Political Quarterly*, Vol.76, No.1, Jan.–Mar. 2005, pp. 3–11.

77 Interview with Clare Short, Oct. 14, 2006.

78 Kampfner, *Blair's Wars*, pp. 302–3.

79 Ewen MacAskill and Nick Watt, "Anger Over Straw's Dossier on Iraqi Human Rights," *Guardian*, Dec. 3, 2002.

80 As it was, at the end of this debate 139 Labour MPs voted against the government—the largest backbench revolt against a government in modern

British history, despite Labour Whips making it clear that Blair would resign if he lost the vote. The question they posed to reluctant backbenchers was: "Do you support regime change in Baghdad or Downing Street?" See Philip Cowley, *The Rebels: How Blair Mislaid His Majority* (London, Politico's, 2005), Ch.5.

6

Australian use of intelligence and the case for war in Iraq

Rodney Tiffen

On November 8, 2001, just days before the federal election, Prime Minister John Howard was making the customary leader's appearance at the National Press Club. The polls showed Howard traveling toward a comfortable victory, one that seemed quite unattainable early that year, when all signs were that his government would suffer a massive defeat.

Through a single-minded effort Howard had retrieved his electoral fortunes. First he had reversed some of his more unpopular domestic policies, but the key turning points came in August and September. On August 26, the Norwegian merchant vessel the *Tampa* properly responded to the distress calls of a sinking boatload of asylum seekers, mainly Afghans and Iraqis who had been heading for the northwest coast of Australia. According to international law and custom, the *Tampa* set out to land at the Australian territory of Christmas Island to offload its extra cargo of 433 people.

This time the Australian government was determined to take decisive action. It refused permission for the *Tampa* to land, saying it had to go back to Indonesia. There then followed a tense stalemate. At one stage Australian SAS troops boarded the boat, and eventually the asylum seekers were transferred to the tiny Pacific Island nation of Nauru. This was the first of several government actions to dramatize the problem of what they called illegal immigrants, and to successfully neutralize what had become a running political sore for it. Two weeks later the terrible events of September 11 made security concerns far more urgent than they had been at least since the end of the Cold War.

These developments transformed the Australian electoral landscape. Moreover, as the election campaign began, another event seemed to dramatize the asylum seeker issue again and to demonstrate the unworthy nature of these unwanted arrivals. It was reported that children had been thrown overboard from one of the boats. Government ministers immediately seized upon this claim and denounced the action and its perpetrators. After an initial flurry of publicity, the incident receded and was overtaken by other campaign events, but as the election was nearing, doubts surfaced from within the navy about the accuracy of government claims. Indeed by this time, the military had reported strongly that the original claim was false, but thoughtful officials kept this inconvenient news from the prime minister.[1]

Howard knew he had to be able to answer questions on the issue at the National Press Club, and he and his staff prepared for the inevitable cross-examination. In his answer he produced a report from the Office of National Assessments (ONA) and read the critical two sentences about the children being thrown into the sea and how these tactics had been used by people smugglers in the Mediterranean. He concluded: "If the Defence Minister and Immigration Minister get verbal advice from Defence sources and the Prime Minister gets that kind of written advice I don't think it's sort of exaggerating or gilding the lily to go out and say what I said." According to Marr and Wilkinson, "the impact was immediate. No one could remember a prime minister reading ONA advice at a press conference before."[2]

After the election, a parliamentary inquiry revealed the truth about the children overboard incident, including the ONA document. It transpired that the prime minister was reading from a fax sent the night before at his request. It came with several caveats—none of which the Prime Minister had made public—including that ONA had compiled the document after ministers had made their public statements, and so could not have been the source for those statements, and that ONA had no independent knowledge of the events. The document had been drawn together from public sources, especially ministers' statements. Howard's and his ministers' "own unsubstantiated claims had been sent back to him in a classified document."[3]

In a defense that prefigured his post-Iraq war statements, the prime minister stressed that, even if now shown to be mistaken, all his claims had been made in good faith, even though his misleadingly selective reading of the document in front of him throws this into severe question. Howard's misrepresentation of the information about children overboard allowed him to escape a momentary political embarrassment, and to change the timing of the revelations to a moment when they would not do the government any lasting electoral damage.

Beyond the picture this episode gives of the prime minister's credibility, however, is the way it exposes dilemmas about the role of intelligence in democratic politics, one that was to become a major issue in Howard's next term of government as he committed Australia to go to war against Iraq. At the center of public debate are claims about information to which the public is denied access. So at its heart the invocation of intelligence material is an appeal to authority rather than evidence. The government is telling the public: if you knew what we know you would have no choice but to agree with us. But the secrecy surrounding intelligence work both permits its public misrepresentation and shields it from the scrutiny and testing that more public documents have, scrutiny and testing which are crucial both to intellectual quality and the health of democracy.

The history of partisan conflicts over the intelligence agencies

For the intelligence agencies themselves, such controversy was an unwelcome throwback. They had done much to dispel the suspicions and criticisms occasioned by the partisan conflicts in which they had sometimes been embroiled during the Cold War, and especially during the long period of conservative rule (1949–72).[4] Then, the major security agency ASIO (the Australian Security and Intelligence Organization) was suspicious that the Labor Party had been infiltrated by Communist Party members, Soviet spies and fellow travelers.

The sharpest controversy erupted spectacularly when a third secretary and spy from the Soviet Embassy, Vladimir Petrov, defected just before the 1954 election. This unprecedented event at the height of the Cold War created a frenzied atmosphere. Labor had been leading substantially, but the Liberals under Robert Menzies ended up winning an extremely close election. The outcome led to severe paranoia among some leftwing figures about ASIO's role, and many on the Labor side blamed the defection and its aftermath for their election loss.

Later, especially during the Vietnam war years, ASIO tended to view peace activists as communist dupes, and again sometimes became a political tool of the government in the vitriolic debates surrounding the war. The first Labor government for 23 years, the Whitlam government, found itself in conflict with the security services over such issues as them failing to monitor the violent activities of rightwing Croatian groups active against the Tito regime in Yugoslavia, and the actions of the Australian Security Intelligence Services (ASIS) in support of American actions against the Allende Government in Chile. Whitlam instituted a Royal Commission, the Hope Commission, to inquire into their functioning, partly to ensure that the agencies were accountable to the government of the day, and not laws unto themselves, but equally to prevent their use for party purposes by the government. One outcome was the formation of the ONA in 1977.

Even the Hawke Labor Government (beginning 1983) had some early entanglements with the security agencies. ASIO thought that former

Labor Party national-secretary-turned-lobbyist David Combe, who was doing work for the Soviets, could become an agent of influence. This again led to a major scandal and a new Royal Commission under Mr. Justice Hope that largely vindicated the government and ASIO.[5]

The key trend throughout this period, and most especially after the end of the Cold War, was the increasing professionalism in the security services, a change away from the cloak-and-dagger melodramas of the past and from the paranoia that viewed anything that was socially or politically nonconformist as suspect and subversive.

Contemporary tensions

As the long countdown to the Iraq war began, Australia's intelligence apparatus seemed to be stable and harmonious, and more professional than it had ever been, but there were undercurrents of tension.[6] Two incidents exhibited just how deep and fraught those currents were—the suicide of Merv Jenkins and the criticisms by Lance Collins. Both involved internal tensions over Indonesia and East Timor.

One of the key tenets of the philosophy of Australian intelligence, as outlined by the Hope Commission and agreed to by all sides of politics, was that intelligence assessment should be kept separate from policy formulation.[7] Collins charged that a pro-Jakarta lobby was damaging intelligence work on East Timor. Jenkins was caught up in the same issue, but his case was further complicated not only by domestic bureaucratic politics but by international intelligence relationships.

The key to Australia's international intelligence gathering and assessments is the Four Eyes relationship with English-speaking allies— America, Britain, and Canada.[8] This gives Australia access to far more intelligence than it could ever gather itself—the US intelligence budget is around 100 times that of Australia, while Britain's is about eight times as large.[9] The benefits to Australia far outweigh the costs, although as in all intelligence work, trust in the reliability of others' information and assessments can be problematic, as they were during the Iraqi WMD debates. Of course, this intimate alliance with other English-speaking democracies does not obviate the need to gather intelligence on them and their intentions as well,[10] so sometimes "Australian (and British) intelligence agencies needed to treat the US more as a focus of intelligence interest than as a close ally," and by late 2002, these agencies were accurately reporting that nothing could stop Washington's countdown to war.[11]

Merv Jenkins who committed suicide in a Washington garage in the northern summer of 1999, leaving a widow and three young children, was a victim of the complex politics of the international intelligence sharing. One area where Australia had primary responsibility was regarding Indonesia and East Timor. However, this was also the issue which caused most contention within the Australian intelligence community. As the situation in East Timor deteriorated sharply in 1999, following President Habibie's announcement of a referendum to determine independence or integration, Australian policy was slow to respond to the increase in militia violence. Issues about the extent of the violence and its links to the Indonesian military became increasingly urgent intelligence and policy issues. Just as ever since 1975 the Australian government's publicity stance was to turn a blind eye to unfavorable developments on East Timor,[12] inside the government there was an ethos that producing evidence of Indonesian atrocities was unwelcome. The increasing scale of the violence and the sense of a gathering climax made this an increasingly inadequate stance. The Americans became increasingly suspicious that Australia was downplaying the seriousness of the situation.

The formal intelligence-sharing arrangements were accompanied by a great deal of informal sharing of material. This proved tragic for the young Australian military attaché. He showed AUSTEO (Australian Eyes Only) material to his American colleagues, something that was routinely done, but now had political ramifications. Threatened with the destruction of his career, Merv Jenkins committed suicide. A few years later Lieutenant-Colonel Lance Collins wrote that Australian intelligence assessments regarding Indonesia and East Timor were being compromised by political acceptability. He was particularly critical of the Defence Intelligence Organization, which he charged was tailoring intelligence to fit government policy. His letters were later leaked, prompting one of the biggest anti-leak operations by the Australian Federal Police.[13]

The Australian politics surrounding Iraqi WMD

The issue of Iraqi WMD put Australian intelligence agencies in a more searing political searchlight than at any time since the end of the Cold War, as the government claimed intelligence justification for its claims about Saddam's arsenal, and as intelligence sources were cited in the press. In key respects the Australian politics surrounding the Iraq war and the issue of Iraqi WMD followed a similar course to its American and British allies,[14] and indeed often Australian debates fed off developments in those countries. As the war approached, there was a high level of commonality in the rhetoric and claims of the three governments.

Iraq's possession of WMD was the central Australian Government rationale for the invasion. As John Howard said on the eve of war, "I would have to accept that if Iraq had genuinely disarmed, I couldn't justify on its own a military invasion of Iraq to change the regime. I've never advocated that, much in all as I despise the regime."[15] In his televised address to the nation about Australia's commitment to the war, Howard said "We are determined to . . . deprive Iraq of its . . . chemical and biological weapons, which even in minute quantities are capable of causing death and destruction on a mammoth scale."[16]

Iraq's possession of WMD was asserted countless times by government ministers, and repeated throughout the media. At least in retrospect a key characteristic of these statements is the complete certainty with which they were uttered. For Prime Minister Howard there was "no doubt on the evidence of the intelligence material available to us that not only does Iraq possess chemical and biological weapons but Iraq also has not abandoned her nuclear aspirations."[17] Similarly he told Parliament in March 2003 that: "The Australian government knows that Iraq has chemical and biological weapons, and that Iraq wants to develop nuclear weapons."[18] He also said the war in 1991 "was suspended on condition that Iraq gave up its weapons of mass destruction. Clearly we all know that this has not happened."[19]

This certainty is often accompanied by the dismissal of all contrary views and impatience with any course of action except invasion. For Foreign Minister Alexander Downer, "the question today is less whether Saddam is guilty of trying to hide his weapons of mass destruction—we know he is. Or why this matters to Australia—we know it does. The real question today is what we—the international community—are going to do about it." Claims about the size of Saddam's arsenal were often phrased in terms of the growing threat, that new activity meant that time was running out, and so that action was urgent. The previous June, Downer argued:

> The world cannot and must not stand idly by while Iraq develops and manufactures weapons of mass destruction . . . Time is running out. The real danger is that Hussein is progressing his comprehensive program to develop and deploy weapons of mass destruction. It is incumbent on the international community to do all within its powers to bring him to heel.[20]

To what extent were these claims based on, or disciplined by, intelligence evidence? Often the rhetoric lacked precision, so that "the extent of Iraq's weapons is sometimes implied rather than stated in the speeches. Iraq's weapons are an 'arsenal' and a 'stockpile'." In 1995, Iraq still had a "massive program" and the quantities unaccounted for were "large."[21]

Moreover, the most terrifying details came from scenarios for the future. A recurring characteristic of the government's rhetoric from the prewar period was the way it moved from established past horrors, through interpreting present uncertainties in the worst possible light, based upon Saddam's undoubted evil, to projecting nightmare scenarios, and so the need for immediate action to stop this future threat. Saddam's provision of WMD to terrorists became for government ministers "the ultimate nightmare," "the ultimate horror," "the sum of all our fears," "nothing [is] out of the question," "a direct, undeniable and lethal threat to Australia"—apocalyptic visions which have moved very far from an embattled dictator unable even to effectively control large parts of his own territory. They all, however, pointed to the need for immediate action, of the dangers of doing nothing and of a growing threat, one that was answered by the March 2003 invasion.

After a period of rejoicing and political triumph after the rapid defeat of Saddam, questions were soon raised about the lack of WMD. The first stage in the government's rhetorical repertoire was procrastination—that it was too soon yet to be definitive. An interview between Howard and ABC TV's Tony Jones[22] demonstrated his essential strategy:

Q: Does it matter if no weapons of mass destruction are found there?
A: Oh, I wouldn't say it doesn't matter . . . And it's too early to make a judgement. I mean, people should be more patient.
. . . I think, Tony, that question should be asked and I'd be very happy to answer it if, after the elapse of a reasonable amount of time, such a conclusion is reached. But it's too early,

Similarly any findings that might indicate WMD were seized upon. Alexander Downer gleefully told Parliament:

Already we have evidence of what appear to be mobile biological laboratories at two sites in Iraq, capable of producing biological materials for use in weapons of mass destruction. I know that is disappointing for the opposition to hear this, but I am afraid this is true.[23]

Downer's triumphalism did not last long. The "biological trailers" proved not to be part of a weapons program, and the Foreign Minister did not refer to them again,[24] although neither did he recant this statement. This may have been the last occasion on which a senior Australian government figure expressed any confidence in finding WMD, in contrast to American leaders who kept up the hope or pretense much longer. So when in October 2003 Brigadier Stephen Meekin, a senior Australian official in the Iraq Survey Group, said that claims Iraq was importing components for a nuclear weapons program were simply wrong, and that "by and large our judgement is that sanctions have been pretty good"; an anonymous US government spokesman responded that Brigadier Meekin was not qualified to make that judgment.[25]

Especially as the mounting disasters in Iraq made the war less politically popular, the pressures for inquiries into the original reasons for going to war at last became irresistible. In all three countries we now know far more about the lead-up to war, the decisionmaking in each, and the interaction between intelligence and policy formulation. Australia had two inquiries—although in sum these have been much less penetrating and revealing than the inquiries held in Britain and America.

The first was forced because the government lacked control of the Senate. The Senate referred the issue to the Joint Parliamentary Committee on ASIO, ASIS, and DSD (Defence Signals Directorate) (the three major intelligence gathering agencies) on June 18, 2003. Unlike its counterparts in Britain and America, the Committee only received excerpts of the assessments made prior to the war. The Committee was evenly split in party terms, and the opposition members included two former ministers for defense, a composition seen as politically favorable for the government. Nevertheless it issued a consensual report which was in key respects quite damning about the government's performance and credibility. In particular it concluded that "the statements by the Prime Minister and Ministers are more strongly worded than most of the AIC [Australian Intelligence Community] judgements."[26] "The case made by the government was that Iraq possessed WMD in large quantities and posed a grave and unacceptable threat to the region and the world, particularly as there was a danger that Iraq's WMD might be passed to terrorist organizations. This is not the picture that emerges from an examination of all the assessments provided to the Committee by Australia's two analytical agencies."[27]

Skilfully the government minimized the political damage from this potentially embarrassing report. Firstly it selectively leaked parts of it, and conditioned expectations in the media that it gave the government a clean bill of health.[28] Moreover, at the same time it informally let it be known—as recommended by the parliamentary committee—that it would immediately launch a second inquiry into the adequacy of the intelligence agencies.

This it did. When the Parliamentary Joint Committee Report was released the prime minister announced another inquiry to be chaired by former senior diplomat and head of Foreign Affairs, Phillip Flood. Flood reported four months later, devoting only a dozen or so pages of his report to issues explicitly concerned with Iraqi WMD, and instead elaborating at length on various bureaucratic arrangements and with the mandarin's gift of making the most urgent issues seem quite bloodless.

In effect, Flood mounts an intelligent defense of the agencies' efforts. Given the absence of Iraqi WMD, he had little choice but to conclude that "ONA and DIO, along with the rest of the international community, failed to judge accurately the extent and nature of Iraq's WMD programmes." However, he attributes this to several causes, especially the thinness of the intelligence and that, on such potentially threatening issues, there is "a proper place" for reporting to cover worst case scenarios. He also notes the complexity of the Iraqi situation and especially "Saddam's history of WMD use, his past and continuing efforts to deceive and obstruct inspection processes, and his perceived strategic ambitions, were key underpinnings of ONA and DIO assessments." Prefiguring a theme that the government would take up, he notes that "ONA's and DIO's key judgments on Iraq's WMD capabilities were relatively cautious," and that "on the whole Australian assessments were more cautious and seem closer to the facts as we know them so far than British and American agencies." He also dismissed any notion of politicization of the assessments. Indeed, "The Inquiry's conclusion that, on the basis of the available information, ONA and DIO drew the most likely conclusions, is consistent with and supports the finding that there was no evidence of politicization."[29] In reaching these reassuring conclusions, he refrains from any detailed review of the many charges and claims regarding WMD in the year leading up to the war.

Accounts by Australian intelligence officials

While Australia's inquiries have been less illuminating than those of its major allies, the politics surrounding the role of the intelligence has been immeasurably assisted by two very senior and experienced officials, who publicly dissented from government claims and policies. Both subsequently wrote excellent and revealing books.

On the eve of war, Andrew Wilkie, a policy analyst at the central intelligence assessment agency, the ONA, resigned and publicly registered his dissent. Wilkie had been a lieutenant-colonel in the army and a senior intelligence officer. He effectively sacrificed his career in order to make his stand of conscience, because "we were on the cusp of waging an unjustified war on the basis of a preposterous lie."[30] "No matter which way I looked at the issue, both the raw intelligence and the assessments of this intelligence indicated clearly that Iraq did not pose a serious enough security threat to justify a war. Iraq's conventional military was weak, its WMD program was disjointed and contained, and there was no active co-operation between it and al Qaida." "By early 2003 Saddam couldn't even control substantial swathes of his own country, or contemplate taking a swipe at his neighbours, let alone mount an attack on more powerful countries further afield."[31]

Wilkie's book systematically goes through the dubious evidence mounted to make the case for war during 2002–3. Rod Barton had a much longer and more intimate acquaintance with the issue. Barton was concerned with Iraqi weapons of mass destruction issues for over two decades. He therefore had a close knowledge of just how awful the regime was, "truly one of the most brutal governments of the twentieth century."[32] Working for Australian intelligence in the 1980s and early 1990s, mainly the DIO, like many others he was alarmed by the extensive WMD arsenal Saddam had built up by the time of the Gulf War. He formed the view that Iraq might have been only a year away from producing a nuclear bomb, although he also thought that the comprehensive allied bombing campaign had destroyed most of Saddam's WMD capacity.[33]

Earlier, Barton had been one of the first analysts to argue, in 1983, that Saddam had started a chemical warfare program, and was planning to manufacture mustard gas.[34] Iraq's use of mustard gas against Iran was confirmed by the UN in the following years. Australia's response to Saddam's CBW [chemical and biological warfare] actions in the 1980s was much more principled than Britain's and America's. Britain, for example, knew of his March 1988 use of poison gas against the Kurdish town of Halabja, but only delivered a very low level diplomatic protest, and six months later was moving to secretly resume arms sales.[35] In contrast, "the Australia Group, now a grouping of 38 countries, was formed in 1985 to strengthen export licencing measures in response to the finding of a UN special investigatory mission that chemical weapons (CW) had been used in the Iran-Iraq war." Australia was also one of the countries supporting the UN Chemical Weapons Convention of 1992, which was given impetus by Iraq's CW program.[36]

After the Gulf War, Barton joined UNSCOM, where with Dr. David Kelly and two others, he formed the Gang of Four who pursued Iraq's biological weapons program. In 1994–95, through diligent on-the-spot monitoring and through tracking imports and many paper trails, they forced Iraq to admit the extent of the program, whose existence it had previously denied. The public climax came with the defection of Saddam's son in law Hussein Kamal, who said his fleeing was prompted by the crisis following from UNSCOM's investigation. In his statement of February 4, 2003, Prime Minister Howard quoted from the debriefing Hussein Kamal gave in 1995, which he said indicated Saddam had "a massive program for developing offensive biological weapons—one of the largest and most advanced in the world." But the program Hussein described related to the period leading up to the Gulf war, and he had said that it no longer existed after the Gulf war, that inspections had been successful.[37]

Barton later came to believe that there was a probability that Iraq still may have had some anthrax. When working with UNMOVIC he became suspicious about an amount of unaccounted for anthrax, small as a proportion but still sufficient to cause great damage.[38] This possibility was included in some public reports and statements by Blix and others. Only after the war was the issue finally resolved with the confession of the chief official, Dr. Taha. She said that during the Gulf war they had tried to move the anthrax on a semi-trailer because of fear of coalition bombing. In July 1991 Hussein Kamal gave the order to destroy it. It had been on a semi-trailer that had broken down outside Radwaniyah Palace, and it was destroyed there without any paper work. Barton and others then visited the site and could see clearly where the anthrax had been destroyed a dozen years earlier. Dr. Taha could not declare this to UNSCOM or UNMOVIC, because "to put it mildly, Saddam would not have been pleased."[39] UNMOVIC had correctly identified Iraq's lack of documentation, and then publicly concluded, "there must be a strong presumption that the anthrax still exists." The truth did not betray the sinister plotting of Saddam so much as the dysfunctionality of a brutal dictatorship, which out of fear was keeping secrets from itself.

Despite his strong sense of the untrustworthiness of the regime, and his determination to track down all unaccounted-for WMD possibilities, Barton's overall judgment, given to an Australian parliamentary committee in the year 2000, was that probably more than 95 percent of Iraq's capabilities had been eliminated, and that Iraq was effectively disarmed. Moreover, he did not think given the parlous state of its industries that Iraq could achieve a large new WMD capacity. "In other words, Iraq was not a threat."[40]

Over the next few years, Barton watched the countdown to war, as one of Blix's most senior assistants in UNMOVIC, and then also witnessed the aftermath as part of the Iraq Survey Group. He notes, for example, that the British dossier of September 2002 "left us bewildered," especially its "unqualified language" about renewed production. They particularly puzzled over the claim given such prominence by Prime Minister Blair that the chemical and biological weapons were deployable within 45 minutes, and after going through several possible meanings, advised Blix that "we did not understand the claim." When David Kelly visited New York, Barton said he seemed embarrassed over the claim and distanced himself from it.[41]

While both the American and British governments made several unqualified statements, which they said were based on their intelligence, the attempts by UNMOVIC to get access to this evidence proved largely fruitless.[42] By the end of 2002, Barton felt that "UNMOVIC had become increasingly irrelevant to the political process, which was now leading inexorably to war. To the US, we were no more than a nuisance and if necessary we, and the UN, would simply be bypassed."[43]

After the first wave of postwar inspections proved fruitless, the Iraq Survey Group was formed, and many old UNMOVIC and UNSCOM hands were to join it, including Barton and Kelly. However, before he could return to Iraq, Kelly committed suicide in July 2003. Barton was devastated: "He was the elite of inspectors . . . the most sane, level-headed and rational person that I had known, and suicide seemed completely inconsistent with this." Barton knew that following the Gilligan BBC story and Kelly's confession to his superiors (volunteered before the story was broadcast) that he had been under pressure "from what should have been an unlikely source: his own government. For a man who had stood up to threats and intimidation from the Iraqis, it was a cruel twist."[44]

Barton's return to Iraq had been delayed, and, although he was returning on David Kay's request, before he arrived in mid-December 2003 Kay returned to America. The senior British official in the ISG told Barton that in the last month, Kay "appeared to be a deeply troubled man." He "had been a strong believer that Iraq had WMD." When he finally realized the weapons did not exist, he became "like a man who had suddenly found there was no God."[45] In late January Kay went public, dramatically declaring "We were nearly all wrong", and in effect forcing an inquiry into the prewar intelligence.

In the vacuum left in the ISG by Kay's departure, Barton came to fill a pivotal role in drafting the report. Despite Kay's public statement, the politics of the report and the absence of any findings of WMD were particularly fraught. The British and American governments were still saying publicly that WMD existed. Barton became impatient with the refusal to state the implications of their investigations. One American official said "you just don't understand how difficult it is to say anything different." Another said they could not state their findings about the mobile trailers alleged to have been biological trailers but were in fact for weather balloons, because "politically it's not possible."[46] Kay's replacement, Charles Duelfer, wanted a non-committal report, and this was done. Barton was very dissatisfied, but stayed to ensure no actual misrepresentations were incorporated. Even then the two major governments exerted some pressure for the draft report to be strengthened. For example, the chair of the UK Joint Intelligence Committee, John Scarlett, thought the report was light on impact, and said the ISG team should pick out some "nuggets," seemingly indifferent to the fact that these nuggets lacked substantiating evidence. In Barton's judgment, Scarlett "was not a fit person to head any intelligence organization."[47]

Some months later, Duelfer, a veteran of the WMD discovery process, was finally ready to write a substantive report. Barton, persuaded by Duelfer that the process would now be objective, participated in this final report. It concluded that although Saddam never gave up his ambition for the weapons and would have resumed his programs if the opportunity arose, he had no definite plans or programs in place at the time of the war in early 2003. Eventually the conclusion was clear, "there were no WMD in Iraq after 1991."[48]

Intelligence assessments and the loaded debate

If by 2004, it was indisputable that the premise for this pre-emptive war was false, what could and should have been known before the war? This was not a small error. Not only were tens of thousands of lives at stake, but the scale of the exaggeration was massive. There were no signs of any imminent attack plans by Saddam, no weapons of mass destruction, no programs to manufacture such weapons. The fact that such a massive sense of threat had been built with so little basis was a surprise to most observers.

Is it sufficient then to say, as John Howard has, that at the time everyone believed that Iraq had WMD?[49] This considerably overstates the degree of consensus. It elides two very different propositions—one, that Iraq had a substantial WMD capacity that was rapidly growing and a threat to its region and the West, and two, that one could say with certainty that Iraq had no WMD capacity. Expert weapons inspectors and others in Western countries were properly reluctant to assert that there was sufficient evidence to say that Iraq had no WMD, but this reluctance is not the same as a positive claim that Iraq did possess a large WMD capacity.

The difference also points to what a loaded political debate occurred in the lead-up to the war. Critics were forced to try to prove a negative, the absence of WMD. No amount of inspections could be taken to confirm this. The absence of evidence was simply taken as evidence of concealment. An unsuccessful search of an alleged weapons site was never sufficient to prove that the weapons were not simply elsewhere. It also meant that it was all but impossible for the Iraqi regime itself to take any action to disprove the charges against it, especially when the even stronger demand was made that they prove they had disarmed. Foreign Minister Downer put this most explicitly in December 2002, "The onus is on Iraq to give concrete evidence that it no longer possesses these weapons or related programs."[50] Or as Defence Minister Robert Hill said, to avoid military intervention, Saddam had to "give real confidence to the Americans that he has stopped his weapons of mass destruction program."[51]

The claims about Iraqi WMD fall into two broad classes—what remained of Saddam's very substantial pre-Gulf war WMD program and second, what new programs were under way, especially in the period since the end of 1998 when UN inspectors had lacked access to the country.

The first chapter of the Australian Parliamentary Report lays out systematically just how much of Iraq's pre-Gulf war WMD capacity had been destroyed, with well over 90 percent known to have been destroyed in most categories.[52] The public focus, however, was on the small proportions not verifiably accounted for, and these were then framed as if they probably still existed and in good working order. Other possibilities—that they had deteriorated or that they had been destroyed but not in a verifiable way, as turned out to be the case with the missing anthrax cited above—received short shrift. Several western analysts, such as Wilkie and Barton, thought there was some possibility that not all the pre-Gulf war materials had been destroyed, but that any residual capacity was too small to constitute a major threat.

Much more problematic were claims about renewed activities in the contemporary era. The evidence adduced to support this has all proved problematic and fallacious, but as Rumsfeld and several others said, the absence of evidence is not evidence of absence. In this sense, the public political debate was only minimally disciplined by the findings of intelligence agencies. The strong general assertions of Iraqi programs were rarely accompanied by detailed evidence, but in the absence of evidence disproving a build-up, ambiguities and areas of ignorance provided the space on which sinister constructions could be built.

Does this mean, as Phillip Flood's inquiry concluded, that the judgments of the Australian intelligence agencies were the best possible given all the available evidence? As Flood and others point out, Australian intelligence was overwhelmingly dependent upon the evidence made available by its senior allies. On the whole it took a more skeptical view of some of the claims than its counterparts. But this was not always so.

Flood found no evidence of politicisation and in a direct sense this seems to be true. However, the influence of the political environment—both international and domestic—on Australian intelligence assessments is also apparent. At the simplest level, it is apparent in the degree of activity on Iraq. "From the beginning of September 2002 the number of intelligence reports on Iraq's WMD increased exponentially."[53] Compared with the eight months from January 1 to August 31, 2002, the following seven and a half months to March 2003 produced a tenfold increase in reporting.[54]

More importantly, the Parliamentary Committee notes that from September, "the language of ONA assessments tends to be much more definitive." "In general, therefore, in [the period up to September 2002], the agencies' view on the existence of Iraq's WMD is that, while there is a capacity to restart programmes, chemical weapons and biological weapons, if they exist at all, would be in small quantities and that the existence of nuclear weapons is doubtful." Changing from these more measured and skeptical views, from September on, ONA's assessments "became more assertive and less qualified."[55]

For analyst Andrew Wilkie, "ONA's sudden shift to a more gung-ho position on Iraq is striking. For years it had treated the CIA's claims about Iraq with great caution. Both ONA and DIO had continued to take a more measured view than the US and UK."[56] On September 13, 2002 an unclassified ONA report prepared at the government's request stated that a range of intelligence and public information suggests that Iraq is highly likely to have chemical and biological weapons. It also said there was no reason to believe that Saddam Hussein has abandoned his ambitions to acquire nuclear weapons. Yet, Wilkie notes, the previous day ONA had reported that there was no firm evidence of new CBW production, and had also said that evidence on Saddam's nuclear capability was patchy and inconclusive.

Wilkie thinks that the government's extraordinary request for an unclassified report for use in the preparation of ministerial speeches "sent a clear signal to ONA to deliver something stronger, something to back up the government's enthusiasm for war."[57] From this time also it is probably clear that America is intent on war, and that Britain and Australia will probably be joining it. This raises the stakes for an intelligence agency very considerably.

Faced with such a strong political consensus, there may be scope to doubt particular details, but perhaps not the general picture. ONA's somewhat curious statement of January 31, 2003[58] almost says as much:

> There is a wealth of intelligence on Saddam's WMD activities, but it paints a circumstantial picture that is conclusive overall rather than resting on a single piece of irrefutable evidence. [However] so far no intelligence has accurately pointed to the location of WMD . . . Such intelligence leaves little room for doubt that Saddam must have something to hide—and confirms that his deception efforts are so systematic that inspectors could not find all his WMD even if given years to do so.

In other words, even though no individual detail is certain, there is no doubt about the total picture. So no rebuttal of an individual claim can refute the central charge.

A process sensitive to the weight of the international consensus seems also to have colored Australian intelligence assessments of the false claim that Iraq had imported uranium from Niger. This became a cause celebre in the United States because of the controversy over Joseph Wilson, a former diplomat with experience in both Niger and Iraq, who went to Niger and discredited the claims in February 2002, exposing forgeries and inconsistencies in the documents. After the war when Wilson published a critical article in the *New York Times*, figures in the administration sought to discredit him by saying he only got the job because his wife, Valerie Plame, worked for the CIA, this disclosure of her identity leading to a long legal inquiry and prosecution.

Despite the fact that Wilson had so thoroughly discredited the claim in February 2002, it kept surfacing in government claims. Indeed a full year later in February 2003 Prime Minister Howard included the claim in a speech to Parliament. Interestingly when ONA first heard the claim it simply noted it, and said simply it has not seen the intelligence on African uranium. However, by January 2003, it told the parliamentary committee that it took the claim on African uranium as "the mainstream view and therefore well founded."[59] The wording of this suggests that perhaps ONA had still not seen the intelligence, but because the claim was widespread ("mainstream") it now accepted it as true.

There is conflicting evidence over when the falsity of the claim was known by Australian intelligence circles. According to Wilkie, the ONA, the Department of Foreign Affairs and Trade and the Defence Department have all publicly acknowledged that they knew before January 2003 that the Niger story was simply wrong. No satisfactory explanation of how the prime minister failed to know has been given.[60]

Eventually, after the war, Foreign Minister Downer discreetly revealed the information about uranium from Niger had proved to be erroneous in an article in the *Sydney Morning Herald* (June 18, 2003). Howard told a press conference on July 10, 2003 that the uranium issue was not a key element in the security assessments made by the intelligence agencies or in the government's decision to go to war, although did not then say why he had included it in a major speech.[61] This easy shifting of ground when a charge was proved false was a recurring feature of government rhetoric.

The other major basis for saying that Iraq was seeking to establish a nuclear program was the issue of the aluminum tubing. Australian intelligence had taken a special interest in the aluminum tubing issue, because it was their efforts in China which had uncovered Iraq's import attempts. There was a "real feeling of accomplishment"[62] in uncovering the convoluted trail to Iraq, leading to the cargo's interception in Jordan in July 2001. Inside Western intelligence circles, there was then an extended debate about what the tubes were intended for, with one faction inside the CIA insistent that they were for a gas centrifuge for uranium enrichment, but with the weight of expert evidence, saying that they were the wrong size, and unsuitable without expensive and substantial modification. These experts were shocked a year later when these tubes suddenly became part of the government's public case against Iraq, and were widely covered as such in news reports from September on. Foreign Minister Downer cited the tubes in Parliament in September 2002, saying they could be used in a uranium enrichment program.[63]

Apart from the debate over the suitability of the tubes, no intelligence evidence of a gas centrifuge facility, which would have been a substantial operation, had come to light anywhere in Iraq. Finally the head of the IAEA Mohammed ElBaradei on January 9, 2003 concluded the aluminum tubes were not part of any uranium enrichment program.[64] Wilkie aptly concluded of this and the Niger uranium claim that "each deception was of course alarming in its own right. Together they were outrageous, because together they meant that the entire case that Saddam was trying to reconstitute his nuclear programme was bogus."[65]

They show how difficult it was in the build-up to war to dispose politically of false charges about Iraqi WMD. Even when there was no evidence linking Iraq to events, it was never proclaimed innocent. When approaching the anniversary of September 11, it was put to Howard that there was no link between Iraq and the September 11 bombing, "Well, I think the true answer is that we can't be certain either way. I'm not asserting conclusively that there is, but I don't think you can assert conclusively without argument that there isn't."[66] Foreign Minister Downer was even more assertive—"Al-Qaida operatives are—or have been—in Baghdad, putting Iraq in breach of UN Security Council Resolutions prohibiting safehavens for terrorists."[67] According to Wilkie, "the US, the UK and Australia never collected any hard intelligence to back up their specific and oft-repeated claim that Saddam's regime was actively co-operating with the broad Islamic extremist movement known as al-Qaida."[68]

Rod Barton had felt at the end of 2002 that UNMOVIC was powerless to stop the inexorable path to war. Certainly UNMOVIC's activities seem to have had little impact in Australia. In the weeks before the war began, on March 11, 2003, ONA declared that "Baghdad remains defiant and claims it has no WMD to declare: US and UNMOVIC assessments say the opposite."[69] While this is an accurate depiction of the American position, it is not that of UNMOVIC. On February 14, for example, Blix's statement had said that searches had now been extensive, that cooperation was now good, and that the results to date have been consistent with Iraq's declarations.[70] This contradiction is consistent with Barton's view that by this stage, no evidence or lack of it could stop the allied march to war.

The intelligence estimates on Iraqi WMD were fundamentally inaccurate. However, the idea that innocent and open-minded governments were misled by poor intelligence into going to war inverts the truth. The invasion of Iraq was a government-led one, not an intelligence-led war. Governments already intent on war used intelligence that suited their preconceived views and ignored that which contradicted or questioned it. In Australia, as in the United States, and Britain, what is needed is not a new inquiry into the intelligence agencies, but one into the dynamics of a political stampede, of how such a huge sense of threat was manufactured from the flimsiest of evidence.

Notes

1 Patrick Weller, *Don't Tell the Prime Minister* (Melbourne, Scribe Publications, 2002).
2 David Marr and Marian Wilkinson, *Dark Victory* (Sydney, Allen & Unwin, 2003), pp. 259–60.
3 Ibid, p. 258
4 David McKnight, *Australia's Spies and their Secrets* (Sydney, Allen & Unwin, 1994).
5 David Marr, *The Ivanov Trail* (Sydney, Allen & Unwin, 1984).
6 Lance Collins and Warren Reed, *Plunging Point: Intelligence Failures, Cover-ups and Consequences* (Sydney, Fourth Estate, Harper Collins, 2005).
7 Phillip Flood, *Report of the Inquiry into Australian Intelligence Agencies* (Canberra, Commonwealth of Australia, 2004).
8 Andrew Wilkie, *Axis of Deceit* (Melbourne, Black Inc., 2004).
9 Flood Report, p. 15.
10 Garry Woodard, "Enigmatic Variations: The Development of National Intelligence Assessment in Australia," *Intelligence and National Security* Vol.16, No.2, Summer 2001.
11 Wilkie, *Axis of Deceit*, pp. 61, 72.
12 Rodney Tiffen, *Diplomatic Deceits: Government, Media and East Timor* (Sydney, University of New South Wales Press, 2001); Desmond Ball and Hamish McDonald, *Death in Balibo, Lies in Canberra* (Sydney, Allen & Unwin, 2000).
13 Collins and Reed, *Plunging Point*.
14 Alan Doig, James Pfiffner, Mark Phythian, and Rodney Tiffen, "Marching in Time: Alliance Politics, Synchrony and the Case for War in Iraq, 2002–2003," *Australian Journal of International Affairs* Vol.61, No.1, Feb. 2007, pp. 23–40.
15 Wilkie, *Axis of Deceit*, p. 128,
16 Howard TV address, March 20, 2003.

17 Interview on ABC radio program *PM*, September 9, 2002. See www.abc. net.au.
18 Geoffrey Barker. *Sexing It Up: Iraq, Intelligence and Australia* (Sydney, University of New South Wales Press, 2003), p. 32.
19 Parliamentary Joint Committee on ASIO, ASIS and DSD, *Intelligence on Iraq's Weapons of Mass Destruction* (Canberra, The Parliament of the Commonwealth of Australia, 2004, p. 90.
20 *The Australian*, 17 June 2002.
21 Parliamentary Joint Committee, p. 90.
22 Interview on ABC TV program *Lateline*, June 11, 2003.
23 Downer Statement to House of Representatives, May 13, 2003, www.aph. gov.au.
24 Rod Barton, *The Weapons Detective. The Inside Story of Australia's Top Weapons Inspector* (Melbourne, Black Inc., 2006), p. 233.
25 Wilkie, *Axis of Deceit*, pp. 110–11.
26 Parliamentary Joint Committee, p. 94.
27 Ibid, p. 93.
28 Peter Browne, "Managing the Economy of Truth," *New Matilda*, September 8, 2004, www.newmatilda.com.
29 Flood Report, pp. 22–8.
30 Wilkie, *Axis of Deceit*, p. 8.
31 Ibid, pp. 10, 66.
32 Barton, *Weapons Detective*, p. 169.
33 Ibid, pp. 60, 80.
34 Ibid, p. 44.
35 Mark Phythian, "Hutton and Scott: A Tale of Two Inquiries," *Parliamentary Affairs*, Vol. 58, No.1, 2005, pp. 124–37.
36 Flood Report, p. 19.
37 Parliamentary Joint Committee, pp. 80, 95.
38 Barton, *Weapons Detective*, pp. 194–5.
39 Ibid, p. 239.
40 Ibid, pp. 190–1.
41 Ibid, p. 201.
42 Ibid, pp. 203, 210, 225.
43 Ibid, p. 212.
44 Ibid, p. 231.
45 Ibid, p. 235.
46 Ibid, pp. 242–6.
47 Ibid, pp. 249–50
48 Ibid, pp. 256, 259.
49 Peter Browne "What Blix told Howard about WMDs," Australian Policy Online, August 19, 2004, www.apo.org.au.
50 Downer, Media release, December 20, 2002.
51 *The Australian* June 29, 2002.
52 Parliamentary Joint Committee, pp. 4f.

53 Ibid, p. 31.
54 Ibid, pp. 45–6.
55 Ibid, pp. 32, 31, 56.
56 Wilkie, *Axis of Deceit*, pp. 141–2.
57 Ibid, p. 57.
58 Parliamentary Joint Committee, p. 35.
59 Ibid, pp. 59, 60.
60 Wilkie, *Axis of Deceit*, p. 98.
61 Ibid, p. 59.
62 Ibid, p. 92.
63 Parliamentary Joint Committee, p. 92.
64 Wilkie, *Axis of Deceit*, pp. 92, 93.
65 Ibid, p. 96.
66 ABC interview, *PM*, September 9, 2002.
67 Downer Speech to Sydney Institute, February 17, 2003.
68 Wilkie, *Axis of Deceit*, p. 90.
69 Parliamentary Joint Committee, p. 35.
70 Ibid, p. 74.

7

The Iraq war and the management of American public opinion

John Mueller

In promoting and prosecuting its war against Iraq, the administration of George W. Bush sought to accomplish two tasks in the management of American public opinion. In the run-up to the war, it tried to rally the public to support its planned venture, and, during the war itself, it tried to maintain public backing for the war even as costs increased.

It failed in both of these endeavors. During the run-up, it was unable to increase enthusiasm for going to war, and during the war, despite continuing efforts to reverse the process, support eroded rather inexorably as American casualties accrued. Moreover, in the process the administration's whole policy approach—often labeled "the Bush Doctrine"—became severely undermined and is likely to be supplanted by an "Iraq Syndrome" that will be hostile to such ventures in the future.

Public opinion and the promotion of war

In its drive toward war with Iraq in 2002, the Bush administration was working from a position of some strength with the public. Hostility toward Saddam Hussein was generated at the time of the 1990–1 Gulf crisis and war following Iraq's August 1990 seizure of neighboring Kuwait, an episode that had been presided over by Bush's father, George H. W. Bush. Throughout, Saddam played the role of demon with consummate skill, and the public responded accordingly. Moreover, the antipathy did not diminish after the event was over. The war succeeded in liberating Kuwait, destroying the Iraqi army, and humiliating Saddam at remarkably low cost in American casualties. Yet, in its aftermath Americans increasingly expressed dissatisfaction because the venture had failed to remove Saddam from office.[1]

In addition, they continued to support a decade of severe economic sanctions on Saddam's regime, and they remained oblivious to reports that the sanctions were a necessary cause of hundreds of thousands of deaths in that country. For example, in 1996 it was put to Madeleine

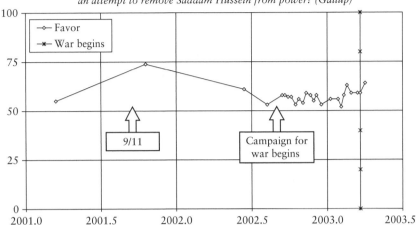

Would you favor or oppose invading Iraq with US ground troops in an attempt to remove Saddam Hussein from power? (Gallup)

Figure 7.1 Support for removing Saddam Hussein, 2001–3

Albright, then America's ambassador to the United Nations, on her country's most popular television news program, *60 Minutes*, that the sanctions had taken the lives half a million Iraqi children, and she was bluntly asked if the price was worth it. Without denying the numbers, Albright acknowledged that " this is a very hard choice," then firmly concluded, " we think the price is worth it." [2] This remarkable conclusion stirred no comment anywhere in the country's media, though it became famous in the Arab world.[3] Generally, politicians seem to have concluded, quite possibly correctly, that any voiced opposition to the sanctions would be politically detrimental since it would imply support for the demonic Saddam Hussein.[4]

In fact, throughout the decade after the Gulf war, polls document a fair degree of support for the use of military force to depose Saddam.[5] As Figure 7.1 documents, in early 2001 55 percent were still responding favorably to the idea of "invading Iraq with US ground troops in an attempt to remove Saddam Hussein from power."

However, despite this potential opening, politicians and others apparently still considered an invasion to be a nonstarter, and few, if any, advocated such a course at the time: there were public declarations and congressional appropriations to support opposition groups, but no one was really calling for a war to depose him. For example, defense department advisor Richard Perle, who would prove to be one of the most ardent proponents of war in 2003, published an article in 2000 that, while strongly advocating a policy hostile toward Saddam, recommended only protecting and assisting resistance movements within Iraq, not anything resembling an invasion by American troops.[6]

As the figure also discloses, this percentage leaped to nearly 75 percent in the wake of the September 11, 2001 terrorist attacks in the United States, a reaction that may have helped encourage the discussions that began at that time within the Bush administration about launching such a war. By January 2002 Bush publicly positioned Iraq prominently on his "axis of evil" hit list and announced that, unlike all of Iraq's neighbors except Israel, the United States had come to imagine that Saddam presented a "grave and growing danger."

However, despite such dramatic fulminations and despite the fact that polls found around half of the population professing to believe Saddam had been personally involved in the 9/11 attacks,[7] support for war against Iraq dwindled during the next several months to about where it had stood before 9/11.

A concentrated campaign to boost support for going to war began in August and September 2002 with speeches by Bush and Vice President Dick Cheney. As can be seen in Figure 7.1, the administration may conceivably have been able to halt further erosion of support, but, despite strenuous efforts, it was unable notably to increase support for going to war: from September 2002 to the launching of war in March 2003, attitudes did not change notably. There was something of a bump upwards to 63 percent at the time of Secretary of State Colin Powell's much-publicized speech at the United Nations on February 5, 2003, but this lift proved to be temporary. There is also an upward push in the last poll of the series, but that one was conducted as the war was beginning in mid-March and represents part of a "rally 'round the flag'" effect as troops were being sent into action. With those exceptions, approval for sending the troops never ranged more than 4 percentage points higher or lower that the 55 percent figure tallied when George W. Bush was taking office, nine months before 9/11.[8]

An interesting comparison can be made with the run-up to the 1991 war presided over by Bush's father. He, too, spent a great deal of time and effort seeking to boost support for sending the American military into action to force Iraq's forces from Kuwait. For the most part, however, during the entire course of the debate over war, there was little change in the degree to which popular opinion supported the idea of initiating a war in the Gulf. People did not become consistently more hawkish or dovish, more war eager or war averse, or more or less supportive of Bush or his policies. And their perceptions of the reasons behind involvement and the reasons for going to war apparently did not change very much either.[9]

Overall, then, neither Bush was able to swing public opinion toward war—though, conceivably, they were able to arrest a deterioration of support for war. This experience suggests there are rather distinct limits to the effectiveness of the bully pulpit.[10]

The president's ability to go to war

Nonetheless, obviously, each president did manage to get his war. But this was because, as president, each was able to order troops into action, not because of his ability to move the public to his point of view. Moreover, they were able to keep the issue brewing as an important one and they could unilaterally commit the country to a path that dramatically increased a sense of fatalism about war and perhaps convinced many that there was no honorable alternative to war. The lessons of the wars suggest, then, that a great deal lies in the president's ability to deploy troops and thus to commit the country's honor and destiny. With such moves he can make an issue important and convey a compelling sense of obligation as well as of entrapment and inevitability.

More generally, it does not appear that the president necessarily needs public support in advance to pull off a military venture.[11] The public generally seems to be willing go along (not that it has much choice), but it reserves the right to object if the cost of the war comes to outweigh its perceived value. Sometimes the public has apparently been quite supportive of going to war, as in World War II (after Pearl Harbor), in Korea (1950), in Vietnam (1965), in Panama (1989), in Somalia (1992–3), and in Afghanistan (2001). At other times, the public has been at best divided as in Lebanon (1958), Grenada (1983), Lebanon (1983), the Gulf war (1991), Haiti (1994), Bosnia (1995), Kosovo (1999), and the Iraq war (2003). In some cases, the ventures have been accomplished at acceptable cost as in World War II, Panama, Lebanon 1958, Grenada, the Gulf War, Haiti, Bosnia, and Kosovo. In others, support dropped as costs grew, as in Korea, Vietnam, and Iraq (and maybe, now, in Afghanistan). And in others, the public's dismay at rising costs was met by abrupt early withdrawal as in Lebanon in 1983 and in Somalia.

But the hope in all this for the president would be that if the venture appears to be worth the cost, the public will accept, even laud, it despite any prewar misgivings. This happened quite clearly in the case of the controversial Gulf war of 1991. Before the war polls found the public split about 50/50 on a question asking whether they preferred continued sanctions or military action. After the war, however, the percentage recalling that they had supported war over sanctions registered at 76 percent.[12]

The extraordinary partisan divide

In one respect there was a great—and rather unexpected—difference in public opinion between the run-ups to the 1991 and 2003 wars against Iraq. In each, Democrats were less likely to support the prospective wars than were Republicans, but what is surprising is that the partisan gap was *far* wider in the 2003 case than in the 1991 one even though the behavior of leading Democrats in Congress would suggest that the relationship should be the reverse. In the earlier war, Democratic leaders stood in strong opposition to going to war, and it was reasonable to expect that many ordinary Democrats would follow their lead. In the later war, by distinct contrast, the leaders mostly remained silent or were even generally supportive of the effort.[13] Yet ordinary Democrats, even though there were few cues being issued by congressional Democrats, departed far more fully from ordinary Republicans on this war.[14]

A truly satisfying explanation for this remarkable finding has yet to be established. There may be some explanation in the very substantial contempt many Democrats harbored for George W. Bush stemming from the controversial 2000 election.[15] However, the gap between Democrats and Republicans on approval of the president greatly diminished for a while after the 9/11 terrorist events, and widened only later.[16] What may have been peculiar to the second war was that George W. Bush was exceptional in that he was much more able to retain the support of the Republicans than was his father. Since it takes *two* to make a gap, some of the differences between the two wars may stem from this.

Public opinion and the prosecution of war

Once the war against Iraq began in March 2003, there was a rally round the flag effect as opinion swung to support the country's military efforts, something that was rather predictable—and predicted. The partisan gap also closed somewhat for a while.[17]

At the outset, the war looked like it might resemble the Gulf war of 1991 as the Iraqi military performed in about the same manner as it had previously: basically, it disintegrated under the onslaught and seems to have lacked any semblance of a coherent strategy of resistance.[18] Indeed, total battle deaths for the invading American and British forces during this period war were well under 150—even lower than had been borne in the Gulf war of 1991. And, as Figure 7.2 demonstrates, public support for the venture during this period remained high and even

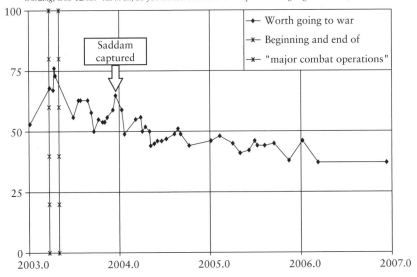

All in all, do you think it was worth going to war in Iraq, or not?
Wording prior to 6/03: "All in all, do you think the current situation in Iraq is worth going to war over, or not?"
Wording, 6/03-12/03: "All in all, do you think the situation in Iraq was worth going to war over, or not?"

Figure 7.2 Value of going to war in Iraq, 2003–6

increased—something that had also happened during the brief war of 1991.[19]

The two wars quickly ceased to resemble each other militarily, however. Once Iraq was summarily expelled from Kuwait in 1991, the Kuwaiti regime came back from exile and took over, and American troops could go home to parade victoriously in American cities. No such pleasant fate awaited their successors in 2003: after President Bush prominently and triumphally declared "major combat operations" to be over on May 1 of that year, the conquerors found they had to hang around and fight in an attempt to build a viable national government out of the rubble that remained after Saddam, economic sanctions, and the war had taken their toll. It had been hoped that the Iraqis would greet the conquerors by dancing happily in the streets and somehow coordinate themselves into a coherent, and appreciative, government. But, although many were glad to see Saddam's tyranny ended, the invaders often found the population resentful and humiliated, rather than gleeful or grateful. Moreover, bringing order to the situation was vastly complicated by the fact that the government-toppling invasion had effectively (and instantly) created a failed state which permitted widespread criminality and looting. In addition some people—including apparently some foreign terrorists drawn opportunistically to the area—were dedicated to sabotaging the victors' peace and to killing the policing forces.[20] Eventually, communal violence and gang warfare were added to the destructive mix.

The decline of support

American troops have been sent into harm's way many times since 1945, but in only three of those ventures—in Korea, Vietnam, and now Iraq— have they been drawn into sustained ground combat and suffered more than 300 deaths in action (though Afghanistan may soon join this list).

Data from questions asking people if the war was a "mistake" allow for a fairly direct comparison of public support for the wars as in Figures 7.3 and 7.4. All three military ventures were quite substantially supported by the public as the troops were sent in and, in all cases, support decreased as casualties—whether of draftees, volunteers, or reservists— were suffered. The decline was steeper in the early stages of the war as reluctant approvers were rather quickly alienated, and the erosion slowed as support progressively became reduced to the harder-core—the pattern is essentially logarithmic.[21] The process is almost uncannily illustrated in Figure 7.5. In addition, Figure 7.6 shows the dramatic dropoff in acceptance of casualties in the Iraq war after the end of "major combat operations" and the slower erosion thereafter as additional casualties continued to be suffered.

There is one important difference between the wars, however: the data suggest the public places a far lower value on the stakes in Iraq than it did in the earlier wars. As Figure 7.4 demonstrates, after two years of war, support for war on this measure had slumped to around 50 percent. However at that point around 20,000 Americans had been killed in Vietnam and Korea, but only about 1,500 in Iraq. Korea and Vietnam were seen, initially at least, to be important and necessary components in dealing with international Communism. In Vietnam, for example, there was widespread agreement with the 1965 views of future war critic David Halberstam that Vietnam was a "strategic country in a key area . . . perhaps one of only five or six nations in the world that is truly vital to US interests." [22] Although Americans eventually soured on the war, it took far more American deaths to accomplish this than in Iraq. That is, casualty for casualty, support dropped off far more quickly in the Iraq war than in either of the earlier two wars.[23]

Contributing to this difference in casualty tolerance may be the fact that the main threats Iraq was deemed to present to the United States when troops were sent in—fears of its "weapons of mass destruction" and of its connections to international terrorism—quickly became, to say

In view of the developments since we first sent our troops to Iraq, do you think the
United States made a mistake in sending troops to Iraq, or not?

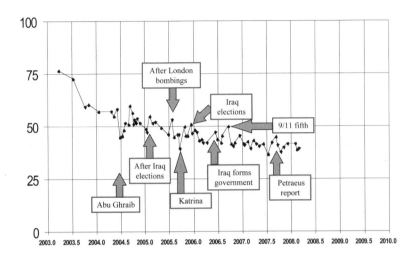

Figure 7.3 Opinion on whether the Iraq war was a mistake, 2003–8 (*percent*
supporting of those with opinion)

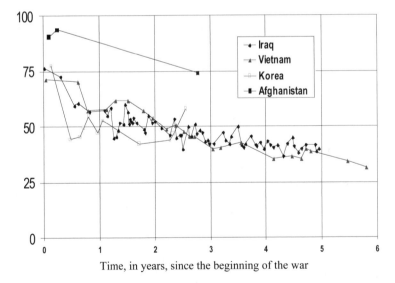

Time, in years, since the beginning of the war

Figure 7.4 Support for wars in Korea, Vietnam, Iraq, and Afghanistan

Suppose President George W. Bush decides to order US troops into a ground attack against Iraqi forces. Would you favor or oppose that decision? (If support) The number of possible casualties in a ground war with Iraq had been estimated at between 100 American soldiers, if the Iraqi military offers little resistance, to as many at 5,000 American soldiers if the Iraqi Republican Guard fight an effective urban defense. With this in mind, would you still support sending ground troops to fight in Iraq if it meant that up to 100 American soldiers would be killed in battle, or not? (If yes) Would you still support sending ground troops if up to 500 American soldiers were killed in battle or not? (If yes) Up to 1,000? (If yes) Up to 5,000? (If yes) Would you say you would support sending ground troops to fight in Iraq no matter what it cost in American casualties, or not? (*Los Angeles Times*)

December 15–17, 2002: before the war
- 35% Oppose war
- 7% Don't know if favor or oppose
- 58% Favor war

- 49% Still favor if any killed
- 46% Still favor if 100 killed
- 43% Still favor if 500 killed
- 37% Still favor if 1,000 killed
- 32% Still favor if 5,000 killed
- 24% Still favor if more than 5,000 but not unlimited
- 17% Still favor no matter the cost in American casualties
- 6% Don't know about casualties

Do you favor or oppose the US war in Iraq? (*Washingon Post*)
December 15–17, 2006: nearly 3,000 US fatalities
- 31% Favor war
- 67% Oppose war
- 8% Unsure

Figure 7.5 Casualty tolerance in Iraq

the least, severely undermined. With those justifications gone, Iraq became something of a humanitarian venture, and, as Francis Fukuyama has put it, a prewar request to spend "several hundred billion dollars and several thousand American lives in order to bring democracy to . . . Iraq" would "have been laughed out of court." [24] However, it should be noted that, applying consistent Cold War standards, the stakes in Korea and Vietnam also declined during the course of the wars there. In the latter

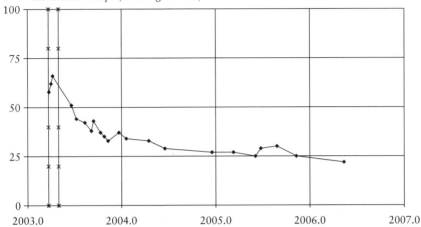

Again thinking about the goals versus the costs of the war, so far in your opinion has there been an acceptable or unacceptable number of US casualties in Iraq? (Washington Post)

Figure 7.6 Opinion on acceptance US casualties, 2003–6 (*percent acceptable*)

war, for example, early fears that Indonesia might fall to Communism unless a stand was taken in Vietnam, evaporated with an antiCommunist coup there after US troops had been committed to Vietnam.[25]

Actually, given the demise of the main reasons for going to war and the subsequent unexpectedly high American casualty levels, it is impressive that support for the war in Iraq remained as high as it did. This may reflect the fact that many people still connect the effort there to the campaign—or " war"—against terror, an enterprise that continues to enjoy huge support, as did World War II or (despite Vietnam) the Cold War. In addition, the toppling of Saddam remains a singular accomplishment, one, as noted earlier, that the American people had been spoiling for at least since 1990. And, despite continual assertions to the contrary from all sides, a fair number of Americans continued to see a connection between Saddam and the events of 9/11: in September 2006, two-and-a-half years into the Iraq war, 38 percent still remained convinced that Saddam Hussein was personally involved in the attacks.[26] However, as Figure 7.7 suggests, the appeal of that result declined as costs grew.

When one shifts from questions about whether the war was a "mistake" or "worth it" to ones about whether the US should get out, much the same pattern holds across Korea, Vietnam, and Iraq: relatively steep declines in support for continuing the war in the early stages, slower erosion later. However, judging how many people want to get out or stay the course at any point in time is essentially impossible because so much

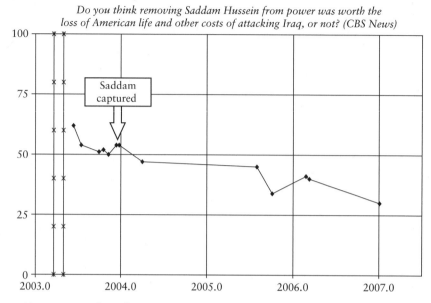

Figure 7.7 Value of removing Saddam Hussein, 2003–7 (*percent worth it*)

depends on the question wording. For example, there is far more support for "gradual withdrawal" or "begin to withdraw" than for "withdraw" or "immediate withdrawal." Thus in June 2005, the *Washington Post* found 58 percent for staying and 41 percent for withdrawing (much the same as in October 2003) when the options were posed this way: "Do you think the United States should keep its military forces in Iraq until civil order is restored there, even if that means continued US military casualties, or, do you think the United States should withdraw its military forces from Iraq in order to avoid further US military casualties, even if that means civil order is not restored there?" But in the same month, the Harris poll tallied only 33 percent for staying and 63 percent for withdrawing (much changed from October 2003) when it asked, "Do you favor keeping a large number of US troops in Iraq until there is a stable government there or bringing most of our troops home in the next year?" All questions, however, have logged substantial increases in withdrawal sentiment over the course of the war.[27]

Insofar as the erosion of support, however measured, is related to casualties, the phenomenon is likely caused by the simple fact of cumulating combat deaths. Pictures of dead bodies, body bags, or flag-draped coffins are not necessary. Somehow, the notion that support declines with casualties became expressed as "support drops when they start seeing the body bags," and this metaphor apparently led, in turn, to the naive notion that for people to become disaffected they actually need to *see* the body bags. In consequence, perhaps, the military in the Iraq War enterprisingly tried to keep people from viewing pictures of body bags and flag-draped coffins presumably in the futile, bizarre hope that this will somehow arrest the decline of support.[28]

The decline in support seems to take place whether there is an active anti-war protest movement or not. There has been little so far for the Iraq war (except within the ranks of the Democratic Party), but there was also little during the Korean war and support for that venture still eroded in very much the same way as in Vietnam where anti-war protest was common. In fact, since the Vietnam protest movement became so associated with anti-American values and activities, it may ultimately have been somewhat counterproductive in its goal of reducing support for the war.[29]

Support can also erode when war opponents simply voice discontent but are unable to come up with specific alternatives. Dwight Eisenhower never seemed to have much of a plan for getting out of the Korean war—though he did say that, if elected, he would visit the place—but discontent with the war still worked well for him in the 1952 election. Richard Nixon's proposals in the 1968 election for fixing the Vietnam mess were distinctly unspecific, though there were some suggestions from time to time that he had a "secret plan."

Politically, the wars seem to have hurt the war-instituting political party not because the opposition comes up with a coherent clashing vision (George McGovern tried that unsuccessfully against Nixon in 1972), but because discontent over the war vaguely, but damagingly, translates into discontent over the capacities of the people in charge and causes people to yearn for a change. Britain's Tony Blair, presiding over a robust economy and a decidedly unpopular war, saw his margin cut very substantially in elections in 2005. In like manner, George W. Bush, with high marks on terrorism, but low ones on the war, would have done considerably better if the war hadn't been there in his reelection campaign of 2004. Examining polls from 1952 to the present, Gary Jacobson reports that the partisan division in the 2004 election was the most intense in the period: almost all the Republicans voted for Bush and almost all the Democrats for John Kerry.[30] Without the war, Bush would have still held the Republicans and would doubtless have done better with Democrats as well as with Independents whose opinion on the war more nearly traces Democratic patterns than Republican ones.[31] Then, in the congressional elections of 2006, Bush's party took a shellacking that seems to have come about substantially because of discontent over the war in Iraq.

Failures of efforts to reverse the decline

The ability of a president to reverse the erosion of support for an increasingly unpopular war seems limited. George W. Bush, like Vietnam's Lyndon Johnson before him, sought many times to turn things around by making speeches explaining what the war is about, urging patience, and repeatedly asserting that progress is being made. He also proved to be particularly adept at hitching the war, often by implication, to the traumatic 9/11 experience. This effort was seen in particular in a set of speeches at the end of 2005 in which Bush repeatedly applied the word, "victory." In one speech, surrounded by signs that said, "Plan for Victory," he used the word fifteen times, twice with the modifier, "complete," as: "Against this adversary there is only one effective response: We will never back down, we will never give in, and we will never accept anything less than complete victory."[32] As with his very considerable efforts to sell his Social Security plan earlier that year (or like Woodrow Wilson's campaign to sell the League of Nations 65 years earlier), this experience suggests once again that the efficacy of the bully pulpit has often been much overrated.[33]

But if the impact of Washington rhetoric is limited at least in situations like this, favorable happenings in the war can boost support from time to time. Figures 7.2 and 7.3 supply evidence for the war in Iraq. There were notable upward shifts in support when Saddam was captured at the end of 2003[34] and when elections were held. The problem for the president and his policy is that these rises proved to be temporary, and support soon relapsed to where it had been before and then continued its generally downward course. The happy events proved more nearly to be bumps on the road than permanent shifts. The same can be seen for negative experiences: a drop in support at the time of the Abu Graib disclosures was eventually mostly reversed. Episodes in 2005 further illustrate the process. Support for the war dropped at the time of Hurricane Katrina as Americans were led to wonder about the nation's priorities, but this was more than reversed by the successful Iraq elections of November 15. Within days, however, war support dropped again to a level slightly lower than was registered before either event took place. In all, the phenomenon suggests that a significant, lasting reversal of the erosion of support is unlikely. Those who now consider the costs of the war already to be too high will probably not permanently reverse their opinion very much even with good news.

Partisan differences regarding Bush and the Iraq war, already seen in the run-up to the war, continued to be incredibly deep as the war progressed. Jacobson has documented that the partisan divide on Iraq is considerably greater than on any military action over the last halfcentury and that the partisan split on presidential approval ratings, despite a major narrowing after 9/11 and at the time of the height of the war in Afghanistan, is greater than for any president over the period—wider than for Reagan, for Clinton, for Nixon.[35] To give an rather extreme example, by the time of the 2004 election, over 80 percent of well-informed Republicans supported the Iraq war while only about 3 percent of well-informed Democrats did so.[36] This means that Bush could scarcely look for increased Republican support because he already had practically all of it, while the Democrats were unlikely to budge much. There might be some hope for him among Independents, but, as noted, their war support patterns more nearly tracked those of the almost completely disaffected Democrats than those of the amazingly loyal Republicans.

In all this, what chiefly matters for public opinion is American losses, not those of the people defended. By some estimates, the number of Iraqis who have died in the upheaval following the invasion has reached well into six figures. As noted earlier, sanctions on Iraq were probably a necessary cause of the deaths of an equally great number of Iraqis, mostly of children, yet little concern is voiced about this. The only cumulative body count that seems to matter, and is routinely reported, is the American one.

This phenomenon is nothing new. The official estimate at the end of the 1991 Gulf war (though later determined almost certainly to be much too high) was that 100,000 Iraqis had been killed in that war.[37] This unpleasant fact scarcely dampened enthusiasm at the victory and "welcome home" parades for returning troops, however. And, although there was considerable support for the wars in Korea and Vietnam, polls make it clear that this was because people saw them as vital to confront the Communist threat: the defense of the South Koreans or the South Vietnamese per se was never perceived to be as remotely important a war goal.[38]

Some scholars have argued that support for war is determined by the prospects for success rather than by casualties—that Americans are "defeat phobic" rather than "casualty phobic." They proclaim it a "myth" that "Americans are casualty shy" and attempt to demonstrate that "a majority of the American people will accept combat deaths—so long as the mission has the potential to be successful." To support their case, they prominently employ results from a poll they conducted indicating that, contra Fukuyama, Americans would on average be entirely willing on average to accept 6,861 battle deaths to "stabilize a democratic government in Congo" and 29,853 battle deaths "to prevent Iraq from obtaining weapons of mass destruction."[39] Essentially, the argument seems to hold that American don't really care how many casualties they suffer so long as their side comes out the winner. In a later book they acknowledge in a footnote that these numbers were "overly susceptible to misinterpretation," and they then rejigger their analysis of the same poll question and essentially conclude that the original figure was some 6,800 percent too high.[40] The damage, however, has already been done: the op-ed had been widely cited and applied (and misinterpreted), particularly in military publications.[41]

In general, it is difficult to separate the effect of casualties from the prospects of success because casualty rates are generally part of what one uses to determine whether the war is going well or not. Where there is a disconnect, however, casualties seem to dominate the consideration. Thus the Tet offensive in Vietnam greatly heightened the public sense that the war was going badly even though American deaths did not surge; yet support for the war (contrary to common assumption) did not drop precipitously in response to the heightened frustration, but rather simply continued to erode tracing casualty patterns (the Tet offensive occurred at the two and a half year mark in Figure 7.4). Similarly, in the spring of 2005 there was a considerable increase in the sentiment that the war in Iraq was going badly or that the United States was becoming bogged down, yet support for the war declined only modestly over the period, as can be seen in Figures 7.2 and 7.3.

There never were periods of continuous good news in the wars in Korea or Vietnam, but should that happen in Iraq—including, in particular, a decline in American casualty rates—it would be more likely to cause the erosion in support to slow or even cease rather than to trigger a large upsurge in support. For support to rise notably, many of those disaffected by the war would need to reverse their position, and that seems rather unlikely: where polls seek to tap intensity of feeling, something over 80 percent of those opposed to the war say they "strongly" feel that way.[42] If you purchase a car for twice what it is worth, you are likely still to consider the deal to have been a mistake even if you come to like the car.

Moreover, it is difficult to see what a spate of continuous good news would look like. Put directly if perhaps a bit confusingly, it may well be that Iraq simply can't not be a mess. The invading forces were too small to establish order and some of the early administrative policies proved misguided (which, however, didn't prevent those chiefly responsible from later being awarded the Medal of Freedom). In effect the invaders almost instantly created a failed state, and clambering out of that condition is going to be difficult in the best of circumstances. If the worst violence diminishes, and therefore Iraq ceases to be quite so much of a *bloody* mess, there is still likely to be plenty of official and unofficial corruption, sporadic vigilantism, police misconduct, militia feuding, political back-stabbing, economic travail, regional separatism, government incompetence, rampant criminality, religious conflict, and posturing by political entrepreneurs who attract votes and support by spouting anti-American and anti-Israeli rhetoric. Under those circumstances Iraq may attract less attention, but the American venture there is unlikely to be seen as a great victory by those who now oppose it.

The politics of debacle

In Iraq, as in Vietnam, Britain and the United States face an armed opposition that is dedicated, resourceful, capable of replenishing its ranks after losses, and seemingly determined to fight forever if necessary. In Vietnam, the hope was that after suffering enough punishment the enemy would reach its "breaking point" and then either fade away or seek accommodation. Great punishment was inflicted, but the enemy never broke; instead it was the United States that faded away after signing a face-saving agreement.[43] Whether the insurgency in Iraq has the same determination and fortitude is yet to be seen, but the signs thus far are not very encouraging.

In the meantime, the policy of Vietnamization has been updated and applied to Iraq—Iraqization, some are calling it, if possible an even uglier word. Thus, strenuous efforts are being made, as in Vietnam, to fabricate a reasonably viable local government, police, and military that can take over the fight, allowing the American and British forces judiciously to withdraw. In Vietnam, of course, that government and military collapsed to the Communists a couple of years after the race-saving agreement. But the enemy they were up against possessed a massive military force backed by, indeed centered in, North Vietnam. The insurgency in Iraq, albeit deadly and dedicated, represents a much smaller and less well organized force and would likely have far more difficulty taking over the country. Moreover, many of the insurgents are probably fighting simply to get the United States out of the country and can be expected to cease doing so when the Americans leave—as happened to some of the insurgents when the Soviets left Afghanistan and when the Israelis left southern Lebanon. To that degree, the insurgency might become more manageable without the American presence there though there could still be a determined effort by at least some of the rebels to go after the remaining, American-fabricated government consisting, in their eyes, of Quislings and collaborators.

It was widely feared that there would be a bloodbath in Vietnam if that country fell to Communism. And indeed upon taking control, the Communists executed tens of thousands, sent hundreds of thousands to "reeducation camps" for long periods, and mismanaged the economy so badly that hundreds of thousands desperately fled the country, often in unseaworthy boats. And what happened in neighboring Cambodia when the Communists took over makes even the word "bloodbath" seem an understatement.[44]

There are understandable and somewhat comparable concerns that Iraq could devolve into full scale civil war after the Americans leave, particularly as conditions considerably worsened in 2006. Much to be feared would be what happened in Afghanistan among those combatants who remained in the fray after the Soviets left in 1989—a cruel, scrabbling conflict between warlord groups, many of them essentially criminal. Images of the lengthy and incredibly chaotic civil war in Lebanon also come to mind.

It is often also argued—including by President Bush—that a precipitous exit from Iraq would be exhilarating to international terrorists who would see it as an even greater victory than the one over the Soviets in Afghanistan. Osama bin Laden's theory that the Americans can be defeated, or at least productively inconvenienced, by inflicting comparatively small, but continuously draining, casualties on them will achieve apparent confirmation. Thus, a venture designed and sold in part as a blow against international terrorists will end up emboldening and energizing them.

The dilemma is that almost any exit from Iraq will have this effect. People like bin Laden believe that America invaded Iraq as part of its plan to control the oil in the Middle East and to dominate the world, a perspective, polls suggest, that enjoys huge popularity in Muslim countries as well as in such nonMuslim ones as France and Germany.[45] But the United States does not intend to do that (at least not in the direct sense bin Laden and others doubtless consider to be its goal), nor does it seek to destroy Islam as many others around the world also bitterly assert. Thus just about any kind of American withdrawal will be seen by such people as a victory for the harassing terrorist insurgents, who, they will believe, are due primary credit for forcing the United States to leave without accomplishing what they take to be its key objectives.

In some important respects, therefore, Iraq is shaping up to be a major debacle, rather like Vietnam. However, on the brighter side for the administration, unless failure in Iraq leads directly to terrorism in the United States, history suggests that the American people are quite capable of taking debacle in their stride—they have not proven to be terribly "defeat phobic." They supported the decision to withdraw policing US troops from Lebanon in 1984 after a terrorist bomb killed 241 of them in the civil war there, and the man who presided over the debacle, Ronald Reagan, readily won reelection a few months later. Something similar happened to Bill Clinton when he withdrew policing troops from Somalia in 1994: by the time the next election rolled around, people had largely forgotten the whole episode.

Most remarkable, and relevant, in this regard, the utter collapse of the American position in Vietnam in 1975 as the Communists won was actually used by the man who presided over it, Gerald Ford, as a point in his favor in his reelection campaign the next year. When he came into office, he proudly pointed out, "we were still deeply involved in the problems of Vietnam;" but now "we are at peace. Not a single young American is fighting or dying on any foreign soil."[46] His challenger, Jimmy Carter, apparently did not think it good politics to point out the essential absurdity of Ford's declaration. Moreover, even if disaster follows in Iraq after American withdrawal—as it did in Lebanon, Somalia, and Vietnam—the people dying will be Iraqis, not Americans. And the deaths of foreigners, as noted earlier, are not what move the public.[47]

Public opinion and the aftermath of war: the Iraq Syndrome

After Vietnam, there was a strong desire—usually called the Vietnam Syndrome—not to do that again, and something similar happened after Korea. And, in fact, there never were other Koreas or Vietnams for the United States during the Cold War. Due to fears of "another Vietnam," the administration was kept by Congress even from rather modest antiCommunist ventures in Africa and, to a lesser extent in Latin America (though there was bipartisan support for aiding the antiSoviet insurgency in Afghanistan, a venture, however, that of course did not involve sending American troops). Meanwhile, Communist genocide in Cambodia after the Vietnam war was studiously ignored in part from fears that paying attention might dangerously lead to the conclusion that American troops should be sent over to rectify the disaster: over most of its course the three network news telecasts devoted a total of twenty-nine minutes to the cataclysm in which millions died.[48]

No matter how the war there comes out, a rather comparable "Iraq Syndrome" seems likely. It probably doesn't matter much how the Bush administration is able to spin the Iraq experience. If a presumed "victory"—or non-defeat—is deemed to have been too costly, any desire for a repeat performance will be, to say the least, attenuated. Thus, a poll in relatively war-approving Alabama in 2005 asked whether America should be prepared to send troops back to establish order if full scale civil war erupted in Iraq after a US withdrawal. Only a third of the respondents favored doing so.[49]

Among the casualties of the Iraq Syndrome for American policy could be the Bush Doctrine, empire, unilateralism, pre-emption (actually, preventive war), last-remaining-superpowerdom, and indispensable-nationhood. Indeed, as the world's last remaining superpower found itself incapable even of supplying Baghdad with reliable electricity, these once-fashionable (and sometimes self-infatuated) concepts are already picking up a patina of quaintness.

Specifically, there will probably be notable increases in skepticism over the notion that the United States should take unilateral military action to correct situations or regimes it considers reprehensible but which present no very direct and very immediate threat to it. As part of this, there will also be very substantial suspicions about any administration claims that such entities do present a threat. In particular, as the Democrats (and quite a few Republicans) strongly opposed other potential Vietnams after the American debacle there, they are hugely likely (as they emerge after the 2006 election out of their self-imposed cage) severely to question any other Iraqs proposed by the administration unless there is severe, unambiguous provocation.

Also declining in force will be the notions that the United States can and should apply its military supremacy to straighten out lesser peoples even if a result of this policy becomes the establishment of something of a new American " empire," that the United States should and can forcibly bring democracy to nations not now so blessed, that it has the duty to bring order to the Middle East, that it should embrace a mission to rid the world of evil, that international cooperation is of only very limited value, and that Europeans and other well-meaning foreigners are naive and decadent wimps. The country may also become more inclined to seek international cooperation, sometimes possibly even showing perceptible signs of humility.

At the end of the Vietnam experience, there was a substantial negative impact on the armed forces of the United States—some people even call it disintegration. Although this seems unlikely to be repeated in the wake of the war in Iraq, there may well be new pressures to reduce the military and to question whether having by far the largest defense budget in the world mostly brings benefits and, in fact, is all that necessary. In addition there will be a tendency (already partly acted upon) to withdraw American troops from overseas and perhaps to putting the frustrating and endless Israel–Palestine turmoil on a back burner.

The chief beneficiaries of the Iraq war are likely to be the rogue/ axis-of-evil (or devil du jour) states of Iran and North Korea. In part because of the American military and financial overextension in Iraq (and Afghanistan), the likelihood of any coherent application of military action or even of focused military threat against these two unpleasant entities substantially diminished, as it has against what at one time seemed to be the next targets: Syria especially, as well as Libya, Saudi Arabia, Egypt, and Lebanon.[50] Accordingly, all such entities have the greatest incentive to make the American experience in Iraq as miserable as possible.

Evidence of the Iraq Syndrome is already emerging. When North Korea abruptly declared in February 2005 that it now actually possessed nuclear weapons, the announcement was officially characterized as "unfortunate" and as "rhetoric we've heard before."[51] Iran has been notable defiant, and its new elected president has actually had the temerity to suggest—surely, the unkindest cut—that he does not consider the United States to be the least bit indispensable.

Notes

1 John Mueller, *Policy and Opinion in the Gulf War* (Chicago, IL: University of Chicago Press, 1994), pp. 88–9.

2 "Punishing Saddam; Sanctions Against Iraq Not Hurting Leaders of the Country, But the Children are Suffering and Dying," *60 Minutes*, CBS Television, May 12, 1996.

3 Andrew Cockburn and Patrick Cockburn, *Out of the Ashes: The Resurrection of Saddam Hussein* (New York: HarperCollins, 1999), p. 263. On this issue more broadly, see John Mueller and Karl Mueller, "The Methodology of Mass Destruction: Assessing Threats in the New World Order," in *Preventing the Use of Weapons of Mass Destruction*, ed. Eric Herring (London: Frank Cass, 2000), pp. 163–87; also in *Journal of Strategic Studies* 23:1 (March 2000).

4 This is particularly impressive because Americans did not blame the people of Iraq—the chief victims of the sanctions—for that country's actions: even at the height of the Gulf war, fully 60 percent said they held the Iraqi people to be *innocent* of *any blame* for their leader's policies. Mueller, *Policy and Opinion*, p. 316.

5 Eric V. Larson and Bodgan Savych, *American Public Support for US Military Operations from Mogadishu to Baghdad* (Santa Monica, CA: RAND Corporation, 2005), pp. 132–8.

6 Richard N. Perle, "Iraq: Saddam Unbound," in *Present Dangers: Crisis and Opportunity in American Foreign and Defense Policy*, ed. Robert Kagan and William Kristol (San Francisco, CA: Encounter Books, 2000), pp. 108–9.

7 Gary C. Jacobson, *A Divider, Not a Uniter: George W. Bush and the American People* (New York: Pearson Longman, 2007), p. 139.

8 For similar data using a wide variety of questions, see Jacobson, *A Divider*, pp. 97, 109. See also Ole R. Holsti, *Public Opinion and American Foreign*

Policy, revised edition (Ann Arbor, MI: University of Michigan Press, 2004, p. 278. By contrast, see Chaim Kaufmann, "Threat Inflation and the Failure of the Marketplace of Ideas: The Selling of the Iraq War," *International Security* 29:1 (Summer 2004), pp. 30–2.

9 Mueller, *Policy and Opinion*, ch. 2.

10 See also George C. Edwards III, *On Deaf Ears: The Limits of the Bully Pulpit* (New Haven, CT: Yale University Press, 2003).

11 See also John Mueller, " Public Support for Military Ventures Abroad," in *The Real Lessons of the Vietnam War: Reflections TwentyFive Years After the Fall of Saigon*, ed. John Norton Moore and Robert F. Turner (Durham, NC: Carolina Academic Press, 2002), pp. 187–9.

12 Mueller, *Policy and Opinion*, pp. 87, 229.

13 The Democrats presumably were more or less expecting a repeat of 1991: Bush would get his war, it would generally be a success, and most American troops would be withdrawn in a few months. Best, then, to be on board for the war and hope, as in 1992, that the brief, successful war would become a distant memory by the time of the next election a year and a half later.

14 Jacobson, *A Divider*, pp. 133, 136.

15 Ibid, pp. 60–7.

16 Ibid, pp. 5, 7.

17 Ibid, p. 5.

18 A reporter's observation from the later war could hold as well for the earlier one: "The battlefields I walked over revealed signs of panicky flight: Iraqi gas masks and uniforms abandoned; armored vehicles left in revetments where they could not see advancing US armor, much less shoot at it; blanket rolls left out in the open. I searched for bodies and bloodstains but saw neither on battlefields where Iraqi vehicles hit by Marines were still smoking. Defenders must have run before Marine fire reached them. Iraqi officers deserted their men. . .and this abandonment almost certainly triggered full flight by all ranks." George C. Wilson, "Why Didn't Saddam Defend His Country?," *National Journal*, April 19, 2003, p. 1222. For similar observations in the earlier war, see John Mueller, "The Perfect Enemy: Assessing the Gulf War," *Security Studies* 5:1 (Autumn 1995), pp. 77–117.

19 Mueller, *Policy and Opinion*, pp. 70–1, 77–8.

20 Something that was predictable, and predicted: John Mueller, "Suicide Watch," *Reason*, January 2003, p. 45.

21 John Mueller, *War, Presidents and Public Opinion* (New York: Wiley, 1973), pp. 59–62.

22 David Halberstam, *The Making of a Quagmire* (New York: Random House, 1965), p. 319.

23 The bump upward in support for the Korean war in early 1953 (at the two-and-a-half year mark in Figure 7.6) was apparently based on wishful thinking as Dwight Eisenhower was elected president and took office. Other related data document a decline again over the course of 1953 to the end of the war: Mueller, *War, Presidents and Public Opinion*, pp. 44–52.

24 Francis Fukuyama, "America's Parties and Their Foreign Policy Masquerade," *Financial Times*, March 8, 2005, p. 21.

25 John Mueller, *Retreat from Doomsday: The Obsolescence of Major War* (New York: Basic Books, 1989), pp. 177–8. Robert J. McMahon, *The Limits of Empire: The United States in Southeast Asia Since World War II* (New York: Columbia University Press, 1999), pp. 119–24.

26 ABC polls under "Iraq" at pollingreport.com.

27 Data at pollingreport.com.

28 Actually, whatever its effect on war support, the best remembered pictorial display during Vietnam was not of coffins or body bags at all. Rather, it was the array in the June 27, 1969 issue of *Life Magazine* of unstaged shots of the 242 young men who had been killed in one week in the war, each smiling or staring awkwardly into the camera not long before their lives were extinguished.

29 Mueller, *War, Presidents and Public Opinion*, pp. 164–5.

30 Jacobson, *A Divider*, pp. 189–90.

31 Ibid, pp. 132, 136.

32 On this development, see Scott Shane, "Bush's Speech on Iraq Echoes Analyst's Voice," *New York Times*, December 4, 2005, p. 1. Bush's speech is at www.cnn.com/2005/POLITICS/11/30/bush.transcript1/index.html.

33 On Bush's ineffective Social Security sales job, see Jacobson, *A Divider*, pp. 206–18.

34 This is seen only in Figure 7.2. The question in Figure 7.4 was not asked at appropriate times to capture the uptick.

35 Jacobson, *A Divider*, p. 7. The gap appears to have been great as well during the Great Depression over the extremely controversial president of the time, Franklin Roosevelt. Three polls conducted in early 1941 found that between 90 and 97 percent of Democrats said they would vote for him as against only 33 to 45 percent of Republicans, generating a gap that approaches, but that still does not reach that obtained by G. W. Bush: Hadley Cantril and Mildred Strunk, *Public Opinion 1935–1946* (Princeton, NJ: Princeton University Press, 1951), p. 758.

36 Jacobson, *A Divider*, pp. 177–8. The group consists of the 8 percent of the sample that got four out of four political identification questions right.

37 The estimate appears to have been too high by a factor of at least 10: Mueller, "Perfect Enemy," pp. 87–95.

38 Mueller, *War, Presidents and Public Opinion*, pp. 44, 48–49, 58, 100–1.

39 Peter D. Feaver and Christopher Gelpi, "Casualty Aversion; How Many Deaths Are Acceptable? A Surprising Answer," *Washington Post*, November 7, 1999, p. B3.

40 Peter D. Feaver and Christopher Gelpi, *Choosing Your Battles: American Civil–Military Relations and the Use of Force* (Princeton, NJ: Princeton University Press, 2004), p. 109n.

41 In *Choosing Your Battles*, Feaver and Gelpi repeatedly declare that "the public is defeat phobic, not casualty phobic." However, their analysis actually

concludes not that the "the public" is defeat phobic, but only some 20 percent of it (p. 145). In their view, this minority group is particularly sensitive to seeming advances or setbacks in the war. My caution is simply to add any such shifts tend to prove temporary when additional American casualties are suffered. The Feaver approach seems to have been at the back of Bush's failed effort to jigger support for his war in Iraq in late 2005: see Shane, "Bush's Speech."

42 Washington Post polls in pollingreport.com.

43 John Mueller, "The Search for the 'Breaking Point' in Vietnam: the Statistics of a Deadly Quarrel," *International Studies Quarterly* 24:4 (December 1980), pp. 497–519.

44 Mueller, *Retreat from Doomsday*, pp. 188–91.

45 Pew Global Attitudes Project, "A Year After Iraq War: Mistrust of America in Europe Ever Higher, Muslim Anger Persists," March 16, 2004.

46 Kraus, Sidney, *The Great Debates: Carter vs. Ford, 1976* (Bloomington, IN: Indiana University Press, 1979), pp. 538–9.

47 In one important respect, withdrawal from Vietnam was much more difficult politically than it would be from Iraq. North Vietnam held some 500 Americans—including John McCain—prisoner in Hanoi, and leaving Vietnam without getting those prisoners back seems to have been a political non-starter. Although 68 percent agreed in a May 1971 poll that US troops should be withdrawn from Vietnam by the end of the year, this number plummeted to 11 when they were asked if they would still favor withdrawal "even if it threatened [not *cost*] the lives or safety of United States POWs held by North Vietnam" (Mueller, *War, Presidents and Public Opinion*, pp. 97–8). There is no comparable problem in Iraq.

48 William C. Adams and Michael Joblove, "The Unnewsworthy Holocaust: TV News and Terror in Cambodia," in *Television Coverage of International Affairs*, ed. William C. Adams (Norwood, NJ: Ablex Publishing, 1982), pp. 217–25.

49 Sean Reilly, "Poll Shows Alabamians Still Support President," *Mobile Register*, May 22, 2005.

50 On these putative targets, see John Mueller, "What if We Leave?," *American Conservative*, February 26, 2007.

51 Sonni Efron and Bruce Wallace, "North Korea Escalates Its Nuclear Threat," *Los Angeles Times*, February 11, 2005, p. A1.

Part III
Intelligence failure

8

Intelligence collection and analysis on Iraq: issues for the US intelligence community

*Richard Kerr, Thomas Wolfe,
Rebecca Donegan, and
Aris Pappas*

The intelligence community's uneven performance on Iraq from 2002 to 2004 raised significant questions concerning the condition of intelligence collection, analysis, and policy support. The discussion of shortcomings and failures that follows is not meant to imply that all surprises can be prevented by even good intelligence. There are too many targets and too many ways of attacking them for even the best intelligence agencies to discover all threats in time to prevent them from happening. Nonetheless, improving performance requires an acknowledgment of past mistakes and a willingness to change.

This report was prepared at a time of a great rush to reorganize and give the leader of the intelligence community new authorities. That probably was a necessary activity. However, to move the organizational boxes and to offer new authorities are not the only answers or perhaps even the best answers. Based on our experience and what we learned during this review, the group believes that the quality of intelligence will be improved only by fundamental changes at the grass roots level. That is, changes in collection, analysis, the nature of the product, and interaction with policymakers and other customers.

The intelligence community itself has made some useful changes and recommended others. Several fixes also have been proposed from outside the community, which might be helpful but do not address some of the core problems identified by the group. This report focuses on the question: does the community's flawed performance on Iraq represent one-time problems, not to be repeated, or is it symptomatic of deeper problems?

Principal findings of the earlier reports

The central focus of national intelligence reporting and analysis prior to the war was the extent of the Iraqi programs for developing weapons of mass destruction (WMD). The analysis on this issue by the intelligence community clearly was wide of the mark. That analysis relied heavily on old information acquired largely before late 1998 and was strongly influenced by untested, long-held assumptions. Moreover, the analytic judgments rested almost solely on technical analysis, which has a natural tendency to put bits and pieces together as evidence of coherent programs and to equate programs to capabilities. As a result the analysis, although understandable and explainable, arrived at conclusions that were seriously flawed, misleading, and even wrong.

Intelligence produced prior to the war on a wide range of other issues accurately addressed such topics as how the war would develop and how Iraqi forces would or would not fight. It also provided perceptive analysis on Iraq's links to al Qaeda; calculated the impact of the war on oil markets; and accurately forecast the reactions of the ethnic and tribal factions in Iraq. Indeed, intelligence assessments on post-Saddam issues were particularly insightful. These and many other topics were thoroughly examined in a variety of intelligence products that have proven to be largely accurate.

The national intelligence produced on the technical and cultural/political areas, however, remained largely distinct and separate. Little or no attempt was made to examine or explain the impact of each area on the other. Thus, perspective and a comprehensive sense of understanding of the Iraqi target per se were lacking. This independent preparation of intelligence products in these distinct but interrelated areas raises significant questions about how intelligence supports policy. In an ironic twist, the policy community was receptive to technical intelligence (the weapons program), where the analysis was wrong, but apparently paid little attention to intelligence on cultural and political issues (post-Saddam Iraq), where the analysis was right.

With respect to the weapons programs, some critics have argued that the off-the-mark judgments resulted largely from reinforcement of the community's assumptions by an audience that was predisposed to believe them. This, however, seems to have been less a case of policy reinforcing "helpful" intelligence judgments than a case of policy deliberations deferring to the community in an area where classified information and technical analysis were seen as giving it unique expertise.

On the other hand, the intelligence community's analysis of post-Saddam Iraq rested on little hard information, was informed largely by strong regional and country expertise developed over time, and yet was on the mark. Intelligence projections in this area, however, although largely accurate, had little or no impact on policy deliberations.

The bifurcation of analysis between the technical and the cultural/political in the analytic product and the resulting implications for policy indicates systemic problems in collection and analysis. Equally important, it raises questions about how best to construct intelligence products to effectively and accurately inform policy deliberations.

The context

Any examination of the intelligence community must acknowledge the impact of more than 10 years of turmoil that adversely affected all collection and analytic efforts, including those on Iraq. The intelligence community was designed to focus on the Soviet Union. It had developed a single-minded rigor and attention to detail that enriched its analysis, particularly with respect to Soviet military issues. The end of the Cold War, however, brought to a close that "stable" bipolar world and left the United States without a principal enemy. Although never perfect, the intelligence community's analytic efforts against the Soviet threat were generally insightful and its collection largely effective, reflecting the accumulation of deep understanding developed over many years.

Absent this singular focus, in the post-Cold War environment the intelligence community struggled to reestablish its identity and purpose in what had become a world of multiple crises and transient threats. The effort to define its priorities was further complicated as policymakers and others raised questions not only about the role of but even the need for intelligence. Accordingly, intelligence came to be seen as an area where the government could reap resource savings. The resulting cutbacks in collection (technical and HUMINT) and analytic resources had a significant adverse impact on intelligence community capabilities.

Nonetheless, during the 1990s the intelligence community confronted numerous crises in which to demonstrate the relevance of intelligence analysis to policy deliberations. Regional conflicts, such as the first Gulf war and follow-on sanctions against Iraq, the breakup of Yugoslavia, and emerging threats from North Korea and Iran provided tests for intelligence. The community's collection and analysis performance over this period, however, was seen as inconsistent and sometimes faulty, leaving important customers still wondering about the relevance of the intelligence input to policy deliberations.

A significant contributor to this uneven performance was, and still is, the community's tendency to establish single-issue centers and crisis-response task forces. By stripping expertise from regional offices, they diminish the overall ability to provide perspective and context for those issues. The resources seldom get returned to the line offices, which historically have been better equipped to provide complete perspectives on country and regional issues.

Although resources increased marginally over the decade, they were not as robust or focused as the capabilities devoted to the Soviet Union and were seen by the intelligence community as inadequate to deal conclusively with the multiplicity of threats. Accordingly, the community in critical situations has faltered in its analyses and failed to collect pertinent information. This has occurred over a length of time and across crises sufficient in number, quite apart from Iraq, to indicate systemic issues rather than just occasional missteps.

Collection impeded and misdirected

Intelligence collection against Iraq fell far short of the mark. The intelligence base for collection and analysis was thin and sketchy. The intelligence community had nothing like the richness, density, and detail that it worked hard to develop and became accustomed to having on Soviet issues during the Cold War. To a significant extent this resulted from the reduction over the past decade of the professional collection management cadre capable of integrating HUMINT, imagery, and signals intelligence capabilities into coherent strategies. This development was compounded by the increased separation of collection professionals from the analytic cadre who had been intimately involved in identifying collection gaps, needs, and priorities and developing collection strategies.

Placing these developments in a broader context, however, is important. Iraq was not the only significant intelligence problem facing the community in the years immediately preceding the war. Counterterrorism and counterproliferation were given higher priority and absorbed much of the clandestine service's capability and leadership attention. Weapons programs in both North Korea and Iran received higher priority than those in Iraq until late 2002. In Iraq, technical collection priorities emphasized coverage of the Iraqi air defense system in southern Iraq in support of US military operations and prevented collection on other important targets in Iraq.

A number of other factors added to the difficulty of clandestine collection on the Iraq target. The Iraqis took pains to carefully hide their WMD programs. People and operations were protected from US intelligence by a variety of methods, including isolating scientists and technicians involved in the programs and employing effective camouflage, concealment, and deception efforts. The Iraqis had learned well about US intelligence during more than 10 years of confrontation and war.

Nevertheless, collection of information on difficult targets is the core mission of intelligence and in the Iraq case it did not measure up. Many of the more sophisticated clandestine technical collection techniques did not produce results. The Iraq WMD target was given a high priority over more than a decade, even if not the highest. Still, the intelligence community did not have conclusive evidence on what the Iraqis were working on, what they had achieved, which programs were ongoing, who was working them, or what the doctrines for use might be. Conversely, the community saw no evidence that WMD programs were slowed, put on hold, or even nonexistent. Nor did it understand why Saddam's devious and obstructionist behavior continued if, as he claimed, he had no stockpiles of banned weapons.

US intelligence collection strategies contributed to the problem. Looking for information on a particular subject with a preconception of what is needed is almost certain to result in data that reinforces existing assumptions. The community directed its collection capabilities to filling in what it thought were gaps in information about WMD programs, monitoring progress, looking for new developments in weapons and delivery systems, and identifying efforts to acquire materiel and technology abroad. Based on the hard information collected by US military forces and UN inspectors during and following the first Gulf war, reinforced by subsequent bits of information, the intelligence community and the US defense establishment had little doubt that Iraq was continuing development of WMD.

Collection was not focused or conceptually driven to answer questions about the validity of the premise that the WMD programs were continuing apace. This problem is well illustrated by a comprehensive collection support brief describing intelligence needs published by the DCI Center for Weapons Intelligence, Nonproliferation, and Arms Control. It was published contemporaneously with the 2002 National Intelligence Estimate (NIE) on WMD. The brief describes in great detail the information required to support analysis of Iraq's weapons programs. The intent of the brief was to expose gaps in knowledge about what was believed to be aggressive, ongoing Iraqi weapons programs. The revealed gaps in knowledge were not, however, raised as requirements to address what was not known nor did such gaps raise doubts about prevailing intelligence judgments.

Discussing largely space-based collection systems at an unclassified level is difficult, but a few observations are possible. Despite a wide variety of technical capabilities available to the US, these systems were able to provide accurate information on relatively few critical issues. Monitoring Iraqi reactions to inspections was informative, as was reporting on Iraqi acquisition efforts. Technical collection lends itself to monitoring large-scale, widespread targets, a condition not met in the Iraqi case. Analysis of Iraq's WMD programs, therefore, provides an excellent case study for an assessment of the limitations of relying too heavily on technical collection systems with little acknowledgement of the political/cultural context in which such programs exist.

Accordingly, surprisingly little collection was directed against several key issues. Neglected topics for collection included the social, cultural, and economic impacts on Iraq of nearly 20 years of war and 10 years of sanctions and isolation. Little attention appears to have been paid, for example, to collecting information on the oil-for-food program. Considerable speculation was voiced that several countries and individuals were profiting from this program. Despite the fact that many of the targets for this subject were outside Iraq, it received only sporadic attention.

Although collection itself was a problem, analysts were led to rely on reporting whose sourcing was misleading and even unreliable. In the case of US clandestine reporting, it too often used different descriptions for the same source, leading analysts to believe they had more corroborative information from more sources than was actually the case. In addition, some critical judgments were made on the basis of intelligence provided by foreign intelligence services. Some of those liaison sources were not available to the US, and some key information obtained from liaison proved to be false.

The intelligence community knows how to collect secret information, even though in the Iraq situation it did not perform this function well. On the other hand, the acquisition of "softer" intelligence on societal issues, personalities, and elites presents an even greater challenge. This latter information can be found in databases, but they are too often only accessible indirectly and with considerable effort. It may also reside in the minds of groups of people who are accessible but not easily approachable and who do not fall into the category of controlled agents. Although there is a strong argument that the clandestine service should not divert its attention away from collecting "secrets," information on the stresses and strains of society may be equally, if not more, important. This type of information, however, does not fit with the reward system in the collection world and can be difficult to fully assess and to integrate with other information.

In the case of Iraq, collection strategies were weak and unimaginative and failed to get the richness and density of information required. A careful examination might have addressed the long-neglected question of the value added by the different types of intelligence—e.g., SIGINT and IMINT—relative to the resources devoted to them. Collection on Iraq also was the victim of inadequate funding and too intense competition between top priority targets. Finally, Iraq demonstrates that collection strategies must take into account that the absence of dangerous activity in a targeted country cannot be convincingly demonstrated in the presence of a secretive and devious regime. Or, put differently, collection strategies should recognize the extreme difficulty of requiring such a regime to prove the negative in the face of assumptions that it is dissembling. Overall, the intelligence community did not acquit itself well in developing collection strategies on Iraq.

Analysis adversely affected

No single act of omission or commission accounts for the inconsistent analytic performance of the intelligence community with regard to Iraq. It appears to be the result of decisions made, and not made, since the fall of the Soviet Union, which had an impact on the analytical environment analogous to the effect of the meteor strikes on the dinosaurs. Nothing was the same afterwards. In response to changed priorities and decreased resources, the intelligence community's analytic cadre underwent changes in both its organization and its methodological orientation. Perhaps the most significant change was the shift away from long-term, in-depth analysis in favor of more short-term products intended to provide direct support to policy. Done with the best of intentions, this shift seems to have had the result of weakening elements of the analytic discipline and rigor that characterized intelligence community products through the Cold War.

The kind of intellectual-capital-intensive analysis that traditionally and effectively preceded policy deliberations was unavailable because of the shift away from research-oriented analytic investments. In reviewing the national intelligence products associated with Iraq, we found that they too often dealt, seriatim, with a broad range of subjects but without extensive cross-reference, and with no attempt to synthesize a broader understanding of Iraq out of the many detailed pieces that were prepared. The absence of such a contextual effort contributed to assessments that failed to recognize the significance of gaps in collection that may have been more evident when viewed from a larger perspective.

The absence of a unifying analysis was also disguised by the rapidity and volume of interactions between intelligence and policy deliberations. Eagerly responsive to quickly developed policy requirements, the quick and assured response gave the appearance of both knowledge and confidence that, in retrospect, was too high.

Of all the methodological elements that contributed, positively and negatively, to the intelligence community's performance, the most important seems to be an uncritical acceptance of established positions and assumptions. Gaps in knowledge were left undiscovered or unattended, which to some degree is explainable by the absence of pervasive, intrusive, and effective collection in Iraq. Although many products were appropriately caveated, the growing need to caveat judgments to explain the absence of direct intelligence did not seem to provoke internal review within the intelligence community. Indeed, although certain gaps were acknowledged, no product or thread within the intelligence provided called into question the quality of basic assumptions, hastening the conversion of heavily qualified judgments into accepted fact.

As noted earlier, the growing use of centers also contributed to what was at best a problematic result. The intelligence community has generally considered centers a useful organizational concept to concentrate analytic and collection capabilities against a carefully defined target set or issue. They also have the effect, however, of drawing resources away from more broadly based organizations. The post-Cold War reductions throughout the intelligence community made this a critical but insidious factor. Analysis of Iraq's weapons of mass destruction thus became the purview of technically competent analysts, but as has been described elsewhere, their efforts were not leavened through review by more broadly based colleagues.

Finally, quality control was weakened. The extensive layers of critical management review that traditionally served to ensure both the validity and standing of finished intelligence products seem to have been ineffective in identifying key issues affecting collection and analysis. Allowing for a satisfying sense of voluminous production, and reflecting the approval of receptive consumers, the policy-heavy process provided positive feedback, while the narrowly focused internal architecture lacked the self-awareness that could otherwise have raised serious and timely warnings.

Interaction with the policy community

Few issues have engaged greater policymaker interest in intelligence than those concerning Iraq—particularly the questions of weapons of mass destruction and Saddam's links to al Qaeda. The demands for intelligence in the months leading up to the war were numerous and intense. The intelligence community responded to the overwhelming consumer demand with an ever-increasing stream of analysis—both written and oral. Neither means of communication, however, served the policy community as well as it might have.

In periods of crisis, when demands are high and response time is short, most written intelligence production is in the form of policy-driven memos and briefs and pieces written for daily publications. The result of this narrowly focused and piecemeal intelligence flow is that it neither fosters continuity of analysis nor provides a context within which to place seemingly unrelated information. In the case of Iraq, national intelligence did not provide a comprehensive picture of how the country functioned as a whole. The intelligence community has made substantial, although sporadic, efforts over the past decade and a half to explore better and more technologically advanced methods of communicating with consumers. The results, however, have been modest at best. The requirement to have background and contextual information available at the policymaker's fingertips in a timely fashion remains unfulfilled.

The policy community was also ill served by the NIE process. NIEs rarely represent new analysis or bring to bear more expertise than already exists in analytic offices; indeed, drafters of NIEs are usually the same analysts from whose work the NIE is drawn. Little independent knowledge or informed outside opinion is incorporated in estimative products. The preparation of an NIE therefore consists primarily of compiling judgments from previous products and debating points of disagreement. The Iraqi WMD estimate of October 2002 was characterized by all of these weaknesses and more. It was done under an unusually tight time constraint—three weeks—to meet a deadline for congressional debate. And it was the product of three separate drafters, each responsible for independent sections, drawing from a mixed bag of analytic product. Consistent application of analytic or evidentiary standards became next to impossible.

The fundamental question is whether national intelligence estimates add value to the existing body of analytic work. Historically, with few exceptions, NIEs have not carried great weight in policy deliberations, although customers have often used them to promote their own agendas. The time may have come to reassess the value of NIEs and the process used to produce them.

Oral communications have their own set of problems. While direct engagement with the policy community is essential for intelligence to have an impact, too close association with policy deliberations can be troublesome. In the case of Iraq, daily briefings and other contacts at the highest levels undoubtedly influenced policy in ways that went beyond the coordinated analysis contained in the written product. Close and continuing personal contact, unfettered by the formal caveats that usually accompany written production, probably imparted a greater sense of certainty to analytic conclusions than the facts would bear.

Some in the intelligence community and elsewhere hold the view that intense policymaker demands in the run-up to the war constituted inappropriate pressure on intelligence analysts. Although viewed in that context as a problem, serious pressure from policymakers almost always accompanies serious issues. The more relevant issue is how the intelligence community responded to the climate of policy-level pressure and expectations. Whether or not this climate contributed to the problem of inconsistent analytic performance, however, remains an open question.

The cases of WMD and Iraq's links to al Qaeda illustrate two different responses to policy pressure. In the case of al Qaeda, the constant stream of questions aimed at finding links between Saddam and the terrorist network caused analysts to take what they termed a "purposely aggressive approach" in conducting exhaustive and repetitive searches for such links. Despite the pressure, however, the intelligence community remained firm in its assessment that no operational or collaborative relationship existed. In the case of Iraq's possession of WMD, on the other hand, analytic judgments and policy views were in accord, so that the impact of pressure, if any, was more nuanced and may have been considered reinforcing. Although it is possible that in the absence of strong policy interest, analysts would have been more inclined to examine their underlying assumptions, it is unlikely that such examination would have changed judgments that were longstanding and firmly held.

Final thoughts

The intelligence world is one of ambiguity, nuance, and complexity. Dealing with these elements is difficult in the world intelligence serves, where success or failure is the uncomplicated measure by which the intelligence community is judged. The controversies over Iraq intelligence can be expressed in the contrast between these two worlds: carefully crafted national intelligence that ultimately failed in its singular mission to accurately inform policy deliberations. This report, the result of over two years of review and consideration, reflects the same contrast. On the one hand, it recognizes the enormous efforts undertaken, the long hours and the intense debate. On the other hand, it describes failures and weaknesses that cannot be ignored or mitigated.

Failures of collection, uncritical analytical assumptions, and inadequate management reviews were the result of years of well-intentioned attempts to do the best job with the resources provided. Decisions were made and their potential risks weighed, but the outcome on important issues proved badly flawed. Recognition of these problems must bring a rapid response. US intelligence is a robust, highly capable, and thoroughly motivated community that represents an invaluable asset to the nation and its citizens. It must reveal itself as sufficiently mature to both adapt to changing circumstances and counteract the evolutionary processes that have conspired to threaten its reputation and its ability to successfully perform its assigned mission. The alternative is unacceptable and unthinkable.

9

The politics and psychology of intelligence and intelligence reform

Robert Jervis

If the US is to employ the tool of pre-emptive war, it "has to be used carefully. One would want to have very good intelligence." (National Security Advisor Condoleezza Rice, Sept. 25, 2002)[1]

Many intelligence reports in war are contradictory; even more are false, and most are uncertain. (Carl von Clausewitz)[2]

Let me tell you about these intelligence guys. When I was growing up in Texas, we had a cow named Bessie. I'd go out early and milk her. I'd get her in the stanchion, seat myself and squeeze out a pail of fresh milk. One day I'd worked hard and gotten a full pail of milk, but I wasn't paying attention, and old Bessie swung her shit-smeared tail through the bucket of milk. Now, you know that's what these intelligence guys do. You work hard and get a good program or policy going, and they swing a shit-smeared tail through it. (Lyndon Johnson)[3]

I could almost stop here because these three quotations summarize the insoluble dilemmas of intelligence and policymaking quite well. Everything else is a gloss on them.

Policymakers say they need and want very good intelligence. They do indeed need it, but often do not want it. They also believe that when intelligence is not out to get them, it is incompetent, and also think that the machinery can be fixed so that it will give them much better answers. Unfortunately, not only will even the best intelligence services be wrong very often, but when they are true to the available evidence their reports are likely to be inconclusive, and when they are right they will often bring disturbing news. Although many things are wrong with American intelligence, they are not likely to be fixed (and certainly will not be fixed by the latest "reforms"), and even if the system were optimally designed, it will still produce many errors. Decisionmakers might be better off if they understood the limitations of intelligence but this would place them under intolerable psychological and political pressures. Similarly, decisionmakers would be better off if they could design their actions with the knowledge that the information and inferences on which they are operating may be incorrect. But this again is extremely difficult. The absence of a Plan B in Iraq is unfortunate, but not atypical.

All students of intelligence realize that errors are unavoidable.[4] The reasons are many, but boil down to incomplete and misleading information and the difficulties in understanding our world. Even intelligence in the sense of our ability to understand our physical environment is limited when we deal with difficult questions. For example, even if all but a few experts believe that the climate is changing, and doing so at least in part because of human activities, an enormous number of puzzles remain. Any ecological experiment or alteration similarly reveals many unexpected connections and consequences. And anyone with an unusual illness knows the limitations of medical diagnoses. Foreign intelligence is, of course, even more difficult still. The adversary is often engaged in concealment and deception, and even when it is not the knowledge that these practices are common degrades much correct information. To give just one example, Stalin initially dismissed the reports of his atomic spies at Los Alamos on the grounds that the Americans could not have been so incompetent as to permit this penetration.

The other side of this coin is that the belief that the other side is deceiving you can account for almost all discrepant information. Thus Stalin rejected the enormous amount of information he received in the spring of 1941 that indicated that Germany was about to attack on the grounds that the British were trying to provoke a war between Germany and the USSR, and that all this information was manufactured for this purpose. One reason for the intelligence errors about Iraq's WMD programs is that the US believed that Iraq had an extensive denial and deception program, and that this explained why we were seeing only scattered signs of the program.

Unless the other's behavior is determined by the situation it is in, and this situation (both internal and external) is readily ascertainable, the state has to understand what the other's goals are and how it sees the world. For reasons too numerous to discuss here, this is extremely difficult. The end of the Cold War has seen a number of conferences bringing together officials from several countries and it is striking how hard it is even in retrospect for them to grasp why the other side was acting as it was.

This is not to say, of course, that the situation is hopeless or that intelligence is always wrong. In fact, studying accuracy is difficult because of selection bias. That is, we are drawn to crises and policy failures, and these are likely to involve intelligence failures. If each side understands the other, they are much more likely to adjust their behavior in a way that minimizes mutually costly conflict, and these cases seem unremarkable and not worth studying. Nevertheless, even routine and successful interactions are often based on limited and faulty understandings. One obvious implication is that policies that are exquisitely sensitive to intelligence are likely to fail. There are many reasons why the policy of preventive war—mislabeled "pre-emptive" by the Bush administration—is likely to be foolish, but if it will work only when intelligence is excellent, as Dr. Rice asserts, then it must be abandoned. We did not need the case of Iraq to show us this, but it is instructive. So is Bush's reply: the war was necessary even if Saddam Hussein did not have active WMD programs because he was a tyrant and eventually could cause great mischief if he was not stopped. This claim may be correct (although I think it is not), but notice that it does not rely on a large and capable intelligence service. The US would not require the sort of information and analysis that Dr. Rice implies we do because all that we would need to know is that Saddam is a tyrant.

Designing policies that are likely to succeed if the intelligence is good but that will not fail disastrously if it is not is difficult. Indeed, in some cases it may be impossible. So it is not surprising that decisionmakers rarely try this or even think in these terms. It is hard enough to carry out a strong and active policy without constantly worrying that your premises may be faulty. It is also psychologically and politically difficult for a leader in a democracy to say that his policy does not rest on a firm foundation of intelligence. When Secretary of State Powell laid out the case against Iraq before the Security Council, he insisted that Director of Central Intelligence Tenet sit right behind him. It might be better if political leaders were able to say something like this: "I think Saddam is a terrible menace. This is a political judgment and I have been elected to make difficult calls like this. Information rarely can be definitive and while I have consulted widely and listened to our intelligence services and other experts, this is my decision, not theirs." This would leave them open to attacks both at home and abroad, however, and so will not be done.

The difficulty in coming to grips with the possibility that one's assumptions, information, and analysis are wrong also inhibits the development of fall-back positions. I will return to the case of Iraq in a minute, but it is worth noting that the Clinton administration did not have a Plan B when it started bombing in Kosovo. Administration officials were quite clear that they thought such a plan was not needed because it was obvious that Milosevic would give in very quickly. In part they believed this because they thought it was the brief and minor bombing that had brought Milosevic to Dayton, an inference that is almost surely incorrect and, even if it were not, would not readily support the conclusion that he would give up Kosovo without a fight. The result was that the administration had to scramble both militarily and politically and was fortunate to be able to end the confrontation as well as it did. (It is worth noting that even in retrospect we do not understand Milosevic's behavior, and the US government has been remarkably incurious in exploring this and several other failures of American threats.)

The most obvious, consequential, and disgraceful recent case of a lack of Plan B, of course, is Iraq. Top administration officials believed that the political and economic reconstruction of Iraq would be easy, that they needed neither short-term plans to maintain order nor long-term plans to put down any insurgency and create a stable and peaceful polity. Furthermore, this negligence cannot be blamed on faulty intelligence. It has been asserted by intelligence officials and not denied by the Bush administration that the former gave ample warnings and good guidance here.[5] The reasons why intelligence was ignored speak volumes about the tensions and ambivalence in policymakers' attitude toward intelligence. For reasons that mercifully lie beyond the scope of this chapter, the Bush administration was set on overthrowing Saddam. This meant that it not only exaggerated intelligence in areas in which the latter did provide significant support for the policy (Iraq's WMD programs) and ignored and twisted it in areas in which it conflicted with policy (the connections between Saddam and al Qaeda), but also that it simply put aside intelligence in areas in which it was raising inconvenient questions. Developing plans for the post-war situation would have been psychologically and politically costly. This kind of planning would have had to recognize that the US might not be greeted as a liberator, that the administration's faith in Ahmad Chalabi might have been misplaced, and that a long occupation might be needed, indeed one that had an uncertain outcome.

Recognizing these possibilities would not have meant that the war was not worth fighting: if Saddam did have WMD and was willing to provide them to terrorists, the threat was great enough to have merited the response. Alternatively, or additionally, if even after a number of years democracy could have been established in Iraq and if such a demonstration project could have had large benign effects throughout the Middle East, then this was an opportunity to be taken. But at minimum realizing that the occupation might be long and difficult would have added significant negative factors that would have made the decision more difficult. The examination of a large number of other cases indicates that people are prone to avoid painful value trade-offs if they possibly can.[6] Decisionmakers talk about how they make hard decisions all the time. But, like the rest of us, they prefer easy ones and will use their great abilities of self-deception in order to turn the former into the latter.

Intelligence, lacking the burden of making the decisions, is much more prone to present dilemmas. CIA found no contradiction in arguing that, on the one hand, Saddam did have active WMD programs but that, on the other hand, he did not have links to al Qaeda and that the aftermath of the overthrow was likely to be very difficult. Even for decisionmakers more thoughtful and open than those in the current administration, being in charge and having responsibility means that they feel psychological pressures to avoid or minimize the costs associated with their behavior. They have to sleep at night, after all.

Their political incentives are similarly aligned. To have acknowledged that the post-war situation might be difficult would have been to give political ammunition to the war's opponents. It is much easier to sell a cheap war than an expensive one: thus the well-known shunting aside and humiliating of military and economic officials who said that the war could prove very costly and that a large occupation force would be needed. To have admitted the possibility that the Iraqi people and the region would be worse off after an American invasion than before it would have multiplied the administration's political problems.

Here as in many cases, policy decisions precede and drive intelligence rather than the other way around. Decisionmakers often act on a combination of longstanding beliefs and intuition and come to cognitive if not political closure long before detailed intelligence estimates land on their desks. This was obviously the case with Bush and Iraq, but characterizes successful as well as unsuccessful policies. Truman's decision to defy the Soviet blockade of Berlin in 1948 was a snap judgment that preceded any governmental analysis.[7]

Indeed, decisionmakers may be correct not to heed the warnings of intelligence and end up being right for the wrong reasons. The classic case is Winston Churchill in the spring of 1940. He prevailed over a great deal of strong sentiment in his Cabinet for a peace agreement with Germany in the wake of the fall of France by arguing that Britain could win because the German economy was badly overstretched and could be broken by a combination of British bombing and guerrilla warfare in the conquered territories. This was a complete fantasy; his foreign secretary was quite correct to say in his diary: "Winston talked the most frightful rot . . . It drives one to despair when he works himself up into a passion of emotion when he ought to make his brain think and reason."[8] Fortunately, Churchill's emotion and force of character carried the day, but intelligence can get no credit.

Of course, intelligence sometimes can be helpful. It can indicate the adversary's vulnerabilities or point to courses of action that may succeed. The breaking of German codes in World War II opened the door to a range of successful military operations, to take an example of invaluable and specific intelligence. It is with good reason that Churchill referred to the code-breakers as his "hens" who brought him "golden eggs." Intelligence in a broader sense was crucial during the deliberations over the Cuban missile crisis. Kennedy had in the room the Soviet expert Llewellyn Thompson who persuaded him that Khrushchev would be willing to remove the missiles from Cuba without an American promise to remove its missiles from Turkey.[9]

But in all too many cases, intelligence will bring leaders bad news, conflicting interpretations, the specter of costs, the dangers of being deceived, and indications that a preferred policy is likely to fail. So it is not surprising that while most leaders, or at least American leaders, often praise intelligence in public and say how much they rely on it, in private they are often scornful. Their claims that intelligence is often wrong, if not incompetent, are correct, but are not the root of the matter. Intelligence, even (or especially) good intelligence, is often highly inconvenient. Johnson's remark quoted earlier was based in part on the propensity of CIA to tell him that his policy was failing, as it did during Vietnam (which led the military services to demand that CIA no longer produce estimates of the military situation, a demand that Secretary of Defense McNamara, who later bemoaned the lack of US information about Vietnam, endorsed). At best intelligence will provide a complicated and nuanced picture. Even if it fundamentally supports policy, it is likely to imply hesitations, costs, and dangers along the way. Although decisionmakers always say they want to be warned and to hear about all the risks and costs of their policy, they rarely do. Intelligence also is likely to introduce or magnify uncertainty by bringing in hedges and qualifications. To heed intelligence often is to raise doubts and the multiple possibilities for alternative interpretations. But decisionmakers have to act, and they probably will act more effectively if they feel confident, even if confidence, especially in the wisdom of a predetermined policy, comes at the price of understanding the environment. This means that while top government officials have at their disposal enormous amounts of information, they often are badly informed, having developed processes for creating and screening news and views that lead them to live in a fantasy world. The Bush administration represents only the most extreme case in which people within the inner circles of power knew less about the problems they were facing than did most informed citizens.

Despite their ambivalence about good intelligence, every president pledges to improve it. The long history is fascinating and dispiriting but will not be rehearsed here. Although the Israeli and British services are often held up as models, it is in fact unclear whether they really have performed any better. But it is clear that the desire to serve multiple political and bureaucratic objectives, combined with the fear of an excessively powerful intelligence service, has produced fragmentation, gaps, and inefficiencies.[10]

The attacks of September 11, 2001 revealed serious problems, of course. Aside from those within CIA, it highlighted what experts had long known: that the FBI was not effectively structured for intelligence work and that coordination and information sharing both within the FBI and between that organization and the CIA were woefully lacking. The mantra of greater sharing of information is an easy and over-simplified solution, however. In what seems like common sense, Pat Roberts, chair of the Senate Select Committee on Intelligence, argues that: "Key terrorism analysts . . . must be given access to every single piece of relevant intelligence data concerning threats to the homeland," and the WMD Commission remarks that the terminology we use may implicitly accept undesirable boundaries within the intelligence community: "To say that we must encourage agencies to 'share' information implies that they have some ownership stake in it."[11] Anyone who has worked in or around CIA knows the proprietary attitude of the Directorates. But, as usual, there are problems with the prescription. Not only will it meet a great deal of resistance, but sharing all information would swamp the system, which, like all organizations, is built on a division of labor. Furthermore, the withholding of information reflects not only the fact that the information is power, but legitimate security concerns. Spies like CIA's Aldrich Ames and FBI's Robert Hanssen would have done even greater damage had there been less compartmentalization. While some barriers need to be broken down, there is no perfect way to balance the competing needs involved and I suspect that some number of years from now a distinguished panel will attribute a security debacle to the excessively free flow of information within the intelligence community.

The main change to come in the aftermath of 9/11 is the establishment of a Director of National Intelligence (DNI) with significant powers over the entire intelligence community. But despite the fact that a number of panels preceding the 9/11 Commission had called for this reform, it was not well thought through and is likely to do more harm than good, which is not surprising in light of the fact that the proposals grew out of the need to meet political pressures. There is no reason to believe that a DNI was needed to meet the problems uncovered by the 9/11 Commission, but an aroused public led by the relatives of the 9/11 victims had sufficient clout so that neither the Congress nor the president could resist. Although the latter had initially—and wisely—said that a DNI was not necessary, he changed his position during the presidential campaign, just as in 2002 he reversed his initial and correct opposition to the establishment of a Department of Homeland Security once the political pressures grew too great.

There is significant merit to the claim that we need a DNI, but the existing statutes provided for one—the title was Director of Central Intelligence (DCI). Most members of the attentive public and even many professionals think that the DCI was the Director of the Central Intelligence Agency (CIA). But he really was supposed to be the director of the entire community. Although in practice it did not work out that way, the reason was not so much a defective statute as it was the political power of other agencies, most obviously the FBI and, even more, the Department of Defense. Without a new law, the president could have given the DCI most of the missing powers by telling the Secretary of Defense that his budget requests in the intelligence area, especially the enormous sums for satellites, had to be approved by the DCI before they went to the White House. Whether the DNI will be able to enforce his will is yet to be seen, but if he can the reason is primarily a changed political climate, not the new law.

The law's proponents said that they did not want the DNI to be an additional layer of bureaucracy on top of all the existing ones. They realized this would degrade rather than improve intelligence. But it is hard to see how the outcome will be anything else. Like it or not, the DNI's office *is* a new layer.

Reforms indeed are possible, but are not likely to be forthcoming. They involve less the dramatic changes that political leaders like to take credit for and more the improvement of collection and analysis within the intelligence agencies, especially CIA. Let me just mention a few. First, unlike the military, CIA does little in the way of continuing education, and while it has some training courses, it lacks a serious focus on improving the skills and analytical abilities of its members. Second and relatedly, little attention is paid to basic methodological questions. I do not mean that intelligence analysts necessarily need to know the latest quantitative techniques, although indeed in some areas this is required. Rather what is needed to start with is a firm grasp of standard social science methods that can move estimates beyond description into a disciplined consideration of alternative interpretations of what the other side is doing and why it is doing. More specifically, there is a lack of understanding of the significance of negative evidence, or "dogs that do not bark."[12] In the case of Iraq's WMD program, what this meant was the ignoring or downgrading of the numerous reports that people who were in positions to know about these programs said that they had seen nothing of interest. Although the desire not to upset the administration which was set on going to war may have played a role here, I think at least as important was the fact that unless one keeps the methodological issue constantly in mind, negative reports will have little impact because they are so undramatic and seemingly without significance. Third, analysts and consumers of intelligence need to work harder to understand the extent to which conclusions are driven by their plausibility rather than by specific bits of evidence. It is not that plausibility is to be put aside, but that if people are unaware of the role it is playing they will fail to understand the grounds for their inferences and conclusions, overestimate the degree to which the evidence supports them, and not properly focus critical scrutiny where it is necessary.[13] Fourth, CIA and other agencies have to work harder to develop the critical habits of mind and supporting institutions to surface assumptions and explore alternative accounts. All post-mortems on intelligence failures stress this, and the difficulty of the task is indicated by the fact that relatively little progress has been made.

To do better, intelligence services need to learn from their past failures—and from their successes as well. In part, this could be an aspect of continuing education, as analysts learn by examining past cases and then bring their new knowledge back to their regular jobs. CIA has recently reconstituted its Product Evaluation Staff, but such offices have withered in the past because of the lack of leadership from the top. It could succeed this time, but the odds against this and the other reforms mentioned in the previous paragraph are quite long. All would require the commitment of resources and attention from the top leadership. Resistance would be significant, the tasks are undramatic, and the effort would bear fruit only slowly. It follows that there is no reason to expect such attempts to be made.

Notes

1 Online NewsHour, "Rice on Iraq. War and Politics," September 25, 2002, available at www.pbs.org/newshour/bb/international/july-dec02/rice_9–25.html.
2 *On War*, ed. and translated by Michael Howard and Peter Paret (Princeton: Princeton University Press, 1976), p. 117.
3 Quoted in Robert Gates, "An Opportunity Unfulfilled: The Use and Perceptions of Intelligence at the White House," *Washington Quarterly*, 1989, vol.1, p. 42.
4 See, for example, Richard Betts, "Analysis, War, and Decisions: Why Intelligence Failures are Inevitable," *World Politics*, vol.31, October 1978, pp. 61–89.
5 See, for example, Paul Pillar in Chapter 13 of this book.
6 See Robert Jervis, *Perception and Misperception in International Politics* (Princeton: Princeton University Press, 1976); also see Philip Tetlock,

"Social-Functionalist Metaphors for Judgment and Choice: The Politician, Theologian and Prosecutor," *Psychological Review*, vol.109, 2002, pp. 451–72, and Tetlock, *Expert Political Judgment: How Good is it? How Can We Know?* (Princeton: Princeton University Press, 2005).

7 For discussion of the role of institutions here and in other cases, see Deborah Larson, "Truman and the Berlin Blockade: The Role of Intuition and Experience in Good Foreign Policy Judgment," in Stanley Renshon and Deborah Larson, eds., *Good Judgment in Foreign Policy* (Lanham, MD: Rowman & Littlefield, 2003), pp. 127–52. For a popular treatment, see Malcolm Gladwell, *Blink: The Power of Thinking Without Thinking* (Boston: Little Brown, 2005).

8 David Reynolds, "Churchill and the British 'Decision' to Fight on in 1940: Right Policy, Wrong Reasons," in Richard Langhorne, *Diplomacy and Intelligence During the Second World War* (New York: Cambridge University Press, 1985), pp. 147–67; quoted in Harold Evans, "His Finest Hour," *New York Times Book Review*, November 11, 2001.

9 Kennedy did make a private commitment to Khrushchev to remove the missiles in the near future, but not only was this a secret pledge, but news of it arrived in Moscow only after Khrushchev had decided to withdraw the missiles in return for Kennedy's pledge not to invade Cuba.

10 For the rational political reasons or any seeming organizational irrationalities, see Amy Zegart, *Flawed by Design: The Evolution of the CIA, JCS and NSC* (Stanford: Stanford University Press, 1999).

11 Pat Roberts, "Comments & Responses: Intelligence Reform," *National Interest*, No.81 (Fall 2005), p. 8; *Report to the President of the United States*, The Commission on the Intelligence Capabilities of the United States Regarding Weapons of Mass Destruction, March 31, 2005, p. 321.

12 For more on this, see Jervis, "Reports, Politics, and Intelligence Failures: The Case of Iraq," *Journal of Strategic Studies*, vol.29, Jan. 2006. pp. 3–52.

13 For further discussion, see ibid.

10

Congress, the Iraq war, and the failures of intelligence oversight

Loch K. Johnson

Introduction

This chapter examines the erroneous US intelligence prediction regarding the likely presence of weapons of mass destruction (WMDs) in Iraq in 2002, and why lawmakers in Washington, D.C., failed to question these estimates more thoroughly before they led the nation into war in the Persian Gulf the following year.

Put simply, the main purpose of intelligence is to provide information to the president and other policymakers that will illuminate their decisionmaking. The assumption is that good—that is, accurate, comprehensive, and timely—information will yield better decisions.[1] Though it is easy to state the purpose of intelligence, the challenge of actually providing useful information to policymakers is a complex matter with many opportunities for error. One of the buccaneers in Robert Louis Stevenson's *Treasure Island* observed, "Wot's wot? Ah, he'd be a lucky one as knowed that." Lucky, indeed, because—as many a grand strategist has lamented—uncertainty and ambiguity dominate the environment in which key foreign policy and security decisions are made.[2]

The first objective in this chapter is to provide a sense of the many potential pitfalls in the conduct of intelligence that make some degree of failure inevitable. Yet, despite the inherent impossibility of perfect intelligence, it is possible to reduce the frequency and severity of failure. One of the key ingredients for more reliable intelligence is the willingness of lawmakers to hold the feet of bureaucrats to the fire, making sure their assumptions and activities are sensible and warranted by the available evidence. This congressional duty is known as accountability or, less formally, "oversight." The purpose is to review executive branch programs and activities. As former US Senate Wyche Fowler (D, Georgia) once put it, oversight is meant to keep "the bureaucrats from doing something stupid"[3]—or, one might add with respect to intelligence bureaucrats, to push them toward the highest possible levels of competence in the collection-and-analysis of information about world events and conditions.

The intelligence cycle

A useful analytic construct for understanding the hazards of intelligence is the so-called intelligence cycle, which traces how America's 16 secret agencies gather, interpret, and disseminate information.[4] The first step in the cycle is known as "planning and direction."

Planning and direction

The world is a large place, with 191 nations and a plethora of groups, factions, and gangs, some of whom have an adversarial relationship with the United States. Unfortunately, no one in the government (or anywhere else) has a crystal ball to predict when and where danger will strike. Part of the dilemma stems from the fact that we live in a world fill not just with secrets, but with mysteries, too.

By secrets, intelligence experts mean something that the United States might be able to find out, even though it is concealed by another nation or group, say, the number of tanks and nuclear submarines in the Chinese weapons inventory. With the use of satellites and other surveillance methods, the United States can determine those figures (although some secrets are much harder to discover, such as the whereabouts of al Qaeda terrorist leaders in the mountains of Afghanistan and Pakistan). In contrast, mysteries are things we will never know about for certain until they happen, because they lie beyond the ken of human capacity to foresee. For example, no one knows who will be the next president of Russia, or, for that matter, of the United States. As former Secretary of State Dean Rusk pointed out, "Fate has not given mankind the capacity to pierce the fog of the future."[5]

Rwanda provides an illustration of how difficult it is to predict the future. The Secretary of Defense in the Clinton Administration, Les Aspin, had never thought much about Rwanda; but when genocide gripped that African nation in 1993 and critics castigated the United States for standing on the sidelines, Rwanda jumped to the top of America's, and therefore Aspin's, international concerns.[6] It stayed there for a period of weeks, then plummeted back into relative obscurity. Rwanda had become the "flavor of the month" for policymakers and, in turn, intelligence officers scrambled to meet the information needs of US government decisionmakers about exactly where this remote country was and why it was in turmoil. Similarly, in 2001, who would have placed Iraq at the pinnacle of America's security concerns, as it would become within a year?

Since the end of the Cold War, the United States has had 11 major inquiries into the US intelligence.[7] Each has concluded that one of the most significant flaws in this secret world has been the failure of policy-makers (including members of Congress) to clarify, during the planning-and-direction phase of the intelligence cycle, exactly what kinds of information they need. All too frequently, intelligence officers are left in the dark about the data requirements of top policy officials, who in turn are inclined to assume that somehow the secret agencies will divine what issues await action in their in-boxes throughout the executive branch and on Capitol Hill.

This failure of effective communication between the producers and the consumers of information results from inadequate liaison bridges between intelligence agencies and policy departments and committees: ongoing conversations between those in the intelligence agencies providing facts and insights, on the one hand, and those making decisions (as well as those reviewing these decisions in Congress), on the one hand. This leads to a lack of "intelligence sharing," in the popular parlance of recent government inquiries, starting at this first step in the intelligence cycle when executive officials and lawmakers inadequately inform intelligence officers about their information needs.

Collection

The second stage in the cycle is intelligence collection. Even wealthy superpowers are unable to saturate the globe with expensive surveillance platforms—reconnaissance aircraft, satellites, ground-based listening posts. Further, such machines have only limited capabilities against some targets. Satellite photography (imagery) helped to dampened down the hair-trigger anxieties of the superpowers during the Cold War; with satellites and high-flying reconnaissance aircraft (like the U-2), both camps could monitor the missilery and armies of their opponents. As a consequence, a surprise attack like Pearl Harbor became an unlikely possibility. Yet cameras on satellites or airplanes are unable to peer inside al Qaeda tents, or into the deep underground caverns where North Koreans construct and hide atomic weapons.

One of the ironies of American intelligence is that the vast percentage of its annual budget—$44 billion—goes into costly intelligence hardware, especially satellites, while the value of these machines is questionable in helping the United States understand such concerns as global terrorism or China's burgeoning economic rivalry. In the case of terrorism, what one would like to have ideally is a human agent well placed in the al Qaeda organization. Such an agent—or "asset," in professional intelligence lingo—could be worth a dozen billion-dollar satellites.

Yet, human intelligence ("HUMINT") also has its limitations. Against closed societies like Iraq in the interwar years, or North Korea and Iran today, local spies are difficult to recruit—especially since Americans have focused for decades on the Communist world and largely ignored the study of languages, history, and culture necessary to operate in such places as Iraqi, Iran, Pakistan, and Afghanistan.[8] How many Americans speak pasto, Arabic, and farsi well (including the nuances of slang and various dialects), and are willing to work in perilous locations for government pay?

Even if successfully recruited, indigenous assets can be unreliable. They are known to fabricate reports, sell information to the highest bidder, and scheme as false defectors or double-agents. These individuals are neither boy scouts nor nuns; they are often driven by greed, with no moral compass. An example of the risks involved in HUMINT is the German agent inside Iraq in 2002, prophetically codenamed "Curveball." He managed to convince the German intelligence service that WMDs did exist in Iraq; and the Central Intelligence Agency (CIA), in turn, took the bait through its ties with the Germans. Only after the war began in Iraq did Curveball's bona fides fall into doubt inside the CIA; and only much later did lawmakers on the intelligence oversight committees get around to questioning the reliability of America's clandestine sources in Iraq.

Processing

In the third stage of the cycle, the intelligence that has been collected—perhaps, intercepted terrorist telephone conversations in farsi or encrypted government documents stolen from Chinese government safes—must be converted into usable information, that is, decoded and translated into English. This conversion of "raw" intelligence into a more useable form is known as processing.

Intelligence pours into America's secret agencies like a stream of water from a firehose held to the mouth. Each day, over 400 satellite photographs arrive at the National Geospatial-Intelligence Agency (NGA), for instance; and millions of telephone intercepts, often in difficult codes that must be broken, descend on the National Security Agency (NSA). The United States finds itself short of translators, photo-interpreters, and code-breaking mathematicians. In response to queries about the major problems facing US intelligence, a recent NSA director responded: "There are three: "processing, processing, and processing."[9]

As things stand today, the vast majority of intelligence gathered by the United States is never examined. It gathers dust in warehouses. This presents a supreme challenge for the government's specialists in information technology (IT): how to improve the nation's capacity to mine intelligence data more rapidly, quickly separating out all the "noise" from the few key "signals" that decisionmakers need to know about. Legislative overseers have shown insufficient interest in this important topic, perhaps because IT is technical and they are rarely trained as scientists or mathematicians; CIA covert actions are much more understandable and "sexier," and more readily draw their attention.

Analysis

At the heart and soul of the intelligence cycle is the phase known as analysis. Here the task is to bring thoughtful insight to the information that has been collected and processed. The method is straightforward enough: hire the smartest people one can recruit to sift through all the information available, from both open and secret sources, in an attempt to make a good educated guess (an "estimate") about what is likely to happen somewhere in the world.

As suggested earlier, here's the bad news: intelligence analysts will always make mistakes, because of human limitations on forecasting events. This brings us back to the dilemma of incomplete information and the uncertain light of the future. To quote Dean Rusk again, all intelligence reports ought to start off with the caveat: "We really don't know what is going to happen, but here is our best guess."[10] The evidence and assumptions that undergird these best guesses are seldom probed by congressional overseers.

Dissemination

In the final phase of the intelligence cycle—and in some ways the most difficult—the secret agencies pass along their findings to those who make decisions on behalf of the United States. Speaking truth to power is a notoriously hard task. In the first place, those in power often do not want to hear facts that run counter to their established policies. In the days of antiquity, the messenger with bad news sometimes had his head removed. According to an old Turkish adage, "Those who speak the truth ought to keep one foot in the stirrup." Further, policymakers frequently convince themselves that they are too busy to read intelligence reports.

The dissemination phase of the intelligence cycle is replete with obstacles. Perhaps the greatest paradox regarding American intelligence is that so much effort and funding go into gathering intelligence for policymakers, only to find at the end that high officials often pay no attention to the results. Nor do legislative overseers. Some of the best assistant secretaries of defense and state, and some of the most highly regarded members of Congress, have conceded they spent, at best, about 10–15 minutes a day scanning intelligence reports. They were simply swamped with other obligations.[11] This would be doubly true of men and women higher up the policy hierarchy (with some exceptions like the Yale history graduate with a Ph.D. in economics from MIT, Les Aspin, who as Secretary of Defense in 1992–93 read every intelligence report in sight). So the first challenge of dissemination is to catch the attention of busy leaders; marketing the information product is a vital part of the intelligence cycle.

Then comes the even more vexatious problem of "politicization"—Sin No. 1 in the secret world of intelligence.[12] The politicization of intelligence can take two forms. Intelligence officers may "cook" information to suit the needs of policymakers, currying the favor of their political superiors in order to advance their own careers—what is known as "intelligence to please." Fortunately, this phenomenon occurs fairly infrequently, since most analysts (like academicians and journalists) are imbued with a sense of professional ethics that shuns this practice.

More common is the second form of politicization, whereby policy officials distort intelligence reports provided to them in those cases where the analytic conclusions fail to support an administration's policy objectives. As a character in John Steinbeck's *The Winter of Our Discontent* sagely noted: "No one wants advice—only corroboration." An illustration is the phenomenon of "cherry picking," that is, when policy officials select from intelligence reports only those snippets of information and analysis that uphold their policy agenda, pushing countervailing facts to the side. Sometimes, even more blatantly, policy officials simply ignore entire intelligence reports, as President Lyndon B. Johnson was inclined to do with CIA analyses that offered a dismal prognosis about the likelihood of US military success in Vietnam; or as the second Bush administration did with CIA reports on the lack of an al Qaeda–Iraq connection. In such instances, the unenviable but important responsibility of intelligence officers is to call policy officials to account for their distortions—publicly if necessary, even though it may place their jobs in jeopardy.

One of the most disquieting outcomes of the Iraqi WMD debates was the unwillingness of either the CIA or its British intelligence counterpart, MI6, to confront policy officials who exaggerated intelligence reporting. This quiescence was particularly egregious in the corridors of Whitehall. Analysts in MI6 had warned Prime Minister Tony Blair that small-scale (tactical) chemical or biological weapons could be used by the Saddam Hussein regime against a front-line Western invasion forces within 45 minutes of an invasion into Iraq. In a press conference, the prime minister's press secretary subsequently inflated this information to imply that Iraqi WMDs could be used strategically against London itself. This hyperbole achieved the desired effect of frightening the British people into support for a UK–US invasion of Iraq. The Bush administration's scare talk of "mushroom clouds" on American soil echoed this approach inside the United States.

The CIA and MI6, both of whom realized that policymakers were expressing an unwarranted alarmist stance toward Iraq, stood by mutely for the most part. An exception occurred when CIA analysts complained publicly (through anonymous media leaks) that Vice President Dick Cheney was wrong to insist on a significant tie between al Qaeda and Saddam. Intelligence reporting had come to just the opposite conclusion, although CIA analysts warned that indeed a bond might be forged between global terrorists and the Iraqi dictatorship (or its insurgent remnants) if the West invaded Iraq. Despite the CIA's findings to the contrary, the vice president continued to argue on television and radio talk shows that al Qaeda and the secular Iraqi regime were secretly allied.

The good news about the intelligence cycle is that for the large sum of money it spends each year, the United States is able to field the largest and (at least in terms of spy machines) the most sophisticated intelligence apparatus in world history. As indicated earlier, this brings in a torrent of information, some of which is quite useful. Further, the federal government has been able to attract into the intelligence agencies many good minds to interpret the findings. The secret agencies are expert as well in packaging and delivering their best judgments to the right people in government in a timely manner. Yet, things still go wrong. Perhaps nothing illustrates this reality better than the misjudgments about the existence of Iraqi WMDs.

The question of Iraqi WMDs

As rumors of war against Iraq circulated around Washington, D.C., in 2002, to its credit Congress (more particularly, the Senate)—not the White House—asked the intelligence agencies to prepare a National Intelligence Estimate (NIE) on the possibility of WMDs in Saddam Hussein's regime. This document was produced, hurriedly, by October. It concluded, as did most intelligence agencies and outside analysts, that WMDs were probably present in Iraq. This judgment, taken too much at face value by lawmakers and others, was based on three primary sources of inaccurate information.

First, because the US intelligence agencies had no significant human assets in Iraq during the interwar years, analysts back in the United States extrapolated from what they knew about Iraq when Americans had entered that rogue nation in 1991 as part of the first Persian Gulf war effort. At that time, the CIA learned that its estimates prior to 1991 regarding Iraqi WMDs were faulty; Saddam's weapons program had advanced far beyond what CIA analysts had anticipated. Now, absent reliable ground-based sources once US troops departed from Iraq after that first invasion, analysts seem to have compensated for their earlier underestimates by this time overestimating the likelihood of WMDs. Of course, every projection into the future is to some extent an extrapolation from the past; but, in this instance, analysts failed to sufficiently flag in the 2002 estimate the large number of deep uncertainties. Even when the analysts who wrote the estimate were guarded on some points, there was a tendency subsequently for lawmakers and other policy officials to "cascade" the intelligence, that is, to treat earlier guarded assertions as if they had become gospel.[13]

Second, the results of two seemingly valuable HUMINT interrogations proved false. Reports from the German asset "Curveball" factored into the CIA's assessments, backed up by assurances from German intelligence officials (at first) that he was a reliable source. Only two years after the war against Iraq started in 2002 did the Germans concede that Curveball had proven to be a fabricator. Moreover, the confessions of a captured al Qaeda member, Ibn al-Shaykh al-Libi, who was interrogated by the Defense Intelligence Agency (DIA), also failed to hold up.[14]

Third, the Iraqi National Congress, led by the Iraqi exile Ahmad Chalabi, claimed to know what was going on in Iraq and encouraged the US intelligence agencies and the second Bush administration to believe that Saddam was hell bent on gaining a nuclear weapons capability. Chalibi's reliability is now in question. His purpose may have been chiefly to push for an American invasion so that he might advance his own personal political agenda: the toppling of Saddam to pave the way for his own hoped for (but feckless) rise to power in Iraq.

On top of this "evidence," CIA analysts were also aware that British intelligence and the intelligence services of several other countries were concerned about the possibility of Iraqi WMDs. Yet, official British government inquiries into this issue (the Butler Report) in 2004 have revealed, recall, that the concerns of British intelligence analysts had more to do with the possible Iraqi use of *tactical* chemical-biological weapons on the battlefield by Saddam if he faced an invasion force, not *strategic* WMDs that could strike the United Kingdom, the United States, or even their support forces at a distance from the immediate battlefield. The speeches of Saddam himself buttressed the WMD hypothesis, since the autocrat often boasted of his capabilities in the realm of unconventional weaponry—perhaps in a misguided rhetorical attempt to deter a US or an Iranian invasion of his nation.

It is often claimed that the second Bush administration pressured intelligence analysts to write intelligence reports that suggested the presence of WMDs in Iraq, thereby providing useful support for a military intervention against Saddam's regime—what some argue was the course of action desired by the Administration in the first place, WMDs aside. Vice President Cheney visited CIA analysts at CIA headquarters an unprecedented eight times leading up to publication of the 2002 NIE, sharply questioning the estimates of analysts whenever they strayed from his conviction that WMDs must surely existing in Iraq. The CIA analysts with whom Cheney visited, though, say they felt no sense of intimidation from the vice president ("despite his perpetually curled lip," as one remembered in June 2005).[15] On the contrary, they were pleased to have such rare, high-level attention paid to their work.

Secretary of State Colin L. Powell also visited with CIA officials more than once to probe the strength of their evidence, especially on the eve of his appearance before the United Nations on February 3, 2003, to make the WMD case to the world on behalf of the administration. In this process, he discovered some disagreement among intelligence analysts, including dissent within his own intelligence shop, the Bureau of Intelligence and Research (INR) in the Department of State, as well as inside the Department of Energy's intelligence unit (an organization notably expert on matters of global nuclear developments, which it tracks closely) and the Air Force's intelligence service. These relatively small agencies presented judgments suggesting that Saddam most likely had never pursued a WMD program after the first Persian Gulf war, despite his boasting. Yet, the analytic behemoths among the intelligence agencies, especially the CIA and the DIA, continued to argue that Saddam probably did have such weaponry. Their argument centered on Iraq's purchase of 60,000 high-strength aluminum tubes, which (they argued) seemed designed for a uranium centrifuge and a nuclear weapons program.[16] Moreover, George J. Tenet, the nation's Director of Central Intelligence (DCI), whose offices were located on the seventh floor of the CIA, backed the majority opinion.

Powell deferred to this powerful coalition, even though analysts in INR and the Department of Energy maintained that the aluminum tubes were probably combustion chambers for conventional rockets. Air Force Intelligence also disputed the administration's assertion that Iraqi's unmanned aerial vehicles (UAVs or drones) had a long-range capability. For the most part, though, these internal debates took place outside the hearing of the American public and were overwhelmed by the views of the largest and most powerful of the intelligence agencies and the DCI. Off went Powell to the UN to make the case for WMD intervention. He now states that his speech at the UN was the biggest mistake of his career.

The president himself, George W. Bush, questioned his intelligence chief, Tenet, directly about his confidence in the conclusion reached in the 2002 NIE that basically supported the WMD hypothesis. Was he sure there were weapons of mass destruction in Iraq? Tenet's now famous response, reported by Bob Woodward of the *Washington Post*, was: "It's a slam dunk, Mr. President."[17] A careful reading of the 2002 NIE indicates, however, that the analysts who wrote it at the request of the Senate were by no means claiming a "slam dunk." They did conclude that, on balance, the odds were in favor of finding WMDs in Iraq; but, the report included some caveats about the softness of the data.

This softness is precisely what Tenet should have underscored for the president and for Congress: that the NIE was hardly a definitive report; that more on-the-ground fact-finding was badly needed; and that the CIA was uneasy about the HUMINT reports from Curveball, al-Libi, and Chalabi. A briefing along these lines from the DCI to the president and to appropriate lawmakers would have highlighted the need for a delay in the invasion plans until UN weapons inspectors had been able to clear up the intelligence ambiguities. Instead, the White House seems to have been all too ready to accept the findings of the intelligence community that conveniently happened to run parallel to their own policy aspirations. As for Congress, its intelligence committees failed to ask the CIA's Iraqi analysts tough questions about the facts and assumptions of the October NIE, and the degree of dissent that it had generated among some significant elements of the intelligence community.

The DCI evidently fell into a beguiling trap that awaits any spymaster: White House politics. Caught up in the administration's euphoria for war against Saddam, along with the pursuit of democracy and nation-building in the Middle East, George Tenet provided the clinching reassurance for the president. In reality, however, the only genuine "slam dunk" conclusion was that war would now come quickly. For its part, the Congress gave only superficial attention to the very NIE the Senate itself had requested. The incentives for fundraising and other reelection stratagems trumped the duties of intelligence oversight.

Earlier, the DCI had failed to correct the record at another important moment in the WMD debate. Inserted into the president's State of the Union address in 2003 was an assertion that Saddam had sought to purchase tons of yellow-cake uranium from Niger, suggesting strongly that the Iraq dictator was indeed pursuing a nuclear weapons program. In fact, the CIA had looked into this allegation, sending a former US ambassador to Niger to make direct inquiries on the ground inside the African nation. The ambassador and CIA analysts found no evidence to support this allegation and reported its finding to the deputy national security advisor,

Steven H. Hadley, well in advance of the State of the Union address. Yet, the speech included the yellow-cake claim anyway, now cloaked in the legitimacy of the president's own word in the nationally televised event. Tenet later claimed that he had never seen an advance copy of the State of the Union remarks (odd for a leading government official) and, therefore, was unable to correct the record before the address to Congress.

Oversight lessons from the Iraqi case

What lessons may be derived from the Iraqi WMD case? First, intelligence officers—most especially the nation's intelligence chief—must be brutally candid with Congress and the White House about the limits of their analyses, raising a bright yellow flag if their conclusions are on shaky grounds. What is firmly rooted in empirical findings and what is largely speculation must be delineated. Intelligence officials probably need some encouragement to do this and executive (closed) session hearings before the congressional oversight committees dedicated to intelligence is a good place for the prodding to take place.

Second, intelligence collectors and analysts—and their overseers in Congress—must be more forceful in vetting their sources. When the Germans balked at allowing the CIA to conduct its own interviews with the asset Curveball, US intelligence officers should have downgraded the quality of this source to a low level. Again, lawmakers can play an important role in testing the reliability of agents, by posing questions to their handlers about the source's past track record, as well as his or her current ability to provide timely and accurate information. This can be probed without getting into the names or precise locations of the agents, since that could jeopardize lives if inadvertently leaked.

Finally, and most importantly, intelligence officials must maintain a wall between themselves and the policy desires of an administration. The siren song of White House politics must be as anathema to intelligence managers and analysts as the beckoning witch with a poisoned apple should have been to Snow White. Legislative overseers must insist on this separation and guard against the "politicization" of intelligence, by cross-examining policymakers and analysts in closed hearing to determine the underlying facts and assumptions that drive their judgments.

Why intelligence oversight fails

Clearly, lawmakers do not pay sufficient attention to their oversight duties, whether the subject is intelligence or practically any other policy dealt with on Capitol Hill. At least this is the case when it comes to day-to-day scrutiny

| | | Responsibility for support | |
		Low	High
		1	2
Responsibility for evaluation	Low	The ostrich	The cheerleader
		3	4
	High	The skeptic	The guardian

Figure 10.1: A typology of roles assumed by intelligence overseers in the US Congress

of executive branch programs and activities—what is sometimes referred to as "police-patrolling" or "institutional" oversight. In times of policy failure or scandal, however, when lawmakers are called upon to perform as "fire-fighters" or "investigators," their record is much better. Members of Congress by and large rise to the occasion in these emergencies, once things have gone wrong. They diligently attend investigative hearings, pose tough questions to bureaucrats, and pass significant remedial legislation in hopes of averting a repeat of the original failure or scandal.[18]

By then, however, the damage has already been done. Preferably, law-makers would perform rigorous program reviews before things when wrong. They would be conscientious police-patrollers, in an effort to avoid in the first place the outbreak of a damaging fire and the need to become firefighters.

One way of looking at the oversight roles that lawmakers play with respect to intelligence (and other policy domains) is to consider the following range of possibilities. One type of overseer is the "ostrich," a label meant to indicate a preference by some members of Congress to embrace a philosophy of benign neglect toward the supervision of the CIA and the other secret agencies (see Figure 10.1). A classic illustration is Senator Barry Goldwater (R, Arizona) when he became chair of the Senate Select Committee on Intelligence (SSCI) in 1981—an ironic historical twist, in light of the fact that he had voted against the creation of the committee in 1976. Predictably, Goldwater largely ignored his oversight responsibilities, at least until late in his tenure when he began to believe that DCI William J. Casey had hoodwinked him with misleading information about CIA operations in Nicaragua.

A second type of legislative overseer for intelligence is the "cheerleader." Here is the member of Congress who has removed his or her head from the sand, but only to cheer more effectively on behalf of the intelligence agencies. This type of lawmaker is interested primarily in the defense of intelligence officers and their decisions, in providing support for intelligence budgets and the quick granting of supplements when needed, and in advancing almost any kind of intelligence operation at home and abroad against those who seek to harm the United States.

During hearings, the cheerleader specializes in "soft ball" pitches—easy questions designed to be hit over the center field fence by witnesses from the intelligence agencies.[19] In press conferences, the cheerleader acts as a kind of defense attorney for the agencies, hinting at their behind-the-scenes, still-secret, "if you only knew" successes; lauding the heroism of intelligence officers and agents in the field, often under conditions of great danger and hardship; castigating journalists for printing leaked secrets that imperil the nation; warning of threats at home and abroad that can lead to more 9/11s or worse, if the intelligence agencies are fettered in any way. Such statements by cheerleaders are often valid, but it is their one-sidedness that characterizes this type.

An illustration of the cheerleader is Representative Edward P. Boland when he became the first chair of House Permanent Select Committee on Intelligence (HISCI) in 1977. Boland had witnessed firsthand how in 1975 the Pike Committee in the House, an investigative panel led by Representative Otis Pike (D, New York), had been excessively critical of intelligence, to the point of a shrill final report that—although it had some insights and fresh historical data—was widely discredited for its strong anti-CIA biases. Appalled by its experience with the Pike Committee, the House refused to create an intelligence oversight committee in 1976 when the Senate established SSCI. It took another year of debate and cooling down before members of the House voted to establish a counterpart to the Senate committee.

As a means of helping to restore the House to a more balance perspective on the value of intelligence, Boland bent over backwards from 1977 to 1982 to display a willingness to cooperate with intelligence officials. He often swallowed his own personal skepticism about some secret operations and expressed his support for the government's secret bureaucracy, just to show that HSPCI could be a partner in the world of intelligence and not a reincarnation of the blunderbuss Pike Committee. Like Goldwater, Boland too would become more aggressive as an overseer when William Casey tried to bypass HPSCI.

A third role type is the "skeptic." This approach is similarly one-sided, only at the opposite extreme from the cheerleader. From the skeptic's point of view, nothing the intelligence agencies do is likely to be good. From this perspective, the secret agencies are inherent immoral: opening and reading other people's mail, listening in on telephone calls, stealing documents, maybe even killing people—all unsavory, not to mention illegal, activities. The secret agencies are also incompetent, continues this argument, with the CIA failing to anticipate the fall of the Soviet Union, the 9/11 attacks, or the absence of WMDs in Iraq. For the most extreme skeptic, there is only one solution: shut down the secret agencies altogether. In 1996, for example, Senator Daniel Patrick Moynihan (D, New York), a member of SSCI dismayed by the CIA's inability to predict the collapse of the Soviet empire, called for the Agency's abolition.[20]

A fourth general type of intelligence overseer is the "guardian." From the normative perspective that runs through the analysis offered here, this model conforms best with the hopes of reformers in 1975, who favored a Congress that conducts a serious review of intelligence programs to prevent (or at least lessen the likelihood of) future domestic spying activities like Operations CHAOS and COINTELPRO.[21] Representative Lee H. Hamilton (D, Indiana), HPSCI chair from 1985–87, maintains that the ideal intelligence overseers are those members of Congress who are both "partners and critics" of the secret agencies.[22] Or as another HPSCI member, Norm Dicks (D, Washington), has put it: "Overseeing the intelligence community is like being a good parent: you have to encourage and discipline."[23]

The dynamic nature of intelligence accountability

Members of SSCI and HPSCI have sometimes displayed more than one approach to intelligence supervision during their tenure on the committees, as suggested by the transformations of Goldwater and Boland from ostriches to guardians as they grew more wary of DCI Casey's activities. Furthermore, even those lawmakers who may generally cluster together in just one of the four cells of Figure 1 can often be far apart within a cell. For example, some cheerleaders may be mild in their cheerleading, while others may be overzealous. The same with the skeptics. Or in the case of the ostriches, some may at least poke their heads out of the sand once in a while. As for guardians, some may be better than others at maintaining an even keel between offering praise and finding fault.

Illustrations of such variations at the time of the WMD intelligence errors are shown in Figure 10.2. The SSCI chairman (2001–2), Bob Graham (D, Florida), for example, moved from cheerleader to skeptic as a result of slights from DCI Tenet. In 2002, Graham served as co-chair of a special joint committee that temporarily combined the membership of SSCI and HPSCI for the purpose of investigating the 9/11 intelligence failure; the other co-chair was the HPSCI leader (1997–2004), Porter J. Goss (R, Florida). Once hearings opened on the events of that tragic terrorist attack, Graham and Tenet began to butt heads over the

Ostrich	*Cheerleader*
Goldwater (1981–84)	Boland (1977–82)
Shelby (1997–9)	Graham (2001–2)
	Goss (2001–4)
	Roberts (2002–3, 2006)

Skeptic	*Guardian*
Goldwater (1984–5)	Hamilton (1985–87)
Boland (1982–5)	Goss (1997–2001)
Shelby (1999–2004)	Roberts (2004–5)
Graham (2002–4)	

Figure 10.2: Illustrations of role migration and stasis
among intelligence overseers*

* The HPSCI Chairman Porter Goss, for example, shifted from the role of guardian in 1997–2001 to (mostly) the role of cheerleader in 2001–4.

committee's authorities and procedures. When Graham asked Tenet to be brief in his introductory remarks before the panel, the DCI instead carried on at length and in a "somewhat defiant tone."[24] Tenet also refused to declassify some materials that Graham thought important for the public record; and the DCI frequently caused havoc in the proceedings by denying the committee access to basic intelligence documents related to the 9/11 attacks, refusing at the last minute to allow scheduled intelligence officers to testify before the committee, and even at the eleventh hour canceling his own appearance before SSCI in executive (closed) session.[25] As DCI Tenet stonewalled and slow-rolled the joint committee, Graham began his transition from cheerleader to skeptic. (Tenet had poked Graham and his panel in the eye one too many times and the Senator went into a boil, accusing the intelligence chief of obstructionism" and "unacceptable" behavior.[26])

Similarly, when SSCI investigated the mistakes surrounding the Iraqi WMD estimate, several Committee members switched from ostriches and cheerleaders to guardians. Even the SSCI chair, Pat Roberts (R, Kansas), normally a dyed-in-the-wool intelligence cheerleader, expressed strong criticism of the CIA's judgments.

Conclusion

The government of the United States is built on a foundation of shared powers among the three branches: the executive, the legislative, and the judicial.[27] Beyond making laws, a primary duty of the legislative branch is to keep watch over the sprawling bureaucracy that lies at the feet of the president. An especially difficult assignment is to keep watch over the dark side of this terrain: the secret agencies. Before 1975, lawmakers largely overlooked the responsibility to supervise these organizations, because the job was daunting in the expertise and time it required.[28] Moreover, it provided little opportunity for credit-claiming; and it was fraught with risk, if things went wrong (such as the Bay of Pigs) and members of Congress might have to share culpability. Better to let the spies go their own way in the noble, if unsavory, war against global Communism fought in the back alleys of the world. The revelation in 1975 that these agencies had engaged in espionage against American citizens—the very people that had been created to protect—changed this attitude of benign neglect on Capitol Hill; the domestic spy scandal forced lawmakers to take intelligence accountability more seriously.

This chapter suggests that members of Congress have displayed a range of responses to the call for greater intelligence accountability, failing dramatically in their ability and willingness to probe the judgments of the CIA and its companion agencies on the question of Iraqi nuclear weapons. Some lawmakers have been throwbacks ("ostriches," in the terminology used here), content to bury their heads in the sand and continue the earlier era of trust when lawmakers deferred to the decisions of the executive branch within the intelligence domain.

Others have chosen to become unabashed boosters for intelligence—"cheerleaders" who view their job primarily as one of explaining the value of intelligence to the American people and supporting intelligence missions with strong funding and encouragement, never mind the careful review of intelligence budgets and programs. Taking the opposite approach, another group of lawmakers (the "skeptics") have been so critical about intelligence that some have even called for the abolition of the CIA. While not going that far, other skeptics have consistently found fault, and little virtue, in America's attempts to spy on adversaries or overthrow regimes that fail to conform with US interests.

Finally, some members of Congress have also been "guardians." They have struck a reasonable balance between serving as partners of the intelligence agencies on Capitol Hill, on the one hand, and demanding competence and law-abiding behavior from these agencies, on the other hand.

From among these roles, the two intelligence committees on Capitol Hill—SSCI and HPSCI—have displayed a scattering of lawmakers across the range of possibilities. Moreover, members of these committees have sometimes migrated from one role to another, say, from adoring cheerleader to dismayed skeptic. One of the main catalysts for motility has been a sense of injured institutional pride, when lawmakers perceive that intelligence officials have failed to treat Congress with appropriate respect. In one instance of role transition, Senator Goldwater shifted from cheerleader to skeptic when DCI William Casey approached hearings with SSCI in a dismissive manner. In other cases, a deteriorating personal relationship between lawmakers and intelligence officials has led to change, as when SSCI Chair Dennis DeConcini (D, Arizona) and DCI R. James Woolsey during the 1990s became estranged from one another on personal grounds. So, more recently, did SSCI Chair Richard C. Shelby (R, Alabama) and DCI Tenet. A dramatic change in policy can also induce changes in oversight behavior, as when HSPCI chair Edward Boland could no longer countenance his role as cheerleader when DCI Casey racheted up the level of violent covert actions in Nicaragua during the 1980s. In the case of the Iraqi WMD mistakes, members of Congress often evolved into guardians when they realized how faulty the intelligence had actually been—a belated metamorphosis that did nothing to prevent the drift toward war in 2002 based on the flawed intelligence.

This analysis only scratches the surface. Much more work remains to be done in the search for a full understanding of how lawmakers choose their oversight roles, and how these roles may change over time. Especially important will be efforts to fathom why so many members of Congress never adopt the role of guardian—the model widely accepted by reformers as the ideal, because it balances support for intelligence with a determination to avoid (through persistent review or "police patrolling") future failures and scandals by the secret agencies. How can lawmakers be urged to spend more time on serious program evaluation? What incentives can be introduced into the culture of Capitol Hill to make accountability a more valued pursuit?

One might think that enough incentives already exist, such as preventing another domestic spy scandal (hints of which emerged in 2005 when it was disclosed that the Bush administration bypassed the warrant procedures for telephone wiretaps),[29] helping to prevent another 9/11 calamity, or eschewing false conclusions on the existence of WMDs abroad of the kind that drew the United States into war with Iraq in 2003. Most observers agree, however, that lawmakers are performing far below their potential when it comes to intelligence accountability and that generally, across the policy board, oversight remains the neglected stepchild of life on Capitol Hill. Correcting this condition is a worthy challenge for educators, journalists, lawmakers, and indeed all public-minded citizens of the United States.

These objectives amount to a tall order, but the United States should set high goals for its intelligence services and legislative oversees if the nation expects to avoid another series of intelligence mistakes like the ones that plague the analysis of Iraqi WMDs. The key to success on the oversight front will be effective leadership on Capitol Hill, especially the development of a system of stronger incentives for good oversight work, and a watchful electorate prepared to vote out of office those lawmakers who neglect their oversight duties.

Notes

1 See Loch K. Johnson, *America's Secret Power: The CIA in a Democratic Society* (New York: Oxford University Press, 1987).
2 See Williamson Murray and Mark Grimsley, "Introduction: On Strategy," in *The Making of Strategy: Rules, States, and War*, Williamson Murray, Alvin Bernstein, and MacGregor Knox, eds. (New York: Cambridge University Press, 1994), 1–23.
3 Author's interview, Washington, D.C. (May 9, 2003).
4 These 16 agencies include eight military organizations: the National Geospatial-Intelligence Agency (NGA), the National Security Agency (NSA), the National Reconnaissance Office (NRO), the Defense Intelligence Agency (DIA), and the intelligence units of the Army, Navy, Air Force, and Marines; seven civilian agencies: the Federal Bureau of Investigation (FBI), the Department of State's Bureau of Intelligence and Research (INR), the intelligence unit of the Department of Homeland Security, the Coast Guard; the Treasury Department, the Energy Department, and the Drug Enforcement Administration (DEA); and one independent agency: the Central Intelligence Agency (CIA).
5 Author's interview, Athens, Georgia (February 21, 1988).
6 Author's interview, Washington, D.C. (March 22, 1995).
7 For an accounting of some, see Amy B. Zegart, "September 11 and the Adaptation Failure of US Intelligence Agencies," 29 *International Security* (Spring 2005), 78–111.
8 See Loch K. Johnson, *Seven Sins of American Foreign Policy* (New York: Longman, 2007).
9 J. M. McConnell, quoted in the author's interview with a senior NSA official, Washington, D.C. (July 14, 1994).
10 Author's interview, Athens, Georgia (July 4, 1988).
11 See, for instance, Loch K. Johnson, *Bombs, Bugs, Drugs, and Thugs: Intelligence and America's Quest for Security* (New York: New York University Press, 2000), 194.
12 See Loch K. Johnson and James J. Wirtz, eds., *Strategic Intelligence: Windows into a Secret World* (Los Angeles: Roxbury, 2004), 167–218.
13 Author's notes on former US intelligence official Mark M. Lowenthal, remarks, conference, Canadian Association of Security and Intelligence Studies (CASIS), Ottawa, Canada (October 28, 2006).
14 See Douglas Jehl, "Report Warned Bush Team About Intelligence Doubts," *New York Times* (November 6, 2005), A14.

15 Author's interviews with CIA analysts in Langley, Virginia, and Washington, D.C. (June 15, 2005).

16 See the account in David Barstow, William J. Broad, and Jeff Gerth," How the White House Used Disputed Arms Intelligence," *New York Times* (October 3, 2004), A1, A 16–18.

17 Bob Woodward, *Plan of Attack* (New York: Simon & Schuster, 2004): 249.

18 See Loch K. Johnson, "Accountability and America's Secret Foreign Policy: Keeping a Legislative Eye on the Central Intelligence Agency," 1 *Foreign Policy Analysis* (March 2005), 99–120.

19 See Loch K. Johnson, *Secret Agencies: US Intelligence in a Hostile World* (New Haven: Yale University Press, 1996): ch. 6.

20 Daniel Patrick Moynihan, "Do We Still Need the CIA? The State Dept. Can Do the Job," *New York Times* (May 19, 1991), E17.

21 See Loch K. Johnson, "Congressional Supervision of America's Secret Agencies: The Experience and Legacy of the Church Committee," *Public Administration Review* 64 (January 2004), 3–14.

22 Quoted by F. Davies, "GOP-Controlled Senate Expected to Give Less Scrutiny to War on Terror," *Miami Herald* (November 7, 2002), p. A1.

23 Interviewed by Cynthia Nolan (Washington, D.C.: October 15, 2003), in "More Perfect Oversight: Intelligence Oversight and Reform," in Loch K. Johnson, ed., *Strategic Intelligence: Accountability*, vol.5 (Westport, CT: Praeger, 2007).

24 K. Guggenheim, "Tenet Defends CIA's Pre-9/11 Efforts," *Washington Post* (October 19, 2002), p. A1.

25 Senate Shelby, who had shifted to the position of SSCI's ranking minority member when the Democrats won back the Senate for a time, complained (in his new role as skeptic): "Witnesses are requested, refused, requested again, granted, and then—at the last minute—refused again" (Congressional Record 148 (2002), p. 590850).

26 Neil A. Lewis, "Senator Insists C.I.A. Is Harboring Iraq Reports, *New York Times* (October 4, 2002), p. A12.

27 See James M. Lindsay, "Deference and Defiance: The Shifting Rhythms of Executive-Legislative Relations in Foreign Policy," *Presidential Studies Quarterly* 33 (September 2003), 530.

28 See David M. Barrett, *The CIA and the Congress* (Lawrence: Kansas University Press, 2005).

29 James Risen and Eric Lichtblau, "Bush Lets US Spy on Callers Without Courts," *New York Times* (December 16, 2005), A1. The two journalists won a Pulitzer Prize for reporting about how the second Bush administration seemed to have violated the 1978 Foreign Intelligence Surveillance Act that requires judicial warrants for national security wiretaps.

11

Flawed intelligence, limited oversight: official inquiries into prewar UK intelligence on Iraq

Mark Phythian

He sat in his room and wrote his negative report to M. He read it through. It would be a depressing signal to get. Should he say anything about the wisp of a lead he was working on? No. Not until he had something solid. Wishful intelligence, the desire to please or reassure the recipient, was the most dangerous commodity in the whole realm of secret information. (Ian Fleming, *Thunderball*)[1]

As Chapter 5 demonstrated, the decision to go to war in Iraq did not arise as a consequence of current intelligence on the threat represented by Iraq's weapons of mass destruction (WMD) programs. However, this should not obscure the fact that UK intelligence on Iraqi WMD was in many key respects inaccurate, and that it played a significant role in the government's presentation of its case for war. In this context, the purpose of this chapter is two-fold. First, it considers both the reliability of UK intelligence on Iraq's WMD programs and explanations for flaws in it. Secondly, it assesses the effectiveness of the different forms of inquiry held into intelligence on Iraqi WMD in providing a full explanation of how the UK came to go to war on what Robin Cook famously termed a "false prospectus."[2] In doing so, this chapter focuses on the inquiries conducted by (in chronological order):

- the Foreign Affairs Committee (FAC), a select committee of the House of Commons;
- the Intelligence and Security Committee (ISC), a committee of parliamentarians but not of Parliament, appointed by and answerable to the prime minister;
- the Butler inquiry, a committee of privy counselors.[3]

At the outset, a brief word about the origins of each of the inquiries will be useful. The 2003 Iraq war had been justified by the government on the grounds that Iraq's WMD represented, to quote from Prime Minister Tony Blair's Foreword to the September 2002 Downing Street dossier, a "current and serious threat to the UK national interest."[4] As the government was advised, these were the only available grounds on which a war could be deemed legal. The post-war failure to find any WMD raised questions about the veracity of the claims underpinning the war. These were posed more frequently as time passed and the failure to locate WMD became more marked. In particular, those MPs who had opposed the war demanded answers, and it was in this context that the FAC decided to investigate the accuracy of governmental claims.[5] One unforeseen outcome of its hearings was the series of events that culminated in the suicide of MoD biological weapons expert Dr. David Kelly.

By the time a second inquiry into the intelligence basis for the war decision, by the ISC, reported in September 2003,[6] Blair had been obliged to set up a further, judicial, inquiry under a former Lord Chief Justice of Northern Ireland, Lord Hutton, to "urgently conduct an investigation into the circumstances surrounding the death of Dr. Kelly." The public hearings conducted by the Hutton inquiry and evidence available to it, notably internal Downing Street email traffic concerning the production of the September 2002 dossier, suggested a critical outcome. However, when the report appeared it exonerated the government of any bad faith in relation to its creation. Any governmental relief at this outcome was short-lived. On the same day Hutton delivered his welcome verdict, January 28, 2004, in Washington, DC arms expert David Kay, the man charged with leading the post-war hunt for Iraq's WMD, testified that Saddam had destroyed all such weapons, possibly even as early as 1991. Blair's post-war public confidence that WMD would be recovered was shown to be misplaced, and the intelligence he had consistently cited as indicating the urgency of dealing with the Iraqi threat was again called into question. Pressure quickly built in the US for an inquiry into prewar intelligence on Iraq, and having failed to dissuade the US from holding its own inquiry, Blair felt obliged to follow suit and announce a fourth inquiry, to be conducted by a team of privy counselors led by former Cabinet Secretary Lord Butler.[7]

The Foreign Affairs Committee inquiry

With few exceptions, House of Commons select committees have found themselves frustrated in investigating issues that require access to intelligence. In 1991–92 the Trade and Industry Select Committee's investigation into the Iraqi supergun affair was seriously compromised by its inability to secure access to intelligence material or personnel.[8] This made it reluctant to take on such work in the future. However, in 1995 it did, at the government's request, investigate allegations that weapons exported from the UK were diverted to a prohibited destination, Iran, but only after receiving assurances that it would have access to all relevant material. Still, it noted in its report:

> We have not had difficulty in obtaining from the Government the witnesses or documents we wanted, with the exception of intelligence material. We received a summary of the intelligence reports, but requests that we be allowed to inspect the intelligence reports, in the form circulated to the Department, under the "Crown jewels procedure", and subsequently that one member of the Committee (a Privy Councillor and former Foreign Office Minister) be allowed to inspect that material, were turned down. While we regret this, we do not believe that it significantly hindered our inquiry, except in several specific areas.[9]

It argued that the "Crown jewels" procedure should be employed more widely where intelligence material was directly relevant to select committee investigations. This procedure related to the FAC's 1984–85 inquiry into the sinking of the *General Belgrano* during the 1982 Falklands war. Then, committee members and staff were allowed to consult intelligence material (the "Crown jewels"), but not permitted to take away any notes. However, the government subsequently argued that this was "always seen as a one-off exception," because "intelligence was at the heart of the matter . . . It was all about the precise intelligence available at that moment."[10] However, this could also be true in other cases, like this and the earlier supergun inquiry. The Committee's Report recorded its, "regret that the Government was not willing to allow the Committee, or even a single member of the Committee . . . to inspect the original intelligence reports."[11]

The FAC inquiry into the decision to go to war in Iraq would represent another textbook illustration of the weaknesses inherent in parliamentary efforts to call the executive to account in relation to intelligence matters. One problem it faced was the familiar one that it could only gain access to those people and papers that the government allowed. While it did interview the Foreign Secretary in closed session it was denied access to the agency heads and John Scarlett, the Chairman of the Joint Intelligence Committee (JIC), the body responsible for coordinating intelligence assessments for ministers and senior officials, and at the center of the controversy over the Downing Street dossier. Additionally, it was denied access to JIC assessments, which would subsequently be made available to the Butler inquiry, although some extracts were read to the committee in private.[12]

Its investigation was conducted rapidly, in not much more than a month, and concluded while that ministers had not misled Parliament, there were areas of concern over the government's presentation of the case for war, particularly in relation to the dossier. These included: the certainty of the assertion that Iraq had sought uranium from Niger; that the "45 minutes" claim—that Iraq could deliver WMD within 45 minutes of an order to do so—did not warrant the prominence given to it in the dossier; and that the language used in the dossier was more assertive than traditionally used in intelligence documents.

Nevertheless, denial of access to intelligence material and personnel meant that the FAC report could never be regarded as definitive. The FAC concluded its report by stating that the, "continued refusal by Ministers to allow this committee access to intelligence papers and personnel, on this inquiry and more generally, is hampering it in the work which Parliament has asked it to carry out", and recommended that:

> the Government accept the principle that it should be prepared to accede to requests from the Foreign Affairs Committee for access to intelligence, when the Committee can demonstrate that it is of key importance to a specific inquiry it is conducting and unless there are genuine concerns for national security. We further recommend that, in cases where access is refused, full reasons should be given.[13]

Of particular concern was the fact that the existence of the ISC seemed to have provided the government with cover for this course of action. The ISC had been created via the 1994 Intelligence Services Act to provide a limited degree of accountability of the intelligence and security services.[14] However, it was no more than a quasi-parliamentary committee, whose members were appointed by and reported to the prime minister, rather than Parliament, and whose reports were reviewed by government prior to their publication to remove any material it wished to remain classified. Whether this arrangement represented a satisfactory one for the oversight of these agencies remained a live question throughout the first decade of the ISC's existence. Calls for it to be reconstituted as a select committee of the House of Commons, and hence be accountable to Parliament rather than the executive, were voiced regularly. In this case, the existence of the ISC allowed the government to claim that it was not essential that the FAC be furnished with access to intelligence personnel and papers for oversight of the agencies to be conducted. This was a source of considerable irritation to the FAC, which regarded the government's, "refusal to grant us access to evidence essential to our inquiries as a failure of accountability to Parliament, the more so as it does not accord entirely with precedent."[15]

The Intelligence and Security Committee inquiry

In its investigation, the ISC sought, "to examine whether the available intelligence, which informed the decision to invade Iraq, was adequate and properly assessed and whether it was accurately reflected in Government publications."[16] It did not consider the decision to go to war *per se*, which fell outside its terms of reference, but this was still controversial territory. It represented the kind of politically sensitive subject that many observers had suggested would represent a litmus test of the ISC's effectiveness as an oversight body. Moreover, the weight of responsibility it bore was made all the greater by the fact that the government had justified its refusal to cooperate with the FAC inquiry on the grounds that the ISC was the appropriate vehicle to undertake such an investigation.

Following a four-month investigation the ISC reported that, based on the intelligence it had seen, "there was convincing intelligence that Iraq had active chemical, biological and nuclear programmes and the capability to produce chemical and biological weapons."[17] The ISC had already commented on the Downing Street dossier in its 2002–3 annual report, stating that it supported, "the responsible use of intelligence and material collected by the Agencies to inform the public on matters such as these."[18] The question here, then, was how far this represented responsible use of the material, and how far it informed the public as opposed to misled them. However, the ISC failed to rise to the challenge. For example, a draft of Tony Blair's Foreword to the dossier acknowledged that there was no threat of nuclear attack on the UK, but this information was excluded from the published version (see Appendix B). This denied the public available reassurance, removed an opportunity to bring some context to bear, and served to heighten the sense of threat conveyed by the dossier. The ISC contented itself with observing that: "It was unfortunate that this point was removed from the published version of the foreword and not highlighted elsewhere."[19] The government's presentation of the claim that Iraq could launch WMD within 45 minutes of an order being given drew similarly mild criticism. The ISC concluded:

> The dossier was for public consumption and not for experienced readers of intelligence material. The 45 minutes claim, included four times, was always likely to attract attention because it was arresting detail that the public had not seen before. As the 45 minutes claim was new to its readers, the context of the intelligence and any assessment needed to be explained. The fact that it was assessed to refer to battlefield chemical and biological munitions and their movement on the battlefield, not to any other form of chemical or biological attack, should have been highlighted in the dossier.

The omission of the context and assessment allowed speculation as to its exact meaning. This was unhelpful to an understanding of this issue.[20]

It also recorded its judgment that the JIC had not been subjected to political pressures.[21] Whether the JIC had felt itself under pressure to conform was a more open question. The Committee was assured by the Ministry of Defence and the Secretary of State for Defence that no one in the Defence Intelligence Staff (DIS) had expressed serious concerns about the drafting of the dossier, only to find out subsequently that two members of DIS had written to their line managers to express their concern at the language being used in the dossier, "which was not in their view supported by the intelligence available to them".[22] The ISC termed this failure of disclosure "unhelpful and potentially misleading."[23]

The government's response to the ISC's report emphasized those aspects that appeared to support its conduct over the production of the dossier, and rejected its criticisms. For example, in response to the charge that the dossier was misleading, it stated:

> the dossier did present a balanced view of Iraq's CBW capability based on the intelligence available. The dossier made clear (paragraph 14, page 16) that the withdrawal of the United Nations Special Commission (UNSCOM) had greatly diminished the ability of the international community to monitor and assess Iraq's continued efforts to reconstitute its programmes. It also noted (paragraph 13, page 16) that UNSCOM was unable to account for significant quantities of agents, precursors and munitions.[24]

But the government could not have it both ways. Either—as this and the objective record both suggest—the intelligence picture on Iraq was characterized by a significant degree of uncertainty, or, as Tony Blair wrote in his Foreword to the dossier, it was known that Iraq represented a "current and serious threat to the UK national interest". The ISC itself was dissatisfied with the government's response which, as it observed, "emphasized only four key conclusions while either rejecting or failing to address fully many of our other conclusions and recommendations. We regard this as extremely unsatisfactory."[25] This did not amount to effective oversight. Key questions had gone unanswered, and the ISC had effectively run out of the options in the face of the government's refusal to engage with it.

Moreover, although the ISC had stated that in producing its report it had seen all JIC assessments on Iraq produced between August 1990 and September 2002, and the eight produced in the period October 2002 to March 2003, it emerged that eight had been withheld—five from the former period, three from the latter. While the Committee was, "satisfied that knowledge of them would not have led us to change the conclusions, including those that were critical, in our Report,"[26] earlier access would have allowed it to include further material, and its conclusions would have been more securely rooted in a fuller picture.

Later, in its 2004–5 annual report, the ISC returned to the issue to report on significant developments regarding intelligence that fed into the dossier. These raised key questions about the accountability of the intelligence services and the possible politicization of intelligence. By this time the Butler inquiry had reported and revealed that on September 11, 2002, the same day as an email appealing for additional intelligence to bolster the in-production Downing Street dossier went out (see Chapter 5), MI6 produced a report containing intelligence from "a new source on trial." This provided "significant assurance to those drafting the Government's dossier that active, current production of chemical and biological agent was taking place."[27] Although neither the Butler Report nor the ISC specifically mentioned it, this report provided apparent validation of the then recently-arrived "45 minutes" claim.[28]

In July 2003 it was withdrawn—that is, it was judged to be untrue.[29] On July 20, 2004, days after the publication of the Butler Report, Foreign Office minister Baroness Symons told the House of Lords that its withdrawal had been kept from the Hutton inquiry (and, of course, the FAC), but had been disclosed to the ISC inquiry on condition that it was not mentioned in its report. Furthermore, Symons revealed that Foreign Secretary Jack Straw was only told about the withdrawal some three months later, and only then because he had to authorize disclosure of the information to the ISC![30] Moreover, the prime minister only learned of this development with the publication of the Butler Report, a year after the intelligence was withdrawn and after he had continued to publicly restate his confidence in the intelligence underpinning the September 2002 dossier.[31]

In October 2004 the Foreign Secretary informed the House of Commons that yet further intelligence, described in the July 2004 Butler Report as being "open to doubt" and "seriously flawed", and which related to Iraq's chemical and biological weapons programs, had been withdrawn by MI6.[32] Hence, less than 18 months after going to war in Iraq, all of the intelligence most heavily relied upon to convey a sense of imminent threat had been withdrawn. The ISC declared itself, "concerned at the amount of intelligence on Iraqi WMD that has now had to be withdrawn by the SIS."[33] It should have been, because this undermined certain of its conclusions—for example, that "there was convincing intelligence that Iraq had active chemical, biological and nuclear programs and the capability to produce chemical and biological weapons"—called into the question the mild language of criticism deployed in relation to the dossier, and suggested grounds for re-visiting the question of political pressure.

The Butler inquiry

Hence, like the earlier FAC inquiry, the ISC's investigation must be considered partial. The most thorough and revealing inquiry into the intelligence underpinning the UK government's case for war was that headed by Lord Butler. The five-member Butler team included just two members of the House of Commons, both members of the ISC which had already investigated the issue of intelligence on Iraqi WMD—senior Conservative backbencher Michael Mates, who had been an ISC member from its creation, and ISC Chair Ann Taylor—along with Sir John Chilcot, a former Northern Ireland permanent secretary, and Field Marshal the Lord Inge, a former chief of defence staff. It was to add valuable information to the public record concerning JIC assessments of Iraqi WMD, the creation of the Downing Street dossier, and the nature of intelligence failure in this case. It also raised, albeit implicitly, the question of politicization of intelligence. At the same time, however, it was clearly reluctant to apportion blame for the Iraq failure.

JIC assessments of Iraqi WMD programs, 1990–2002

By virtue of its access to JIC assessments, regular distillations and evaluations of all available intelligence on specific issues of immediate and long-term importance to UK national security, Butler was able to chart the development of assessments of Iraq's WMD and ballistic missile programs. In terms of Iraq's nuclear weapons program, at the time of the 1990 invasion of Kuwait, the JIC's assessment was that Iraq, without significant external assistance, was some four years away from being able to produce sufficient weapons-grade fissile material to produce a single nuclear device. This understanding was confirmed in a December 1990 assessment:

> We have no intelligence that would cause us to change our assessment of Iraq's current nuclear capability. Without significant foreign assistance, Iraq is still at least three years away from the capability to produce fissile material itself; and at least a further year away from being able to turn it into a weapon.[34]

However, post-war International Atomic Energy Authority (IAEA) inspections suggested that Iraq might have produced more fissile material than previously suspected. Had it not invaded Kuwait, Iraq might have been able to produce its first nuclear weapon by 1993. This information, together with the revelation that in August 1990 Iraq had attempted, but abandoned, a crash program to develop a nuclear weapon within a year, suggested that Iraq's capabilities may have been underestimated. It now seemed that Iraq had successfully concealed the full scale of its pre-war nuclear weapons program. This possibility impacted on subsequent JIC assessments, encouraging a tendency toward greater conservatism.

Still, by February 1998, some ten months before the withdrawal of the UNSCOM weapons inspection regime, the JIC assessment was that; "UNSCOM and the IAEA have succeeded in destroying or controlling the vast majority of Saddam's 1991 weapons of mass destruction capability."[35] This assessment also covered chemical and biological weapons. By 1998 the JIC assessed that most of these holdings had been destroyed, although some small stocks probably remained hidden.

More significant than any remaining stocks was the obvious fact that, having previously developed these weapons programs, Iraq would be able to do so again at short notice once sanctions were lifted. An August 24, 1995 JIC assessment concluded that Iraq; "may also have hidden some specialized equipment and stocks of precursor chemicals but it is unlikely they have a covert stockpile of weapons or agent in any significant quantity; Hussein Kamil claims there are no remaining stockpiles of agent."[36] In a sense, Iraq did not need them, because it "could begin to make chemical weapons within a matter of weeks, and produce sufficient quantities within months, if UN constraints were removed."[37] Similarly with regard to biological weapons, capacity to re-start production in a post-sanctions environment was assessed to be of greater concern than any possible current holdings. Hence, a December 1997 JIC assessment judged that Iraq "may have retained hidden BW production equipment, agent and delivery systems," but that in any case, it could "regenerate a significant offensive BW capability within months" if it so desired.[38]

However, the Butler Report was critical of the quality of assessments relating to Iraqi chemical and biological weapons during this period. Assessments of Iraq's nuclear capabilities, it found:

> were generally thorough; drew fully on both secret and open material; brought together human and technical intelligence; offered a view where appropriate on the quality of the underlying intelligence sources; were balanced and measured; identified explicitly those areas where previous assessments had been wrong, and the reasons why, to correct the record; and at each significant stage included consideration of alternative hypotheses and scenarios, and provided an explanation of the consequences were any to arise, to aid readers' understanding.[39]

By contrast, assessments relating to Iraqi chemical and biological weapons programs were judged: "less complete, especially in their considerations of alternative hypotheses; used a different "burden of proof" in testing Iraqi declarations; and hence inclined towards over-cautious or worst case estimates, carrying with them a greater sense of suspicion and an accompanying propensity to disbelieve."[40]

After the departure of UNSCOM from Iraq at the end of 1998, gathering intelligence on Iraq's WMD programs, always one of the hardest of targets, became even more challenging. In an environment where it was more difficult to report developments with certainty, a May 2001 JIC assessment represented what the Butler Report termed a "clear change" in its perception of Iraqi efforts to reconstitute its WMD programs. While this conceded that, "our knowledge of developments in Iraq's WMD and ballistic missile programs since *Desert Fox* air operations in December 1998 is patchy" and that "we have no clear intelligence" on Iraq's nuclear programs, it also included a Key Judgement referring to Iraqi research and development into uranium enrichment which, "could reduce the time needed to develop a nuclear warhead once sanctions were lifted."[41] The Butler Report was critical of the weight attached to the intelligence underpinning this judgement, which was based on two human intelligence reports, both from new sources, and neither of whom were reporting from direct experience.[42]

At the same time, the JIC's assessment of Iraq's chemical weapons program began to reach firmer judgments about the likelihood that Iraq was engaged in continuing research and development into chemical weapons, although this was based on essentially historical evidence provided by two new, untested, sources, which the Butler report considered "by no means conclusive."[43] Crucially, this assessment made no comment on the limitations of the intelligence base underpinning the judgment. Similarly, judgments on biological weapons became somewhat firmer during this period. The Key Judgement of a April 19, 2000 assessment that there was "clear evidence of continuing Iraqi biological warfare activity, including BW related research and the production of BW agent"[44] was informed by the claims of the agent Curveball, subsequently exposed as a fabricator, whose claims of mobile biological warfare facilities also infected US intelligence assessments during this period (see Chapter 12). Moreover, acceptance of the veracity of Curveball's account of mobile biological warfare facilities had, by the time of a February 2002 JIC assessment, led to the downward revision of the estimated timescale within which Iraq could produce significant quantities of biological warfare agent from weeks to days.[45]

This flawed intelligence was not without significance. It fed into interdepartmental advice for government ministers and so helped shape their views of Iraqi capabilities and intent. For example, a March 2002 briefing judged the containment policy to have been essentially successful in that it had "effectively frozen Iraq's nuclear programme"; prevented Iraq "from rebuilding its chemical arsenal to pre-Gulf War levels"; hindered chemical and biological weapons programmes; and "severely restricted" ballistic missile programmes. However, it also warned that: "Iraq continues with its BW and CW programmes and, if it has not already done so, could produce significant quantities of BW agents within days and CW agent within weeks of a decision to do so. . .There are also some indications of a continuing nuclear programme."[46]

Intelligence and the Downing Street dossier

The decision to publish summaries of intelligence material in a dossier designed to generate support for the government's policy is one which the Butler Report criticizes. It echoed the ISC's criticism that the Downing Street dossier gave no indication of existing gaps or uncertainties in intelligence, or of the thin base of some judgments, thereby creating the impression of a more solid intelligence base than actually existed. Moreover, it found that the dossier simply omitted reference to JIC judgments which would not advance the government's case, but which were essential to a balanced understanding of the overall picture. The structure of the dossier and the language used within it seemed to have one purpose, to persuade the reader of the imminence of the Iraqi threat and so increase support for the government's still undeclared policy of regime change. The Butler Report concluded that:

> The dossier did include a first chapter on the role of intelligence, as an introduction for the lay reader. But, rather than illuminating the limitations of intelligence either in the case of Iraq or more generally, the language in that Chapter may have had the opposite effect on readers. Readers may, for example, have read language in the dossier about the impossibility for security reasons of putting all the detail of the intelligence into the public domain as implying that there was fuller and firmer intelligence behind the judgements than was the case: our view, having reviewed all of the material, is that judgements in the dossier went to (although not beyond) the outer limits of the intelligence available.[47]

Essentially, then, it was a piece of advocacy. The inquiry team concluded that, "in the particular circumstances, the publication of such a document in the name and with the authority of the JIC had the result that more weight was placed on the intelligence than it could bear."[48] Whether these two judgments, appearing over 130 paragraphs apart, are entirely compatible is a very good question, and may well indicate divisions within the inquiry team. Beyond the dossier itself, the report was also critical of Tony Blair's parliamentary presentation of the intelligence underpinning it as "extensive, detailed and authoritative"—something which proved not to be the case.[49]

Human sources, validation and the question of politicization

Human intelligence sources proved highly unreliable in this case. MI6 had five main sources of human intelligence inside Iraq but, as noted above, the majority of these were subsequently deemed to be unreliable, leading to the post-war withdrawal of intelligence that had underpinned the Downing Street dossier and the public case for war. Why was this? MI6 told the Butler inquiry that it had, "for half a century been viscerally wary of émigré organisations,"[50] and while the Butler Report concludes that overreliance on such sources was not a "major cause" of the weakness in human intelligence, it is nevertheless true that a refugee—Curveball—and an influential subsource linked to opposition groups did provide intelligence subsequently deemed unreliable. At the same time, Curveball was a German intelligence source to whom UK officials had no direct prewar access, highlighting the risks of reliance on intelligence sharing.

The length of reporting chains was a further problem. Because there were so few human sources reporting from within Iraq, they came to be asked to gather intelligence on areas outside their usual expertise. This resulted in them moving beyond first-hand knowledge or experience and drawing on subsources and even subsubsources, heightening the risk of inaccurate or unreliable reporting. This became a more acute problem in the context of the decision to produce what became the Downing Street dossier and, as outlined in Chapter 5, the urgent requirement to secure material to bolster its thin intelligence base. This created the kind of pressure described by Ian Fleming in *Thunderball*, to meet and satisfy the requirement, to please. Butler notes the possibility that this pressure led to more credence being given to untried sources than would usually be the case.[51]

The Butler Report had warned that the process of assessing the validity of a source and the intelligence emanating from it must be "informed by an understanding of policy-makers' requirements for information, but must avoid being so captured by policy objectives that it reports the world as policy-makers would wish it to be rather than as it is."[52] Having issued this warning, how did it explain the validation failures relating to intelligence that fed into the Downing Street dossier?

In part, Butler offers an explanation rooted in budgetary cuts leading to organizational change that impacted negatively on validation processes. However, the answer could also lie in perceptions of political pressure infecting the intelligence process, although the possibility of politicization is not referred to explicitly in the report (indeed, the word does not appear once in the 216-page Report). Still, it is not insignificant that Butler identified "a strong case for the post of Chairman of the JIC being held by someone with experience of dealing with Ministers in a very senior role, and who is demonstrably beyond influence, and thus probably in his last post."[53] Perceptions of political pressure could help also explain why there was no JIC reassessment of Iraq's WMD programmes once the Blix UNMOVIC weapons inspection team was admitted to the country and failed to locate the previously reported program, an omission the Butler Report termed "odd."[54]

Another possible example of politicization of the intelligence process related to the way in which, during the production of the Downing Street dossier, evidence was kept from experts who may have questioned it, risking its withdrawal and thereby diluting the government's case. DIS scientist Dr. Brian Jones returned from annual leave to find the dossier in production and, in light of the limited intelligence base, raised concerns about the certainty of language being employed to support key claims. The Butler Report focuses on one intelligence report, kept from Jones, used to justify the "45 minutes" claim and withdrawn by MI6 in July 2003 (discussed above). It concluded that putting this information in the dossier and bypassing the technical experts had "resulted in a stronger assessment in the dossier in relation to Iraqi chemical weapons production than was justified by the available intelligence."[55] This report, Jones subsequently wrote, "was critical in silencing dissenting intelligence experts, and allowed the dossier to be published on time and on message."[56] The imperative of finding the kind of material needed to bolster the dossier meant that established procedures were bypassed. As Jones notes, the report:

> came from "a new source on trial", which means it should have been treated with suspicion. Instead it was shown to [David] Manning [the prime minister's foreign policy advisor], who saw to it that the prime minister was told two days later, on 12 September—before most members of the JIC even knew of its existence. Clearly, policy and intelligence were hopelessly entangled at this stage. Before the chief of Defence Intelligence, who was also deputy chairman of the JIC, had even seen [the report], it was being used to silence intelligence experts and facilitate the dossier.[57]

Given this, it is reasonable to ask how far the Butler Report pulled its punches? Lord Butler was himself asked about this in October 2004, when he gave evidence to the Public Administration Select Committee. Chairman Tony Wright put it to Butler that:

> You seemed to keep stopping short in your Report when you entered the policy arena. It is very interesting to deconstruct the text. It is as though you saw red lights flashing when the policy arena appeared, we only get little

glimpses of it, in so far as it relates to what you are going to say about assessment. Can you see how tantalising and unsatisfactory that is to a reader who wants to know what happened?[58]

However, Butler's view was that it was not the inquiry team's job to bring down the government. Once it had been presented with the information by the inquiry that would be the job of either Parliament or the public. After all, the inquiry team had clearly reported that the intelligence picture in mid-2002 would not of itself have "given rise to a conclusion that Iraq was of more immediate concern than the activities of some other countries". What was new was the prime minister's post-9/11 unwillingness, in line with shifts in the Bush administration, to tolerate a continuation of the Iraq situation and the risks inherent in it. As Butler told Wright:

> As regards the policy aspects, I think it is not quite fair to say we drew back from the policy aspects because we did try to give a full account of how the policy developed, how the decision came to be taken, but having given a full account of those facts, we left it to Parliament and the public to draw their conclusions about it. That was the right thing to do. As I say, I think it is not really for a Committee of this sort to enter into the political debate. Our purpose was to enable everybody to know all they needed to know about how the decision had come about.[59]

And again:

> We felt the proper place where government should survive or fall was in Parliament or with the electorate. It would have been a heavy responsibility and one where I think it would have been improper for us to say the government should resign on this matter . . . Whether the prime minister survived was not really an issue for us. What we wanted to do was to give a balanced, factual picture. I return to the balance and the balance was that we believed that the prime minister and the government acted in good faith when they said that they believed that Saddam had proscribed weapons including biological and chemical weapons. We believed that they should at the same time have said that the intelligence which underlies this is thin. We wanted to give that balanced, fair, factual picture and then I think it is a matter for political debate and for Parliament and the public to take it on from there.[60]

Also relevant to this question is the fact that the inquiry team clearly saw the minute of the 23 July 2002 Downing Street meeting at the heart of the subsequently leaked Downing Street memos (see Appendix B), where the prime minister was informed that the US was fixing the intelligence and facts around the policy. Nevertheless, it kept this policy dimension from its Report, instead providing an anodyne one-paragraph account of the meeting.[61] At the same time, it seems clear that Butler himself felt there was a case to be made that the prime minister had misled Parliament and the public by not revealing the thin basis of the intelligence underlying his government's claims about Iraqi WMD programs.[62]

Conclusion

Clearly, there were a number of intelligence failures in this case, stretching from collection and analysis to the user-customer interface where intelligence management comes under the spotlight. Following the publication of the Iraq Survey Group report and post-war inquiries by MI6, it is clear that:

- the July 2002 JIC conclusion that, "Iraq is pursuing a nuclear weapons programme" was wrong;
- the 2002 JIC judgment that Iraq "retains up to 20 missiles over 1000 km" was wrong;
- the judgement that "Iraq could produce significant quantities of mustard [gas] within weeks, significant quantities of Sarin and VX within months and in the case of VX may already have done so" was speculative and not supported by post-war investigation;
- the 2002 JIC judgment that "Iraq currently has available, either from pre-Gulf War, or more recent production, a number of biological agents . . . Iraq could produce more of these biological agents within days", overstated the case.
- The "45 minutes" claim was wrong.

Additionally, the government continued to insist that the claim included in the dossier relating to alleged Iraqi attempts to procure uranium from Niger was based on (unspecified) intelligence other than documents easily exposed as forgeries by the IAEA. In this it was supported by both the ISC and Butler. However, in the context of the conclusions reached by former US Ambassador Joseph Wilson following his fact-finding mission and the general skepticism of the US intelligence community (see Chapter 4), serious questions remain about this claim. Notwithstanding these, in each area of WMD concern—nuclear, chemical, biological, and missile development—UK intelligence had been somewhat wide of the mark.

In explaining why, the Butler inquiry team identified a tendency for earlier errors in estimation, for example, surrounding Iraq's nuclear weapons programme in 1990–91, to result in subsequent over-compensation in the form of the adoption of estimates approaching worst-case scenarios. In this respect, the Butler Report observed that:

> It is reasonable for assessments requested by the MOD for planning purposes relating to potential military activity to consider worst case scenarios. The burden of proof in such cases may reasonably be lower than in normal circumstances and assessments may reasonably be made on a more precautionary basis. But JIC assessments that take this approach should state the fact explicitly. So should assessments and analysis derived from them, then and subsequently. Care should be taken to ensure that worst case analysis is not carried forward into assessments except those (like assessments of enemy capabilities) that warrant such an approach.[63]

It also suggested that gaps and uncertainties needed to be consistently flagged up in reports to allow readers to appreciate the full intelligence picture, and believed that understanding of Iraqi politics and the Iraqi regime could have been better. Collecting intelligence on these was accorded a lower priority than intelligence on WMD. While understandable at one level, this impeded a full understanding of Iraqi intent and the regime's world view, dimensions only fully revealed by the Iraq Survey Group in 2004.

A number of failures were common in both the US and the UK experiences. These included compartmentalization of, or a reluctance to share, intelligence, and managerial reluctance to accommodate dissenting views once the policy direction had been fixed on regime change. Of course, these could be linked and symptomatic of a different problem. The absence of any competitive analysis was another common feature. On this, the Butler Report recommended that, "all reasonably sustainable hypotheses should not be dismissed finally until there is sufficient information to do so," and that, "challenge should be an accepted and routine part of the assessment process as well as an occasional formal exercise, built into the system."[64]

A linked failure was the unchallenged belief that the failure by UNMOVIC to find any WMD in Iraq was attributable to Iraq's sophisticated deception techniques rather than the fact that they did not exist. Both the Butler Report and US inquiries vaguely attributed this type of failure to groupthink, but none explored the appropriateness or implications of this diagnosis in any detail. However, some of the Butler inquiry's firmest criticisms are reserved for the prime minister's approach to decisionmaking over Iraq, what one commentator has termed the "mismanagement of the interface between the community and its consumers in government—that is, mismanagement of that interface by the *consumers themselves*."[65] In this sense Butler did stray into the policy arena, rather than halt at its water's edge. To paraphrase Butler himself, he went to the outer limits of, but not beyond, his terms of reference.

Significantly, when Butler appeared before the Public Administration Select Committee and was asked about the high proportion of human intelligence sources in Iraq who proved unreliable, but had supplied what might be considered the more alarming intelligence to emerge from the country, he was quick to remind MPs; "that what we discovered was that the government did not go to war on the basis of those intelligence reports. It went to war on wider grounds and the intelligence reports were not the basis for the decision."[66] Hence, Robin Cook's view that, "Downing Street did not worry that the intelligence was thin and inferential or that the sources were second-hand and unreliable, because intelligence did not play a big part in the real reason why we went to war,"[67] emerges as a reliable one. Nevertheless, in another sense the intelligence failures were highly significant. As Robin Cook further claimed: "it is embarrassingly clear that Parliament was misled into voting for war on the basis of unreliable sources and overheated analysis, producing between them false intelligence."[68] Flawed intelligence, in particular that produced in response to the last calls for intelligence that could feed into the September 2002 Downing Street dossier, provided the backbone of the case with which the government carried key votes in the House of Commons in late 2002 and early 2003. These votes paved the way for British participation in the Iraq war, but may well not have been carried if politicians had not had at their disposal alarming intelligence that was subsequently proved wrong. This fact that should not be overlooked in acknowledging the limited role intelligence played in the prime minister's own war decision.

Notes

1 Ian Fleming, *Thunderball* (London, Penguin, 2006 ed.), p. 188.
2 See, for example, Robin Cook, *The Point of Departure* (London, Simon & Schuster, 2003), p. 2.
3 Primarily for reasons of space it does not consider the Hutton inquiry, which looked at the production of the September 2002 Downing Street dossier as part of its investigation into the circumstances surrounding the death of Dr David Kelly. See Lord Hutton, *Report of the Inquiry into the Circumstances Surrounding the Death of Dr. David Kelly CMG* (HC 247, London, HMSO, 2004). For a discussion of the effectiveness of this inquiry and the issues raised, see Alan Doig, "45 Minutes of Infamy? Hutton, Blair and the Invasion of Iraq," *Parliamentary Affairs*, Vol.58, No.1, Jan. 2005, pp. 109–23; and Anthony Glees, "Evidence-Based Policy or Policy-Based Evidence? Hutton and the Government's Use of Secret Intelligence," ibid, pp. 138–55.

4 *Iraq's Weapons of Mass Destruction: The Assessment of the British Government*, Sep. 2002, www.number-10.gov.uk/output/Page271.asp.

5 Foreign Affairs Committee (FAC), *The Decision to go to War in Iraq* (London, The Stationery Office, HC 813–1), 7 Jul. 2003, para.3.

6 Intelligence and Security Committee, *Iraqi Weapons of Mass Destruction—Intelligence and Assessments* (Cm 5972, London, HMSO, 2003)

7 See, John Kampfner, *Blair's Wars* (London, Free Press, 2004 ed.), pp. 369–72. Only one member, Ann Taylor, was a privy counselor prior to the inquiry, the other members were made privy counselors in order to carry out the inquiry.

8 See Mark Phythian, "Intelligence Oversight in the UK: The Case of Iraq," in Loch K. Johnson (ed.), *Handbook of Intelligence Studies* (New York, Routledge, 2007), pp. 301–14.

9 Trade and Industry Select Committee, *Export Licensing and BMARC* (London, The Staionery Office, 1996, HC 87-I), para.6.

10 Ibid, para.168.

11 Ibid.

12 FAC, *The Decision to go to War*, para.6.

13 Ibid, paras. 168–9.

14 See, Mark Phythian, "The British Experience with Intelligence Accountability," *Intelligence and National Security*, Vol.22, No.1, Feb. 2007, pp. 75–99.

15 FAC, *The Decision to go to War*, para. 163.

16 ISC, *Iraqi Weapons of Mass Destruction*, para. 11.

17 Ibid, para. 66.

18 Intelligence and Security Committee, *Annual Report 2002–03*, Cm 5837, June 2003, para 81.

19 ISC, *Iraqi Weapons of Mass Destruction*, para. 83.

20 Ibid, para. 86.

21 Ibid, paras. 107–8.

22 Ibid, para. 101.

23 Ibid, para. 104.

24 Government Response to ISC Report on Iraqi Weapons of Mass Destruction—Intelligence and Assessments, Cm 6118, Feb. 2004, para. 13.

25 Intelligence and Security Committee, *Annual Report 2003–04*, Cm 6240, June 2004, para. 87.

26 Ibid, para. 146.

27 Lord Butler, *Review of Intelligence on Weapons of Mass Destruction* (London, The Stationery Office, July 2004, HC 898), para. 405.

28 Brian Jones, "What They Didn't Tell Us About WMD," *New Statesman*, Dec. 11, 2006, pp. 18–20.

29 Butler Report, para.405. Post-war, the alleged subsource for the claims contained in the Report had denied providing the information.

30 Hansard (Lords), Jul. 20, 2004, cols. 98–9.

31 Ibid. In late April 2003, for example, Blair told the *Financial Times*: "There is no doubt that Iraq has had these weapons of mass destruction, no doubt

about that at all. They engaged in a six-month campaign of concealment before the inspectors went in. It is not in the least surprising it is going to take time for us to unearth this, but I have no doubt that we will." Philip Stephens and Cathy Newman, "Hidden Saddam Arsenal Will be Found," *Financial Times*, Apr. 28, 2003.

32 Hansard, Oct. 12, 2004, col.153.
33 Intelligence and Security Committee, *Annual Report 2004–05*, Cm 6510, April 2005, para. 63.
34 Cited in the Butler Report, para.159.
35 Ibid, para. 171.
36 Ibid, para.177.
37 Ibid, para.178.
38 Ibid, para.187.
39 Ibid, para.208.
40 Ibid, para.209.
41 Ibid, paras. 221–4.
42 Ibid, para.225.
43 Ibid, para.235.
44 Ibid, para.238.
45 Ibid, paras.244–5.
46 Ibid, para.261.
47 Ibid, para.331.
48 Ibid, para.466.
49 Hansard, Sep. 24, 2002, col.3.
50 Butler Report, para.29, footnote 7.
51 Ibid, paras. 438–42.
52 Ibid, para.58.
53 Ibid, para.597.
54 Ibid, para.364.
55 Ibid, paras. 452, 577.
56 Jones, "What They Didn't Tell Us," p. 20.
57 Ibid. Additional questions about the initial authorship of the dossier remain unanswered, which may reveal a higher degree of politicization and failure at the level of the customer-intelligence community interface. See Martin Bright, "Iraq: The New Cover-Up—The Riddle of the Missing WMD Document," *New Statesman*, Nov. 13, 2006, pp. 12–15; Martin Bright, "Iraq: The Guns Continue to Smoke," ibid, Nov. 20, 2006, p. 10.
58 Public Administration Select Committee, Minutes of Evidence, Oct. 21, 2004, www.publications.parliament.uk/pa/cm200304/cmselect/cmpub-adm/606/4102102.htm
59 Ibid.
60 Ibid.
61 Butler Report, para. 287.
62 In September 2004, he told the House of Lords: "the Government's dossier in September 2002 did not make clear that the intelligence underlying those

conclusions was very thin, even though the JIC assessments had been quite clear about that. How grave a fault that was in the context of the lead-up to the war is a matter on which people will and should reach their own conclusions. But we regard it as a serious weakness—a weakness which subsequently came home to roost as the conclusion about deployable stocks of chemical and biological weapons have turned out to be wrong." Hansard (Lords), Sep 7, 2004, col.463.

63 Butler Report, para.605.
64 Ibid.
65 Philip H. J. Davies, "Spin Versus Substance: Intelligence Reform in Britain After Iraq," *WeltTrends*, Vol.51, Summer 2006, pp. 25–35. On this point, see the discussion in Chapter 5.
66 Public Administration Select Committee, Minutes of Evidence, Oct. 21, 2004,   www.publications.parliament.uk/pa/cm200304/cmselect/cmpub-adm/606/4102106.htm
67 Robin Cook, "The Die Was Cast: The Dossiers Were Irrelevant," *Independent on Sunday*, Jul. 18, 2004.
68 Robin Cook, "Britain's Worst Intelligence Failure, and Lord Butler Says No One is to Blame," *Independent*, Jul. 15, 2004.

Part IV
Policy failure

12

Decisionmaking, intelligence, and the Iraq war

James P. Pfiffner

In his decision to go to war in Iraq, President Bush did not follow the same path that he did during his decision to attack the Taliban and al Qaeda in Afghanistan. Immediately after 9/11 he met with his major national security policy team, deliberated with them about what to do, and made clear decisions about how to proceed in Afghanistan. In contrast, the decision to go to war in Iraq was seemingly spread over the course of a year or more. President Bush and his major advisors carefully considered operational decisions as well as the short-term military aspects of an invasion. But the overall decision about whether to go to war in Iraq, was not explicitly confronted in any formal NSC or cabinet meeting.

President Bush's decisionmaking (as far as we know, based on public sources) was non-deliberative, sequential, and informal. The administration neglected to plan for an occupation of the country, the creation of a new Iraqi government, or the political implications of a power vacuum after Saddam Hussein had been deposed.[1] In addition, President Bush did not heed the advice of many in the professional officer corps about the wisdom of invading Iraq, the number of troops necessary, or the need for planning for a lengthy occupation of the country.[2] Neither did he listen to the advice from many intelligence professionals who called into doubt the supposed link between Saddam and al Qaeda and Iraq's nuclear capacity.[3]

This chapter will begin with an account of the run-up to the war in Iraq. It will then turn to a critique of the national security decisionmaking process that led up to the war. Next, it will take up the role of intelligence and how it was used before the war. Finally, the conclusion will abstract some lessons that might be learned about presidential decision making about going to war.

The march to war

As has been mentioned above, in contrast to the president's decision to go to war in Afghanistan, which was made during a relatively short time period, the decision to invade Iraq seems to have been made during the course of a year or so and was characterized by incremental decision-making along the way, with no formal cabinet-level debate about the overall wisdom of initiating the war. President Bush was aware of disagreements with his seeming intention to go to war, but most of these came from outside the administration. The only serious reservation from within was voiced by Colin Powell during a dinner with President Bush (and Rice) in August of 2002.[4]

It is not clear when President Bush finally decided to go to war with Iraq, but his orders for planning for war began shortly after the terrorist attacks of 9/11.[5] Security advisor Richard Clarke reported that the president ordered him to find any ties between 9/11 and Saddam Hussein, even though Clarke had told the president that such links had been explored and not found.[6] At the war cabinet meeting at Camp David on September 15, 2001, the issue of Iraq was raised by Deputy Secretary of Defense Paul Wolfowitz who strongly favored going after Saddam Hussein and argued that war in Iraq might be easier than war in Afghanistan. Powell argued that the coalition backing the United States would not hold if the target was shifted to Iraq. Cheney said, "If we go after Saddam Hussein, we lose our rightful place as good guy." Tenet and Card agreed against attacking Iraq. The president finally decided not to pursue Iraq at that time and recalled, "If we tried to do too many things . . . the lack of focus would have been a huge risk."[7]

On September 17, 2001, President Bush signed a top-secret plan for the war in Afghanistan that also contained a direction for the Defense Department to begin to plan for a war with Iraq.[8] In 2003 White House officials said that Bush decided soon after the terrorist attacks that Iraq had to be confronted, but that he did not make his decision public because "he didn't think the country could handle the shock of 9/11 and a lot of talk about dealing with states that had weapons of mass destruction."[9]

The president decided to take more concerted action on November 21, 2001, when he told Secretary of Defense Rumsfeld to develop operational plans for war with Iraq.[10] General Tommy Franks's initial reaction to Rumsfeld's order to shift priorities was consternation, because it would detract significantly from the war he was then conducting in Afghanistan; but he set up top-secret teams in the Pentagon to develop the plans. On February 7, General Franks presented to President Bush the formal plan in operational form, that is, rather than a working draft, Franks presented a concrete set of plans that could be carried out.[11]

President Bush hinted in public about his decision to pursue Iraq in the State of the Union message on January 29, 2002. His reference was somewhat vague about the way in which he stated his intention, imbuing it with a high level of generality with his inclusion of Iraq, Iran, and North Korea in what he called an "axis of evil."[12] In the speech Bush declared: "I will not wait on events while dangers gather. I will not stand by as peril draws closer and closer."[13] In April the administration started talking about "regime change" in Iraq, and Bush told a British reporter, "I made up my mind that Saddam needs to go."[14]

Senator Bob Graham reported that he was shocked when he visited US Central Command in Florida on February 19 and spoke with General Tommy Franks about the war in Afghanistan. Franks told him that the war was being scaled back to a manhunt and that resources were being shifted to Iraq. According to Graham, Franks did not see Iraq as the next logical move in the war on terror. Graham said, "I had been informed that the decision to go to war with Iraq had not only been made but was being implemented, to the substantial disadvantage of the war in Afghanistan."[15] On the weekend of April 6–7 at Crawford, Texas, when he was hosting Prime Minister Tony Blair, President Bush told a British news reporter, "I have no plans to attack on my desk." Later, on May 23 and 26, he repeated this at press conferences: "I have no war plans on my desk."[16]

The next major public pronouncement by the president on national security and Iraq came at the June 1, 2002, commencement address he gave at the US Military Academy at West Point. The president said: "The war on terror will not be won on the defensive. We must take the battle to the enemy."[17] The president was narrowing his consideration of ways of dealing with Iraq. According to State Department Director of Policy and Planning Richard Haass (who had worked on the NSC staff on Middle East issues for George H. W. Bush), Condoleezza Rice told him that the president had made up his mind by July 2002. Haass said that he broached the issue of war with Iraq with Rice: "I raised this issue about were we really sure that we wanted to put Iraq front and center at this point, given the war on terrorism and other issues. And she said, essentially, that that decision's been made, don't waste your breath."[18]

During the summer of 2002 some of the professional military began to voice reservations about US plans to attack Iraq. *Washington Post* articles cited "senior US military officers" and "some top generals and admirals in the military establishment, including members of the Joint Chiefs of Staff," who argued for a cautious approach to Iraq. They were not convinced that Iraq had any connection to the 9/11 terrorist attacks; they believed that containment had worked up until then; they thought a military invasion would be costly; and they thought that a likely US victory would entail a lengthy occupation of Iraq.[19] Echoing another president from Texas, Lyndon Johnson, who similarly minimized the concerns of opponents of the Vietnam War, George Bush dismissed the concerns of the professional military: "There's a lot of nervous nellies at the Pentagon."[20]

In August, members of former President George H. W. Bush's administration came out publicly against war with Iraq. Brent Scowcroft, the senior Bush's national security advisor and Rice's mentor, wrote an op-ed piece entitled "Don't Attack Saddam."[21] James Baker, secretary of state for G. H. W. Bush, also expressed reservations about an attack on Iraq: "If we are to change the regime in Iraq, we will have to occupy the country militarily. The costs of doing so, politically, economically and in terms of casualties, could be great."[22] Reservations about an attack on Iraq were also expressed by retired General Anthony Zinni (senior advisor to Secretary of State Powell and former chief of US Central Command),[23] General Wesley Clark (former NATO Supreme Allied Commander),[24] and General H. Norman Schwarzkopf (commander of US forces in the 1991 Gulf war).[25]

The Bush administration sensed that opposition to war with Iraq was building and had to be countered, so Vice President Cheney took the occasion of an address to the Veterans of Foreign Wars convention on August 26, 2002, to lay out the administration's case in blunt terms: "Saddam Hussein could . . . be expected to seek domination of the entire Middle East . . . and subject the United States or any other nation to nuclear blackmail."[26]

After the administration convinced Congress to give the president authority to attack Iraq, Colin Powell and US diplomats went to work building a coalition to convince the UN Security Council to pass a new resolution on Iraq. After the resolution passed, the UN weapons inspectors searched Iraq with seeming carte blanche, making surprise visits to sites of possible weapons manufacture, but by late January they had found no "smoking gun." Chief UN inspector Hans Blix said that he needed more time to do a thorough job, but the United States began to deploy troops to the Middle East in preparation for war with Iraq.[27] In his State of the Union address on January 28, 2003, President Bush said that the UN had given Saddam Hussein his "final chance to disarm."[28]

The decisionmaking process

The striking thing about the decision to go to war was that there seemed to be no overall meeting of the principals in which the issue of whether to go to war with Iraq was debated. As mentioned, when Haass wanted to raise the question of the wisdom of invading Iraq in July 2002, Rice told him that the decision had already been made. One of the few points at which a high-level aide to President Bush raised objections was in the summer of 2002 when Secretary of State Powell questioned the wisdom of invading Iraq during a meeting with the president and Rice.

On August 5, 2002, at Powell's initiative, Rice arranged for him to spend two hours with the president in order to explain his own reservations about war with Iraq. He argued that war with Iraq would destabilize the whole Middle East, an American occupation would be seen as hostile by the Muslim world, and an invasion of Iraq should not be undertaken by the United States unilaterally. Powell didn't think the president understood the full implications of an American invasion. He told the president that if the United States invaded Iraq, it would tie down most of the army and the United States would be responsible for twenty-five million people: "You will become the government until you get a new government."[29]

Part of the reason for the lack of systematic analysis of the need for war with Iraq (as opposed to operational plans) was the lack of a regularized national security policy process, which was consistent with the general approach of the Bush administration to policy making. In most presidencies, there is a systematic way that policy options are developed and evaluated. President Eisenhower initiated a national security policy making process that was based on his extensive experience with large organizations and international relations. [30]

The Eisenhower process was relatively formal, with the second-level Planning Board reporting policy options to the principals on the National Security Council, and then the Operations Coordinating Board would deal with implementation of policy. Eisenhower expected full and open debate among his staffers, but more importantly, he encouraged it and sent clear signals to his advisors that disagreement would not be punished and that frank analysis would be rewarded. In his words:

> I know of only one way in which you can be sure you've done your best to make a wise decision. That is to get all of the people who have partial and definable responsibility in this particular field, whatever it may be. Get them with their different viewpoints in front of you, and listen to them debate. I do not believe in bringing them in one at a time, and therefore being more impressed by the most recent one you hear than the earlier ones. You must get courageous men, men of strong views, and let them debate and argue with each other.[31]

According to Burke and Greenstein, Eisenhower's policy deliberations "put a high premium on vigorous, informed debate . . . the advisors managed to state their disagreements with one another and with the president clearly and forcefully in Eisenhower's presence."[32]

President Kennedy learned a difficult lesson in the disaster of the Bay of Pigs invasion, due in part to the lack of a coherent policy process. He put that hard lesson to work during the Cuban Missile Crisis, when careful deliberations led him to change his mind from his initial inclination to order a military attack on Cuba. The deliberations of his civilian and military advisors led him to impose a blockade on Cuba rather than commence a military attack, thus averting a possible nuclear war. One measure of the effectiveness of the deliberations over the 13 days of the crisis was that most of the member of the Ex Comm changed their minds at least once over the course of their deliberations.[33] The Nixon, Ford, Carter, Reagan, and George W. Bush presidencies all developed a systematic national security policy process.

In contrast, the Bush White House did not adhere to any regularized policy development process. The president eschewed detailed deliberation, and preferred to consult with only a small group of advisors before making policy decisions. Treasury Secretary Paul O'Neill thought that the Bush White House had no serious domestic policy process. "It was a broken process . . . or rather no process at all; there seemed to be no apparatus to assess policy and deliberate effectively, to create coherent governance."[34] John DiIulio, who worked in the Bush White House on faith-based initiatives for the first eight months of the administration, said: "There is no precedent in any modern White House for what is going on in this one: a complete lack of a policy apparatus."[35]

The national security policy process was even worse. According to Lawrence Wilkerson, chief of staff to Colin Powell, what "I saw for four-plus years was a case that I have never seen in my studies of aberrations, bastardizations, perturbations, changes to the national security decision-making process. What I saw was a cabal between the vice president of the United States, Richard Cheney, and the secretary of Defense, Donald Rumsfeld on critical issues that made decisions that the bureaucracy did not know were being made . . . the bureaucracy often didn't know what it was doing as it moved to carry them out."[36] His judgment was echoed by Deputy Secretary of State Richard Armitage, who when asked about the Bush administration policy process, said: "There was never any policy process to break, by Condi or anyone else." "There was never one from the start. Bush didn't want one, for whatever reason."[37] Henry Kissinger, who had been advising President Bush on Iraq, felt that in contrast to previous administrations there was no regularized process or attempt to evaluate the possible pitfalls of invading Iraq. Chief of staff Andrew Card admitted to Bob Woodward that he could not remember any formal meetings that evaluated the overall wisdom of going to war.[38]

The lack of a formal process of decision making is highlighted by the fact that the president had to be prompted by Rice to inform Powell that he had made up his mind to go to war. (The president had already asked Rice and White House counselor Karen Hughes their opinion.) So, on January 13 the president brought Powell in for a 12-minute meeting to inform him of the decision to go to war and ask him to support his decision. The president stressed that it was a "cordial" conversation and that "I didn't need his permission."[39] Interestingly, the president informed Prince Bandar, the Saudi Arabian ambassador to the United States, of his decision before he informed Powell.[40] What is striking about all of this is that the deliberations about war were not definitive enough or inclusive enough for the secretary of state (the only principal with combat experience) to know that the decision had been made.

The president thought that he did not need to ask Cheney, Powell, or Rumsfeld about their judgments because "I could tell what they thought . . . I think we've got an environment where people feel free to express themselves."[41] Though there were many meetings on tactical and operational decisions, there seemed to be no meetings where the entire staff engaged in face-to-face discussions about all the options including the pros and cons of whether to go to war. In part, this may have been due to the shift in Rice's role away from the honest broker role she played in the decisions about Afghanistan. According to John Burke, in the decisions about Iraq, Rice did not act as a broker.[42] Instead, the president decided to use her talents as an advisor.

In addition to the overall lack of deliberate decisionmaking about whether to go to war, several other aspects of the administration's deliberations were problematic:

1 Condoleezza Rice said that she was not aware, and thus did not tell the president, of doubts in the Departments of State and Energy (expressed in the National Intelligence Estimate of October 2002) about the existence of a nuclear weapons program in Iraq.

2 Some dissenting views from within the administration were ignored or met with hostility. General Eric Shinseki's congressional testimony that about 200,000 troops would be needed in Iraq was denounced, and he was forced to retire without the customary honors. After White House economic advisor Lawrence Lindsey predicted that the war would cost about $200 billion, he was fired. Planning for the occupation and reconstruction of Iraq by the State Department was ignored or suppressed.[43]

3 After his top two CIA officials gave a presentation of evidence for WMD in Iraq, President Bush told them, "Nice try. I don't think this is quite—it's not something that Joe Public would understand or would

gain a lot of confidence from . . . is this the best we've got?" [44] But this was not followed up by a high-level reevaluation of the evidence.

In making the decision to invade Iraq, the administration would have benefited from a more thorough deliberation of the issues, such as that employed in making the decision to invade Afghanistan. It is quite possible Bush really did not know what to do about Afghanistan and so went into his sessions with his war cabinet with an open mind and chose the best solution. By contrast, when making his decision on Iraq, he did not fully consider dissenting opinions like those of Powell, Haass, or Scowcroft. Bush and his neoconservative advisors were committed to regime change in Iraq for a variety of reasons and thus did not approach the question of whether to invade Iraq with open minds.

The use of intelligence

The lack of deliberation about whether to go to war with Iraq was compounded by the administration's use and abuse of intelligence in the year before the war.[45] The administration was so convinced that Iraq was an imminent threat to the United States that it attempted to use the intelligence process to bolster its case for war. Some of its pressure on the intelligence community was legitimate, but some of it went beyond the normal relationship between intelligence professionals and their political superiors. In the end, the distortions of intelligence about Iraq led to the United States going to war based in part on incorrect assumptions.

When Senator Biden held hearings on WMD, he asked CIA Director Tenet if the intelligence community had any "technically collected" evidence concerning Iraqi WMD. That is, he wanted to know if there was any physical evidence, such as electronic intercepts, radioactive readings, or biological agents. Director Tenet replied, "None, Senator."[46] The committee's science advisor who had a PhD in physics, Peter Zimmerman, was at the hearing and asked to see one of the aluminum tubes that the CIA claimed Saddam was going to use for nuclear centrifuges. The State and Energy Departments had argued that the tubes wee not suitable for nuclear centrifuges, and Zimmerman's personal inspection confirmed their judgment for himself. Thus the Bush administration was relying on circumstantial evidence based on Saddam's pre-1991 capabilities, the human intelligence it got from the suspect Iraqi defectors brought to the Defense Department by Chalabi, and Curveball, the fabricating Iraqi defector the Germans were holding. Zimmerman concluded that "They're going to war and there's not a damn piece of evidence to substantiate it."[47]

In addition to using dubious evidence to support its intention of going to war with Iraq, the Bush administration attempted to politicize the intelligence process in the run-up to the Iraq war in several ways: 1) by creating new bureaucratic units to bypass the intelligence community; 2) by "stovepiping" raw intelligence directly to the White House; and 3) by pressuring the CIA to adjust its analysis to support the administration's policy goal of war with Iraq. The traditional public administration division of labor calls for career professionals to give their best judgment to their political superiors and for political officials to make policy decisions. It is the prerogative of political appointees to make policy decisions, whether or not their decisions seem to be supported by the analysis of the career professionals. But politicians are often tempted to try to distort the evidence in order to make their policy decisions seem to be based on solid evidence and advice from the career experts.

The obligation of career professionals in this dichotomy is to "speak truth to power." That is, to present their best professional analysis and judgment to political leaders whether or not it seems that their conclusions support the politicians' policy preferences, and then to carry out legitimate orders regardless of their own judgments about the wisdom of the order.

A more pithy definition of the politicization in the WMD case was articulated by the head of Britain's Secret Intelligence Service (MI6) when he reported in July 2002 that, after his meeting in Washington with US officials, "Military action was now seen as inevitable. Bush wanted to remove Saddam, through military action, justified by the conjunction of terrorism and WMD. *But the intelligence and facts were being fixed around the policy.*"[48] (emphasis added) Thus the judgment at the highest levels of the British government, the most important ally of the United States, was that the intelligence upon which the Bush administration was acting was not solid.

The normal intelligence process calls for all "raw" reports from the field to be carefully vetted by analysts to ensure that the sources are credible and that the information fits with what else is known about the particular issue. This might include examining the history of the issue or checking with other US or allied intelligence agencies. In 2002 the political leadership in the Department of Defense and in the White House had become convinced that the US intelligence community, and the CIA in particular, was discounting the link between Saddam and Osama bin Laden and ignoring the information coming from Ahmad Chalabi and his associates.

This led Undersecretary of Defense for Policy Douglas Feith to use the Office of Special Plans and the Policy Counterterrorism Evaluation Group, created shortly after 9/11, to provide alternative analytic perspectives to those being produced by the CIA.[49] Feith's units had close working relationship with the Iraqi National Congress, which the United States had funded, and which was headed by Ahmad Chalabi. The CIA, Defense Intelligence Agency (DIA), and the Bureau of Intelligence and Research (INR) at the State Department, however, had become skeptical of the reliability of Chalabi and the defectors from Iraq that he referred to Feith's office. The other intelligence agencies concluded that Chalabi was unreliable and that the defectors had a stake in overthrowing Saddam and thus were exaggerating or fabricating reports of Saddam's WMD. Feith, however, thought the defectors were reporting accurately and that the CIA was ignoring a valuable intelligence source.

So instead of allowing the CIA to vet the intelligence from Chalabi and the defectors, Feith "stovepiped" the reports of the Iraqi defectors straight to the White House (Vice President's staff and NSC staff) without any opportunity for comments by career intelligence professionals. According to Kenneth Pollack, who wrote a book supporting the war with Iraq, the Bush administration: "dismantled the existing filtering process that for fifty years had been preventing the policy makers from getting bad information. They created stovepipes to get the information they wanted directly to the top leadership. Their position is that the professional bureaucracy is deliberately and maliciously keeping information from them."[50]

The point here is not that White House officials should not get raw intelligence or direct reports from the field, but rather that to be fully informed, they ought to also get the best judgment of career intelligence professionals about the credibility of the sources and interpretation of the information. Thus the White House officials, who were predisposed to believe Feith and Chalabi and pressured the CIA to support their predispositions, used faulty evidence and non-credible intelligence in decisionmaking about going to war with Iraq and obtaining public support for it.

In 2007, the Department of Defense Inspector General criticized Feith's use of the specially created units to send intelligence directly to the White House without any input from the CIA. The IG concluded that, "While such actions were not illegal or unauthorized, the actions were, in our opinion, inappropriate given that the intelligence assessments were intelligence products and did not clearly show the variance with the consensus of the intelligence Community."[51] The point here is not that the special units' views were inconsistent with the conclusions of the intelligence community; disagreement and questioning assumptions are healthy. But in this case, policymakers were deprived of the considered judgment of career intelligence professionals on the reliability of Chalabi and the Iraqi exiles.

Intelligence may also have been politicized by pressure placed upon intelligence analysts to arrive at the conclusions favored by political levels of the Bush administration. During the summer and fall of 2002 Vice President Cheney made multiple visits to CIA headquarters in Langley in order to ask sharp questions about CIA analysis of intelligence relating to Iraq. Although it is appropriate for the vice president or other high level officials to question intelligence conclusions, there is a fine line between skeptical questioning and pressure for a specific outcome.[52]

Despite the findings of no political interference by the Senate Select Committee and the Robb-Silberman Commission, some intelligence officials said they felt pressure from these visits to write reports that would help the administration make the case for war.[53] One senior Bush administration official told Seymour Hersh: "They got pounded on, day after day . . . Pretty soon . . . they began to provide the intelligence that was wanted."[54] Some intelligence professionals felt that "intense questioning" and "repetitive tasking" created pressure to conform with administration expectations. One intelligence veteran said that the pressure on analysts was greater than what he had seen at the CIA in his 32-year career.[55] "They were the browbeaters," according to a former DIA official who was at some of the meetings. "In interagency meetings Wolfowitz treated the analysts' work with contempt."[56]

In one important case of political priorities driving the intelligence process was the case of a supposed Iraqi defector that the Germans held. This source, codenamed Curveball, provided virtually all of the contemporary evidence for Saddam's biological weapons program. Curveball was the source of Colin Powell's claim in his speech to the United Nations on February 5, 2003 that Saddam possessed biological weapons. Despite doubts about his reliability, the CIA assured Colin Powell before his UN speech that the sources were multiple and credible.[57] Yet senior German officials of the Federal Intelligence Service (BND) said that they had warned US intelligence officials in the fall of 2002 that Curveball was unreliable. According to them, Curveball was "not a stable, psychologically stable guy." "This was not substantial evidence. We made it clear that we could not verify the things he said." After hearing the US claims about chemical and biological weapons, the Germans said "We were shocked. Mein Gott! We had always told them it was not proven . . . It was not hard intelligence."[58]

When one DOD biological weapons analyst (the only US intelligence official who had met the only source of the Iraqi biological weapons, Curveball) went over Colin Powell's draft speech to the UN, he felt he had to warn Powell that Curveball, the source of the reports of the mobile biological weapons labs, was not reliable. But the deputy chief of the Iraqi Task Force wrote him an email saying: "Let's keep in mind the fact that this war's going to happen regardless of what Curveball said or didn't say, and that the Powers That Be probably aren't terribly interested in whether Curveball knows what he's talking about."[59] The CIA later admitted that the mobile trailers were intended for producing hydrogen rather than biological weapons.

The German judgment that Curveball was not reliable was also passed on to the CIA through Tyler Drumheller, chief of the Directorate of Operations of the European Division of the CIA.[60] After he had read a draft of Colin Powell's upcoming speech to the United Nations, Drumheller tried to warn Deputy CIA Director John McLaughlin that the Germans doubted Curveball's mental stability and reliability. McLaughlin reportedly said that Curveball was at "the heart of the case" for Iraq's biological weapons programs. Drumheller also warned Tenet on the night before Powell's speech that Curveball's information was not reliable. Later, Tenet and McLaughlin told the Robb-Silberman Commission that they did not remember Drumheller's warnings about Curveball.[61]

One of the major criticisms of the CIA regarding the Iraq war was the lack of "HUMINT," that is human agents who have penetrated the enemy's government. But in several cases, the CIA did have inside information based on human contacts. In the summer of 2002 the CIA located relatives of Iraqi scientists and convinced them to contact their relatives in Iraq to get information on Saddam's WMD programs. One of them was Dr. Sawsan Alhaddad whose brother had worked in Saddam's nuclear program in the 1980s. She traveled to Baghdad to talk with her brother and reported back to the CIA that her brother said that Iraq's nuclear program had been abandoned in the 1990s. In total, 30 relatives of Iraqi scientists reported back to the CIA that Saddam had no nuclear programs of which the scientists were aware. The CIA, however, was convinced that Saddam was pursuing a nuclear program, and they did not forward the reports to senior policymakers in the administration.[62]

In another case, the United States had a source inside Saddam's regime. The political levels of the Bush administration, however, did not pay attention to the accurate intelligence from this source when it did not fit their own preconceptions about Saddam's regime. The French intelligence agency had managed to recruit a source at the highest levels of Saddam's government: the Foreign Minister, Naji Sabri. There could be few more valuable intelligence sources of inside information about Iraq. The implication from the intelligence from Sabri was that Saddam did not possess WMD, especially nuclear, and that they had been destroyed after the first Gulf War.[63] This meant that Saddam was bluffing about his WMD, probably in order to scare his enemies in the Middle East.

But when this crucial intelligence was communicated back to CIA headquarters and the White House, it was ignored. The administration was interested in the source if he wanted to defect, but not in his information that Saddam was bluffing about his supposed WMD. (Sabri refused to defect for fear that Saddam would kill his family.) When asked why the CIA was not following up on this important (and accurate) intelligence, Drumheller's CIA colleague was told: "It's time you learned it's not about intelligence anymore. It's about regime change."[64] Drumheller said that "President Bush heard directly about our attempts to talk to the Iraqi, who knew the weapons programs were virtually nonexistent, and our leader was clearly not interested in pursuing him."[65]

Drumheller, a 30-year veteran of the CIA who had served on several continents and in its highest post in Europe, concluded in his memoirs after he retired, that the political leadership of the Bush administration did not use intelligence from the CIA in a responsible way: "the CIA has been made a scapegoat for one foreign policy disaster after another . . . never have I seen the manipulation of intelligence that has played out since the second President Bush took office . . . the White House deliberately tried to draw a cloak over its own misjudgments."[66] Although Drumheller admits that the CIA made mistakes in its intelligence conclusions about Iraq, the most important problem with prewar intelligence was "that the policy was shaping the intelligence and not the other way around."[67] Drumheller concluded that the White House saw the CIA "as a political tool rather than a place to turn for information," and that before the war, "the nation was about to embark on a war based on intelligence I knew was false."[68]

Perhaps the most authoritative evidence that political officers of the Bush administration tried to politicize intelligence prior to the Iraq war is the testimony of Paul R. Pillar. Pillar was the National Intelligence Officer for Near East and South Asia who directed the coordination of the intelligence community's assessments of Iraq. In an article originally published in *Foreign Affairs*, Pillar charged that 1) "official intelligence analysis was not relied on in making even the most significant national security decisions;" 2) "intelligence was misused publicly to justify decisions already made"; and 3) "the intelligence community's own work was politicized."[69] Pillar concluded: "The administration used intelligence not to inform decision-making, but to justify a decision already made. It went to war without requesting—and evidently without being influenced by—any strategic-level intelligence assessments on any aspect of Iraq."[70]

Conclusion: lessons about national security decisionmaking

President Bush's decision to go to war in Iraq was based in part on several faulty assumptions, some of which were pointed out in advance. The assumption that the war would be easily successful in deposing Saddam and replacing his tyrannical regime with a democratic government was questioned by Colin Powell (as well as other former generals with experience in Iraq). But President Bush did not directly confront the issues in a cabinet or NSC meeting. The assumption that Saddam had robust biological weapons stockpiles and capabilities was undercut by the unreliability of the source of that intelligence (Curveball). But the CIA was so certain of the president's determination to go to war that it did not heed the warnings of Drumheller and others about the unreliability of Curveball. The assumption that Saddam was rebuilding his nuclear capacity was undercut by the intelligence analysis of the Departments of Energy and State, but these assessments were not weighted heavily by President Bush.

The inaccuracy of these assumptions might have been exposed, or at least their consequences explored through the use of a systematic policy process. In deliberations about war and peace the president can benefit from formal meetings with his principal advisors. The deliberations should be marked by face-to-face give-and-take and frank evaluations of the range of options available to the president, as President Eisenhower advocated. President Bush, in contrast, made his decision about going to war over an extended period of time. Each step may have been considered carefully by itself, but the broader strategic context was neglected.[71]

President Bush's White House might also have benefited from the presence of a "neutral broker" to ensure that the process benefited from "multiple advocacy," an idea developed by Alexander George. He argued that it is useful to have a "custodian manager" of the decisionmaking process in order to insure that the advocates for different policy positions have comparable resources and sufficient opportunity to present their views to the president.[72] The natural person to take this role is the National Security Advisor, but Condoleezza Rice did not play that role in the run-up to the Iraq war.[73] Another device that might have been used is the "devil's advocate," in which one presidential advisor is assigned the role of arguing against the group consensus in order to force members of the group to reexamine their basic premises. Colin Powell, in a sense, played this role for President Bush by taking a less hawkish position on Iraq. But he did not make his arguments with the rest of the advisors present. Powell's decision to support President Bush rather than object publicly was paralleled by the ambiguous position of CIA Director George Tenet.

In April 2007 George Tenet's book, *At the Center of the Storm*, was released to the public. Shortly afterwards, several former CIA and intelligence officers wrote a public letter charging Tenet with abdicating his duty to the country in supporting the Bush administration's decision to go to war with Iraq. They charged that the CIA had solid evidence that Saddam had no stockpiles of WMD, but that Tenet did not convey this fully to the president. They also charged that CIA officers had learned from a high level official in Saddam's inner circle that there was no collaboration between Saddam and al Qaeda, and that al Qaeda was seen as an enemy by Saddam. On the basis of these and other charges, the former officers argued that Tenet should have resigned in 2003, and called on him to return the Medal of Freedom that President Bush had awarded him. Although embarrassing to Tenet, this alternative perspective demonstrates the difficulty faced by intelligence agencies when faced with a political leader fixed upon a certain policy objective. Specifically, it points to the pressure that can exist at the intelligence community–customer interface, and it expresses the anger which some in the intelligence community felt toward what they perceived to be a failure of Tenet to convey to the president an objective analysis of the evidence and intelligence analysis.[74] (The letter is reproduced in Appendix E.)

Finally the experience of the Bush administration illustrates the importance of questioning the basic assumptions upon which the decisions rest. In revisiting the mistakes that were made by the United States before the war in Vietnam, Robert McNamara stressed the importance of taking a close look at the fundamental reasoning in the case for war. He noted that the United States had few allies who supported the war in Vietnam and said, 'if we can't convince our allies of the merit of our cause, we had better reexamine our reasoning.'[75]

The design of the policy process and presidential use of advisors, however, cannot guarantee good decisions. At the end of the day, the president has to make the crucial decisions about war (subject to congressional agreement), and there is no substitute for good judgment on the part of the president.

Notes

1 This does not mean that no planning was done. The Department of State conducted a large planning exercise; the CIA did planning for the aftermath of war; and army analysts at the Strategic Studies Institute at Carlisle Barracks in Pennsylvania did planning before the invasion. The administration, however, did not take any of these efforts seriously. See James P. Pfiffner,

"The First MBA President," *Public Administration Review* (January/February 2007), pp. 6–20, esp. p. 9.

2 For an argument that President Bush often ignored the advice of career professionals, see Pfiffner, "The First MBA President."

3 For an analysis of how the Bush administration used intelligence before the war in Iraq, see James P. Pfiffner, "The Use of US Intelligence Before the War with Iraq," in George C. Edwards and Desmond King (eds.), *The Polarized Presidency of George W. Bush* (Oxford: Oxford University Press, 2007).

4 Secretary of State Powell was the only top level official in the Bush administration with combat experience. President Bush was in the National Guard, Vice President Cheney had "other priorities" during the Vietnam war, neither Condoleezza Rice nor Paul Wolfowitz had military experience, and Donald Rumsfeld flew jets for the Navy in the 1950s but not in combat.

5 Bush's Secretary of the Treasury, Paul O'Neill, reported that Iraq was a major focus of the Bush administration's first two meetings of the NSC on January 30 and February 1 of 2001. Ron Suskind, *The Price of Loyalty: George W. Bush, the White House, and the Education of Paul O'Neill* (New York: Simon & Schuster, 2004), pp. 70–4, 82–6.

6 Richard Clarke, *Against All Enemies: Inside America's War on Terror* (New York: Free Press, 2004), pp. 32–3.

7 Bob Woodward, *Bush at War* (New York: Simon & Schuster, 2005), pp. 84–91.

8 Glenn Kessler, "US Decision on Iraq Has Puzzling Past: Opponents of War Wonder When, How Policy Was Set," *Washington Post* (January 12, 2003), pp. 1, A20.

9 Kessler, "US Decision on Iraq," p. A20.

10 Bob Woodward, *Plan of Attack* (New York: Simon and Schuster, 2004), pp. 30–1.

11 Woodward, *Plan of Attack*, pp. 77, 80, 96, 98. On March 21, 2003, General Franks told his top commanders that the United States was going to war with Iraq unless Saddam left the country. To emphasize his seriousness, he said: "You know, if you guys think this is not going to happen, you're wrong." CIA Director George Tenet in March also told Kurdish leaders that there would be a military attack in Iraq. Woodward, *Plan of Attack*, pp. 115–16.

12 According to David Frum, a speechwriter was assigned to "provide a justification for war" with Iraq. David Frum, *The Right Man: The Surprise Presidency of George W. Bush* (New York: Random House, 2003), pp. 224, 238–40.

13 Weekly Compilation of Presidential Documents, *Administration of George W. Bush, 2002* (January 29, 2002), pp. 133–9.

14 Kessler, "US Decision on Iraq," p. A20; Woodward, *Plan of Attack*, p. 119.

15 Bob Graham with Jeff Nussbaum, *Intelligence Matters: The CIA, the FBI, Saudi Arabia, and the Failure of America's War on Terror* (New York: Random House, 2004), p. 126.

16 Woodward, *Plan of Attack*, pp. 120, 127. General Franks also stated on May 21 that "my boss has not yet asked me to put together a plan to do that [attack Iraq]," p. 130.

17 Weekly Compilation of Presidential Documents, *Administration of George W. Bush, 2002*, "Commencement Address at the United States Military Academy in West Point, New York" (June 1, 2002), pp. 944–8.

18 Nicholas Lemann, "How It Came to War," *New Yorker*, Vol.79, No.6 (March 31, 2003), p. 36. For Haass's criticisms of the decision to go to war with Iraq, see Richard Haass, *The Opportunity: America's Moment to Alter History's Course* (New York: Public Affairs, 2005), pp. 182–94.

19 Thomas E. Ricks, "Some Top Military Brass Favor Status Quo in Iraq: Containment Seen Less Risky Than Attack," *Washington Post* (July 28, 2002), pp. 1, A23. Also, Thomas E. Ricks, "Timing, Tactics on Iraq War Disputed; Top Bush Officials Criticize Generals' Conventional Views," *Washington Post* (August 1, 2002), p. 1, A24, in which he says, "Much of the senior uniformed military, with the notable exception of some top Air Force and Marine generals, opposes going to war anytime soon, a stance that is provoking frustration among civilian officials in the Pentagon and in the White House."

20 Weisman, Steven R., "History Lessons for Wartime Presidents and Their Generals," *New York Times* (September 15, 2002), section 4, p. 14.

21 Brent Scowcroft, "Don't Attack Saddam," *Wall Street Journal* (August 15, 2002), p. A12.

22 James A. Baker III, "The Right Way to Change a Regime," *New York Times* (August 25, 2002), section 4, p. 9.

23 *Washington Post*, "Powell Aide Disputes Views on Iraq" (August 28, 2002), p.A16.

24 Tara Tuckwiller, "Don't Invade Yet, Ex-NATO Chief Says," *Charleston Gazette* (15 October 2002), p. 1A.

25 Thomas E. Ricks, "Desert Caution: Once 'Stormin' Norman,"Gen. Schwarzkopf Is Skeptical About US Action in Iraq," *Washington Post* (January 28, 2003), p. C1. Schwarzkopf remarked that "the thought of Saddam Hussein with a sophisticated nuclear capability is a frightening thought, okay?" Nevertheless, he argued that UN weapons inspectors should be given more time to determine if Saddam Hussein really had weapons of mass destruction.

26 Dana Milbank, "Cheney Says Iraqi Strike Is Justified: Hussein Poses Threat, He Declares," *Washington Post* (August 27, 2002), pp. 1, A8.

27 Erick Schmitt, "US Force in Gulf Is Said to be Rising to 150,000 Troops," *New York Times* (January 12, 2003), p. 1.

28 State of the Union Address (28 January 2003), printed in *Washington Post* (January 29, 2003), pp. A10–A11.

29 Woodward, *Plan of Attack*, pp. 150–1.

30 An excellent account of the Eisenhower administration's deliberations about whether to intervene in Vietnam in 1953 is John Burke and Fred Greenstein, *How Presidents Test Reality: Decisions on Vietnam, 1954 and 1965* (New York: Russell Sage Foundation, 1991), upon which much of this discussion is based.

31 Quoted in Burke and Greenstein, *How Presidents Test Reality*, pp. 54–5.
32 Ibid, p. 288.
33 Irving L. Janis, *Victims of Groupthink* (New York, Houghton Miffline, 1973), p. 152.
34 Suskind, *The Price of Loyalty*, p. 97.
35 Ron Suskind "Why Are These Men Laughing?" *Esquire* (January 1, 2003), posted on Ron Suskind website.
36 Lawrence Wilkerson, "Weighing the Uniqueness of the Bush Administration's National Security Decision-Making Process: Boon or Danger to American Democracy?" *New America Foundation Policy Forum* (October 19, 2005), transcript of remarks, p. 8.
37 Quoted by Mark Danner, "Iraq: The War of the Imagination," *New York Review of Books* (December 21, 1006), p. 87.
38 Bob Woodward, *State of Denial* (NY: Simon & Schuster, 2006), p. 455.
39 Woodward, *Plan of Attack*, pp. 269–74.
40 Ibid, pp. 251–2, 265.
41 Ibid, pp. 251–2.
42 John Burke, "The Contemporary Presidency: Condoleezza Rice as NSC Advisor: A Case Study of the Honest Broker Role," *Presidential Studies Quarterly*, Vol.35, No.3 (September 2005), pp. 554–75.
43 See James Fallows, "Blind Into Baghdad," *Atlantic Monthly*, Vol.293, No.1 (January/February 2004), pp. 52–74. See also Woodward, *Plan of Attack*, pp. 280–5.
44 Woodward, *Plan of Attack*, p. 249.
45 This section is based on the analyses in Pfiffner, "The First MBA President," and "The Use of Intelligence Before the War with Iraq."
46 Michael Isikoff and David Corn, *Hubris* (NY: Crown Publishers, 2006), p. 118.
47 Ibid, p. 119.
48 Downing Street Memo. 2002. Memo: 23 July 2002 "Secret and Strictly Personal—UK Eyes Only. To: David Manning, From Matthew Rycroft S 195/02l Re: Iraq: Prime Minister's Meeting, 23 July." Published by *The Times* (London) (www.timesonline.co.uk) accessed June 21, 2005.
49 See Jeffrey Goldberg, "A Little Learning," *New Yorker* (May 9, 2005), pp. 36–41; Seymour Hersh, "The Stovepipe" *New Yorker* (October 27, 2005), p. 87; David Phillips, "Listening to the Wrong Iraqi" *New York Times* (September 20, 2003).
50 Hersh, "The Stovepipe", p. 87.
51 Department of Defense Office of Inspector General, "Review of Pre-Iraqi War Activities of the Office of the Under Secretary of Defense for Policy," Report No. 07–INTEL-04 (February 9, 2007), Executive Summary (the Executive Summary was the only part of the report that was declassified and made public).
52 Tyler Drumheller, *On the Brink* (NY Carroll & Graf Publishers, 2006), p. 43.

53 James Risen, "CIA Aides Feel Pressure In Preparing Iraqi Reports, *New York Times* (March 23, 2003), p. B10.
54 Hersh, "The Stovepipe", p. 80.
55 T. Christian Miller and Maura Reynolds, "Senate Intelligence Report: Question of Pressure Splits Panel, *Los Angeles Times*, July 10, 2004), website.
56 Walter Pincus and Dana Priest, "Some Iraq Analysts Felt Pressure From Cheney Visits," *Washington Post* (June 5, 2003), p. 1.
57 The Kerr Report said that "different descriptions of the same source," i.e. "Curveball," often led "analysts to believe they had more corroborative information from more sources than was actually the case." Powell believed that the CIA had several sources for the information, when, in fact, there was only one—Curveball. See Chapter 8 in the volume, p. 156.
58 Bob Drogin and John Goetz, "How US Fell Under the Spell of 'Curveball,'" *Los Angeles Times* (November 20, 2005), Los Angeles Times website, accessed November 27, 2005. Also, Bob Drogin and John Goetz, "CIA Was Warned On Iraq Informer," *Washington Post* (November 21, 2005), p. A10. David Kay raised the interesting question that "if the BND [German intelligence service] thought he was a fabricator why did not they just throw him to the US instead of trying to protect him as if he was a valuable source??" Personal email to the author, December 13, 2005.
59 David Johnston, "Powell's 'Solid' CIA Tips Were Soft, Committee Says," *New York Times* (July 11, 2004), p. 11.
60 In explaining the problems with Curveball's stories, Drumheller said that "Curveball had neglected to mention that he had been fired from the job that supposedly gave him access to sensitive sites and that he had been out of the country [Iraq] on the date he claimed to have witnessed the 1998 accident that killed twelve of his fellow workers." Drumheller, *On the Brink*, p. 105.
61 James Risen, *State of War* (NY: Free Press, 2006), pp. 116–20. In the fall of 2003, the CIA discovered that Curveball had been fired in 1995, before the time that he claimed to have been working on biological weapons in Iraq. In May 2004 the CIA sent out a notice admitting the Curveball was not a solid source: "Discrepancies surfaced regarding the information provided by . . . Curveball in this stream of reporting, which indicate that he lost his claimed access in 1995. Our assessment, therefore, is that Curveball appears to be fabricating in this stream of reporting." Drogin and Goetz, "How US Fell Under the Spell of 'Curveball,'" p. 14. See also, Bob Drogin and Greg Miller, "'Curveball' Debacle Reignites CIA Feud," *Los Angeles Times* (April 2, 2005).
62 Risen, *State of War*, pp. 106, 185–208.
63 Drumheller, *On the Brink*, pp. 89–97; neither Sabri's name nor the nation of the intelligence service was mentioned in Drumheller's book.
64 Ibid, p. 95.
65 Ibid, p. 194.
66 Ibid, pp. 2, 4, 5.

67 Ibid, p. 77.
68 Ibid, pp. 104, 107.
69 See Chapter 13.
70 Ibid, pp. 234–5.
71 For an analysis of presidential decisionmaking, see the special issue of Presidential Studies Quarterly, edited by James P. Pfiffner: *Presidential Studies Quarterly*, Vol.35, No.2 (June 2005). See particularly, Andrew Rudalevige, "The Structure of Leadership: Presidents, Hierarchies, and Information Flow," pp. 333–60; and Matthew J. Dickinson, "Neustadt, New Institutionalism, and Presidential Decision Making: A Theory and Test," pp. 259–88.
72 Alexander George, "The Case for Multiple Advocacy in Making Foreign Policy", *American Political Science Review*. Vol.66, No.3 (1972); and *Presidential Decisionmaking in Foreign Policy* (Boulder, CO: Westview Press, 1980).
73 For a thorough analysis of the neutral or honest broker role, see John Burke, "The Neutral/Honest Broker Role in Foreign-Policy Decision Making: A Reassessment," *Presidential Studies Quarterly*, Vol.35, No.2 (June 2005), pp. 229–58. For an insightful application of the concept to Condoleezza Rice during President Bush's first term, see Burke, "The Contemporary Presidency: Condoleezza Rice as NSC Advisor."
74 Michael Hirsh, "Intel Agents Call for Tenet's Medal," *Newsweek*, website, April 30, 2007: www.msnbc.msn.com/id/18399374/site/newsweek/?nav= slate?from=rss.
75 The quote comes from the documentary film, *Fog of War*. Single quotation marks are used because McNamara's words were written down by the author as he watched the film and may be accurate and not verbatim.

13

Intelligence, policy, and the war in Iraq
Paul R. Pillar

A dysfunctional relationship

The most serious problem with US intelligence today is that its relationship with the policymaking process is broken and badly needs repair. In the wake of the Iraq war, it has become clear that official intelligence analysis was not relied on in making even the most significant national security decisions, that intelligence was misused publicly to justify decisions already made, that damaging ill will developed between policymakers and intelligence officers, and that the intelligence community's own work was politicized. As the national intelligence officer responsible for the Middle East from 2000 to 2005, I witnessed all of these disturbing developments.

Public discussion of prewar intelligence on Iraq has focused on the errors made in assessing Saddam Hussein's unconventional weapons programs. A commission chaired by Judge Laurence Silberman and former Senator Charles Robb usefully documented the intelligence community's mistakes in a solid and comprehensive report released in March 2005. Corrections were indeed in order, and the intelligence community has begun to make them.

At the same time, an acrimonious and highly partisan debate broke out over whether the Bush administration manipulated and misused intelligence in making its case for war. The administration defended itself by pointing out that it was not alone in its view that Saddam had weapons of mass destruction (WMD) and active weapons programs, however mistaken that view may have been.

In this regard, the Bush administration was quite right: its perception of Saddam's weapons capacities was shared by the Clinton administration, congressional Democrats, and most other Western governments and intelligence services. But in making this defense, the White House also inadvertently pointed out the real problem: intelligence on Iraqi weapons programs did not drive its decision to go to war. A view broadly held in the United States and even more so overseas was that deterrence of Iraq was working, that Saddam was being kept "in his box," and that the best way to deal with the weapons problem was through an aggressive inspections program to supplement the sanctions already in place. That the administration arrived at so different a policy solution indicates that its decision to topple Saddam was driven by other factors—namely, the desire to shake up the sclerotic power structures of the Middle East and hasten the spread of more liberal politics and economics in the region.

If the entire body of official intelligence analysis on Iraq had a policy implication, it was to avoid war—or, if war was going to be launched, to prepare for a messy aftermath. What is most remarkable about prewar US intelligence on Iraq is not that it got things wrong and thereby misled policymakers; it is that it played so small a role in one of the most important US policy decisions in recent decades.

A model upended

The proper relationship between intelligence gathering and policymaking sharply separates the two functions. The intelligence community collects information, evaluates its credibility, and combines it with other information to help make sense of situations abroad that could affect US interests. Intelligence officers decide which topics should get their limited collection and analytic resources according to both their own judgments and the concerns of policymakers. Policymakers thus influence which topics intelligence agencies address but not the conclusions that they reach. The intelligence community, meanwhile, limits its judgments to what is happening or what might happen overseas, avoiding policy judgments about what the United States should do in response.

In practice, this distinction is often blurred, especially because analytic projections may have policy implications even if they are not explicitly stated. But the distinction is still important. National security abounds with problems that are clearer than the solutions to them; the case of Iraq is hardly a unique example of how similar perceptions of a threat can lead people to recommend very different policy responses. Accordingly, it is critical that the intelligence community not advocate policy, especially not openly. If it does, it loses the most important basis for its credibility and its claims to objectivity. When intelligence analysts critique one another's work, they use the phrase "policy prescriptive" as a pejorative, and rightly so.

The Bush administration's use of intelligence on Iraq did not just blur this distinction; it turned the entire model upside down. The administration used intelligence not to inform decisionmaking, but to justify a decision already made. It went to war without requesting—and evidently without being influenced by—any strategic-level intelligence assessments on any aspect of Iraq. (The military made extensive use of intelligence in its war planning, although much of it was of a more tactical nature.) Congress, not the administration, asked for the now-infamous October 2002 National Intelligence Estimate (NIE) on Iraq's unconventional weapons programs, although few members of Congress actually read it. (According to several congressional aides responsible for safeguarding the classified material, no more than six senators and only a handful of House members got beyond the five-page executive summary.) As the national intelligence officer for the Middle East, I was in charge of coordinating all of the intelligence community's assessments regarding Iraq; the first request I received from any administration policymaker for any such assessment was not until a year into the war.

Official intelligence on Iraqi weapons programs was flawed, but even with its flaws, it was not what led to the war. On the issue that mattered most, the intelligence community judged that Iraq probably was several years away from developing a nuclear weapon. The October 2002 NIE also judged that Saddam was unlikely to use WMD against the United States unless his regime was placed in mortal danger.

Before the war, on its own initiative, the intelligence community considered the principal challenges that any post-invasion authority in Iraq would be likely to face. It presented a picture of a political culture that would not provide fertile ground for democracy and foretold a long, difficult, and turbulent transition. It projected that a Marshall Plan-type effort would be required to restore the Iraqi economy, despite Iraq's abundant oil resources. It forecast that in a deeply divided Iraqi society, with Sunnis resentful over the loss of their dominant position and Shiites seeking power commensurate with their majority status, there was a significant chance that the groups would engage in violent conflict unless an occupying power prevented it. And it anticipated that a foreign occupying force would itself be the target of resentment and attacks—including by guerrilla warfare—unless it established security and put Iraq on the road to prosperity in the first few weeks or months after the fall of Saddam.

In addition, the intelligence community offered its assessment of the likely regional repercussions of ousting Saddam. It argued that any value Iraq might have as a democratic exemplar would be minimal and would depend on the stability of a new Iraqi government and the extent to which democracy in Iraq was seen as developing from within rather than being imposed by an outside power. More likely, war and occupation would boost political Islam and increase sympathy for terrorists' objectives—and Iraq would become a magnet for extremists from elsewhere in the Middle East.

Standard deviations

The Bush administration deviated from the professional standard not only in using policy to drive intelligence, but also in aggressively using intelligence to win public support for its decision to go to war. This meant selectively adducing data—"cherry picking"—rather than using the intelligence community's own analytic judgments. In fact, key portions of the administration's case explicitly rejected those judgments. In an August 2002 speech, for example, Vice President Dick Cheney observed that "intelligence is an uncertain business" and noted how intelligence analysts had underestimated how close Iraq had been to developing a nuclear weapon before the 1991 Persian Gulf war. His conclusion—at odds with that of the intelligence community—was that "many of us are convinced that Saddam will acquire nuclear weapons fairly soon."

In the upside-down relationship between intelligence and policy that prevailed in the case of Iraq, the administration selected pieces of raw intelligence to use in its public case for war, leaving the intelligence community to register varying degrees of private protest when such use started to go beyond what analysts deemed credible or reasonable. The best-known example was the assertion by President George W. Bush in his 2003 State of the Union address that Iraq was purchasing uranium ore in Africa. US intelligence analysts had questioned the credibility of the report making this claim, had kept it out of their own unclassified products, and had advised the White House not to use it publicly. But the administration put the claim into the speech anyway, referring to it as information from British sources in order to make the point without explicitly vouching for the intelligence.

The reexamination of prewar public statements is a necessary part of understanding the process that led to the Iraq war. But a narrow focus on rhetorical details tends to overlook more fundamental problems in the intelligence–policy relationship. Any time policymakers, rather than intelligence agencies, take the lead in selecting which bits of raw intelligence to present, there is—regardless of the issue—a bias. The resulting public statements ostensibly reflect intelligence, but they do not reflect intelligence analysis, which is an essential part of determining what the pieces of raw reporting mean. The policymaker acts with an eye not to what is indicative of a larger pattern or underlying truth, but to what supports his case.

Another problem is that on Iraq, the intelligence community was pulled over the line into policy advocacy—not so much by what it said as by its conspicuous role in the administration's public case for war. This was especially true when the intelligence community was made highly visible (with the director of central intelligence literally in the camera frame) in an intelligence-laden presentation by Secretary of State Colin Powell to the UN Security Council a month before the war began. It was also true in the fall of 2002, when, at the administration's behest, the intelligence community published a white paper on Iraq's WMD programs—but without including any of the community's judgments about the likelihood of those weapons' being used.

But the greatest discrepancy between the administration's public statements and the intelligence community's judgments concerned not WMD (there was indeed a broad consensus that such programs existed), but the relationship between Saddam and al Qaeda. The enormous attention devoted to this subject did not reflect any judgment by intelligence officials that there was or was likely to be anything like the "alliance" the administration said existed. The reason the connection got so much attention was that the administration wanted to hitch the Iraq expedition to the "war on terror" and the threat the American public feared most, thereby capitalizing on the country's militant post-9/11 mood.

The issue of possible ties between Saddam and al Qaeda was especially prone to the selective use of raw intelligence to make a public case for war. In the shadowy world of international terrorism, almost anyone can be "linked" to almost anyone else if enough effort is made to find evidence of casual contacts, the mentioning of names in the same breath, or indications of common travels or experiences. Even the most minimal and circumstantial data can be adduced as evidence of a "relationship," ignoring the important question of whether a given regime actually supports a given terrorist group and the fact that relationships can be competitive or distrustful rather than cooperative.

The intelligence community never offered any analysis that supported the notion of an alliance between Saddam and al Qaeda. Yet it was drawn into a public effort to support that notion. To be fair, Secretary Powell's presentation at the UN never explicitly asserted that there was a cooperative relationship between Saddam and al Qaeda. But the presentation was clearly meant to create the impression that one existed. To the extent that the intelligence community was a party to such efforts, it crossed the line into policy advocacy—and did so in a way that fostered public misconceptions contrary to the intelligence community's own judgments.

Varieties of politicization

In its report on prewar intelligence concerning Iraqi WMD, the Senate Select Committee on Intelligence said it found no evidence that analysts had altered or shaped their judgments in response to political pressure.

The Silberman–Robb commission reached the same conclusion, although it conceded that analysts worked in an "environment" affected by "intense" policymaker interest. But the method of investigation used by the panels—essentially, asking analysts whether their arms had been twisted—would have caught only the crudest attempts at politicization. Such attempts are rare and, when they do occur (as with former Undersecretary of State John Bolton's attempts to get the intelligence community to sign on to his judgments about Cuba and Syria), are almost always unsuccessful. Moreover, it is unlikely that analysts would ever acknowledge that their own judgments have been politicized, since that would be far more damning than admitting more mundane types of analytic error.

The actual politicization of intelligence occurs subtly and can take many forms. Context is all-important. Well before March 2003, intelligence analysts and their managers knew that the United States was heading for war with Iraq. It was clear that the Bush administration would frown on or ignore analysis that called into question a decision to go to war and welcome analysis that supported such a decision. Intelligence analysts—for whom attention, especially favorable attention, from policymakers is a measure of success—felt a strong wind consistently blowing in one direction. The desire to bend with such a wind is natural and strong, even if unconscious.

On the issue of Iraqi WMD, dozens of analysts throughout the intelligence community were making many judgments on many different issues based on fragmentary and ambiguous evidence. The differences between sound intelligence analysis (bearing in mind the gaps in information) and the flawed analysis that actually was produced had to do mainly with matters of caveat, nuance, and word choice. The opportunities for bias were numerous. It may not be possible to point to one key instance of such bending or to measure the cumulative effect of such pressure. But the effect was probably significant.

A clearer form of politicization is the inconsistent review of analysis: reports that conform to policy preferences have an easier time making it through the gauntlet of coordination and approval than ones that do not. (Every piece of intelligence analysis reflects not only the judgments of the analysts most directly involved in writing it, but also the concurrence of those who cover related topics and the review, editing, and remanding of it by several levels of supervisors, from branch chiefs to senior executives.) The Silberman–Robb commission noted such inconsistencies in the Iraq case but chalked it up to bad management. The commission failed to address exactly why managers were inconsistent: they wanted to avoid the unpleasantness of laying unwelcome analysis on a policymaker's desk.

Another form of politicization with a similar cause is the sugarcoating of what otherwise would be an unpalatable message. Even the mostly prescient analysis about the problems likely to be encountered in postwar Iraq included some observations that served as sugar, added in the hope that policymakers would not throw the report directly into the burn bag, but damaging the clarity of the analysis in the process.

But the principal way that the intelligence community's work on Iraq was politicized concerned the specific questions to which the community devoted its energies. As any competent pollster can attest, how a question is framed helps determine the answer. In the case of Iraq, there was also the matter of sheer quantity of output—not just what the intelligence community said, but how many times it said it. On any given subject, the intelligence community faces what is in effect a field of rocks, and it lacks the resources to turn over every one to see what threats to national security may lurk underneath. In an unpoliticized environment, intelligence officers decide which rocks to turn over based on past patterns and their own judgments. But when policymakers repeatedly urge the intelligence community to turn over only certain rocks, the process becomes biased. The community responds by concentrating its resources on those rocks, eventually producing a body of reporting and analysis that, thanks to quantity and emphasis, leaves the impression that what lies under those same rocks is a bigger part of the problem than it really is.

That is what happened when the Bush administration repeatedly called on the intelligence community to uncover more material that would contribute to the case for war. The Bush team approached the community again and again and pushed it to look harder at the supposed Saddam-al Qaeda relationship—calling on analysts not only to turn over additional Iraqi rocks, but also to turn over ones already examined and to scratch the dirt to see if there might be something there after all. The result was an intelligence output that—because the question being investigated was never put in context—obscured rather than enhanced understanding of al Qaeda's actual sources of strength and support.

This process represented a radical departure from the textbook model of the relationship between intelligence and policy, in which an intelligence service responds to policymaker interest in certain subjects (such as "security threats from Iraq" or "al Qaeda's supporters") and explores them in whatever direction the evidence leads. The process did not involve intelligence work designed to find dangers not yet discovered or to inform decisions not yet made. Instead, it involved research to find evidence in support of a specific line of argument—that Saddam was cooperating with al Qaeda—which in turn was being used to justify a specific policy decision.

One possible consequence of such politicization is policymaker self-deception. A policymaker can easily forget that he is hearing so much about a particular angle in briefings because he and his fellow policymakers have urged the intelligence community to focus on it. A more certain consequence is the skewed application of the intelligence community's resources. Feeding the administration's voracious appetite for material on the Saddam–al Qaeda link consumed an enormous amount of time and attention at multiple levels, from rank-and-file counterterrorism analysts to the most senior intelligence officials. It is fair to ask how much other counterterrorism work was left undone as a result.

The issue became even more time-consuming as the conflict between intelligence officials and policymakers escalated into a battle, with the intelligence community struggling to maintain its objectivity even as policymakers pressed the Saddam–al Qaeda connection. The administration's rejection of the intelligence community's judgments became especially clear with the formation of a special Pentagon unit, the Policy Counterterrorism Evaluation Group. The unit, which reported to Undersecretary of Defense Douglas Feith, was dedicated to finding every possible link between Saddam and al Qaeda, and its briefings accused the intelligence community of faulty analysis for failing to see the supposed alliance.

For the most part, the intelligence community's own substantive judgments do not appear to have been compromised. (A possible important exception was the construing of an ambiguous, and ultimately recanted, statement from a detainee as indicating that Saddam's Iraq provided jihadists with chemical or biological training.) But although the charge of faulty analysis was never directly conveyed to the intelligence community itself, enough of the charges leaked out to create a public perception of rancor between the administration and the intelligence community, which in turn encouraged some administration supporters to charge intelligence officers (including me) with trying to sabotage the president's policies. This poisonous atmosphere reinforced the disinclination within the intelligence community to challenge the consensus view about Iraqi WMD programs; any such challenge would have served merely to reaffirm the presumptions of the accusers.

Partial repairs

Although the Iraq war has provided a particularly stark illustration of the problems in the intelligence–policy relationship, such problems are not confined to this one issue or this specific administration. Four decades ago, the misuse of intelligence about an ambiguous encounter in the Gulf of Tonkin figured prominently in the Johnson administration's justification for escalating the military effort in Vietnam. Over a century ago, the possible misinterpretation of an explosion on a US warship in Havana harbor helped set off the chain of events that led to a war of choice against Spain. The Iraq case needs further examination and reflection on its own. But public discussion of how to foster a better relationship between intelligence officials and policymakers and how to ensure better use of intelligence on future issues is also necessary.

Intelligence affects the nation's interests through its effect on policy. No matter how much the process of intelligence gathering itself is fixed, the changes will do no good if the role of intelligence in the policymaking process is not also addressed. Unfortunately, there is no single clear fix to the sort of problem that arose in the case of Iraq. The current ill will may not be reparable, and the perception of the intelligence community on the part of some policymakers—that Langley is enemy territory—is unlikely to change. But a few steps, based on the recognition that the intelligence–policy relationship is indeed broken, could reduce the likelihood that such a breakdown will recur.

On this point, the United States should emulate the United Kingdom, where discussion of this issue has been more forthright, by declaring once and for all that its intelligence services should not be part of public advocacy of policies still under debate. In the United Kingdom, Prime Minister Tony Blair accepted a commission of inquiry's conclusions that intelligence and policy had been improperly commingled in such exercises as the publication of the "dodgy dossier," the British counterpart to the United States' Iraqi WMD white paper, and that in the future there should be a clear delineation between intelligence and policy. An American declaration should take the form of a congressional resolution and be seconded by a statement from the White House. Although it would not have legal force, such a statement would discourage future administrations from attempting to pull the intelligence community into policy advocacy. It would also give some leverage to intelligence officers in resisting any such future attempts.

A more effective way of identifying and exposing improprieties in the relationship is also needed. The CIA has a "politicization ombudsman," but his informally defined functions mostly involve serving as a sympathetic ear for analysts disturbed by evidence of politicization and then summarizing what he hears for senior agency officials. The intelligence oversight committees in Congress have an important role, but the heightened partisanship that has bedeviled so much other work on Capitol Hill has had an especially inhibiting effect in this area. A promised effort by the Senate Intelligence Committee to examine the Bush administration's use of intelligence on Iraq got stuck in the partisan mud. The House committee has not even attempted to address the subject.

The legislative branch is the appropriate place for monitoring the intelligence–policy relationship. But the oversight should be conducted by a nonpartisan office modeled on the Government Accountability Office (GAO) and the Congressional Budget Office (CBO). Such an office would have a staff, smaller than that of the GAO or the CBO, of officers experienced in intelligence and with the necessary clearances and access to examine questions about both the politicization of classified intelligence work and the public use of intelligence. As with the GAO, this office could conduct inquiries at the request of members of Congress. It would make its results public as much as possible, consistent with security requirements, and it would avoid duplicating the many other functions of intelligence oversight, which would remain the responsibility of the House and Senate intelligence committees.

Beyond these steps, there is the more difficult issue of what place the intelligence community should occupy within the executive branch. The reorganization that created the Office of the Director of National Intelligence (DNI) is barely a year old (at the time of writing), and yet another reorganization at this time would compound the disruption. But the flaws in the narrowly conceived and hastily considered reorganization legislation of December 2004—such as ambiguities in the DNI's authority—will make it necessary to reopen the issues it addressed. Any new legislation should also tackle something the 2004 legislation did not: the problem of having the leaders of the intelligence community, which is supposed to produce objective and unvarnished analysis, serve at the pleasure of the president.

The organizational issue is also difficult because of a dilemma that intelligence officers have long discussed and debated among themselves: that although distance from policymakers may be needed for objectivity, closeness is needed for influence. For most of the past quarter century, intelligence officials have striven for greater closeness, in a perpetual quest for policymakers' ears. The lesson of the Iraq episode, however, is that the supposed dilemma has been incorrectly conceived. Closeness in this case did not buy influence, even on momentous issues of war and peace; it bought only the disadvantages of politicization.

The intelligence community should be repositioned to reflect the fact that influence and relevance flow not just from face time in the Oval Office, but also from credibility with Congress and, most of all, with the American public. The community needs to remain in the executive branch but be given greater independence and a greater ability to communicate with those other constituencies (fettered only by security considerations, rather than by policy agendas). An appropriate model is the Federal Reserve, which is structured as a quasi-autonomous body overseen by a board of governors with long fixed terms.

These measures would reduce both the politicization of the intelligence community's own work and the public misuse of intelligence by policymakers. It would not directly affect how much attention policymakers give to intelligence, which they would continue to be entitled to ignore. But the greater likelihood of being called to public account for discrepancies between a case for a certain policy and an intelligence judgment would have the indirect effect of forcing policymakers to pay more attention to those judgments in the first place.

These changes alone will not fix the intelligence–policy relationship. But if Congress and the American people are serious about "fixing intelligence," they should not just do what is easy and politically convenient. At stake are the soundness of US foreign-policy making and the right of Americans to know the basis for decisions taken in the name of their security.

Part V

Excerpts from key speeches and documents

Appendix A

Excerpts from key US speeches before the war in Iraq

Excerpts from President George W. Bush, State of the Union Address, January 29, 2002

Our military has put the terror training camps of Afghanistan out of business, yet camps still exist in at least a dozen countries. A terrorist underworld—including groups like Hamas, Hezbollah, Islamic Jihad, Jaish-i-Mohammed—operates in remote jungles and deserts, and hides in the centers of large cities.

While the most visible military action is in Afghanistan, America is acting elsewhere. We now have troops in the Philippines, helping to train that country's armed forces to go after terrorist cells that have executed an American, and still hold hostages. Our soldiers, working with the Bosnian government, seized terrorists who were plotting to bomb our embassy. Our Navy is patrolling the coast of Africa to block the shipment of weapons and the establishment of terrorist camps in Somalia.

My hope is that all nations will heed our call, and eliminate the terrorist parasites who threaten their countries and our own. Many nations are acting forcefully. Pakistan is now cracking down on terror, and I admire the strong leadership of President Musharraf. [Applause]

But some governments will be timid in the face of terror. And make no mistake about it: If they do not act, America will. [Applause]

Our second goal is to prevent regimes that sponsor terror from threatening America or our friends and allies with weapons of mass destruction. Some of these regimes have been pretty quiet since September the 11th. But we know their true nature. North Korea is a regime arming with missiles and weapons of mass destruction, while starving its citizens.

Iran aggressively pursues these weapons and exports terror, while an unelected few repress the Iranian people's hope for freedom.

Iraq continues to flaunt its hostility toward America and to support terror. The Iraqi regime has plotted to develop anthrax, and nerve gas, and nuclear weapons for over a decade. This is a regime that has already used poison gas to murder thousands of its own citizens—leaving the bodies of mothers huddled over their dead children. This is a regime that agreed to international inspections—then kicked out the inspectors. This is a regime that has something to hide from the civilized world.

States like these, and their terrorist allies, constitute an axis of evil, arming to threaten the peace of the world. By seeking weapons of mass destruction, these regimes pose a grave and growing danger. They could provide these arms to terrorists, giving them the means to match their hatred. They could attack our allies or attempt to blackmail the United States. In any of these cases, the price of indifference would be catastrophic.

We will work closely with our coalition to deny terrorists and their state sponsors the materials, technology, and expertise to make and deliver weapons of mass destruction. We will develop and deploy effective missile defenses to protect America and our allies from sudden attack. [Applause] And all nations should know: America will do what is necessary to ensure our nation's security.

We'll be deliberate, yet time is not on our side. I will not wait on events, while dangers gather. I will not stand by, as peril draws closer and closer. The United States of America will not permit the world's most dangerous regimes to threaten us with the world's most destructive weapons. [Applause]

Our war on terror is well begun, but it is only begun. This campaign may not be finished on our watch—yet it must be and it will be waged on our watch.

We can't stop short. If we stop now—leaving terror camps intact and terror states unchecked—our sense of security would be false and temporary. History has called America and our allies to action, and it is both our responsibility and our privilege to fight freedom's fight. [Applause]

Vice President Cheney's Remarks at the Veterans of Foreign Wars Convention, August 26, 2002 (excerpts)

The case of Saddam Hussein, a sworn enemy of our country, requires a candid appraisal of the facts. After his defeat in the Gulf War in 1991, Saddam agreed under to U.N. Security Council Resolution 687 to cease all development of weapons of mass destruction. He agreed to end his nuclear weapons program. He agreed to destroy his chemical and his biological weapons. He further agreed to admit U.N. inspection teams into his country to ensure that he was in fact complying with these terms.

In the past decade, Saddam has systematically broken each of these agreements. The Iraqi regime has in fact been very busy enhancing its capabilities in the field of chemical and biological agents. And they continue to pursue the nuclear program they began so many years ago. These are not weapons for the purpose of defending Iraq; these are offensive weapons for the purpose of inflicting death on a massive scale, developed so that Saddam can hold the threat over the head of anyone he chooses, in his own region or beyond.

On the nuclear question, many of you will recall that Saddam's nuclear ambitions suffered a severe setback in 1981 when the Israelis bombed the Osirak reactor. They suffered another major blow in Desert Storm and its aftermath.

But we now know that Saddam has resumed his efforts to acquire nuclear weapons. Among other sources, we've gotten this from the first-hand testimony of defectors—including Saddam's own son-in-law, who was subsequently murdered at Saddam's direction. Many of us are convinced that Saddam will acquire nuclear weapons fairly soon.

Just how soon, we cannot really gauge. Intelligence is an uncertain business, even in the best of circumstances. This is especially the case when you are dealing with a totalitarian regime that has made a science out of deceiving the international community. Let me give you just one example of what I mean. Prior to the Gulf War, America's top intelligence analysts would come to my office in the Defense Department and tell me that Saddam Hussein was at least five or perhaps even 10 years away from having a nuclear weapon. After the war we learned that he had been much closer than that, perhaps within a year of acquiring such a weapon.

Saddam also devised an elaborate program to conceal his active efforts to build chemical and biological weapons. And one must keep in mind the history of U.N. inspection teams in Iraq. Even as they were conducting the most intrusive system of arms control in history, the inspectors missed a great deal. Before being barred from the country, the inspectors found and destroyed thousands of chemical weapons, and hundreds of tons of mustard gas and other nerve agents.

Yet Saddam Hussein had sought to frustrate and deceive them at every turn, and was often successful in doing so. I'll cite one instance. During the spring of 1995, the inspectors were actually on the verge of declaring that Saddam's programs to develop chemical weapons and longer-range ballistic missiles had been fully accounted for and shut down. Then Saddam's son-in-law suddenly defected and began sharing information. Within days the inspectors were led to an Iraqi chicken farm. Hidden there were boxes of documents and lots of evidence regarding Iraq's most secret weapons programs. That should serve as a reminder to all that we often learned more as the result of defections than we learned from the inspection regime itself.

To the dismay of the inspectors, they in time discovered that Saddam had kept them largely in the dark about the extent of his program to mass produce VX, one of the deadliest chemicals known to man. And far from having shut down Iraq's prohibited missile programs, the inspectors found that Saddam had continued to test such missiles, almost literally under the noses of the U.N. inspectors.

Against that background, a person would be right to question any suggestion that we should just get inspectors back into Iraq, and then our worries will be over. Saddam has perfected the game of cheat and retreat, and is very skilled in the art of denial and deception. A return of inspectors would provide no assurance whatsoever of his compliance with U.N. resolutions. On the contrary, there is a great danger that it would provide false comfort that Saddam was somehow "back in his box."

Meanwhile, he would continue to plot. Nothing in the last dozen years has stopped him—not his agreements; not the discoveries of the inspectors; not the revelations by defectors; not criticism or ostracism by the international community; and not four days of bombings by the U.S. in 1998. What he wants is time and more time to husband his resources, to invest in his ongoing chemical and biological weapons programs, and to gain possession of nuclear arms.

Should all his ambitions be realized, the implications would be enormous for the Middle East, for the United States, and for the peace of the world. The whole range of weapons of mass destruction then would rest in the hands of a dictator who has already shown his willingness to use such weapons, and has done so, both in his war with Iran and against his own people. Armed with an arsenal of these weapons of terror, and seated atop ten percent of the world's oil reserves, Saddam Hussein could then be expected to seek domination of the entire Middle East, take control of a great portion of the world's energy supplies, directly threaten America's friends throughout the region, and subject the United States or any other nation to nuclear blackmail.

Simply stated, there is no doubt that Saddam Hussein now has weapons of mass destruction. There is no doubt he is amassing them to use against our friends, against our allies, and against us. And there is no doubt that his aggressive regional ambitions will lead him into future confrontations with his neighbors—confrontations that will involve both the weapons he has today, and the ones he will continue to develop with his oil wealth.

President Bush Outlines Iraq Threat, Remarks in Cincinnati, Ohio, October 7, 2002 (excerpts)

The threat comes from Iraq. It arises directly from the Iraqi regime's own actions—its history of aggression, and its drive toward an arsenal of terror. Eleven years ago, as a condition for ending the Persian Gulf War, the Iraqi regime was required to destroy its weapons of mass destruction, to cease all development of such weapons, and to stop all support for terrorist groups. The Iraqi regime has violated all of those obligations. It possesses and produces chemical and biological weapons. It is seeking nuclear weapons. It has given shelter and support to terrorism, and practices terror against its own people. The entire world has witnessed Iraq's eleven-year history of defiance, deception and bad faith.

We also must never forget the most vivid events of recent history. On September the 11th, 2001, America felt its vulnerability—even to threats that gather on the other side of the earth. We resolved then, and we are resolved today, to confront every threat, from any source, that could bring sudden terror and suffering to America.

[. . .]

Iraq could decide on any given day to provide a biological or chemical weapon to a terrorist group or individual terrorists. Alliance with terrorists could allow the Iraqi regime to attack America without leaving any fingerprints.

Some have argued that confronting the threat from Iraq could detract from the war against terror. To the contrary; confronting the threat posed by Iraq is crucial to winning the war on terror. When I spoke to Congress more than a year ago, I said that those who harbor terrorists are as guilty as the terrorists themselves. Saddam Hussein is harboring terrorists and the instruments of terror, the instruments of mass death and destruction. And he cannot be trusted. The risk is simply too great that he will use them, or provide them to a terror network.

Terror cells and outlaw regimes building weapons of mass destruction are different faces of the same evil. Our security requires that we confront both. And the United States military is capable of confronting both.

Many people have asked how close Saddam Hussein is to developing a nuclear weapon. Well, we don't know exactly, and that's the problem. Before the Gulf War, the best intelligence indicated that Iraq was eight to ten years away from developing a nuclear weapon. After the war, international inspectors learned that the regime has been much closer—the regime in Iraq would likely have possessed a nuclear weapon no later than 1993. The inspectors discovered that Iraq had an advanced nuclear weapons development program, had a design for a workable nuclear weapon, and was pursuing several different methods of enriching uranium for a bomb.

Before being barred from Iraq in 1998, the International Atomic Energy Agency dismantled extensive nuclear weapons-related facilities, including three uranium enrichment sites. That same year, information from a high-ranking Iraqi nuclear engineer who had defected revealed that despite his public promises, Saddam Hussein had ordered his nuclear program to continue.

The evidence indicates that Iraq is reconstituting its nuclear weapons program. Saddam Hussein has held numerous meetings with Iraqi nuclear scientists, a group he calls his "nuclear mujahideen"—his nuclear holy warriors. Satellite photographs reveal that Iraq is rebuilding facilities at sites that have been part of its nuclear program in the past. Iraq has attempted to purchase high-strength aluminum tubes and other equipment needed for gas centrifuges, which are used to enrich uranium for nuclear weapons.

If the Iraqi regime is able to produce, buy, or steal an amount of highly enriched uranium a little larger than a single softball, it could have a nuclear weapon in less than a year. And if we allow that to happen, a terrible line would be crossed. Saddam Hussein would be in a position to blackmail anyone who opposes his aggression. He would be in a position to dominate the Middle East. He would be in a position to threaten America. And Saddam Hussein would be in a position to pass nuclear technology to terrorists.

Some citizens wonder, after 11 years of living with this problem, why do we need to confront it now? And there's a reason. We've experienced the horror of September the 11th. We have seen that those who hate America are willing to crash airplanes into buildings full of innocent people. Our enemies would be no less willing, in fact, they would be eager, to use biological or chemical, or a nuclear weapon.
[. . .]

Knowing these realities, America must not ignore the threat gathering against us. Facing clear evidence of peril, we cannot wait for the final proof—the smoking gun—that could come in the form of a mushroom cloud. As President Kennedy said in October of 1962, "Neither the United States of America, nor the world community of nations can tolerate deliberate deception and offensive threats on the part of any nation, large or small. We no longer live in a world," he said, "where only the actual firing of weapons represents a sufficient challenge to a nation's security to constitute maximum peril."
[. . .]

The attacks of September the 11th showed our country that vast oceans no longer protect us from danger. Before that tragic date, we had only hints of al Qaeda's plans and designs. Today in Iraq, we see a threat whose outlines are far more clearly defined, and whose consequences could be far more deadly. Saddam Hussein's actions have put us on notice, and there is no refuge from our responsibilities.

President Bush, State of the Union Address, January 28, 2003 (excerpts)

The International Atomic Energy Agency confirmed in the 1990s that Saddam Hussein had an advanced nuclear weapons development program, had a design for a nuclear weapon and was working on five different methods of enriching uranium for a bomb. The British government has learned that Saddam Hussein recently sought significant quantities of uranium from Africa. Our intelligence sources tell us that he has attempted to purchase high-strength aluminum tubes suitable for nuclear weapons production.

Saddam Hussein has not credibly explained these activities. He clearly has much to hide.

The dictator of Iraq is not disarming. To the contrary; he is deceiving. From intelligence sources we know, for instance, that thousands of Iraqi security personnel are at work hiding documents and materials from the U.N. inspectors, sanitizing inspection sites and monitoring the inspectors themselves. Iraqi officials accompany the inspectors in order to intimidate witnesses.

Iraq is blocking U-2 surveillance flights requested by the United Nations. Iraqi intelligence officers are posing as the scientists inspectors are supposed to interview. Real scientists have been coached by Iraqi officials on what to say. Intelligence sources indicate that Saddam Hussein has ordered that scientists who cooperate with U.N. inspectors in disarming Iraq will be killed, along with their families.

Year after year, Saddam Hussein has gone to elaborate lengths, spent enormous sums, taken great risks to build and keep weapons of mass destruction. But why? The only possible explanation, the only possible use he could have for those weapons, is to dominate, intimidate, or attack.

With nuclear arms or a full arsenal of chemical and biological weapons, Saddam Hussein could resume his ambitions of conquest in the Middle East and create deadly havoc in that region. And this Congress and the America people must recognize another threat. Evidence from intelligence sources, secret communications, and statements by people now in custody reveal that Saddam Hussein aids and protects terrorists, including members of al Qaeda. Secretly, and without fingerprints, he could provide one of his hidden weapons to terrorists, or help them develop their own.

Before September the 11th, many in the world believed that Saddam Hussein could be contained. But chemical agents, lethal viruses and shadowy terrorist networks are not easily contained. Imagine those 19 hijackers with other weapons and other plans—this time armed by Saddam Hussein. It would take one vial, one canister, one crate slipped into this country to bring a day of horror like none we have ever known. We will do everything in our power to make sure that that day never comes. [Applause]

Some have said we must not act until the threat is imminent. Since when have terrorists and tyrants announced their intentions, politely putting us on notice before they strike? If this threat is permitted to fully and suddenly emerge, all actions, all words, and all recriminations would come too late. Trusting in the sanity and restraint of Saddam Hussein is not a strategy, and it is not an option. [Applause]

The dictator who is assembling the world's most dangerous weapons has already used them on whole villages—leaving thousands of his own citizens dead, blind, or disfigured. Iraqi refugees tell us how forced confessions are obtained—by torturing children while their parents are made to watch. International human rights groups have catalogued other methods used in the torture chambers of Iraq: electric shock, burning with hot irons, dripping acid on the skin, mutilation with electric drills, cutting out tongues, and rape. If this is not evil, then evil has no meaning. [Applause]

And tonight I have a message for the brave and oppressed people of Iraq: Your enemy is not surrounding your country—your enemy is ruling your country. (Applause.) And the day he and his regime are removed from power will be the day of your liberation. [Applause]

Appendix B

Excerpts from key UK speeches and documents before the war in Iraq

Tony Blair, 'Doctrine of the International Community' Speech, Economic Club, Chicago, April 24, 1999 (excerpt)

We now have a decade of experience since the end of the Cold War. It has certainly been a less easy time than many hoped in the euphoria that followed the collapse of the Berlin Wall. Our armed forces have been busier than ever—delivering humanitarian aid, deterring attacks on defenceless people, backing up UN resolutions and occasionally engaging in major wars as we did in the Gulf in 1991 and are currently doing in the Balkans.

Have the difficulties of the past decade simply been the aftershocks of the end of the Cold War? Will things soon settle down, or does it represent a pattern that will extend into the future?

Many of our problems have been caused by two dangerous and ruthless men—Saddam Hussein and Slobodan Milosevic. Both have been prepared to wage vicious campaigns against sections of their own community. As a result of these destructive policies both have brought calamity on their own peoples. Instead of enjoying its oil wealth Iraq has been reduced to poverty, with political life stultified through fear. Milosevic took over a substantial, ethnically diverse state, well placed to take advantage of new economic opportunities. His drive for ethnic concentration has left him with something much smaller, a ruined economy and soon a totally ruined military machine.

One of the reasons why it is now so important to win the conflict is to ensure that others do not make the same mistake in the future. That in itself will be a major step to ensuring that the next decade and the next century will not be as difficult as the past. If NATO fails in Kosovo, the next dictator to be threatened with military force may well not believe our resolve to carry the threat through.

At the end of this century the US has emerged as by far the strongest state. It has no dreams of world conquest and is not seeking colonies. If anything Americans are too ready to see no need to get involved in affairs of the rest of the world. America's allies are always both relieved and gratified by its continuing readiness to shoulder burdens and responsibilities that come with its sole superpower status. We understand that this is something that we have no right to take for granted, and must match with our own efforts. That is the basis for the recent initiative I took with President Chirac of France to improve Europe's own defence capabilities.

As we address these problems at this weekend's NATO Summit we may be tempted to think back to the clarity and simplicity of the Cold War. But now we have to establish a new framework. No longer is our existence as states under threat. Now our actions are guided by a more subtle blend of mutual self interest and moral purpose in defending the values we cherish. In the end values and interests merge. If we can establish and spread the values of liberty, the rule of law, human rights and an open society then that is in our national interests too. The spread of our values makes us safer. As John Kennedy put it "Freedom is indivisible and when one man is enslaved who is free?"

The most pressing foreign policy problem we face is to identify the circumstances in which we should get actively involved in other people's conflicts. Non-interference has long been considered an important principle of international order. And it is not one we would want to jettison too readily. One state should not feel it has the right to change the political system of another or foment subversion or seize pieces of territory to which it feels it should have some claim. But the principle of non-interference must be qualified in important respects. Acts of genocide can never be a purely internal matter. When oppression produces massive flows of refugees which unsettle neighbouring countries then they can properly be described as "threats to international peace and security". When regimes are based on minority rule they lose legitimacy—look at South Africa.

Looking around the world there are many regimes that are undemocratic and engaged in barbarous acts. If we wanted to right every wrong that we see in the modern world then we would do little else than intervene in the affairs of other countries. We would not be able to cope.

So how do we decide when and whether to intervene. I think we need to bear in mind five major considerations

First, are we sure of our case? War is an imperfect instrument for righting humanitarian distress; but armed force is sometimes the only means of dealing with dictators. Second, have we exhausted all diplomatic options? We should always give peace every chance, as we have in the case of Kosovo. Third, on the basis of a practical assessment of the situation, are there military operations we can sensibly and prudently undertake? Fourth, are we prepared for the long term? In the past we talked too much of exit strategies. But having made a commitment we cannot simply walk away once the fight is over; better to stay with moderate numbers of troops than return for repeat performances with large numbers. And finally, do we have national interests involved? The mass expulsion of ethnic Albanians from Kosovo demanded the notice of the rest of the world. But it does make a difference that this is taking place in such a combustible part of Europe.

I am not suggesting that these are absolute tests. But they are the kind of issues we need to think about in deciding in the future when and whether we will intervene.

Any new rules however will only work if we have reformed international institutions with which to apply them.

If we want a world ruled by law and by international co-operation then we have to support the UN as its central pillar. But we need to find a new way to make the UN and its Security Council work if we are not to return to the deadlock that undermined the effectiveness of the Security Council during the Cold War. This should be a task for members of the Permanent Five to consider once the Kosovo conflict is complete.

Memorandum from Foreign Policy Adviser David Manning to the Prime Minister, March 14, 2002 (excerpt)

YOUR TRIP TO THE US

I had dinner with Condi on Tuesday; and talks and lunch with her an NSC team on Wednesday (to which Christopher Meyer also came). These were good exchanges, and particularly frank when we were one-on-one at dinner. I attach the records in case you want to glance.

IRAQ

We spent a long time at dinner on IRAQ. It is clear that Bush is grateful for your support and has registered that you are getting flak. I said that you would not budge in your support for regime change but you had to manage a press, a Parliament and a public opinion that was very different than anything in the States. And you would not budge either in your insistence that, if we pursued regime change, it must be very carefully done and produce the right result. Failure was not an option.

Condi's enthusiasm for regime change is undimmed. But there were some signs, since we last spoke, of greater awareness of the practical difficulties and political risks. (See the attached piece by Seymour Hersh which Christopher Meyer says gives a pretty accurate picture of the uncertain state of the debate in Washington.)

From what she said, Bush has yet to find the answers to the big questions:

– how to persuade international opinion that military action against Iraq is necessary and justified;

– what value to put on the exiled Iraqi opposition;

– how to coordinate a US/allied military campaign with internal opposition (assuming there is any);

– what happens on the morning after?

Bush will want to pick your brains. He will also want to hear whether he can expect coalition support. I told Condi that we realised that the Administration could go it alone if it chose. But if it wanted company, it would have to take account of the concerns of its potential coalition partners. In particular:

– the Un [*sic*] dimension. The issue of the weapons inspectors must be handled in a way that would persuade European and wider opinion that the US was conscious of the international framework, and the insistence of many countries on the need for a legal base. Renwed refused [*sic*] by Saddam to accept unfettered inspections would be a powerful argument'

– the paramount importance of tackling Israel/Palestine. Unless we did, we could find ourselves bombing Iraq and losing the Gulf.

YOUR VISIT TO THE RANCH

No doubt we need to keep a sense of perspective. But my talks with Condi convinced me that Bush wants to hear you [*sic*] views on Iraq before taking decisions. He also wants your support. He is still smarting from the comments by other European leaders on his Iraq policy.

This gives you real influence: on the public relations strategy; on the UN and weapons inspections; and on US planning for any military campaign. This could be critically important. I think there is a real risk that the Administration underestimates the difficulties. They may agree that failure isn't an option, but this does not mean that they will avoid it.

Memorandum from British Ambassador to the US, Sir Christopher Meyer, March 18, 2002

1. Paul Wolfowitz, the Deputy Secretary of Defense, came to Sunday lunch on 17 March.

2. On Iraq I opened by sticking very closely to the script that you used the Condi Rice last week. We backed regime change, but the plan had to be clever and failure was not an option. It would be a tough sell for us domestically, and probably tougher elsewhere in Europe. The US could

go it alone if it wanted to. But if it wanted to act with partners, there had to be a strategy for building support for military action against Saddam. I then went through the need to wrongfoot Saddam on the inspectors and the UN SCRs and the critical importance of the MEPP as an integral part of the anti-Saddam strategy. If all this could be accomplished skilfully [*sic*], we were fairly confident that a number of countries would come on board.

3. I said that the UK was giving serious through to publishing a paper that would make the case against Saddam. If the UK were to join with the US in any operation against Saddam, we would have to be able to take a critical mass of parliamentary and public opinion with us. It was extraordinary how people had forgotten how bad he was.

4. Wolfowitz said that he fully agreed. He took a slightly different position from others in the Administration, who were forccused [*sic*] on Saddam's capacity to develop weapons of mass destruction. The WMD danger was of course crucial to the public case against Saddam, particularly the potential linkage to terrorism. But Wolfowitz thought it indispensable to spell out in detail Saddam's barbarism. This was well documented from what he had done during the occupation of Kuwait, the incursion into Kurdish territory, the assault on the Marsh Arabs, and to hiw [*sic*] own people. A lot of work had been done on this towards the end of the first Bush administration. Wolfowitz thought that this would go a long way to destroying any notion of moral equivalence between Iraq and Israel. I said that I had been forcefully struck, when addressing university audiences in the US, how ready students were to gloss over Saddam's crimes and to blame the US and the UK for the suffering of the Iraqi people.

5. Wolfowitz said that it was absurd to deny the link between terrorism and Saddam. There might be doubt about the alleged meeting in Prague between Mohammed Atta, the lead hijacker on 9/11, and Iraqi intelligence (did we, he asked, know anything more about this meeting?). But there were other substantiated cases of Saddam giving comfort to terrorists, including someone involved in the first attack on the World Trade Center (the latest New Yorker apparently has a story about links between Saddam and Al Qaeda operating in Kurdistan).

6. I asked to Wolfowitz's take on the struggle inside the Administrations between the pro- and anti- INC lobbies (well documented in Sy Hersh's recent New Yorker piece, which I gave you). He said that he found

himself between the two sides (but as the conversation developed, it became clear that Wolfowitz was far more pro-INC than not). He said that he was strongly opposed to what some were advocating: a coalition including all outside the factions except the INC (INA, KDP, PUK, SCRI). This would not work. Hostility towards the INC was in reality hostility toward Chalabi. It was true that Chalabi was not the easiest person to work with. Bute [*sic*] had a good record in bringing high-grade defectors out of Iraq. The CIA stubbornly refused to recognize this. They unreasonably denigrated the INC because of their fixation with Chalabi. When I mentioned that the INC was penetraded [*sic*] by Iraqi intelligence, Wolfowitz commented that this was probably the case with all the opposition groups: it was something we would have to live with. As to the Kurds, it was true that they were living well (another point to be made in any public dossier on Saddam) and that they feared provoking an incursion by Baghdad. But there were good people among the Kurds, including in particular Salih (?) of the PUK. Wolfowitz brushed over my reference to the absence of Sunni in the INC: there was a big difference between Iraqi and Iranian Shia. The former just wanted to be rid of Saddam.

7. Wolfowitz was pretty dismissive of the desirability of a military coup and of the defector generals in the wings. The latter had blood on their hands. The important thing was to try to have Saddam replaced by something like a functioning democracy. Though imperfect, the Kurdish model was not bad. How to achieve this, I asked? Only through a coalition of all the parties was the answer (we did not get into military planning).

Minutes: Iraq—Prime Minister's Meeting, July 23, 2002

cc: Defence Secretary, Foreign Secretary, Attorney-General, Sir Richard Wilson, John Scarlett, Francis Richards, CDS, C, Jonathan Powell, Sally Morgan, Alastair Campbell

IRAQ: PRIME MINISTER'S MEETING, 23 JULY

Copy addressees and you met the Prime Minister on 23 July to discuss Iraq.

This record is extremely sensitive. No further copies should be made. It should be shown only to those with a genuine need to know its contents.

John Scarlett summarised the intelligence and latest JIC assessment. Saddam's regime was tough and based on extreme fear. The only way to overthrow it was likely to be by massive military action. Saddam was worried and expected an attack, probably by air and land, but he was not convinced that it would be immediate or overwhelming. His regime expected their neighbours to line up with the US. Saddam knew that regular army morale was poor. Real support for Saddam among the public was probably narrowly based.

C reported on his recent talks in Washington. There was a perceptible shift in attitude. Military action was now seen as inevitable. Bush wanted to remove Saddam, through military action, justified by the conjunction of terrorism and WMD. But the intelligence and facts were being fixed around the policy. The NSC had no patience with the UN route, and no enthusiasm for publishing material on the Iraqi regime's record. There was little discussion in Washington of the aftermath after military action.

CDS said that military planners would brief CENTCOM on 1–2 August, Rumsfeld on 3 August and Bush on 4 August.

The two broad US options were:

(a) Generated Start. A slow build-up of 250,000 US troops, a short (72 hour) air campaign, then a move up to Baghdad from the south. Lead time of 90 days (30 days preparation plus 60 days deployment to Kuwait).
(b) Running Start. Use forces already in theatre (3 × 6,000), continuous air campaign, initiated by an Iraqi casus belli. Total lead time of 60 days with the air campaign beginning even earlier. A hazardous option.

The US saw the UK (and Kuwait) as essential, with basing in Diego Garcia and Cyprus critical for either option. Turkey and other Gulf states were also important, but less vital. The three main options for UK involvement were:

(i)   Basing in Diego Garcia and Cyprus, plus three SF squadrons.
(ii) As above, with maritime and air assets in addition.
(iii) As above, plus a land contribution of up to 40,000, perhaps with a discrete role in Northern Iraq entering from Turkey, tying down two Iraqi divisions.

The Defence Secretary said that the US had already begun "spikes of activity" to put pressure on the regime. No decisions had been taken, but he thought the most likely timing in US minds for military action to begin was January, with the timeline beginning 30 days before the US Congressional elections.

The Foreign Secretary said he would discuss this with Colin Powell this week. It seemed clear that Bush had made up his mind to take military action, even if the timing was not yet decided. But the case was thin. Saddam was not threatening his neighbours, and his WMD capability was less than that of Libya, North Korea or Iran. We should work up a plan for an ultimatum to Saddam to allow back in the UN weapons inspectors. This would also help with the legal justification for the use of force.

The Attorney-General said that the desire for regime change was not a legal base for military action. There were three possible legal bases: self-defence, humanitarian intervention, or UNSC authorisation. The first and second could not be the base in this case. Relying on UNSCR 1205 of three years ago would be difficult. The situation might of course change.

The Prime Minister said that it would make a big difference politically and legally if Saddam refused to allow in the UN inspectors. Regime change and WMD were linked in the sense that it was the regime that was producing the WMD. There were different strategies for dealing with Libya and Iran. If the political context were right, people would support regime change. The two key issues were whether the military plan worked and whether we had the political strategy to give the military plan the space to work.

On the first, CDS said that we did not know yet if the US battleplan was workable. The military were continuing to ask lots of questions.

For instance, what were the consequences, if Saddam used WMD on day one, or if Baghdad did not collapse and urban warfighting began? You said that Saddam could also use his WMD on Kuwait. Or on Israel, added the Defence Secretary.

The Foreign Secretary thought the US would not go ahead with a military plan unless convinced that it was a winning strategy. On this, US and UK interests converged. But on the political strategy, there could be US/UK differences. Despite US resistance, we should explore discreetly the ultimatum. Saddam would continue to play hard-ball with the UN.

John Scarlett assessed that Saddam would allow the inspectors back in only when he thought the threat of military action was real.

The Defence Secretary said that if the Prime Minister wanted UK military involvement, he would need to decide this early. He cautioned that many in the US did not think it worth going down the ultimatum route. It would be important for the Prime Minister to set out the political context to Bush.

Conclusions:

(a) We should work on the assumption that the UK would take part in any military action. But we needed a fuller picture of US planning before we could take any firm decisions. CDS should tell the US military that we were considering a range of options.

(b) The Prime Minister would revert on the question of whether funds could be spent in preparation for this operation.

(c) CDS would send the Prime Minister full details of the proposed military campaign and possible UK contributions by the end of the week.

(d) The Foreign Secretary would send the Prime Minister the background on the UN inspectors, and discreetly work up the ultimatum to Saddam.

He would also send the Prime Minister advice on the positions of countries in the region especially Turkey, and of the key EU member states.

(e) John Scarlett would send the Prime Minister a full intelligence update.

(f) We must not ignore the legal issues: the Attorney-General would consider legal advice with FCO/MOD legal advisers.

(I have written separately to commission this follow-up work.)
MATTHEW RYCROFT

Prime Minister's Foreword to the September 2002 Downing Street Dossier (excerpt)

It is unprecedented for the Government to publish this kind of document. But in light of the debate about Iraq and Weapons of Mass Destruction (WMD), I wanted to share with the British public the reasons why I believe this issue to be a current and serious threat to the UK national interest.

In recent months, I have been increasingly alarmed by the evidence from inside Iraq that despite sanctions, despite the damage done to his capability in the past, despite the UN Security Council Resolutions expressly outlawing it, and despite his denials, Saddam Hussein is continuing to develop WMD, and with them the ability to inflict real damage upon the region, and the stability of the world.

Gathering intelligence inside Iraq is not easy. Saddam's is one of the most secretive and dictatorial regimes in the world. So I believe people will understand why the Agencies cannot be specific about the sources, which have formed the judgements in this document, and why we cannot publish everything we know. We cannot, of course, publish the detailed raw intelligence. I and other Ministers have been briefed in detail on the intelligence and are satisfied as to its authority. I also want to pay tribute to our Intelligence and Security Services for the often extraordinary work that they do.

What I believe the assessed intelligence has established beyond doubt is that Saddam has continued to produce chemical and biological weapons, that he continues in his efforts to develop nuclear weapons, and that he has been able to extend the range of his ballistic missile programme. I also believe that, as stated in the document, Saddam will now do his utmost to try to conceal his weapons from UN inspectors.

The picture presented to me by the JIC in recent months has become more not less worrying. It is clear that, despite sanctions, the policy of containment has not worked sufficiently well to prevent Saddam from developing these weapons. I am in no doubt that the threat is serious and current, that he has made progress on WMD, and that he has to be stopped.

Saddam has used chemical weapons, not only against an enemy state, but against his own people. Intelligence reports make clear that he sees the building up of his WMD capability, and the belief overseas that he would use these weapons, as vital to his strategic interests, and in particular his goal of regional domination. And the document discloses that his military planning allows for some of the WMD to be ready within 45 minutes of an order to use them.

I am quite clear that Saddam will go to extreme lengths, indeed has already done so, to hide these weapons and avoid giving them up.

In today's inter-dependent world, a major regional conflict does not stay confined to the region in question. Faced with someone who has shown himself capable of using WMD, I believe the international community has to stand up for itself and ensure its authority is upheld.

The threat posed to international peace and security, when WMD are in the hands of a brutal and aggressive regime like Saddam's, is real. Unless we face up to the threat, not only do we risk undermining the authority of the UN, whose resolutions he defies, but more importantly and in the longer term, we place at risk the lives and prosperity of our own people.

The case I make is that the UN Resolutions demanding he stops his WMD programme are being flouted; that since the inspectors left four years ago he has continued with this programme; that the inspectors must be allowed back in to do their job properly; and that if he refuses, or if he makes it impossible for them to do their job, as he has done in the past, the international community will have to act.

I believe that faced with the information available to me, the UK Government has been right to support the demands that this issue be confronted and dealt with. We must ensure that he does not get to use the weapons he has, or get hold of the weapons he wants.

Prime Minister's Iraq Statement to Parliament, September 24, 2002 (excerpts)

Mr. Speaker, thank you for recalling Parliament to debate the best way to deal with the issue of the present leadership of Iraq and Weapons of Mass Destruction.

Today we published a 50 page dossier detailing the history of Iraq's WMD, its breach of UN resolutions and the current attempts to rebuild the illegal WMD programme . . .

. . . [Saddam's] chemical, biological and nuclear weapons programme is not an historic leftover from 1998. The inspectors aren't needed to clean up the old remains. His WMD programme is active, detailed and growing. The policy of containment is not working. The WMD programme is not shut down. It is up and running.

The dossier is based on the work of the British Joint Intelligence Committee. For over 60 years, beginning just prior to WWII, the JIC has provided intelligence assessments to British Prime Ministers. Normally its work is secret. Unusually, because it is important we explain our concerns over Saddam to the British people, we have decided to disclose these assessments. I am aware, of course, that people are going to have to take elements of this on the good faith of our intelligence services. But this is what they are telling me the British Prime Minister and my senior colleagues. The intelligence picture they paint is one accumulated over the past four years. It is extensive, detailed and authoritative.

It concludes that Iraq has chemical and biological weapons, that Saddam has continued to produce them, that he has existing and active military plans for the use of chemical and biological weapons, which could be activated within 45 minutes, including against his own Shia population; and that he is actively trying to acquire nuclear weapons capability.

On chemical weapons, the dossier shows that Iraq continues to produce chemical agent for chemical weapons; has rebuilt previously destroyed production plants across Iraq; has bought dual-use chemical facilities; has retained the key personnel formerly engaged in the chemical weapons programme; and has a serious ongoing research programme into weapons production, all of it well funded.

In respect of biological weapons, again production of biological agents has continued; facilities formerly used for biological weapons have been rebuilt; equipment has been purchased for such a programme; and again Saddam has retained the personnel who worked on it, pre 1991. In particular, the UN inspection regime discovered that Iraq was trying to acquire mobile biological weapons facilities which are easier to conceal.

Present intelligence confirms they have now got such facilities. The biological agents we believe Iraq can produce include anthrax, botulinum, toxin, aflatoxin and ricin. All eventually result in excruciatingly painful death.

As for nuclear weapons, Saddam's previous nuclear weapons programme was shut down by the inspectors, following disclosure by defectors of the full, but hidden, nature of it. That programme was based on gas centrifuge uranium enrichment. The known remaining stocks of uranium are now held under supervision by the International Atomic Energy Agency.

But we now know the following. Since the departure of the inspectors in 1998, Saddam has bought or attempted to buy: specialised vacuum pumps of the design needed for the gas centrifuge cascade to enrich uranium; an entire magnet production line of the specification for use in the motors and top bearings of gas centrifuges; dual use products such as Anhydrous Hydrogen Fluoride and fluoride gas, which can be used both in petrochemicals but also in gas centrifuge cascades; a filament winding machine, which can be used to manufacture carbon fibre gas centrifuge rotors; and has attempted, covertly, to acquire 60,000 or more specialised aluminium tubes, which are subject to strict controls due to their potential use in the construction of gas centrifuges.

In addition, we know Saddam has been trying to buy significant quantities of uranium from Africa, though we do not know whether he has been successful. Again key personnel who used to work on the nuclear weapons programme are back in harness. Iraq may claim that this is for a civil nuclear power programme but it has no nuclear power plants . . .

. . . Why now? People ask. I agree I cannot say that this month or next, even this year or next, that he will use his weapons. But I can say that if the international community having made the call for his disarmament, now, at this moment, at the point of decision, shrugs its shoulders and walks away, he will draw the conclusion dictators faced with a weakening will, always draw. That the international community will talk but not act; will use diplomacy but not force; and we know, again from our history, that diplomacy, not backed by the threat of force, has never worked with dictators and never will work. If we take this course, he will carry on, his efforts will intensify, his confidence grow and at some point, in a future not too distant, the threat will turn into reality. The threat therefore is not imagined. The history of Saddam and WMD is not American or British propaganda. The history and the present threat are real

. . . Finally, there are many acts of this drama still to be played out. I have always said that Parliament should be kept in touch with all developments, in particular those that would lead us to military action. That remains the case. To those who doubt it, I say: look at Kosovo and Afghanistan. We proceeded with care, with full debate in this House and when we took military action, did so as a last resort. We shall act in the same way now. But I hope we can do so, secure in the knowledge that should Saddam continue to defy the will of the international community, this House, as it has in our history so many times before, will not shrink from doing what is necessary and right.

Appendix C

October 2002 National Intelligence Estimate: Key Judgments (excerpts): Iraq's Continuing Programs for Weapons of Mass Destruction

We judge that Iraq has continued its weapons of mass destruction (WMD) programs in defiance of UN resolutions and restrictions. Baghdad has chemical and biological weapons as well as missiles with ranges in excess of UN restrictions; if left unchecked, it probably will have a nuclear weapon during this decade. (See INR alternative view at the end of these Key Judgments.)

We judge that we are seeing only a portion of Iraq's WMD efforts, owing to Baghdad's vigorous denial and deception efforts. Revelations after the Gulf war starkly demonstrate the extensive efforts undertaken by Iraq to deny information. We lack specific information on many key aspects of Iraq's WMD programs.

Since inspections ended in 1998, Iraq has maintained its chemical weapons effort, energized its missile program, and invested more heavily in biological weapons; in the view of most agencies, Baghdad is reconstituting its nuclear weapons program.

- Iraq's growing ability to sell oil illicitly increases Baghdad's capabilities to finance WMD programs; annual earnings in cash and goods have more than quadrupled, from $580 million in 1998 to about $3 billion this year.
- Iraq has largely rebuilt missile and biological weapons facilities damaged during Operation Desert Fox and has expanded its chemical and biological infrastructure under the cover of civilian production.
- Baghdad has exceeded UN range limits of 150 km with its ballistic missiles and is working with unmanned aerial vehicles (UAVs), which allow for a more lethal means to deliver biological and, less likely, chemical warfare agents.

- Although we assess that Saddam does not yet have nuclear weapons or sufficient material to make any, he remains intent on acquiring them. Most agencies assess that Baghdad started reconstituting its nuclear program about the time that UNSCOM inspectors departed— December 1998.

How quickly Iraq will obtain its first nuclear weapon depends on when it acquires sufficient weapons-grade fissile material.

- If Baghdad acquires sufficient fissile material from abroad it could make a nuclear weapon within several months to a year.
- Without such material from abroad, Iraq probably would not be able to make a weapon until 2007 to 2009, owing to inexperience in building and operating centrifuge facilities to produce highly enriched uranium and challenges in procuring the necessary equipment and expertise.
  - Most agencies believe that Saddam's personal interest in and Iraq's aggressive attempts to obtain high-strength aluminum tubes for centrifuge rotors—as well as Iraq's attempts to acquire magnets, high-speed balancing machines, and machine tools—provide compelling evidence that Saddam is reconstituting a uranium enrichment effort for Baghdad's nuclear weapons program. (DOE agrees that reconstitution of the nuclear program is underway but assesses that the tubes probably are not part of the program.)
  - Iraq's efforts to re-establish and enhance its cadre of weapons personnel as well as activities at several suspect nuclear sites further indicate that reconstitution is underway.
  - All agencies agree that about 25,000 centrifuges based on tubes of the size Iraq is trying to acquire would be capable of producing approximately two weapons' worth of highly enriched uranium per year.
- In a much less likely scenario, Baghdad could make enough fissile material for a nuclear weapon by 2005 to 2007 if it obtains suitable centrifuge tubes this year and has all the other materials and technological expertise necessary to build production-scale uranium enrichment facilities.

We assess that Baghdad has begun renewed production of mustard, sarin, GF (cyclosarin), and VX; its capability probably is more limited now than it was at the time of the Gulf war, although VX production and agent storage life probably have been improved.

- An array of clandestine reporting reveals that Baghdad has procured covertly the types and quantities of chemicals and equipment sufficient to allow limited CW agent production hidden within Iraq's legitimate chemical industry.
- Although we have little specific information on Iraq's CW stockpile, Saddam probably has stocked at least 100 metric tons (MT) and possibly as much as 500 MT of CW agents—much of it added in the last year.
- The Iraqis have experience in manufacturing CW bombs, artillery rockets, and projectiles. We assess that they possess CW bulk fills for SRBM warheads, including for a limited number of covertly stored Scuds, possibly a few with extended ranges.

We judge that all key aspects—R&D, production, and weaponization—of Iraq's offensive BW program are active and that most elements are larger and more advanced than they were before the Gulf war.

- We judge Iraq has some lethal and incapacitating BW agents and is capable of quickly producing and weaponizing a variety of such agents, including anthrax, for delivery by bombs, missiles, aerial sprayers, and covert operatives.
  - o Chances are even that smallpox is part of Iraq's offensive BW program.
  - o Baghdad probably has developed genetically engineered BW agents.
- Baghdad has established a large-scale, redundant, and concealed BW agent production capability.
  - o Baghdad has mobile facilities for producing bacterial and toxin BW agents; these facilities can evade detection and are highly survivable. Within three to six months [Corrected per Errata sheet issued in October 2002] these units probably could produce an amount of agent equal to the total that Iraq produced in the years prior to the Gulf war.

Iraq maintains a small missile force and several development programs, including for a UAV probably intended to deliver biological warfare agent.

- Gaps in Iraqi accounting to UNSCOM suggest that Saddam retains a covert force of up to a few dozen Scud-variant SRBMs with ranges of 650 to 900 km.
- Iraq is deploying its new al-Samoud and Ababil-100 SRBMs, which are capable of flying beyond the UN-authorized 150-km range limit;

Iraq has tested an al-Samoud variant beyond 150 km—perhaps as far as 300 km.
- Baghdad's UAVs could threaten Iraq's neighbors, U.S. forces in the Persian Gulf, *and if brought close to, or into, the United States, the U.S. Homeland.*
  - An Iraqi UAV procurement network attempted to procure commercially available route planning software and an associated topographic database that would be able to support targeting of the United States, according to analysis of special intelligence.
  - The Director, Intelligence, Surveillance, and Reconnaissance, U.S. Air Force, does not agree that Iraq is developing UAVs *primarily* intended to be delivery platforms for chemical and biological warfare (CBW) agents. The small size of Iraq's new UAV strongly suggests a primary role of reconnaissance, although CBW delivery is an inherent capability.
- Iraq is developing medium-range ballistic missile capabilities, largely through foreign assistance in building specialized facilities, including a test stand for engines more powerful than those in its current missile force.

We have low confidence in our ability to assess when Saddam would use WMD.

- Saddam could decide to use chemical and biological warfare (CBW) preemptively against U.S. forces, friends, and allies in the region in an attempt to disrupt U.S. war preparations and undermine the political will of the Coalition.
- Saddam might use CBW after an initial advance into Iraqi territory, but early use of WMD could foreclose diplomatic options for stalling the US advance.
- He probably would use CBW when be perceived he irretrievably had lost control of the military and security situation, but we are unlikely to know when Saddam reaches that point.
- We judge that Saddam would be more likely to use chemical weapons than biological weapons on the battlefield.
- Saddam historically has maintained tight control over the use of WMD; however, he probably has provided contingency instructions to his commanders to use CBW in specific circumstances.

Baghdad for now appears to be drawing a line short of conducting terrorist attacks with conventional or CBW against the United States, fearing that exposure of Iraqi involvement would provide Washington a stronger cause for making war.

Iraq probably would attempt clandestine attacks against the U.S. Homeland if Baghdad feared an attack that threatened the survival of the regime were imminent or unavoidable, or possibly for revenge. Such attacks—more likely with biological than chemical agents—probably would be carried out by special forces or intelligence operatives.

- The Iraqi Intelligence Service (IIS) probably has been directed to conduct clandestine attacks against US and Allied interests in the Middle East in the event the United States takes action against Iraq. The US probably would be the primary means by which Iraq would attempt to conduct any CBW attacks on the US Homeland, although we have no specific intelligence information that Saddam's regime has directed attacks against US territory.

Saddam, if sufficiently desperate, might decide that only an organization such as al-Qa'ida—with worldwide reach and extensive terrorist infrastructure, and already engaged in a life-or-death struggle against the United States—could perpetrate the type of terrorist attack that he would hope to conduct.

- In such circumstances, he might decide that the extreme step of assisting the Islamist terrorists in conducting a CBW attack against the United States would be his last chance to exact vengeance by taking a large number of victims with him.

State/INR Alternative View of Iraq's Nuclear Program

The Assistant Secretary of State for Intelligence and Research (INR) believes that Saddam continues to want nuclear weapons and that available evidence indicates that Baghdad is pursuing at least a limited effort to maintain and acquire nuclear weapons-related capabilities. The activities we have detected do not, however, add up to a compelling case that Iraq is currently pursuing what INR would consider to be an integrated and comprehensive approach to acquire nuclear weapons. Iraq may be doing so, but INR considers the available evidence inadequate to support such a judgment. Lacking persuasive evidence that Baghdad has launched a coherent effort to reconstitute its nuclear weapons program, INR is unwilling to speculate that such an effort began soon after the departure of UN inspectors or to project a timeline for the completion of activities it does not now see happening. As a result, INR is unable to predict when Iraq could acquire a nuclear device or weapon.

In INR's view Iraq's efforts to acquire aluminum tubes is central to the argument that Baghdad is reconstituting its nuclear weapons program, but INR is not persuaded that the tubes in question are intended for use as centrifuge rotors. INR accepts the judgment of technical experts at the U.S. Department of Energy (DOE) who have concluded that the tubes Iraq seeks to acquire are poorly suited for use in gas centrifuges to be used for uranium enrichment and finds unpersuasive the arguments advanced by others to make the case that they are intended for that purpose. INR considers it far more likely that the tubes are intended for another purpose, most likely the production of artillery rockets. The very large quantities being sought, the way the tubes were tested by the Iraqis, and the atypical lack of attention to operational security in the procurement efforts are among the factors, in addition to the DOE assessment, that lead INR to conclude that the tubes are not intended for use in Iraq's nuclear weapon program.

Confidence Levels for Selected Key Judgments in This Estimate

High Confidence:

- Iraq is continuing, and in some areas expanding, its chemical, biological, nuclear and missile programs contrary to UN resolutions.
- We are not detecting portions of these weapons programs.
- Iraq possesses proscribed chemical and biological weapons and missiles.
- Iraq could make a nuclear weapon in months to a year once it acquires sufficient weapons-grad fissile material

Moderate Confidence:

- Iraq does not yet have a nuclear weapon or sufficient material to make one but is likely to have a weapon by 2007 to 2009. (See INR alternative view, page 84).

Low Confidence

- When Saddam would use weapons of mass destruction.
- Whether Saddam would engage in clandestine attacks against the US Homeland.
- Whether in desperation Saddam would share chemical or biological weapons with al-Qa'ida.

[NIE page 24]

[. . .]

Uranium Acquisition. Iraq retains approximately two-and-a-half tons of 2.5 percent enriched uranium oxide, which the IAEA permits. This low-enriched material could be used as feed material to produce enough HEU for about two nuclear weapons. The use of enriched feed material also would reduce the initial number of centrifuges that Baghdad would need by about half. Iraq could divert this material—the IAEA inspects it only once a year—and enrich it to weapons grade before a subsequent inspection discovered it was missing. The IAEA last inspected this material in late January 2002.

Iraq has about 500 metric tons of yellowcake[1] and low enriched uranium at Tuwaitha, which is inspected annually by the IAEA. Iraq also began vigorously trying to procure uranium ore and yellowcake; acquiring either would shorten the time Baghdad needs to produce nuclear weapons.

- A foreign government service reported that as of early 2001, Niger planned to send several tons of "pure uranium" (probably yellow-cake) to Iraq. As of early 2001, Niger and Iraq reportedly were still working out arrangements for this deal, which could be for up to 500 tons of yellowcake. We do not know the status of this arrangement.
- Reports indicate Iraq also has sought uranium ore from Somalia and possibly the Democratic Republic of the Congo.

We cannot confirm whether Iraq succeeded in acquiring uranium ore and/or yellowcake from these sources. Reports suggest Iraq is shifting from domestic mining and milling of uranium to foreign acquisition. Iraq possesses significant phosphate deposits, from which uranium had been chemically extracted before Operation Desert Storm. Intelligence information on whether nuclear-related phosphate mining and/or processing has been reestablished is inconclusive, however.

[. . .]
[NIE page 84]

---

[1] A refined form of natural uranium.

Annex A

Iraq's Attempts to Acquire Aluminum Tubes

(This excerpt from a longer view includes INR's position on the African uranium issue)

INR's Alternative View: Iraq's Attempts to Acquire Aluminum Tubes

Some of the specialized but dual-use items being sought are, by all indications, bound for Iraq's missile program. Other cases are ambiguous, such as that of a planned magnet-production line whose suitability for centrifuge operations remains unknown. Some efforts involve non-controlled industrial material and equipment—including a variety of machine tools—and are troubling because they would help establish the infrastructure for a renewed nuclear program. But such efforts (which began well before the inspectors departed) are not clearly linked to a nuclear end-use. Finally, the claims of Iraqi pursuit of natural uranium in Africa are, in INR's assessment, highly dubious.

Appendix D

Excerpts from post-war US investigations

The Commission on the Intelligence Capabilities of the United States Regarding Weapons of Mass Destruction, *Report to the President of the United States* (March 31, 2005) [the Silberman–Robb Commission]

Letter of transmittal (excerpt):

Mr President:

With this letter, we transmit the report of the Commission on the Intelligence Capabilities of the United States Regarding Weapons of Mass Destruction. Our unanimous report is based on a lengthy investigation, during which we interviewed hundreds of experts from inside and outside the Intelligence Community and reviewed thousands of documents. Our report offers 74 recommendations for improving the US Intelligence Community (all but a handful of which we believe can be implemented without statutory change). But among these recommendations a few points merit special emphasis.

We conclude that the Intelligence Community was dead wrong in almost all of its pre-war judgments about Iraq's weapons of mass destruction. This was a major intelligence failure. Its principal causes were the Intelligence Community's inability to collect good information about Iraq's WMD programs, serious errors in analysing what information it could gather, and a failure to make clear just how much of its analysis was based on assumptions, rather than good evidence. On a matter of this importance, we simply cannot afford failures of this magnitude.

After a thorough review, the Commission found no indication that the Intelligence Community distorted the evidence regarding Iraq's weapons of mass destruction. What the intelligence professionals told you about Saddam Hussein's programs was what they believed. They were simply wrong.

Laurence H. Silberman
Charles S. Robb

Overview of the Report (excerpt):

On the brink of war, and in front of the whole world, the United States government asserted that Saddam Hussein had reconstituted his nuclear weapons program, had biological weapons and mobile biological weapons production facilities, and had stockpiled and was producing chemical weapons. All of this was based on the assessments of the US Intelligence Community. And not one bit of it could be confirmed when the war was over.

While the intelligence services of many other nations also thought that Iraq had weapons of mass destruction, in the end it was the United States that put its credibility on the line, making this one of the most public—and most damaging—intelligence failures in recent American history.

This failure was in large part the result of analytical shortcomings; intelligence analysts were too wedded to their assumptions about Saddam's intentions. But it was also a failure on the part of those who collect intelligence—CIA's and the Defense Intelligence Agency (DIA) spies, the National Security Agency's (NSA) eavesdroppers, and the National Geospatial-Intelligence Agency's (NGA) imagery experts. In the end, those agencies collected precious little intelligence for the analyst to analyse, and much of what they did collect was either worthless or misleading. Finally, it was a failure to communicate effectively with policymakers; the Intelligence Community didn't adequately explain just how little good intelligence it had—or how much its assessments were driven by assumptions and inferences rather than concrete evidence.

Was the failure in Iraq typical of the Community's performance? Or was Iraq, as one senior intelligence official told the Commission, a sort of "perfect storm"—a one-time breakdown caused by a rare confluence of events that conspired to create a bad result? In our view, it was neither.

The failures we found in Iraq are not repeated everywhere. The Intelligence Community played a key role, for example, in getting Libya to renounce weapons of mass destruction and in exposing the long-running A. Q. Khan nuclear proliferation network. It is engaged in imaginative, successful (and highly classified) operations in many parts of the world. Tactical support to counter terrorism efforts is excellent, and there are signs of a boldness that would have been unimaginable before September 11, 2001.

But neither was Iraq a "perfect storm." The flaws we found in the Intelligence Community's Iraq performance are still all too common. Across the board, the Intelligence Community knows disturbingly little about the nuclear programs of many of the world's most dangerous actors. In some cases, it knows less now than it did five or ten years ago.

As for biological weapons, despite years of Presidential concern, the Intelligence Community has struggled to address this threat.

To be sure, the Intelligence Community is full of talented, dedicated people. But they seem to be working harder and harder just to maintain a *status quo* that is increasingly irrelevant to the new challenges presented by weapons of mass destruction. Our collection agencies are often unable to gather intelligence on the very things we care the most about. Too often, analysts simply accept these gaps; they do little to help collectors identify new opportunities, and they do not always tell decision-makers just how limited their knowledge really is.

Taken together, these shortcomings reflect the Intelligence Community's struggle to confront a environment that has changed radically over the past decade. For almost 50 years after the passage of the National Security Act of 1947 the Intelligence Community's resources were overwhelmingly trained on a single threat—the Soviet Union, its nuclear arsenal, its massive conventional forces, and its activities around the world. By comparison, today's priority intelligence targets are greater in number (there are dozens of entities that could strike a devastating blow against the United States) and are often more diffuse in character (they include not only states but also nebulous transnational terror and proliferation networks). What's more, some of the weapons that would be most dangerous in the hands of terrorists or rogue nations are difficult to detect. Much of the technology, equipment, and materials necessary to develop biological and chemical weapons, for example, also has legitimate commercial applications. Biological weapons themselves can be built in small-scale facilities that are easy to conceal, and weapons-grade uranium can be effectively shielded from traditional detection techniques. At the same time, advances in technology have made the job of technical intelligence collection exceedingly difficult.

The demands of this new environment can only be met by broad and deep change in the Intelligence Community. The Intelligence Community we have today is buried beneath an avalanche of demands for "current intelligence"—the pressing need to meet the tactical requirements of the day. Current intelligence in support of military and other action is necessary, of course. But we also need an Intelligence Community with *strategic* capabilities: it must be equipped to develop long-term plans for penetrating today's difficult targets, and to identify political and social trends shaping the threats that lie over the horizon. We can imagine nothreat that demands greater strategic focus from the Intelligence Community than that posed by nuclear, biological, and chemical weapons.

The Intelligence Community is also fragmented, loosely managed, and poorly coordinated; the 15 intelligence organizations are a "Community" in name only and rarely act with a unity of purpose. What we need is an Intelligence Community that is *integrated*: the Community's leadership must be capable of allocating and directing the Community's resources in a coordinated way. The strengths of our distinct collection agencies must be brought to bear together on the most difficult intelligence problems. At the same time we need a Community that preserves diversity of analysis, and that encourages structured debate among agencies and analysts over the interpretation of information.

Perhaps above all, the Intelligence Community is too slow to change the way it does business. It is reluctant to see new human and technical collection methods; it is behind the curve in applying cutting-edge technologies; and it has not adapted its personnel practices and incentive structures to fit the needs of a new job market. What we need is an Intelligence Community that is flexible—able to respond nimbly to an ever-shifting threat environment and to the rapid pace of today's technological changes.

In short, to succeed in confronting today's and tomorrow's threats, the Intelligence Community must be transformed—a goal that would be difficult to meet even in the best of all possible worlds. And we do not live in the best of worlds. The CIA and NSA may be sleek and omnisicient in the movies, but in real life they and other intelligence agencies are vast government bureaucracies. They are bureaucracies filled with talented people and armed with sophisticated technological tools, but talent and tools do not suspend the iron laws of bureaucratic behavior. Like government bodies everywhere, intelligence agencies are prone to develop self-reinforcing, risk averse cultures that take outside advice badly. While laudable steps were taken to improve our intelligence agencies after September 11, 2001, the agencies have done less in response to the failures over Iraq, and we believe that many within those agencies do not accept the conclusion that we reached after our year of study: that the Community needs fundamental change if it is to successfully confront the threats of the 21st century.

We are not the first to say this. Indeed, commission after commission has identified some of the same fundamental failings we see in the Intelligence Community, usually to little effect. The Intelligence Community is a closed world, and many insiders admitted to us that *it has an almost perfect record of resisting external recommendations.*

But the present moment offers an unprecedented opportunity to overcome this resistance. About halfway through our inquiry, Congress passed the *Intelligence Reform and Terrorism Prevention Act of 2004*, which became a sort of a *deus ex machina* in our deliberations. The Act created a Director of National Intelligence (DNI). The DNI's role could have been a purely coordinating position, with a limited staff and authority to match. Or it could have been something closer to a "Secretary of Intelligence," with full authority over the principal intelligence agencies and clear responsibility for their actions—which also might well have been consistent with a small bureaucratic super-structure. In the end, the DNI created by the intelligence reform legislation was neither of these things; the office is given broad responsibilities but only ambiguous authorities. While we might have chosen a different solution, we are not writing on a blank slate. So our focus has been in large part on how to make the new intelligence structure work, and in particular on giving the DNI tools (and support staff) to match his large responsibilities.

We are mindful, however, that there is a serious risk in creating too large a bureaucratic structure to serve the DNI: the risk that decision-making in the field, which sometimes requires quick action, will be improperly delayed. Balancing these two imperatives—necessary agility of operational execution and thoughtful coordination of intelligence activities—is, in our view, the DNI's greatest challenge.

In considering organizational issues, we did not delude ourselves that organizational structure alone can solve problems. More than many parts of government, the culture of the Intelligence Community is formed in the field, where organizational changes at headquarters are felt only lightly. We understand the limits of organizational change, and many of our recommendations go beyond organizational issues and would, if enacted, directly affect the way that intelligence is collected and analyzed. But we regret that we were not able to make such detailed proposals for some of the most important technical collection agencies, such as NSA and NGA. For those agencies, and for the many other issues that we could only touch upon, we must trust that our broader institutional recommendations will enable necessary reform. The DNI that we envision will have the budget and management tools to dig deep into the culture of each agency and to force changes where needed.

Case Study of Iraq, an Overview (excerpt)

In October 2002, at the request of members of Congress, the National Intelligence Council produced a National Intelligence Estimate (NIE) —the most authoritative intelligence assessment produced by the Intelligence Community—which concluded that Iraq was reconstituting its nuclear weapons program and was actively pursuing a nuclear device. According to the exhaustive study of the Iraq Survey Group, this assessment was almost completely wrong. The NIE said that Iraq's biological weapons capability was larger and more advanced than before the Gulf War and that Iraq possessed mobile biological weapons production facilities. This was wrong. The NIE further stated that Iraq had renewed production of chemical weapons, including mustard, sarin, GF and VX, and that it had accumulated chemical stockpiles of between 100 and 500 metric tons. All of this was also wrong. Finally, the NIE concluded that Iraq had unmanned aerial vehicles that were probably intended for the delivery of biological weapons, and ballistic missiles that had ranges greater than the United Nations' permitted 150 kilometer range. In truth, the aerial vehicles were not for biological weapons; some of Iraq's missiles were, however, capable of traveling more than 150 kilometers. The Intelligence Community's Iraq assessments wee, in short, riddled with errors.

Contrary to what some defenders of the Intelligence Community have since asserted, those errors were *not* the result of a few harried months in 2002. Most of the fundamental errors were made and communicated to policymakers well before the now-infamous NIE of October 2002, and were not corrected in the months between the NIE and the start of war. They were not isolated or random failings. Iraq had been an intelligence challenge at the forefront of the US attention for over a decade. It was a known adversary that had already fought one war with the United States and seemed increasingly likely to fight another. But, after ten years of effort, the Intelligence Community still had no good intelligence on the status of Iraq's weapons programs. Our full report examines these issues in detail. Here we limit our discussion to the central lessons to be learned from this episode.

The first lesson is that the Intelligence Community cannot analyze and disseminate information that it does not have. The Community's Iraq assessment was crippled by its inability to collect meaningful intelligence on Iraq's nuclear, biological, and chemical weapons programs. The second lesson follows from the first: lacking good intelligence, analysts and collectors fell back on old assumptions and inferences drawn from Iraq's past behavior and intentions.

The Intelligence Community had learned a hard lesson after the 1991 Gulf War, which revealed that the Intelligence Community's pre-war assessments had underestimated Iraq's nuclear program and had failed to identify all of its chemical weapons storage sites. Shaken by the magnitude of their errors, intelligence analysts were determined not to fall victim again to the same mistake. This tendency was only reinforced by later events. Saddam acted to the very end like a man with much to hide. And the dangers of underestimating our enemies were deeply underscored by the attacks of September 11, 2001.

Throughout the 1990s, therefore, the Intelligence Community assumed that Saddam's Iraq was up to no good—that Baghdad had maintained its nuclear, biological, and chemical technical expertise, had kept its biological and chemical weapons production capabilities, and possessed significant stockpiles of chemical agents and weapons precursors. Since Iraq's leadership had not changed since 1991, the Intelligence Community also believed that these capabilities would be further revved up as soon as inspectors left Iraq. Saddam's continuing cat-and-mouse parrying with international inspectors only hardened these assumptions.

These experiences contributed decisively to the Intelligence Community's erroneous National Intelligence Estimate of October 2002. That is not to say that its fears and assumptions were foolish or even unreasonable. At some point, however, these premises stopped being working hypotheses and became more or less unrebuttable conclusions; worse, the intelligence system became too willing to find confirmations of them in evidence that should have been recognized at the time to be of dubious reliability. Collectors and analysts too readily accepted any evidence that supported their theory that Iraq had stockpiles and was developing weapons programs, and they explained away or simply disregarded evidence that pointed in the other direction.

Even in hindsight, those assumptions have a powerful air of common sense. If the Intelligence Community's estimate and other pre-war intelligence had relied principally and explicitly on inferences the Community drew from Iraq's past conduct, the estimate would still have been wrong, but it would have been far more defensible. For good reason, it was hard to conclude that Saddam Hussein had indeed abandoned his weapons programs. But a central flaw of the NIE is that it took these defensible assumptions and swathed them in the mystique of intelligence, providing secret information that seemed to support them but was in fact nearly worthless, if not misleading. The NIE simply didn't communicate how weak the underlying intelligence was.

This was, moreover, a problem that was not limited to the NIE. Our review found that *after* the publication of the October 2002 NIE but *before* Secretary of State Colin Powell's February 2003 address to the United Nations, intelligence officials within the CIA failed to convey to policymakers new information casting serious doubt on the reliability of a human intelligence source known as "Curveball." This occurred despite the pivotal role Curveball's information played in the Intelligence Community's assessment of Iraq's biological weapons programs, and in spite of Secretary Powell's efforts to strip every dubious piece of information out of his proposed speech. In this instance, once again, the Intelligence Community failed to give policymakers a full understanding of the frailties of the intelligence on which they were relying.

Finally, we closely examined the possibility that intelligence analysts were pressured by policymakers to change their judgments about Iraq's nuclear, biological, and chemical weapons programs. The analysts who worked Iraqi weapons issues universally agreed that in no instance did political pressure cause them to skew or alter any of their analytical judgments. That said, it is hard to deny the conclusion that intelligence analysts worked in an environment that did not encourage skepticism about the conventional wisdom.

United States Senate, Select Committee on Intelligence, 109th Congress (September 8, 2006), *Postwar Findings About Iraq's WMD Programs and Links to Terrorism and How They Compare with Prewar Assessments* (excerpts)

Section II: Iraq's WMD Capabilities—Conclusion

Conclusion 1: Postwar findings do not support the 2002 National Intelligence Estimate (NIE) judgment that Iraq was reconstituting its nuclear weapons program. Information obtained after the war supports the State Department's Bureau of Intelligence and Research's (INR) assessment in the NIE that the Intelligence Community lacked persuasive evidence that Baghdad had launched a coherent effort to reconstitute its nuclear weapons program.

Conclusion 2: Postwar findings do not support the 2002 National Intelligence Estimate (NIE) assessment that Iraq's acquisition of high-strength aluminum tubes was intended for an Iraqi nuclear program. The findings do support the assessment in the NIE of the Department of Energy's Office of Intelligence and the State Department's Bureau of Intelligence and Research (INR) that the aluminum tubes were likely intended for a conventional rocket program.

Conclusion 3: Postwar findings do not support the 2002 National Intelligence Estimate (NIE) assessment that Iraq was "vigorously trying to procure uranium ore and yellowcake" from Africa. Postwar findings support the assessment in the NIE of the State Department's Bureau of Intelligence and Research (INR) that claims of Iraqi pursuit of natural uranium in Africa are "highly dubious."

Conclusion 4: Postwar findings do not support the 2002 National Intelligence Estimate (NIE) assessment that "Iraq has biological weapons" and that "all key aspects of Iraq's offensive biological weapons (BW) program are larger and more advanced than before the Gulf war."

Conclusion 5: Postwar findings do not support the 2002 National Intelligence Estimate (NIE) assessment that Iraq possessed, or ever developed, mobile facilities for producing biological warfare (BW) agents.

Conclusion 6: Concerns existed within the Central Intelligence Agency's (CIA) Directorate of Operations (DO) prior to the war about the credibility of the mobile biological weapons program source code-named CURVE BALL. The concerns were based, in part, on doubts raised by the foreign intelligence service that handled CURVE BALL and a third service. The Committee has no information that these concerns were conveyed to policymakers, including members of the U.S. Congress, prior to the war. The Committee is continuing to investigate issues regarding prewar concerns about CURVE BALL's credibility.

Conclusion 7: Postwar findings do not support the 2002 National Intelligence Estimate (NIE) assessments that Iraq "has chemical weapons" or "is expanding its chemical industry to support chemical weapons (CW) production."

Conclusion 8: Postwar findings support the 2002 National Intelligence Estimate (NIE) assessment that Iraq had missiles which exceeded United Nations (UN) range limits. The findings do not support the assessment that Iraq likely retained a covert force of SCUD variant short range ballistic missiles (SRBMs).

Conclusion 9: Postwar findings do not support the 2002 National Intelligence Estimate (NIE) assessments that Iraq had a developmental program for an Unmanned Aerial Vehicle (UAV) "probably intended to deliver biological agents" or that an effort to procure U.S. mapping software "strongly suggests that Iraq is investigating the use of these UAVs for missions targeting the United States." Postwar findings support the view of the Air Force, joined by the DIA and the Army, in an NIE published in January 2003, that Iraq's UAVs were primarily intended for reconnaissance.

Section III: Iraqi Links to al-Qa'ida—Conclusion

Conclusion 1: Postwar findings indicate that the Central Intelligence Agency's (CIA) assessment that the relationship between Iraq and al-Qa'ida resembled "two independent actors trying to exploit each other," accurately characterized bin Laden's actions, but not those of Saddam Hussein. Postwar findings indicate that Saddam Hussein was distrustful of al-Qa'ida and viewed Islamic extremists as a threat to his regime, refusing all requests from al-Qa'ida to provide material or operational support.

Conclusion 2: Postwar findings have identified only one meeting between representatives of al-Qa'ida and Saddam Hussein's regime reported in prewar intelligence assessments. Postwar findings have identified two occasions, not reported prior to the war, in which Saddam Hussein rebuffed meeting requests from an al-Qa'ida operative. The Intelligence Community has not found any other evidence of meetings between al-Qa'ida and Iraq.

Conclusion 3: Prewar Intelligence Community assessments were inconsistent regarding the likelihood that Saddam Hussein provided chemical and biological weapons (CBW) training to al-Qa'ida. Postwar findings support the Defense Intelligence Agency (DIA) February 2002 assessment that Ibn al-Shaykh al-Libi was likely intentionally misleading his debriefers when he said that Iraq provided two al-Qa'ida associates with chemical and biological weapons (CBW) training in 2000. The Central Intelligence Agency's January 2003 assessment said that the al-Libi claim was credible, but included the statement that al-Libi was not in a position to know whether the training had taken place. Postwar findings do not support the CIA's assessment that his reporting was credible. No postwar information has been found that indicates CBW training occurred and the detainee who provided the key prewar reporting about this training recanted his claims after the war.

Conclusion 4: Postwar findings support the April 2002 Defense Intelligence Agency (DIA) assessment that there was no credible reporting on the al-Qa'ida training at Salman Pak or anywhere else in Iraq.

Conclusion 5: Postwar information supports the Intelligence Community's assessments that Abu Musab al-Zarqawi, using an alias, and members of his network, were present in Baghdad in 2002. Postwar findings indicate al-Zarqawi was in Baghdad from May 2002 until late November 2002, when he traveled to Iran and north eastern Iraq. Prewar assessments expressed uncertainty about Iraq's complicity in their presence, but overestimated the Iraqi regime's capabilities to locate them. Postwar information indicates that Saddam Hussein attempted, unsuccessfully, to locate and capture al-Zarqawi and that the regime did not have a relationship with, harbor, or turn a blind eye toward Zarqawi.

Conclusion 6: Postwar information indicates that the Intelligence Community accurately assessed that al-Qa'ida affiliate group Ansar al-Islam operated in Kurdish-controlled northeastern Iraq, an area that Baghdad had not controlled since 1991. Prewar assessments reported on Iraqi Intelligence Service (IIS) infiltrations of the group, but noted uncertainty regarding the purpose of the infiltrations. Postwar information reveals that Baghdad viewed Ansar al-Islam as a threat to the regime and that the IIS attempted to collect intelligence on the group.

Conclusion 7: Postwar information supports prewar Intelligence Community assessments that there was no credible information that Iraq was complicit in or had foreknowledge of the September 11 attacks or any other al-Qa'ida strike. These assessments discussed two leads which raised the possibility of ties between Iraqi officials and two of the September 11 hijackers. Postwar findings support CIA's January 2003 assessment, which judged that "the most reliable reporting casts doubt" on one of the leads, an alleged meeting between Muhammad Atta and an Iraqi intelligence officer in Prague, and confirm that no such meeting occurred. Prewar intelligence reporting cast doubt on the other lead as well.

Conclusion 8: No postwar information indictates that Iraq intended to use al-Qa'ida or any other terrorist group to strike the United States homeland before or during Operation Iraqi Freedom.

Conclusion 9: While document exploitation continues, additional reviews of documents recovered in Iraq are unlikely to provide information that would contradict the Committee's findings or conclusions.

Appendix E

Open Letter to George Tenet from US intelligence professionals, April 28, 2007

Dear Mr. Tenet:

We write to you on the occasion of the release of your book, *At the Center of the Storm*. You are on the record complaining about the "damage to your reputation." In our view the damage to your reputation is inconsequential compared to the harm your actions have caused for the U.S. soldiers engaged in combat in Iraq and the national security of the United States. We believe you have a moral obligation to return the Medal of Freedom you received from President George Bush. We also call for you to dedicate a significant percentage of the royalties from your book to the U.S. soldiers and their families who have been killed and wounded in Iraq.

We agree with you that Vice President Dick Cheney and other Bush administration officials took the United States to war for flimsy reasons. We agree that the war of choice in Iraq was ill-advised and wrong headed. But your lament that you are a victim in a process you helped direct is self-serving, misleading and, as head of the intelligence community, an admission of failed leadership. You were not a victim. You were a willing participant in a poorly considered policy to start an unnecessary war and you share culpability with Dick Cheney and George Bush for the debacle in Iraq.

You are not alone in failing to speak up and protest the twisting and shading of intelligence. Those who remained silent when they could have made a difference also share the blame for not protesting the abuse and misuse of intelligence that occurred under your watch. But ultimately you were in charge and you signed off on the CIA products and you briefed the President.

This is not a case of Monday morning quarterbacking. You helped send very mixed signals to the American people and their legislators in the fall of 2002. CIA field operatives produced solid intelligence in September 2002 that stated clearly there was no stockpile of any kind of WMD in Iraq. This intelligence was ignored and later misused. On

October 1 you signed and gave to President Bush and senior policy makers a fraudulent National Intelligence Estimate (NIE)-which dovetailed with unsupported threats presented by Vice President Dick Cheney in an alarmist speech on August 26, 2002.

You were well aware that the White House tried to present as fact intelligence you knew was unreliable. And yet you tried to have it both ways. On October 7, just hours before the president gave a major speech in Cincinnati, you were successful in preventing him from using the fable about Iraq purchasing uranium in Africa, although that same claim appeared in the NIE you signed only six days before.

Although CIA officers learned in late September 2002 from a high-level member of Saddam Hussein's inner circle that Iraq had no past or present contact with Osama bin Laden and that the Iraqi leader considered bin Laden an enemy of the Baghdad regime, you still went before Congress in February 2003 and testified that Iraq did indeed have links to Al Qaeda.

You showed a lack of leadership and courage in January of 2003 as the Bush Administration pushed and cajoled analysts and managers to let them make the bogus claim that Iraq was on the verge of getting its hands on uranium. You signed off on Colin Powell's presentation to the United Nations. And, at his insistence, you sat behind him and visibly squandered CIA's most precious asset—credibility.

You may now feel you were bullied and victimized but you were also one of the bullies. In the end you allowed suspect sources, like Curveball, to be used based on very limited reporting and evidence. Yet you were informed in no uncertain terms that Curveball was not reliable. You broke with CIA standard practice and insisted on voluminous evidence to refute this reporting rather than treat the information as suspect. You helped set the bar very low for reporting that supported favored White House positions, while raising the bar astronomically high when it came to raw intelligence that did not support the case for war being hawked by the president and vice president.

It now turns out that you were the Alberto Gonzales of the intelligence community – a grotesque mixture of incompetence and sycophancy shielded by a genial personality. Decisions were made, you were in charge, but you have no idea how decisions were made even though you were in charge. Curiously, you focus your anger on the likes of Dick Cheney, Don Rumsfeld, and Condi Rice, but you decline to criticize the President.

Mr. Tenet, as head of the intelligence community, you failed to use your position of power and influence to protect the intelligence process and, more importantly, the country. What should you have done? What could you have done?

For starters, during the critical summer and fall of 2002, you could have gone to key Republicans and Democrats in the Congress and warned them of the pressure. But you remained silent. Your candor during your one-on-one with Sir Richard Dearlove, then-head of British Intelligence, of July 20, 2002, provides documentary evidence that you knew exactly what you were doing; namely, "fixing" the intelligence to the policy.

By your silence you helped build the case for war. You betrayed the CIA officers who collected the intelligence that made it clear that Saddam did not pose an imminent threat. You betrayed the analysts who tried to withstand the pressure applied by Cheney and Rumsfeld.

Most importantly and tragically, you failed to meet your obligations to the people of the United States. Instead of resigning in protest, when it could have made a difference in the public debate, you remained silent and allowed the Bush Administration to cite your participation in these deliberations to justify their decision to go to war. Your silence contributed to the willingness of the public to support the disastrous war in Iraq, which has killed more than 3300 Americans and hundreds of thousands of Iraqis.

If you are committed to correcting the record about your past failings then you should start by returning the Medal of Freedom you willingly received from President Bush in December 2004. You claim it was given only because of the war on terror, but you were standing next to General Tommy Franks and L. Paul Bremer, who also contributed to the disaster in Iraq. President Bush said that you:

> played pivotal roles in great events, and [your] efforts have made our country more secure and advanced the cause of human liberty.

The reality of Iraq, however, has not made our nation more secure nor has the cause of human liberty been advanced. In fact, your tenure as head of the CIA has helped create a world that is more dangerous. The damage to the credibility of the CIA is serious but can eventually be repaired. Many of the U.S. soldiers maimed in the streets of Fallujah and Baghdad cannot be fixed. Many will live the rest of their lives missing limbs, blinded, mentally disabled, or physically disfigured. And the dead have passed into history.

Mr. Tenet, you cannot undo what has been done. It is doubly sad that you seem still to lack an adequate appreciation of the enormous amount of death and carnage you have facilitated. If reflection on these matters serves to prick your conscience we encourage you to donate at least half of the royalties from your book sales to the veterans and their families, who have paid and are paying the price for your failure to speak up when you could have made a difference. That would be the decent and honorable thing to do.

Sincerely yours,

Phil Giraldi

Ray McGovern

Larry Johnson

Jim Marcinkowski

Vince Cannistraro

David MacMichael

UPDATE: Signatories who were not CIA officers but worked in high level intelligence and national security positions.

W. Patrick Lang (Colonel, retired, US Army and former Chief of Middle East Division, DIA)

Thomas R. Maertens (Director for nonproliferation and homeland defense under Presidents Bill Clinton and George W. Bush)

Index